Section D for Destruction

Section D for Destruction

Forerunner of SOE

Malcolm Atkin

Pen & Sword
MILITARY

First published in Great Britain in 2017 by
PEN & SWORD MILITARY
An imprint of
Pen & Sword Books Ltd
47 Church Street
Barnsley
South Yorkshire
S70 2AS

Copyright © Malcolm Atkin, 2017

ISBN 978-1-47389-260-6

Typeset by Concept, Huddersfield HD4 5JL.
Printed and bound by TJ International Ltd, Padstow, Cornwall

Pen & Sword Books Limited incorporates the imprints of Atlas, Archaeology, Aviation, Discovery, Family History, Fiction, History, Maritime, Military, Military Classics, Politics, Select, Transport, True Crime, Air World, Frontline Publishing, Leo Cooper, Remember When, Seaforth Publishing, The Praetorian Press, Wharncliffe Local History, Wharncliffe Transport, Wharncliffe True Crime and White Owl.

For a complete list of Pen & Sword titles please contact
PEN & SWORD BOOKS LIMITED
47 Church Street, Barnsley, South Yorkshire, S70 2AS, England
E-mail: enquiries@pen-and-sword.co.uk
Website: www.pen-and-sword.co.uk

Contents

List of Plates

List of Figures

Acknowledgements

The starting point for this book was the manuscript history of Section D by SOE, largely written by a former Section D officer, Anthony Samuel (Pl. 6) during the latter half of 1943 (TNA HS 7/3 and HS 7/4). Samuel could directly reference many documents that have since been destroyed. I could not have undertaken this project without the services of Lee Richards of ARCRE who made available copies of documents in The National Archives to the comfort of my armchair! Both Lee and I wish to thank the staff of The National Archives for their unfailing assistance. I was also able to enjoy many fruitful discussions of the sources with Lee, and share his knowledge of wartime propaganda. Dr C.G. McKay kindly commented upon an earlier draft of Chapter 8 and provided valuable insight into the Rickman affair. Paul McCue provided information on Marcel Clech in advance of his own publication as part of the Valençay 104 project and Michael Van Moppes shared his knowledge of the diamond-processing industry and his family history.

It was a particular pleasure to meet the daughter of Laurence Grand, Lady Bessborough, and his grandsons Hon. Matthew and Hon. Charles Ponsonby and to correspond with Jacqueline O'Halloran, the daughter of Anthony Samuel. Such contact helped provide an insight into the character of extraordinary men.

Thanks are owed to all of the copyright owners of the illustration for permission to publish. These are acknowledged in the individual captions. Special thanks are owed to my daughter, Kate, for some of the photography, including the basis of the cover montage. Rupert Harding and Sarah Cook of Pen & Sword have been supportive throughout and guided the project expertly through the publication process. As ever, final thanks go to my wife Susanne, for her patience and support, for trying to correct my grammar and for the index.

The responsibility for any errors, speculation and conclusions remain my own.

Malcolm Atkin
March 2017

Abbreviations and Acronyms

AAF	Auxiliary Air Force.
Abwehr	German Military Intelligence.
BEF	British Expeditionary Force (France 1939–1940).
BSC	British Security Coordination (in USA).
BUF	British Union of Fascists.
CIGS	Chief of the Imperial General Staff.
COS	Chiefs of Staff Committee.
CSS	Chief of the Secret Service (SIS). Commonly further abbreviated to 'C'.
DCO	Director of Combined Operations.
DDMI	Deputy Director of Military Intelligence.
DMI	Directorate of Military Intelligence.
DNI	Directorate of Naval Intelligence.
EH	Electra House: the Department of Publicity in Enemy Countries.
FSS	Field Security Sections of the Military Intelligence Corps. Until July 1940 part of D Division, MI5.
GHQ	General Headquarters, Home Forces.
GS(R)	General Service (Research). Original name for what became D/MI(R) and then MI(R).
HDE	Home Defence Executive. Created on 10 May 1940 under chairmanship of General Ironside, C-in-C Home Forces, to coordinate anti-invasion planning.
HDS	Home Defence Scheme. Intelligence and sabotage organisation created in 1940 by Section D of SIS. Otherwise known in 1940 as the Regional D Scheme.
HD(S)E	Home Defence (Security) Executive. Created on 28 May 1940 to consider matters of internal security and defence against the Fifth Column.
IRA	Irish Republican Army.
ISPB	Inter-Services Project Board. Created in April 1940 to coordinate proposals between the War Office, Naval and Air Force Intelligence services and SIS for the development of British irregular warfare.
ITF	International Transport Workers Federation.
JBC	Joint Broadcasting Committee.
JIC	Joint Intelligence Committee.

LDV	Local Defence Volunteers, forerunner of Home Guard.
MAP	Ministry of Aircraft Production.
MEW	Ministry of Economic Warfare.
MI5	Secret Security Service, responsible for counter-espionage operations within the UK. Ceased to be a section of the War Office in 1931 and henceforth its official title became the Security Service, as an inter-departmental intelligence agency. The name MI5 was retained as a popular abbreviation and it took some while for the War Office to realise that the change had been made.
MI6	Alternative name of Secret Intelligence Service (SIS).
MI(R)	Military Intelligence (Research).
MOI	Ministry of Information.
MTB	Motor Torpedo Boat.
PCO	Passport Control Officer (usual cover for pre-war SIS officers abroad).
RAAF	Royal Australian Air Force.
RSHA	*Reichssicherheitshauptamt* (Reich Main Security Office).
RSLO	Regional Security Liaison Officer (MI5).
SAS	Special Air Service.
SCU	Special Communications Unit of SIS.
SD	*Sicherheitsdienst*. Intelligence agency of the SS.
SDB	Special Duties Branch of GHQ Auxiliary Units.
Section D	Sabotage section of SIS, 1938–1940 (aka Section IX of SIS or the Statistical Research Department of the War Office).
Section V	Counter-espionage section of SIS.
SIS	Secret Intelligence Service (aka MI6).
SLU	Special Liaison Unit of SIS. Responsible for deciphering intelligence received by SCU and passing it on to the military.
SOE	Special Operations Executive.
SOPADE	Organisation of exiled German Social Democrats.
SPD	German Social Democratic Party (*Sozialdemokratische Partei Deutschlands*).
SPP	Serbian Peasant Party.
TIGR	Revolutionary Organisation of the Julian March – Trieste, Istria, Gorizia and Rijeka (Slovenian nationalist movement).
TNA	The National Archives.
TRD	Duplex wireless set developed for the Special Duties Branch of the GHQ Auxiliary Units.

In the original documents Section D officers and agents are usually referred to merely by their alphabetic codes. For simplicity, in the text these have been translated into their actual names. The original codes can be found in TNA HS 8/965-984, and are published in Atkin (2017b).

Preface

This study arose out of research on the planning for clandestine warfare in Britain during the Second World War (Atkin, 2015). It soon became apparent that SIS, and Section D in particular, had a much more central role than had been previously acknowledged. The wider history of Section D has attracted little attention in the historical literature, usually only as a preamble to accounts of SOE and negative in tone, fossilising the opinion of earlier writers. The present work has, wherever possible, returned to the original documents that are now publicly available in the National Archives and elsewhere. Yet even in 2017, some documents relating to the work of Section D have been redacted on national security grounds and some personnel files are subject to data protection. The story remains incomplete but it is now possible to offer a much broader picture of the work of Section D than has been possible hitherto, and a reassessment of its impact on the development of irregular warfare. It is also a story of the machinations and rivalries of the British government and its intelligence services in the early years of the war and the reluctance amongst many to engage with the consequences of 'total war'.

The policy of SIS is not to comment on the existence of its officers and agents, present or past. There are obvious security considerations in wishing to keep the identity of such people secret for as long as possible but this has meant that the contribution of SIS during the Second World War has been under-estimated, in favour of the flood of books dealing with its rivals in SOE. It has also meant that the contribution of many individuals, including those who worked for Section D, has never been publicly acknowledged. A further problem in trying to unravel the history of Section D in Eastern Europe and in the Middle East is that its work, and the identity of its agents, became entangled in post-war politics. The history of resistance to the Nazis in the Balkans was heavily rewritten to give maximum credit to the Communist parties that subsequently took power, whereas those groups that worked with Section D before the Communist Party took up the struggle risked being persecuted as agents of a foreign power. Such times have passed and hopefully this book will help give better appreciation for their efforts.

The British Foreign Office and War Office of the time did not take kindly to unorthodox thinkers and every effort was made at the time to systematically destroy the reputation of Laurence Grand, the head of Section D.[1] The attacks have largely been taken at face value in post-war historiography but, although

Grand certainly had his flaws, many criticisms were politically motivated and undeserved. An unknown civil servant appended to the brusque letter of dismissal of Grand in September 1940 'a word of thanks would not have come amiss'.[2] Hopefully the present work will allow the contribution of Laurence Grand to irregular warfare to be considered in a kinder light.

Malcolm Atkin
March 2017

Introduction

Germany annexed Austria in March 1938 (the *Anschluss*) and then made claim to the Czech Sudetenland. The British government desperately sought a diplomatic solution to the rising international crisis and on 30 September 1938 the Prime Minister, Neville Chamberlain, famously declared 'Peace in Our Time' (Pl. 2). Ignoring such optimism, few people were aware that, in the darkest depths of Whitehall, the recently formed Section D of the Secret Intelligence Service (SIS, *aka* MI6), was already preparing to go to war.

Section D (D for Destruction – also known as the 'Sabotage Service') was formed in April 1938 by Major Laurence Grand, under orders from the Chief of the Secret Service, Admiral Hugh Sinclair, and in March 1939, five months before war was officially declared, it was given formal approval to begin action. Grand's agents spread across Europe, creating a separate network from the existing intelligence-gathering operations of SIS and by 1940 it was ruthlessly pursuing what was now a no-holds-barred crusade against the Nazis that encompassed sabotage, political warfare and subversion. It shaped the course of irregular warfare during the Second World War and beyond, which was at odds with the 'softly softly' approach of appeasement and the 'phoney war', and questioned how far the concept of neutrality could be protected in a world war. Suspicion and distaste for this 'ungentlemanly' war then turned to envy as the War Office and Ministry of Economic Warfare looked upon its resources with greedy intent.

The whole ethos of Section D appeared 'un-British' and interfered with the mechanisms of official foreign policy. The staff were the anarchists of the British establishment and their simplistic ethos of 'the enemy of my enemy is my friend' brought them into bitter conflict with local diplomats. Efforts at political subversion irritated the Foreign Office, whilst the organisation of sabotage outside the military establishment offended the traditionally minded War Office. Section D was also an anathema to many in SIS, whose main purpose was the quiet gathering of intelligence. Every opportunity was taken to cast scorn on its efforts, especially, after the war, by those wishing to build the myth of its successor, the Special Operations Executive (SOE).

The sources are disjointed. Many SIS documents were destroyed as a matter of course once they had been read, were burnt during the invasion scares of 1940, or were destroyed post-war in a wholesale purge of secret service documents. To give an idea of the scale of what has now been lost, the Balkans section sent weekly reports back to London but few have survived. The SOE history of Section D remarked:

> The files of the French Office were destroyed at the time of the hasty evacuation of France, similar wholesale destruction took place in the London office during the invasion scare. It must also be admitted that with the re-organisation, new personnel inclined to discard all previous records as being useless either as past evidence of operations or as future guidance for planning.[1]

An unknown number of records were destroyed in a fire in 1946 at the former Baker Street HQ of SOE and in 1949 another weeding of documents resulted in the destruction of a reputed 100 tons of material.[2] A key source is the SOE history of Section D compiled during the summer of 1943 by former Section D officer Anthony Samuel (Pl. 6) and it makes frequent references to SIS correspondence files, memos and reports that are no longer available.[3]

Mackenzie's official *Secret History of SOE* has been the most comprehensive study of Section D to date. It was written in 1948 but not published until 2000, and several pages were still marked '[PASSAGE DELETED ON GROUNDS OF NATIONAL SECURITY]'. Many of these relate either to the activities of foreign groups operating in what was in 1948 part of the Eastern Bloc or in Palestine, or to the propaganda role of Section D. Even in 2017, some documents relating to this work remain classified on the grounds of national security, or are heavily redacted. Autobiographies of those concerned in the story of Section D have proved to be of dubious reliability. In his account of his work as an SIS agent in the Balkans, David Walker wrote:

> No successful agent writes a book. After years of espionage his mounting knowledge and experience commit him more and more to silence. Much of his success is in any case due to an acquired or natural preference for a life behind the scenes.[4]

Yet publishers demanded spy stories with dramatic tales of derring-do to match the fiction of James Bond-type characters. With no expectation in the 1960s and 1970s that official records would ever be released, many authors of autobiographies were tempted to embellish their stories. Similarly, biographers sanctified their secret agent subjects and more attention was given to stories of personal heroism and suffering than to an objective assessment of their strategic contribution. Already the fragility of memory was causing the sequence of events to be muddled, and fact and fiction began to be intertwined to a degree that would give pride to any exponent of black propaganda. There is always a risk of autobiographies being egocentric and, at the extreme, the memoirs of Section D agent John Toyne (1962) and Naval Intelligence's Merlin Minshall (1977) see both men apparently winning the war single-handedly, vying with each other to claim a source of the James Bond character created in 1953. Former Section D and SOE officer Leslie Humphreys provided what might be taken as the official view in September 1945:

> Any history of SOE would seem to be in the nature of self-vindication which as a secret service is in my opinion undesirable and unnecessary. That other people will seek to claim the honour and glory should, I think, leave us unmoved.[5]

The issue of objectivity became particularly relevant with histories written by those who had close links to wartime operations, or who later had to tread the delicate path as 'official historians'.

Section D was innovative and this brought risks. Criticism focused on the exuberant Laurence Grand but was rarely objective, driven by a wider political agenda. Far from the stereotype of the thoughtless maverick, the official documents show Grand repeatedly warning about the risk in what was expected of the Section. He was, however, impatient of delays caused by Foreign Office bureaucracy, which at times seemed to fear Section D as much as the Nazis – going to great lengths to contain, delay and thwart its plans. One particular area of suspicion was that Section D relied on foreign nationals for the success of its plans. Former First World War intelligence agent George Hill (who became a senior officer of Section D) wrote in 1932:

> the espionage agent finds himself again and again compelled to resort to the employment of nationals. It is because of this part of his work, because of the necessity imposed on him of associating with traitors, that a certain odium has come to be attached to the name of spy.[6]

Suspicion could be mutual. Anti-Nazi activists in Germany, Austria and Italy were wary of assisting a foreign power which might not have their own national interests as a priority. One problem in acknowledging the work of agents who collaborated with Section D in the Balkans came after the communist ascendancy post-war; the early work of Yugoslavs and Romanians with British intelligence was suppressed. Across the borders in Austria, it took decades to properly acknowledge the role of their native resistance, with many still regarding them as traitors. In 1953, in the town of Maria Gail, resistance fighters and victims of the Nazis were omitted from the new war memorial unveiled by former SS *Sturmbannführer* Karl Fritz, who in 1940 had hunted down the Austrian and Slovenian partners of Section D. Some of the most effective work of Section D was carried out by their Slovenian and Czech partners in Austria and the Balkans but the work of such early resistance groups is often overlooked in favour of stories of dashing British agents parachuted in to rescue the poor foreigners.

The story of Section D has become entwined in the later story of SOE and has principally been used as part of the apologia of the latter. The doyen of SOE historians, M.R.D. Foot, influenced by Bickham Sweet-Escott's whimsical account of his own experiences, claimed Section D had only one serious triumph

– the rescue of the industrial diamonds from Amsterdam by Montagu Chidson. There is no mention of the pioneering first raid into occupied Europe or its contribution to political warfare or to propaganda. He wrote off as incompetent Section D's attempts to create stay-behind units in Britain during the fraught months of 1940. This was all part of the necessary background to his thesis that SOE was 'starting from scratch, or very near it' and conveniently drew attention away from SOE's own failures.[7] Cruickshank's 1977 history of psychological warfare makes no mention at all of Section D, although he reproduced one of its propaganda leaflets.[8] Such early distortions have become fossilised in the scholarly record. Even in 2016, Lett could assert that 'One major problem was that SOE had to start from absolutely nothing … SOE had to start from scratch.'[9] Lindeman repeated Foot's contention that Section D was 'too imprac-tical' for the coming conflict. In his biography of Colin Gubbins, he saw Section D as 'chasing ghosts' as opposed to the more 'practical' efforts of MI(R), although the truth was far more complicated.[10] Nonetheless, as other sources became publicly accessible, other historians have been more charitable about the work of Section D. In 2004 Davies suggested that, with the popular focus on SOE, there had been a 'systematic undervaluation' of the achievements of Section D, particularly in regard to clandestine political warfare.[11] In 2006 Mark Seaman commented on 'the remarkable contribution of Section D and MI(R) to SOE's eventual success'.[12]

The breadth of activity of Section D was indeed remarkable during its period of active operation in 1939–1940. It operated across national borders, linking activists from diverse communities and political agendas. Any apparent chaos in its work must be judged within the fraught context of those times and the speed of Nazi invasions which left many schemes unfinished at the point of Section D's takeover by SOE. Sadly, the stories of those men and women involved can now only be partially reconstructed, largely from those who transferred to SOE and whose personnel files have survived. To accompany the present book, a bio-graphical database of Section D officers, agents and key contacts has been pub-lished online (Atkin 2017b).

The Special Operations Executive (SOE) was formally created on 22 July 1940 but Section D maintained an independent existence until 18 August and the structure did not change until after the dismissal of Laurence Grand a month later. Even then, in the Middle East the new organisation did not have an impact on the division between Section D and its military rival MI(R) until the end of the year and some staff continued to be employed by SIS until that date.

For convenience, ranks are not generally given in the text. The use of substan-tive, temporary and acting ranks were used in cavalier fashion by SIS and can be confusing, especially where officers were recommissioned in 1940 but preferred to use their higher ranks from the First World War.

Chapter 1

Creating the 'Fourth Arm' – 1938

Everything you do is going to be disliked by a lot of people in Whitehall –
some in this building. The more you succeed, the more they will dislike you
and what you are trying to do.

(Admiral Hugh Sinclair, Chief of the SIS, 1 April 1938)[1]

The British government had considered the possibility of a war with Germany
as soon as Hitler took power in 1933, with a chillingly accurate estimate that
Germany would be ready to take the offensive in 1938 or 1939.[2] The task of
gathering intelligence on the rise of the Nazi war machine was that of the Secret
Intelligence Service (SIS, *aka* MI6). But SIS was starved of resources during the
inter-war period and, as the estimate for the outbreak of war drew closer, Admiral
Hugh Sinclair, Chief of SIS (CSS), tried to put the organisation onto a better
war footing. The intelligence operations of SIS would remain pre-eminent but
Sinclair also wanted SIS to take a more aggressive role, arguing in 1935 that
Britain needed the capability to retaliate against any threat of sabotage.[3] In 1937
Claude Dansey, head of the Z network, suggested to Sinclair that SIS should
recruit sabotage agents who would be kept distinct from SIS intelligence-
gathering networks. They would be 'agents we have employed from time to time
[who] were more fitted for this kind of action than they were for obtaining information'. In January 1938 Section III (Naval) and Section VI (Industrial) endorsed
the concept, but to Dansey's dismay Sinclair went further and in April 1938 he
created Section D with a broader remit to include propaganda and political warfare.[4] Its agents would become the 'Fourth Arm' of warfare, a clandestine civilian
force supplementing the three regular services. The task was fundamentally at
odds with the primary role of SIS in quietly collecting and assessing intelligence;
it also carried huge risks of precipitating diplomatic incidents. Bickham Sweet-
Escott, an officer in Section D and later SOE, put it thus:

> The man who is interested in obtaining intelligence must have peace and
> quiet, and the agents he employs must never, if possible, be found out. But
> the man who has to carry out operations will produce loud noises if he is suc-
> cessful, and it is only too likely that some of the men he uses will not escape.[5]

Section D was conceived as a weapon of offence. The concept of organising subversion and sabotage before any declaration of war caused distaste within both

SIS and the Foreign Office, especially as targets included neutral countries having trading interests with the anticipated enemy. The tendency was for those few officials and politicians who were aware of its activities to look the other way, producing a lack of engagement that was later to have serious consequences. As the 1940 Hankey Inquiry into SIS commented:

> At first sight the natural instinct of any humane person is to recoil from this undesirable business [sabotage] as something he would rather know nothing about.[6]

In early March 1938, just before the *Anschluss*, 40-year-old Major Laurence Grand, then Deputy Assistant Director of Mechanisation at the War Office, was asked if he would be interested in a secondment to SIS to advise on sabotage.[7] Later that day, he was collected by Stewart Menzies (then head of SIS Section II (Military) and Sinclair's deputy) and taken to meet Admiral Sinclair at his house at Queen Anne's Gate (connected to the rear of SIS HQ at Broadway Buildings). A professional soldier in the Royal Engineers, Grand had served during the First World War in France and North Russia, and subsequently in Kurdistan, where his work with the irregular Iraq levies earned him an MBE. After a series of staff appointments and work with Imperial Chemical War Research, in 1938 he was coming to the end of a four-year posting at the War Office. He was looking forward to being posted to Egypt in command of an engineering unit and was assured by his commanding officer that his attachment to SIS would be short and would not affect the Middle East posting.[8] Speaking after the war, Colonel Leslie Wood of Aston House mistakenly believed that Grand came to the attention of SIS through an incident on India's North-West Frontier, where he 'doctored' ammunition that he knew would be stolen by the Pathans and would lead to the rifles blowing up in the thieves' faces, which was regarded as ungentlemanly behaviour by his fellow officers. However, Grand did not serve in India until later in his service and this story might instead refer to events in Kurdistan, thereby forming the inspiration for Section D booby trap experiments whereby detonators were inserted into .303 rounds with explosive results! More prosaically, Grand had written a paper on irregular warfare whilst at the War Office in 1937, which brought him to the attention of Stewart Menzies, who suggested him for the new post.[9] Although not a career intelligence officer, he did have a reputation for being inventive and a skilled engineer with a knowledge of demolition. The immediate enthusiasm of Grand for the task proved disconcerting.

Grand was tall, handsome and armed with a sharp wit (Pl. 1). He abandoned his army uniform whilst with SIS and was always elegantly dressed with a red carnation in his lapel, and chain-smoking cigarettes from a long, black, cigarette holder. He was a free thinker, not something that sat easily within the corridors of power in either the War Office or SIS HQ, and he was not gifted with tact. Kim Philby, one-time Section D officer, described him thus: 'his mind was certainly not clipped. It ranged free and handsome over the whole field of his awesome responsibilities, never shrinking from an idea, however big or wild'.[10] Such men inspire and infuriate in equal measure. To the Director of Military Intelligence, General Pownall, Grand was 'gifted, enthusiastic and persuasive, but I do not regard him as being well-balanced or reliable'.[11] Ever optimistic, for Joan Bright Astley he was a 'volatile dreamer':

> His imagination flaring ahead of our schemes, each one of which seemed to him a war-stopper. If, as so often happened, one of his schemes or ours [MIR] came to nothing, he showed no disappointment, called for more and never let his enthusiasm descend to the level of a cautious 'Wait and see'.[12]

Grand attracted fierce loyalty from his staff but a deep suspicion from others. For Eric Maschwitz he was a remarkable man: 'Like the rest of the staff I adored him to the point of hero-worship.'[13] Grand was loyal in return, necessarily giving staff considerable discretion in a flat organisational structure that otherwise placed a huge personal responsibility on Grand. His principle of defending his staff 'through thick and thin whatever mistakes you might make' could, however, be dangerous, as events in Sweden were to show.[14] Grand's theatrical nature found the air of secrecy surrounding SIS appealing and his officers were not supposed to acknowledge each other if they met in the street. His friend and colleague, Lieutenant Colonel Jo Holland of MI(R), was amused by such behaviour and sometimes used to shout 'Boo' to members when he passed them in the street. The mischievous John Walter, former *Times* journalist and now Section D officer, once got into trouble for lack of respect when he did not acknowledge Sinclair when he paid a visit to the office. 'I'm sorry,' said Walter, 'but I thought we were not supposed to know who he was.'[15]

Colin Gubbins, the future head of SOE but then sharing offices with Section D as part of the War Office MI(R) (*see* p. 22), was aghast at what he saw as the amateurishness and extravagance of some of the wilder projects of Section D, but at the same time he found the risk-taking attitude of the young ex-businessmen refreshing in contrast to the ponderous hierarchy of the War Office.[16] In the immediate frustration of his wartime politicking, Gladwyn Jebb of the Foreign Office (first CEO of SOE) complained that Grand's judgement 'is almost always wrong, his knowledge wide but alarmingly superficial, his organisation in many respects a laughing stock, and he is a consistent and fluent liar'.[17] This came after Grand and Stewart Menzies together concocted a series of paper-thin lies for the Foreign Office, to try to provide plausible deniability for the Oxelösund sabotage scheme (*see* Chapter 9). Jebb's attitude later mellowed and whilst still describing Grand as 'rather theatrical and James Bondish', he now admitted that Grand was 'impressive' and 'an able man who inspired loyalty'.[18] Grand's citation for the award of CBE in 1943, when he was Chief Engineer for 4 Corps in India, not only offered what was a universal acknowledgement of his drive and imagination but also significantly complimented his organisational skills – proof of the political nature of earlier criticism. It stated:

> Owing to lack of resources, much improvisation has been necessary. His drive and energy has reflected itself in those working under him. ... He has shown great ability as an organiser under difficult conditions and a determination to attain his object. His work merits recognition.[19]

Grand's successful career as an engineering officer, retiring as Director of Fortifications and Works with the rank of major general, certainly demonstrates that he was not the uncontrollable maverick that might be inferred from some of his detractors.

At his interview in early March, Sinclair told Grand that he wanted someone to 'look after sabotage'. Grand's first question was 'Is anything banned?', to which came the blunt reply: 'Nothing at all.' He began work on 1 April and, prophetically, Sinclair warned the task would not be popular: 'Don't have any illusions. Everything you do is going to be disliked by a lot of people in Whitehall – some in this building. The more you succeed, the more they will dislike you and what you are trying to do.' In what became a mantra for Grand, Sinclair added 'There are a lot of jealous people about so don't tell anyone more than you have to.'[20] Jebb wrote after the war: 'The great criticism of the old D Organisation had been that nobody knew what it was up to and that none of those departments which should have been consulted was consulted.'[21] As will be shown, such criticism (of a policy encouraged by Sinclair) was often unfair. Having been given an office on the ground floor of SIS HQ in Broadway Buildings (Pl. 9), with a desk and chair but little else, he admitted 'we were starting from scratch with a vengeance'.[22] Grand was originally appointed for just two months and had no staff. His initial task was to write a feasibility study of a new type of warfare and he admitted the concept was 'peculiarly disreputable'.[23] Grand's report of 31 May 1938 was a comprehensive plan for encouraging internal revolt against the Nazis. The potential targets, which were both broad and shocking to those who still clung to a gentlemanly vision of war, encompassed not only sabotage of electricity supplies, telephones, railways, dockyards and airfields, but also considered starting forest and crop fires, poisoning food supplies and the introduction of disease into animals and crops. This focus on economic warfare, rather than purely military targets, was a core element of British strategic planning during the first two years of war, deriving from the widespread belief that in the First World War it was the economic blockade that finally broke Germany, rather than the fighting on the Western Front. Resources to develop such work were slender and it was envisaged that existing foreign anti-Nazi groups would be the main mechanism of delivery.

Grand's report was approved and in June 1938 he became Head of the new Section D, *aka* Section IX, *aka* the 'Sabotage Service', *aka* the 'Statistical Research Department of the War Office', reporting directly to the Chief of SIS.

Its offices were originally in the shabby basement of SIS HQ at 54 Broadway Buildings which, despite its pre-war cover of the 'Minimax Fire Extinguisher Company', was an address known to London taxi drivers and German agents alike as the home of Britain's secret intelligence service (Pl. 9). In April 1939 Section D moved around the corner from Broadway to the 6th floor of a Victorian mansion block at 2 Caxton Street, connected by a passage to the St Ermin's Hotel where Grand later maintained an apartment funded by Section D (Pl. 10). Eric Maschwitz described the early premises in Caxton Street as a cramped little office where the security was somewhat weakened by the staff cars and uniformed dispatch riders that were constantly parked outside it. The original charter of Section D stated it was 'to investigate every possibility of attacking potential enemies by means other than the operation of military forces'.[24] Its twin aims were to:

1. undertake sabotage and create anti-German political unrest in neutral and occupied countries, and
2. provide lines of communication from neutral countries into enemy countries for introduction of propaganda (produced by Section D or from other departments).

Such aims not only challenged the accepted concepts of neutrality and diplomatic process but also raised concern in official circles regarding the moral consequences of guerrilla warfare fought by civilians with no visible chain of command, which was illegal under The Hague Convention and was a form of warfare that Britain condemned when conducted against itself by the IRA. This was to be a political, as much as a sabotage, campaign, drawing inspiration from previous campaigns of irregular warfare in Russia, Arabia, Kurdistan and Ireland, and recognised that Section D would be reliant on the participation of local groups driven by their own political agenda. The obvious allies to oppose the Nazi state were socialists, communists, Jews and trade unions. The May report envisaged communists as carrying out general sabotage, together with the recruitment of 'lone wolves' to attack specific targets. There was also to be 'moral sabotage' (which Grand believed was best undertaken by Jewish groups) comprising 'whisperings' and even the first use of automatic nuisance telephone calls. It was hoped that, collectively, such work 'would create a feeling of disquiet' within Germany, divert large numbers of troops for internal security duties and lead to a popular revolt, so obviating the need for a British expeditionary force to fight abroad.[25] There was a problem in that the British establishment tended to view any group of foreigners as inherently untrustworthy and unreliable. Grand himself recognized the need and the problems of recruiting from such groups:

> This started us on a maze, from the original occasional and tenuous contacts, through masses of wishful thinking and exaggerated claims to a few important and serious bodies.[26]

In July 1940 the Minister in charge of the new SOE, Hugh Dalton, would appropriate the methodology as an explicitly socialist agenda but Laurence Grand was no socialist, driven rather by a calculating practicality. Grand had ambitions as a prospective Conservative MP and in 1939 his wife Irene worked for the Conservative Party Central Office whilst his chief of staff in Section D was Marjorie Maxse, the redoubtable chief organising officer of the Conservative Party.

Operations would rely on the establishment in Germany and surrounding neutral countries of agent networks and supply dumps of sabotage material. In Scandinavia, agents would target Swedish iron ore shipments, Finnish food shipments and the passing of supplies to German workers in Hamburg, Kiel, etc. In the Balkans, agents would attempt to interrupt oil from Romania and Russia, and food supplies from Italy. Agents in Belgium or Switzerland would attempt to supply sabotage devices to workers in southern Germany, the Ruhr and the Saar.[27] The immediate priority in 1938 was research into sabotage devices and their production, the identification of targets and the organisation of contacts and supply dumps in neutral countries. Not surprisingly the plan was met 'with a combination of alarm and fascination'.[28] For some it was ambitious, for others 'it merely scratched the surface'. It was 'too wide' or of 'doubtful practicality'. It would eventually develop into the D Plan of March 1939 (*see* p. 22).

Propaganda

In the wake of Hitler's success in promoting his view of the Munich crisis, on 26 September 1938 Sinclair expanded the remit of Section D into black propaganda, 'to form immediately a section for the dissemination through all channels outside this country of material to enemy and neutral countries'.[29] This had been anticipated by Grand and an immediate success was the broadcast into Germany of Neville Chamberlain's speech outlining the British position in the negotiations (Pl. 2). It was broadcast illegally on Radio Luxembourg on 28 September 1938, to immediate protests from Berlin. On 30 September both the existence of Section D and its new role were introduced to Stephen Tallents, then Director-Designate of the proposed Ministry of Information (the MOI) via a meeting with his liaison officer, A.P. Ryan.[30] A puzzled Ryan was introduced to Grand and two of his new officers, a Major 'Thornton' (? Thornley) and Walter Wren, and was told that a propaganda leaflet, printed in German, was already due for distribution. Ryan explained: 'The first two of these [Grand and Thornton] are soldiers who took me to see some of their foreign contacts. Major Grand expressed strong views on how this type of propaganda should be conducted.'[31] Grand explained that the propaganda work of Section D would fall into four areas:

a) broadcasting, using foreign radio stations;
b) making an index of foreign newspapers and their journalists to direct material to them;
c) leaflets 'distributed by any and every means' and written appropriately for the group that would be distributing them; and

d) whispering campaigns of the type that had been effective in the First World War.[32]

There was a subsequent briefing with Grand on 5 October when Ryan had to admit, 'I am still not certain to whom Major Grand is responsible. He told me that he was not directly under either the War Office or the Foreign Office.'[33] Ryan would have realised that it was not going to be easy to unravel Grand's chain of command when asked whether a new Section D officer, John Walter (formerly of *The Times*), might be given cover as a member of the MOI or the BBC. Work to establish the MOI was still in the preparatory stage but Grand tactfully stressed that he would not wish to cut across its work when finally mobilised, acknowledging that the MOI would be responsible for determining policy as well as the preparation of material, with the main role of Section D being to act as a covert channel of distribution. Admiral Sinclair, however, made clear that any material to be secretly distributed needed to be suitable for the local target group – if necessary by Section D being involved in its production. This would have consequences for future relations. Sinclair informed Tallents:

> Although the matter to be disseminated will come from the Ministry of Information or other authority, the actual printing and the form in which it is produced will be a matter for liaison between ourselves and the Ministry of Information, and although we shall of course use their printing when possible, we must obviously be empowered to convey the matter which they wish disseminated, in whatever form we may find possible.[34]

Grand was equally punctual in explaining the propaganda role of Section D to the embryonic Department of Publicity in Enemy Countries, better known simply as Electra House or EH, under Sir Campbell Stuart. The two men dined together in April 1939, when they not only discussed their respective plans but also interviewed Robert Walmsley, described as 'the best German leaflet writer in the UK', whom Grand asked to join Section D as an interim measure until EH could mobilise. Grand explained that Section D would be responsible for propaganda against Germany up to the outbreak of war, at which point EH would take over but, as with the MOI, Section D would still have a role in distribution.[35] In September 1939 Walmsley was still on the fringes of Section D as an editorial consultant, but transferred to EH soon afterwards. Dansey was annoyed by the widening brief of Section D:

> I immediately realised that, far from confining his [Grand's] activities and thoughts to the original purpose, he had got tied up with propaganda interests and 'whispers' and such-like ideas, which he was pleased to term 'The 4th Arm' ...[36]

Sinclair and Grand saw no such limitations, directing Section D towards 'influencing events in any part of the world as to be favourable to the policy of His

Majesty's Government', and this was the context for the recruitment of highly experienced advertising executives and journalists, although they sometimes seemed out of their depth when later drawn into the organisation of sabotage.[37] There was no comparable body in any other branch of war planning and for Grand this was a crusade, with political warfare at its heart, that demanded a total, uncompromising, commitment.

> It was soon realised that against such an enemy as Hitler who harnessed to his war chariot the four horses of treacherous diplomacy, lying propaganda, racial persecutions and economic blackmail, sabotage must in turn be spiritual, political and economic, as well as merely physical.[38]

Direct broadcasting into a foreign country had been made illegal in 1936, but time could be bought on foreign commercial radio stations that broadcast into Germany (i.e. Radios Luxembourg, Strasbourg and Liechtenstein). In October 1938 Grand created the Joint Broadcasting Committee (JBC) to organise broadcasting into Germany using those radio stations as well as secret radio stations within Germany. The members of the JBC, under the chairmanship of Lord Rothes, were chosen by Grand as being 'biddable' and had close, if complicated, personal ties. They were orchestrated by Guy Burgess, who was recruited to Section D in December 1938 and was liaison officer from the JBC to Electra House under the cover of being employed by the Ministry of Information.[39] The Broadcasting Director was Miss Hilda Matheson, formerly Talks Director at the BBC. She was in a relationship with the ex-wife of another committee member, Harold Nicolson, whilst Harold was a close friend, if not lover, of Burgess. Keeping order was the committee secretary, Elizabeth Hodgson, a pre-war SIS officer now in Section D. Funding was provided through the expedient of gold sovereigns from the Section D 'slush' fund which so irritated critics. A complication was that the BBC had long been fighting to get Radio Luxembourg off the air, claiming that it lost over half its audience to the station at the weekends. To avoid embarrassment, Grand (minuted as being from the 'Communications Department' of the Foreign Office) attended meetings of the Cabinet Committee on Overseas Broadcasting and was asked to work with J.W. Philips from the GPO to find a diplomatic solution. The answer was typically machiavellian. Grand suggested that any questions on the subject in Parliament should be met with the response that the government was getting nowhere in its negotiations with Luxembourg and that, for the moment, no good purpose would be served by pursuing the matter. The British delegates to the forthcoming Wavelength Conference should also refrain from any attack on Luxembourg and avoid any position on advertising policies.[40] Writer W.J. West has described Grand's use of Radio Luxembourg as 'objectionable and scurrilous', with the JBC being 'the most daring excursion by the British into secret illegal broadcasting'.[41]

In March 1939 Hilda Matheson formed an overt element of the JBC as a 'goodwill committee' to develop 'closer intercourse between the Nations of

Europe'. It was hoped that 'cultural propaganda' would overcome the objections of owners of foreign stations to broadcasting explicit political propaganda. Meanwhile, Section D continued to use the facilities of the JBC to secretly produce gramophone records of anti-Nazi propaganda that it could distribute through its own channels. By early 1940 Section D material was being broadcast to fourteen countries from Europe to South America. Hundreds of recordings were made each month and thousands of gramophone records of them were then distributed. Those sent to neutral countries were distributed by the JBC, whilst Section D secretly distributed German language records within Germany and Austria, including special 4-inch-diameter flexible records that could be hidden in a rolled-up newspaper.[42] To make the propaganda more appealing, the recordings included variety programmes with selections of popular music, produced by Guy Burgess. Small portable transmitters were produced that included a record player, the idea being that if enough broadcasts were made across Germany on short-range mobile transmitters, the overall impression would be of a major 'freedom' radio station.[43] Success may be judged by the fact that the German government complained to the British Embassy in Berlin and made attacks in speeches and in the press on the British propaganda emanating from Radio Luxembourg. The Foreign Office referred all complaints to the BBC, who legitimately denied all knowledge of the origin! The JBC was funded by a £2,000 grant from the MOI and £800 from Section D but by August 1940 the Ministry suspected that Section D was siphoning off the MOI grant to subsidise the covert operations of JBC. Matheson died in October 1940 and full control of the JBC finally passed to the MOI in February 1941.

By April 1939 the propaganda work of Section D was well established and Grand took the lead in proposing the establishment of a policy committee to consider the future organisation of British propaganda. His enthusiasm may well have been considered overbearing by the members of the proto-MOI and EH who were yet to properly enter the field.[44] He put down a clear marker for the work of Section D, highlighting its work to date and, although stressing that Section D would cooperate with the MOI and EH in time of war, pointing out that these bodies were not yet in formal existence. This meant that Section D was, in practice, the lead agency for the distribution of propaganda by leaflet and broadcast, while the frustrated MOI and EH watched from the sidelines.

The expanding scope of work of Section D, as defined by Sinclair, was well beyond its meagre resources. In 1946 Grand ruefully reflected: 'Examining such an enormous task, one felt as if one had been told to move the Pyramids with a pin.'[45] One consequence of the novelty of Section D was that he had to spend an inordinate amount of time dissipating his energies by justifying its existence.[46] Here, Grand's greatest asset also proved to be his curse with Julian Amery describing him as having unusual powers of persuading his superiors as well as enthusing his subordinates.[47] The reaction from within SIS in May 1938 to this pro-active programme had been mixed and confused.

This survey was passed to the various sections of the Secret Service, who commented variously that it was ambitious, that it merely scratched the surface, that it went too far and too fast, that it was too wide or that too much of it was of doubtful practicality. One officer took the line that he was against active preparations in peacetime; another declared that there were no communist or anti-Hitler organisations in Germany, while a third thought that the organisation of sabotage within Germany should be left to the anti-Nazi organisations, one of which he had reason to believe was considering the problem.[48]

Sabotage and subversion

On 2 October 1938 the *News of the World* reported Chamberlain's return from the four-power Munich conference with an agreement that brought 'peace with honour' even though it hinged on the cession of the Czech Sudetenland to the Germans.[49] Unimpressed with this public declaration of world peace, two weeks later on 19 October Laurence Grand reported to Admiral Sinclair his progress in developing Section D to make war against Nazi Germany including:

1. The establishment of secure lines of communications into Germany from surrounding neutral countries.
2. Appointment of three officers covering
   a) Scandinavia and the Baltic,
   b) Romania, Hungary and Yugoslavia, and
   c) Holland, Luxembourg and Switzerland.
3. A Fleet Street agency had begun work on a survey of the international press to identify all the anti-Nazi movements throughout Europe.
4. A card index was established of potential contacts in bodies such as the Vatican, the Communist Party, the trade union movement, etc.
5. £2,000 to be spent on experimental work concerning explosive devices, with £1,000 required to produce initial stocks.
6. Appointment of an officer to investigate the transport of sabotage material from England to representatives abroad.[50]

Here was the beginning of a process that was to see Section D outstrip the size of the rest of SIS. It was viewed, by its detractors, as being beyond control but this was not the case during the lifetime of Admiral Sinclair, who had inspired its foundation and early development. Even under his successor, Stewart Menzies, there was a structured system of project vetting and monthly reports to CSS. In November plans to develop a sabotage network were stepped up when Grand asked Colonel Dansey whether he had any contacts in industries connected with oil, rubber, aluminium, railways, margarine and edible oils, power houses, naval engine rooms and foundries. The aim was to establish sympathetic contacts in those industries connected to likely future sabotage targets. Events were certainly to show that the Section D organisation relied heavily on the type of commercial contacts that Dansey had been cultivating over many years, including those of Chester Beatty through his Selection Trust Group, the Unirea Oil Company of T.S. Masterson, and Viscount Bearsted's Shell Oil. Dansey was fearful that Section D was about to conduct its own foreign policy which risked arming foreign anti-Nazi groups whose primary interest might be to disrupt Chamberlain's efforts for peace. Grand's pointed response was that he was merely following the orders of the head of SIS (therefore, by implication, so should Dansey) but he offered reassurance that his work was still only at a preparatory stage. His response to Dansey was, however, somewhat economical with the truth as both Grand and Sinclair were well aware that they were acting in anticipation of an eventual change to official government policy.

> In 1938 CSS [Admiral Sinclair] knew that, barring a miracle, war was coming. The Government was warned in general terms and with detailed reports of preparations. But there was no overall government policy of resistance to Germany. Hence all the time our efforts in Section D were in effect against one of the policies HBMG [His Britannic Majesty's Government] was pursuing, that in Foreign Affairs, though our efforts were in-keeping with, and may perhaps have been regarded as part of, the rearmament programme which was just beginning to pursue its leisured way.[51]

Preparations for underground warfare had already gone beyond the theoretical model that Grand had admitted to Dansey. In August Section D had made a preliminary survey of Narvik harbour in Norway to establish options for sabotage. Even as the Munich crisis developed, Grand made a personal visit to the Skoda armaments works in Czechoslovakia (Pl. 17) to discuss, with Czech intelligence, the core of a future sabotage network.[52] It was the first link between British intelligence and the future European resistance movement; Czech agents were to provide a mainstay of saboteurs in Section D. In February 1939 the then Deputy Head of SIS, Stewart Menzies, briefed his opposite numbers in the French 2ième Bureau on the ethos of Section D. He spoke of the need for both propaganda and 'terrorism' (as he put it) against Germany and Italy. Menzies admitted that SIS had been studying the options for sabotage for more than a year and he believed that 'acts of terrorism' would

> crystallise opposition to the Nazi regime and profoundly disrupt military and economic life in Germany. Potential targets (such as factories and communications) had already been identified, as had the personnel to mount attacks (for example Communists and anarchists).[53]

Having briefed its ally, on 23 March 1939 Section D received its authorisation to go to war (*see* Chapter 2). The history of Section D by SOE was clear in blaming many of the subsequent failings of Section D on the reluctance of the Foreign Office to accept this new form of warfare and a similar criticism came from within, levelled by Gladwyn Jebb: 'To be candid, I thought it was a weakness of the FO that it tended to be more critical than constructive.'[54] Grand's own assessment put the blame on a broader scale:

> as a nation, we had not only distrusted political propaganda and felt a traditional distaste for it, but we had obstinately refused to comprehend it.[55]

As Section D agents deployed around the neutral countries of Europe they caused horror in the traditionalist world of the Legations. Their work was designed to be carried out at a distance from the normal diplomatic business and to be capable of being disavowed, but at the same time they needed contact with the Legation, which provided wireless communications through the SIS station and could provide protection through the granting of diplomatic status as local vice-consuls. The greatest temptation was to use the diplomatic immunity of the Legation to provide safe storage of explosives, risking embarrassment to the diplomatic establishment.

Staffing

The first recruits to Section D were Commander John Langley, an explosives expert, and Edward 'Dead-eye Dick' Schröter, a civilian expert in telecommunications. From such small beginnings Section D grew rapidly in a number of sub-sections (Fig. 1) with a flat organisational structure that was difficult to co-ordinate, expanding to the point where it was difficult for contemporaries to establish its true size. There were both full-time and part-time British officers, volunteer agents and a range of foreign partner groups. Some officers were recruited to Section D on a 'Territorial' basis to be given minimal training in peacetime and then co-opted as full-time intelligence officers in time of war (when they would be given an army commission).[56] Some officers had private means and did not require a salary. They were the traditional 'honourable correspondents' of SIS, drawn from a tight social circle bound by schooling and family, who would discreetly carry out secret missions when required. Grand became expert in persuading newspapers and commercial bodies to continue at least part-paying other officers as part of their cover and it is a moot point as to whether the British Council realised that several of its lecturers in Italy and the Balkans were Section D agents.[57] Where possible, the officers were given diplomatic status as a measure of protection, as assistant consuls or assistant press officers, although this was greatly resented by local Ministers.

The long-established tradition of amateurism in British intelligence would soon become apparent. According to Maschwitz, the staff of Section D were a mixed bunch, including an advertising copywriter, ballistics expert, racing driver, oil millionaire, lawyers, real estate agents and journalists as well as men in 'mufti' from the services. Fortunately, there were also experienced intelligence officers, with service dating back to the First World War. For Langley, they were 'rather strange people'.[58] Men were particularly sought from the industrial sector for their specialized technical knowledge and for their international contacts. The preponderance of SIS officers acting under the cover of 'journalist' was so common in the Balkans that any British journalist was likely to come under suspicion. George Lofoglu was a Greek who had worked for the British intelligence service during the period of British occupation (1919–1923). He was sent to Turkey in March under the cover of being a special correspondent for Reuters but his fellow reporters saw through his cover and threatened to resign since he was jeopardising their own legitimate activities.[59] Overall, the officers tended to be in their early 40s – younger, fitter men would stand out for not being in the services.

Women were mainly in administrative and secretarial positions but they included several key personalities. Marjorie Maxse, chief organising officer of the Conservative Party and vice-chair of the WVS, was the chief recruiting officer and Grand's first Chief of Staff. A remarkable trio of female officers, whose experience with SIS went back to the First World War, were Evelyn Stamper, Clara Holmes and Elizabeth 'Bessie' Hodgson. These became senior officers of the Section D Propaganda and Austrian sections with Stamper salaried as a major, Holmes and Hodgson as captains.[60] They were the longest-serving female intelligence officers of the Second World War and deserve greater recognition for their quiet dedication and skill. Holmes (Pl. 4) had been forced to flee Austria in 1938 and in 1940 was liaising with German émigrés in Paris. She and Stamper became mainstays of the Austrian section of SOE. Elizabeth Hodgson also joined SOE and in 1943 was obliged to avoid arrest in Switzerland by a perilous journey through occupied France and across the Pyrenees to Spain. She later served in Italy providing black propaganda to Italian partisans. Several family partnerships were recruited, including Mary, the wife of Gerard Holdsworth, who later managed the accommodation of the Helston Flotilla; Bickham Sweet-Escott employed his sister, Lutie, as a secretary in the Balkans and Middle East; Leslie Sheridan's wife Doris organised transport arrangements for couriers. One of the most intriguing is 'Mrs Douglas', who was a finance officer in London. Douglas was an alias of Laurence Grand and she may have been his wife, Irene. If the value of secret agents is assessed on the basis of their strategic value rather than their suffering, such women deserve as much attention as later SOE female agents such as Krystyna Skarbek (Christine Granville), who launched her controversial and semi-mythical career in Section D.

Grand admitted that it was difficult to find qualified staff for the salaries offered. There were, however, some perks to working for an organisation that did not officially exist. Staff were paid in cash and paid no income tax. Some business accounts were settled in gold sovereigns![61] Grand told a story of once being in Sinclair's office when he was asked if he needed any money for entertaining. Sinclair then pulled out £100 in notes from a desk drawer.[62] Annual salaries of officers averaged £500–£600 in 1939 but showed little discernible pattern. Arnold Lawrence moved from a salary of £350 with the University of Cambridge to £650 with Section D. R.J. Barwell was recruited with a salary of £720 at the same time as Nigel Westall at £264. John Hackett had a salary of £800.[63] Some foreign partners were paid bonuses upon satisfactory results from either sabotage or passing propaganda into Germany, providing a sometimes irresistible financial temptation to exaggerate successes.

The traditional SIS method of recruitment was from a known school, family or business circle. Grand's old school of Rugby featured prominently and most recruits were university-educated. The advertising firm J. Walter Thompson promised to put its whole organisation at the disposal of Section D, including the Chief Executive Douglas Saunders, Director of the film unit Gerard Holdsworth, Art Director George Butler, and advertising executives Ingram Fraser and Hratchia Paniguian. Viscount Bearsted recruited several friends and colleagues from the banking world and Shell Oil. Engineer Walter T. Wren did not fit the normal profile of the stereotypical SIS recruit but was a pre-war friend of Grand who had sold him an Aga cooker. A simple security enquiry to MI5 would normally report 'nothing against', followed by a discreet phone call to one's place of work and an informal interview at a convenient club or restaurant, or simply in the forecourt of the St Ermin's Hotel. After receiving a mysterious telephone call from the War Office asking if he was interested in some undisclosed work, Kim Philby had his first interview with Chief of Staff, Marjorie Maxse.

> I found myself in the forecourt of St Ermin's Hotel, near St James's Park station, talking to Miss Marjorie Maxse. She was an intensely likeable elderly lady (then almost as old as I am now). I had no idea then, as I have no idea now, what her precise position in government was. But she spoke with authority, and was evidently in a position at least to recommend me for interesting employment.[64]

William Berington first came to the notice of SIS in 1937 when he answered an enigmatic advertisement in *The Times*: 'A few vacancies exist in employment requiring gentlemen of Public School education with a knowledge of European languages. Commencing salary £500 p.a.'[65] The address was an anonymous London PO Box but was a trawl for possible future officers who could speak foreign languages; Berington's name went onto a card index and led to him being approached to join Section D in August 1939. He became liaison officer to the German and Italian opposition groups in France.

An essential element of Section D was the partnership of paid British officers with a wide range of activists of differing national backgrounds and life experience – from academics and journalists to smugglers and those who had lived for many years as refugees from the Nazis. They brought a harder, uncompromising edge to the work of Section D and were responsible for much of the operational activity. Until the establishment of the 'D School' in July 1940 (*see* Chapter 3), training of the British officers was minimal and well educated academics or businessmen, however enthusiastic, did not necessarily make the best spies. At first, the intention was to use experienced foreign anti-Nazi groups to conduct sabotage and, other than the recruitment of mining engineers in the Balkans, recruitment was geared towards men who might be well suited to subversion and propaganda, taken from the advertising or journalist professions as well as the less-likely profession of chartered accountants. Hugh Seton-Watson (SOE officer in Romania in late 1940) characterised the Section D recruits as follows:

> nearly all the earlier recruits lacked the habit of subordination to a regular hierarchy; were disciplined by no mandarin ethos; and were impatient or even contemptuous of the bureaucratic conventions of the diplomatic service and its auxiliaries. To the diplomats, they often appeared brash, ignorant of things which diplomats were trained to regard as important, and at times a positive menace.[66]

There was a tradition of heavy drinking in the intelligence community that, as ever, could cause security issues. There were repeated complaints of drunken Naval Intelligence and Section D officers in Romania, and in England Special Branch arrested a drunken, voluble, member of Section D in a public house:

> A man called Thomas [XXXXX] who had been working in SIS has been interned under Emergency Regulation 18(b) for gross indiscretion when in a state of intoxication. He is a member of Laurence Grand's party and was telling everybody exactly what he was going to do.[67]

In September 1940 Guy Burgess appeared before Marlborough Street Magistrates Court in London, charged with driving a War Office car whilst under the influence of drink. The defence case was that Burgess was under the strain of working fourteen hours a day on 'rather confidential' work and had just been caught up in an air raid. The case was dismissed with the payment of 5 guineas costs by Burgess, but the magistrate declared the real 'villain of the piece' was a 'high War Office official'. So discreetly put, this was Laurence Grand. Burgess had been returning home from a dinner party at Grand's St Ermin's Hotel apartment and the magistrate made the point: 'Judging by the rank of your chief, he is an older man than you; and it was very wrong of him to send a young man out with a car, having given him more drink than was advisable.'[68] It would, however, have taken a truly remarkable man to have curtailed the alcoholic excesses of Guy Burgess. It is debatable whether this really was a simple 'dinner party'. Also in the car was a Swiss diplomat friend and one-time lover of Burgess. Grand and Burgess may have been trying to secure his cooperation for Section D operations in Switzerland, where the authorities were being difficult. If so, the fact that his name was kept out of the court proceedings would have been a bonus in securing his gratitude. Guy Burgess was a well-known homosexual and, it being illegal at the time, in normal circumstances it would have flagged up a security risk, but Burgess was so widely considered a disreputable person that the risk of blackmail was slight. To fellow officer H. Montgomery Hyde, Burgess was 'a blatant homosexual, an alcoholic, and distinctly unclean in his personal habits'.[69] Who would have thought such a person would be a spy – never mind a double agent! Confounding expectation, however, is a necessary skill of a good intelligence agent.

By December 1939 Section D acknowledged 43 officers.[70] Grand was deliberately vague as to the staffing levels but in an interview in 1973 he estimated that the final total strength was around three hundred.[71] Staff moved between the individual sub-sections (whose work, especially in propaganda, often overlapped), and until April 1940 they relied on the personal ability of Laurence Grand to coordinate their work in a system that was still rooted in the small beginnings of the organisation. Fig. 1 is an attempt to reconstruct the constituent sub-sections of the organisation in so far as they are known.

The pattern of recruitment and lack of systematic training caused wide variations of expertise across the regions in which Section D operated. Grand relied heavily on former Shell executive George Taylor, who led the huge Section D/H covering the Balkans, part of East Europe and the Middle East, and who played a major role in developing the policy of Section D. He became Grand's deputy and had a largely unheralded role in the management of SOE. For Sweet-Escott: 'It was certainly due more to him [Taylor] than to any other one person that the theory and practice of what eventually became SOE was in the end accepted by

Figure 1. Section D administrative codes and section heads.

D	Head of Section D	Laurence Grand
D/A	Administrative Section	George Courtauld
D/B	Finance section	'Mrs Douglas'
D/C	Agent documents; London Communications; small arms	James Tomlinson
		Hugh Pollard
D/D	Research and Development (engineering and small devices)	Leslie Wood
D/DB	Balloons	Walter Wren
		James O'Hea
D/E	Wireless development	Edward Schröter
D/F	France	Leslie Humphreys
D/G	Scandinavia	Ingram Fraser
D/H	The Balkans, East Europe and Middle East	George Taylor
D/I	Belgium and Holland	Norman Hope
D/K	Abyssinia and propaganda in the Middle East	Stephen Longrigg
D/L	Postal Censorship (clandestine letter opening)/Plans	Walter Wren
D/M	Military liaison group and liaison with MI(R)	Jo Holland
D/P	Neutral Countries Propaganda	Walter Wren
D/Q	Press Propaganda and 'rumours'	Douglas Saunders
		Leslie Sheridan
D/R	Germany and Austria	Monty Chidson
D/T	Liaison to SIS	Everard Calthrop
D/U	Potential Sabotage Plans/Training school	Guy Burgess
D/V	Russian section	George Hill
D/X	Research and Development (Scientific)	John Langley
D/Y	Home Defence Scheme	Viscount Bearsted
D/Z	Germany and Austria	Monty Chidson

our detractors and competitors, as well as by our supporters.'[72] Taylor gathered together experienced SIS officers, soldiers, academics, journalists and engineers. Western Europe and the USA were also under long-time SIS officers Montagu Chidson and Leslie Humphreys. The smallest and least experienced team was in Scandinavia, under advertising executive Ingram Fraser. Here, there were no professional intelligence officers, no former army officers and not even mining engineers who understood explosives. Operations in Britain, under Shell director Viscount Bearsted (Pl. 5), are the least understood but did include several existing SIS officers. Despite a small number of security breaches, the mystery of the Home Defence Scheme is a tribute to their professionalism. However imperfect, it was Section D staff who then went on to form the core of the early SOE.

Chapter 2

Section D goes to War

All I can say is that if you join us, you mustn't be afraid of forgery and you mustn't be afraid of murder.

(Arthur Goodwill to Bickham Sweet-Escott, March 1940)[1]

On 16 March 1939 the Nazis completed the occupation of Czechoslovakia. One week later Laurence Grand persuaded the SIS, Foreign Office and War Office that Section D should begin operational activity against Germany. 'Scheme D for Europe-wide sabotage and subversive operations' was intended to encourage large-scale risings in already-occupied countries and prepare resistance in countries that might be over-run in the future. Reflecting the contemporary and wildly optimistic opinion about the fragility of the Nazi state, Grand proposed being ready for a general uprising in German-occupied territory in just three or four months, whilst a 'combination of guerrilla and IRA tactics' could bring about the collapse of Romania in just three weeks.[2] The methodology drew on the practical experience of the British army in confronting irregular warfare in India, Russia, Iraq and Ireland but debate on the philosophy of irregular warfare was confined to its champions in Section D and MI(R) and there was little wider analysis of the potential effectiveness of political warfare or popular revolt.[3] A series of country-by-country objectives were outlined, including the assassination of Gestapo agents in Romania; supplying guerrilla organisations in Denmark, Holland and Poland; supplying arms to Bohemia to enable the inhabitants 'to commence operations on the lines of the Irish Terror in 1920–21'; supplying arms to resistance groups within Germany and Austria; and encouraging popular risings in Italian-held Libya and Abyssinia. The overall aim was

> it should be possible, if not to avoid war itself, since this is somewhat late, to ensure that no military effort could be made by the German Army without giving opportunity for such turmoil on its lines of communication as to render continued effort impossible.[4]

Scheme D had been drafted in partnership with Lieutenant Colonel Jo Holland of what was then GS(R), later D/MI(R) and then simply MI(R), and it thereby combined civilian and military irregular warfare in a single plan. MI(R) originated in 1936 as a small research unit of the War Office, providing a fellowship for officers to carry out a period of research into a topic that interested them.

Early topics included army education and medical services. From December 1938 GS(R) came under Jo Holland, then recovering from illness. He was another Royal Engineer officer and near-contemporary of Laurence Grand at Woolwich Military College. As Foot pointed out, Grand and Holland might both be taken as exceptions to Field Marshal Montgomery's dictum that 'all sappers are mentally constipated'.[5] Holland chose to research military-based irregular warfare in contrast to the civilian, agent-led, work being simultaneously developed by Section D.[6] The mandate of MI(R) was the research and preparation of projects involving the employment of military forces in guerrilla warfare. But in Holland's view, its work was essentially theoretical, and he was content to let Section D get involved with the dirtier aspects of irregular warfare, becoming irritated when MI(R) was drawn into an operational role with the management of the Independent Companies (precursor of the Commandos). This is clear from Holland's memo of April 1939 in which he outlined the objectives of MI(R):

a. to study guerrilla methods and produce a guerrilla 'manual';
b. to evolve destructive devices suitable for the use of guerrillas; and
c. to evolve procedure and machinery for operating guerrilla activities.[7]

There were clear points of common interest with the work of Section D, and SIS therefore provided funding and shared accommodation with Section D to exercise a measure of oversight. In his 5 June 1939 report Grand claims the work of MI(R) was carried out 'under the aegis of Section D', referring both to the joint planning of Scheme D and the need for MI(R) to use Section D communication lines.[8] The distinction between Section D and MI(R) could certainly blur in practice. Peter Wilkinson admitted 'as much of my time was spent at the headquarters of Section D in Caxton Street as in MI(R). I was given a desk in their Balkan section and allotted the secret symbol DH/M.'[9] In February 1940 he reported spending three hours a day working under George Taylor.[10] Importantly, MI(R) officers who were installed at Legations frequently provided a mechanism of liaison at an official level with agents of Section D.

For Holland's secretary, Joan Bright Astley, 'he [Holland] and Grand got on well together' and they remained close friends after the war.[11] Holland was very different from Grand – a burly, chain-smoking, unsmiling visionary with a fiery temper and a calculating mind.[12] He had experienced guerrilla warfare in Ireland and India and had contributed to an early War Office paper on 'An Investigation of the Possibilities of Guerrilla Activities'. The relationship between MI(R) and Section D was much closer than the War Office later cared to admit, trying to avoid any suggestion that its research section might have been subservient to SIS. The MI(R) Charter of June 1939 clearly describes Section D and MI(R) as distinct entities with the role of MI(R) to earmark staff for training in sabotage and the theory of guerrilla warfare.[13] It is true that Holland reported to the Deputy Chief of the Imperial General Staff and the Director of Military

Intelligence but Grand was adamant that, until the outbreak of war, MI(R) was a functional element of Section D as Section D/M under Holland.

> Jo Holland joined almost immediately and it was agreed that a new sub-section 'DM' should be formed which would in general deal with all activities that could be carried out by uniformed troops, the initial contacts and acquisition of information being obtained by any methods (uniformed or secret) that were most appropriate.[14]

SIS, in July 1946, confirmed Grand's opinion: 'To it [Section D], the War Office attached a military section (MIR) in 1939, responsible for study and preparation of guerrilla warfare.'[15] Joan Bright Astley was originally recruited to Section D but worked as secretary to Jo Holland and simply stated: 'We became part of Section D.'[16] The fact that Holland was the more senior officer would not necessarily contradict this arrangement as seniority within SIS did not relate to military rank.[17] Even Colin Gubbins' account of his recruitment to MI(R) is ambiguous as to who was actually in charge. He says he was invited to a lunch by his friend Jo Holland but,

> In a private room at St Ermin's Hotel I found that the real host, who was waiting for us there, was another sapper officer whom I also knew well. Over lunch he told us that he was the head of Section D and explained his charter.[18]

The key to the relationship of the two bodies was the launch of Scheme D in March 1939. The language and framing suggests it was jointly drafted by Grand and Holland but the latter was content for it to be seen as being under Section D ownership, with Grand being the one to present it to government. Gubbins, later deputy to Holland, described Holland as being 'completely unselfish' with 'no intention of building an empire for himself'.[19] Similarly, for Joan Astley he 'never sought personal aggrandisement'.[20] MI(R) was, in any case, constrained by its charter to remain on the side-lines of the scheme until the declaration of war with any particular country. 'Scheme D for Europe-wide sabotage and subversive operations' was first presented to Stewart Menzies, then head of Section II (Military) of SIS, by Grand on 20 March 1939.[21] Menzies advised that the scheme should be submitted to the War Office via the DDMI, W.E. van Cutsem. Just two days later the scheme had reached the Chief of the Imperial General Staff (Lord Gort) and the Director of Military Operations (Sir Henry Pownall).[22] From there, it went to the Foreign Office, with a meeting on 23 March attended by the Foreign Secretary (Lord Halifax) and Colonial Secretary (Lord Cadogan) as well as the CIGS, Menzies and Grand. Gort gave formal War Office approval for the scheme but Grand asked for the matter to be kept secret, except for the Prime Minister. The CIGS even specifically agreed that there should be no consultation with his Chiefs of Staff Committee (a source of their later resentment towards Section D). As part of Scheme D, Grand asked for the attachment of twenty-six army officers, including Jo Holland, to Section D. The purpose was to build a wing to study the military use of guerrilla warfare, using uniformed troops, and to ensure coordination with the War Office. Here was the birth of D/M Section/MI(R), recognisably under Section D's aegis and Grand's summary of the meeting is included in the MI(R) files without dissent.[23] Even the War Diary of MI(R) includes a note of officers working on schemes for Romania being 'under Colonel Holland in D' and the War Diary noted that 'MIR funds are allocated by C' ('C' being an alternative code for the Chief of the SIS).[24] At the end of the war Grand took the commanding officer's role and recommended Holland for a decoration.[25] In return for accepting Section D's oversight, MI(R) received the necessary funding from SIS to expand its work beyond parliamentary scrutiny. Joan Bright Astley, who witnessed the, at times, mutual bewilderment of the Section D spies and military men of MI(R) working alongside each other, summed up the distinction thus:

> Grand's Section D deeds would be done by undercover men, spies and sabo-teurs, who, if caught, would be neither acknowledged nor defended by their government. Holland's MI(R) plans would be subject to proper strategic and tactical requirements and carried out by men in the uniform of the established Armed Services for whom the normal conventions of war would operate.[26]

Grand did not spare the War Office and Foreign Office representatives any details of the brutal methodology that would be employed under Scheme D. In Romania, 'Where possible they would endeavour to execute members of the Gestapo with as much show as possible, to produce in the minds of the local inhabitants that the guerrillas were more to be feared than the occupying secret police'.[27] It was said that this was a lesson taken from the IRA. A horrified Lord Halifax said that 'he agreed in principle with the scheme, which he now intended to forget'.[28] The decision of the Foreign Office not to engage with the process of Scheme D was to create future problems. Repeatedly, when confronted with the need to commit to time-limited plans for sabotage, the Foreign Office shied away from a decision. To Sweet-Escott, the Foreign Office did not seem anxious to suggest exactly what Section D ought to be doing but rather 'seemed to restrict themselves to telling us what not to do'.[29] A key obstacle was the fact that requests for funding from the Treasury had to be funnelled through Gladwyn Jebb of the Foreign Office. He had a great dislike of Section D, and of Grand in particular, and was repeatedly accused of delaying payments. Somewhat ironic-ally, he was later to become the Chief Executive Officer of SOE. A frustrated Grand wrote, 'although our existence was accepted, our activities at times met with obstruction when official assistance was required or could at least have helped'.[30]

In typical Grand fashion, the approval for Scheme D had already been pre-empted. On 10 March Julius Hanau had been recruited as head agent in Yugo-slavia (Pl. 3). He immediately went to war by organising the sabotage of German arms supplies travelling through the region. German intelligence retaliated and, in turn, Grand authorised his agents to use lethal force.

> The Gestapo were reinforced strongly and tried strong-arm methods. ... I therefore directed that violence would not be met with violence, but with elimination and that for every casualty on our side, British or Serb, one Nazi should disappear. This was achieved with great care and discretion, but the Nazis were informed of the tariff that had been laid down. This put an end to violence within two months and from May 1939 to July 1940 we had no casualties in Yugoslavia.[31]

By May 1939 the sabotage manual *Home Hints* had been produced, illustrated by Mary Holdsworth, and translated into German, Polish, French and Czech. One of its key principles was instruction on how to make explosives from everyday items that would not excite suspicion in a cursory search. Many of the groups given *Home Hints* were socialists and providing them with the means to commit sabotage would previously have been viewed with horror by the Foreign Office and British Intelligence. Grand acknowledged the 'high degree of violence from Whitehall' but commented on the complexities of the anti-Nazi struggle that 'You cannot half-resist (or is the verb "to Munich?")'.[32] He proposed an

> International Sixth Column which would aim to encourage national parties in every Nazi-controlled territory ... and at a given signal revolt together against German oppression, cutting lines of communication and committing internal sabotage in their respective territories. These political risings would considerably impede German efforts at defence against coinciding naval, military, and air attack.[33]

Once Scheme D was approved, Grand's arch-enemy, Claude Dansey, demanded instant results. Rather, he wanted it to fail enough for him to say to Sinclair 'I told you so'. He later wrote one of his famously caustic memos on the subject:

> In the spring of 1939 Admiral Sinclair sent for me and said he was not entirely happy about the activities of his Section D and he wished me to spend a day in the offices at St Ermin's, finding out what was actually going on. Then Major Grand gave me an exposé of his activities. I was not impressed. There were many ideas, but it did not seem to me that practical possibilities had been examined ... I further said that the original idea had long been lost sight of. The number of appliances or aids to sabotage that I could be shown was very small. ... I heard little more about this Organisation until I returned to England at the end of 1939, when it had grown beyond all knowledge, and, as far I could determine, nothing was ever accomplished.[34]

Dansey wrote of a period when Section D had only just been authorized to commence operations and his comment on 'appliances', as produced by the technical section at Aston House, was clearly to prove incorrect (*see* Chapter 3). Dansey was not an objective commentator and was more than ready to destroy anyone whose views differed from his own. He found Grand infuriating, complaining (with great irony given his own reputation) of the mystery surrounding his funding and believing that Grand should 'conform and co-operate' rather than 'galloping about the world at his own gait'. It was the principle of Section D that was at the heart of Dansey's complaints and he attacked the later SOE in the same vein. Hugh Trevor Roper called Dansey 'an utter sh*t, corrupt, incompetent, but with a certain low cunning'. Edward Crankshaw described him as 'the sort of man who gives spying a bad name'.[35]

In June, as war became ever more likely, Grand further considered the organisational implications for Scheme D and, over a year before the formation of SOE, proposed that all irregular warfare should be put under the tight control of an inter-services body. Grand (still, it should be remembered, a serving army officer merely on secondment to SIS) suggested CSS as the central coordinating authority between army, navy, a future ministry of propaganda and SIS. Section D would serve directly under CSS as an executive section to implement the preparatory plans of the other services until war was declared. Unfortunately, Sinclair died before he could progress this radical vision of clandestine warfare firmly under SIS control.[36] The first joint Section D/MI(R) training course was held at Caxton Hall, adjacent to their offices, in July 1939. It was entirely lecture-based and outlined the principles of guerrilla warfare, demolition and radio communications. Peter Wilkinson was not impressed, commenting that the weekend would have been better spent reading T.E. Lawrence's *Seven Pillars of Wisdom*.[37] Within three weeks of the outbreak of war, D/MIR became simply MI(R) and moved to separate offices within the War Office.[38] Sadly, the two organisations drifted apart at a time when they should have been working more closely together. To forestall confusion, the out-going Director of Military Intelligence, Lieutenant General Henry Pownall, attempted a definition of the wartime roles of Section D and MI(R). A memo on 3 September 1939 stated:

> Clearly there must be the very closest liaison between MI(R) and Section D. They will equally be studying possibilities and preparing for action where it is more appropriately in their sphere. Research must therefore be carried on together. As to the resultant action, broadly it is for Section D when action must be subterranean, i.e., in countries which are in effective occupation, and it is for us, when the action is a matter of military missions, whether regular or irregular.[39]

The theoretical nature of much of MI(R)'s work prior to the start of formal military operations in any particular country was later written into the Hankey

Inquiry of SIS in March 1940, establishing that MI(R) would only organise sabotage in arenas where regular British forces were directly involved, whilst Section D undertook operations in areas under enemy occupation or in neutral countries.[40] This division of responsibilities did not work as anticipated, its first test being operations in Poland, and followed the recruitment to MI(R) and the Polish Mission of Colin Gubbins, not a party to the creation of Scheme D and far more ambitious than Holland. Writing in May 1941 Robert Bruce Lockhart (Director-General of the Political Warfare Executive) commented, 'Jebb had said the other day that Gubbins was the most ambitious man he knew. If that is Jebb's verdict, you know what Gubbins must be!'[41] Jo Hollis, secretary to the Chiefs of Staff Committee, went further and declared (in the context of the replacement of Hambro as head of SOE by Gubbins), that Gubbins was evil.[42] His colleagues and biographers, Wilkinson and Astley strongly refuted any suggestion that Gubbins was capable of such disloyalty, although admitting that the rumour had currency at the time.[43] Gubbins wanted a greater operational role for MI(R) and with the Polish Mission being a formal military initiative under the terms of the DMI statement, Gubbins could feel justified in taking a proprietorial view towards the Polish resistance. He was, however, frustrated by the necessity of relying on Section D supply lines. Equally, Poland being an occupied territory, Grand could interpret the DMI policy statement as authority for work in Poland falling within the remit of Section D. The same argument would occur later between Grand and Gubbins over plans for resistance in Britain (*see* Chapter 10). SIS also saw Section D as a convenient arms-length means of maintaining contacts with the Polish resistance independently of the Polish General Staff. Gubbins continued to test the boundaries of working between MI(R) and Section D but could not compete with the latter's expansion. In July 1940 the official War Establishment of MI(R) was still set at only one lieutenant colonel, four majors, nine captains and one clerk. This remained largely unchanged until its disbandment in October.[44] It consequently had little influence in the early direction of SOE. The long-standing antipathy of Gubbins towards SIS was to have personal consequences when SOE was eventually absorbed into SIS and, although a temporary major general, he was retired on the pension of his substantive rank of colonel by a vengeful Menzies.

On a war footing

In August 1939 both Laurence Grand and his then deputy, Monty Chidson, were party to high-level discussions in the Foreign Office on the progress of negotiations for an Anglo-Soviet friendship pact which would, *inter alia*, help guarantee the sovereignty of Poland. However, the government view was that, as it would be difficult to provide practical opposition to any German expansion against Russia, an Anglo-Soviet pact might be an embarrassment. War with Germany to protect Poland was seen as inevitable – but going to war to protect Communist

Russia was a step too far. The negotiations with Stalin would, however, be pro-longed until the intentions of Germany were clearer. Grand and Chidson shared this interpretation with the Section D officer responsible for secret broadcasting in Europe, to ensure that nothing was broadcast which might conflict with British foreign policy. Unfortunately, that man was Soviet spy Guy Burgess, who had joined Section D in December 1938. Their information confirmed other Foreign Office sources and Burgess duly forwarded the intelligence to Moscow.[45] With hopes of any alliance with the Western powers dashed, on 23 August Stalin entered a non-aggression pact with Germany. With its eastern flanks now secure, Germany invaded Poland on 1 September and the Soviet Union followed a similar course on 17 September. Soviet intelligence believed that this was the most important intelligence that Burgess ever delivered to them. He also passed on the weekly intelligence bulletins of Section D and details of operations, including the debate in December 1939 over whether to endorse a plan to assas-sinate Hitler and plans to foment a Swedish miners' strike.[46] A fear at the time was that the Soviets were sharing intelligence with their German allies but fortu-nately the capture in 1944 of *Abwehr* documents suggests that German intelli-gence still relied principally on the out-of-date information extracted from kidnapped SIS agents Sigismund Best and Richard Stevens in November 1939.[47]

The declaration of war on 3 September heralded a series of crises for SIS. Admiral Sinclair died on 4 November and Stewart Menzies became the new CSS. Sinclair had been the guiding hand of Section D, he and Grand becoming good friends. Menzies never showed the same level of commitment and was described as being 'obviously uneasy' about Section D.[48] By late July 1940 Lord Cadogan acknowledged that Menzies, who disliked dealing with personnel matters or administration, found it difficult to control Grand.[49] On the heels of Sinclair's death came the capture, on 9 November 1939, of Best and Stevens at Venlo in Holland. The two men confessed the basic structure of SIS, including the exis-tence of Section D under Grand. Stevens identified it only as a propaganda department but Best admitted its true purpose was to organise sabotage.[50]

Meanwhile, Section D frantically tried to complete its mobilisation, establish-ing secret lines of communication into Germany and Austria and potential coastal insertion points using the survey work organised by Frank Carr along the west coast from Norway, through Denmark into Holland and Belgium (*see* Chapter 9). During August 1939, as the international situation worsened, 2.5 tons of material (mostly propaganda) was run into Germany, Austria and Czechoslovakia using contacts in Switzerland, Belgium and Holland, with the French section acting as the major hub of communication.[51] Some was distributed into north German ports by eel boats sailing from Essex.[52] Unfortunately, the Gestapo were well-prepared and many key collaborators in Germany were arrested in the first ten days of war. Another recurring problem was the difficulty of getting travel visas into neutral countries for agents who were still German nationals or stateless refugees, without arousing the suspicion of the receiving country. On the outbreak of war, Section D officers began to be given army commissions to provide cover and a degree of legal protection if captured. In some cases, this followed a three-month abbreviated course at either Aldershot or the 110th (Horsed Cavalry) OCTU at Weedon, Northamptonshire, in what was unofficially known as the 'M.I. Troop' (Military Intelligence), where, alongside recruits to MI(R), an attempt was made to give these exponents of 'ungentlemanly' warfare the semblance of being an 'officer and gentleman'. At Weedon this included a month-long intensive course in horsemanship but no specialised training that might be useful in their future work. From July 1940 they could choose to appear on the General Service list or be nominally badged to the new Intelligence Corps. A discreet entry in the *London Gazette* for 5 September 1939 announcing the latest army commissions reads like a 'Who's Who' of Section D.[53]

> The undermentioned from Army Officers Emergency Reserve to be Lts. 2nd Sept. 1939:–
>
> | | | |
> |---|---|---|
> | E. Schröter. | A. Courtauld. | W. Berington. |
> | L.A.L. Humphreys. | R. Riley. | G.F. Taylor. |
> | W.T. Wren. | C.R. Bailey. | C.H.E. Phillips. |
> | R. Cliveley. | T. Fairley. | L. Sheridan. |
> | G. Courtauld. | Ingram Fraser. | |

By July 1940 Grand acknowledged having 140 British officers on his staff. However, SIS never admitted to its full strength, which was complicated by its use of both unpaid volunteers, paid foreign agents and contracted foreign groups.[54] In an interview in 1973 Grand estimated the total number as about 300 officers.[55] There were well over 60 agents in the Balkans alone. It had become a self-sufficient department of SIS with direct access to the Prime Minister, and its staffing levels rivalled the entire strength of the rest of SIS, with corresponding mistrust and envy.[56]

With the outbreak of war imminent, and expecting an immediate bombing campaign, Squadron Leader Rowe was sent to look for countryside war stations to supplement the Caxton Street offices. An out-of-London HQ was established on 1 September 1939 under Monty Chidson at the neo-Gothic Frythe Hotel, Welwyn (Station IX). The Frythe was the main HQ until much of the section returned to London in March 1940 and remained the Emergency War Station that would function as HQ if London ever became untenable.[57] Wealthy members of the section loaned their cars for the regular commutes to London. The former manager of the hotel vented his frustration at losing his job by baiting the army guards. He negotiated the various trip wires and uttered ghostly wailing and whistles whilst prowling the grounds before escaping down what was already known as 'Spook Alley'.[58] The 'production organ' of the propaganda section – six men, three women and four typists, originally under Walter 'Freckles' Wren – moved to Woburn alongside Electra House, under cover of the 'Neutral

Countries section' (D/P) but Campbell Stuart was not greatly interested in 'black propaganda' and resented their presence. They comprised

Walter Wren	Robert Walmsley
Douglas Saunders	Clara Holmes
Anthony Wyatt Parker	Miss Stanhope [? Evelyn Stamper]
George Butler	'a senior woman'[59] [? Elizabeth Hodgson]
Frederick Voigt	

The section was heavily reliant on former members of the J. Walter Thompson advertising agency, including Douglas Saunders, George Butler and Anthony Parker. The latter joined Section D in July 1939 and was described as having 'a very acute mind' but was 'fantastically lazy'.[60] Frederick Voigt was a British journalist born of German parents, who had been diplomatic correspondent for the *Manchester Guardian* and a regular broadcaster on foreign affairs for the BBC. Part of his role within Section D was as a 'cut-out' for new recruits. Clara Holmes and Evelyn Stamper were mainstays of the German and Austrian sections of Section D and SOE for the rest of the war. Clara Holmes had worked intermittently for SIS since 1917. It may be presumed that her senior officer throughout the war, Evelyn Stamper (age 55), a pre-war translator of German and Austrian texts, was also a long-standing SIS officer. The 'senior woman' may be Elizabeth Hodgson, who was also in the pre-war SIS and co-wrote a number of pre-war translations with Stamper. She became the secretary of the Joint Broadcasting Committee and then served with SOE in Zurich. Sir Campbell Stuart may have thought that this was a bridgehead for the well-established Section D to take over his new organisation. Clearly not welcome, they soon established themselves in The Old Rectory, Hertingfordbury ('a beautiful little house in delightful grounds') in mid-September, under Douglas Saunders (future head of the press propaganda Section D/Q). A house in Lexham Gardens was also used as a production office by the propaganda section, run by Evelyn Stamper and Clara Holmes.

The original base for the technical section was at Bletchley Park (Station X) but in October a new base was found for its noisy work in testing explosives at Aston House, Stevenage (Station XII), close to the Frythe Hotel (Station IX). It had the cover of the 'Inter-Service Experimental Department' or the 'War Department Signals Development Branch' (*see* Chapter 3). Much of the early, ad hoc, agent training was carried out at Aston House, in advance of the creation of the formal training school at Brickendonbury (Station XVII).[61]

In March 1940, with no sign of the expected Luftwaffe bombing campaign, many staff moved back to London, leaving the technical section at Aston House. The HQ of Section D now expanded to fill both the 5th and 6th floor offices at 2 Caxton Street and the 4th floor of the St Ermin's Hotel, where the entrance was guarded by a burly ex-Royal Navy petty officer called Cornelius.[62] Disconcertingly, a 4th floor storeroom in the hotel was used to store and pack explosives, from where they were handed over to couriers, taken by taxi to Victoria station and shipped around Europe. Private meetings and entertainment were held in Grand's Section D-funded suite of apartments in the St Ermin's Hotel (Pl. 10), linked by private corridor to the Caxton Street offices. Here, under the name of 'Mr Douglas', he ran up weekly bills of £40 that included laundry, fruit, biscuits and taxis. A more curious expense was the serviced flat provided for Desmond Morton, an important ally and intermediary with the Prime Minister (now special adviser to Churchill and formerly head of the Intelligence Division of the Ministry of Economic Warfare). His flat at 110 Whitehall Court was rented from 26 May in the name of 'Colonel L. Graham' (another of Grand's aliases) but Morton's tastes were less extravagant. The weekly rent was £6.6s.0d with total weekly costs amounting to £16 including meals, drinks and cigarettes.[63] SOE unknowingly continued to pay for the flat until December 1940 and when finally confronted with the charge, Morton was neither 'candid or helpful'.[64] In June 1940 an emergency HQ was established at an undisclosed small country house near Cheltenham for Grand and his immediate staff – cryptically stated to be for use if the government had to move in case of enemy occupation.[65]

Section D did not sit easily within the traditionalist Whitehall establishment. Grand paid tribute to the 'imaginative capacities of its personnel and the comparative freedom from the inertia that is born of a profitless adherence to the book of rules'.[66] But to Claude Dansey, Assistant Chief of SIS, it was 'mafia-like'.[67] The formal declaration of war brought its work more clearly into focus and fundamentally altered the relationship between the activities of Section D and those of the armed forces and other government departments. The latter had a chance to express their resentment as evidence to the Inquiry on SIS conducted by Lord Hankey (War Cabinet advisor on intelligence), completed in March 1940. The War Office naturally wanted to take full strategic control of the war effort and some within it were not yet ready to embrace the new form of warfare that Section D represented. In 1946 SIS noted,

> It was painfully evident that Commanders-in-Chief in the early years of the War without exception regarded the clandestine effort not only as a nuisance but also as a serious handicap.[68]

Section D was defended in the Hankey Inquiry by Desmond Morton, Churchill's security adviser, who confirmed that, despite their complaints to the contrary, Grand's sabotage plans 'were put into effect by agreement with the Ministry, the Service departments and the Foreign Office'.[69] Morton's evidence continued: 'This system, in Mr Morton's opinion, worked well and he had no complaints to make, though the dynamic personality of Major Grand was in some respects a difficulty.'[70] Grand's 'dynamic personality' was again mentioned by the Director of Military Intelligence as the core of the War Office criticism of Section D.[71] His enthusiasm did not fit easily in the cautious context of the 'phoney war'. The Inquiry confirmed the basic division of responsibility between Section D and

MI(R), with Pownall's successor as Director of Military Intelligence, Major General Frederick Beaumont-Nesbitt, explaining,

> There was one side of SIS work which up till recently had given rise to particular difficulties and to a certain amount of friction. This was sabotage; and the friction was perhaps, to a certain extent, due to the dynamic personality of Major Grand. It had however now been arranged in principle that MIR ... should devote itself primarily to plans and research and that actual sabotage in enemy countries should be undertaken by the SIS. If, however, there was a possibility of our own troops acting in conjunction with the local government, then the actual work of sabotage should more properly be entrusted to MIR.[72]

Overall, the Hankey Inquiry was complimentary about the early sabotage operations of Section D, describing the plans as well devised and backed up by a wide range of supporting documentation.[73] Demands from the fighting services continued to increase, straining the resources of Section D to the limit. The Minutes of the ISPB meeting on 14 May included requests for Section D to

- prepare plans for an attack on the Brenner Pass should Italy enter the war;
- arrange for the supply of demolition materials to Libya and Abyssinia and plan minor sabotage;
- sabotage any German planes landing in Spain;
- submit a plan for the delaying of US airmail traffic to the USA; and
- consider Foreign Office proposals for sabotage in Denmark and Norway.[74]

The declaration of war had triggered the mobilisation of Electra House and the MOI to organise propaganda but both were hazy as to what Section D had been doing for the past year.[75] Even in February 1940, whilst collecting evidence for his Inquiry, Hankey wrote that Campbell Stuart (head of Electra House) seemed to have 'only a very slight knowledge of what (or at any rate what we are told) is being done, and what Grand is doing and has done for him'.[76] The brief of Electra House was to be responsible for propaganda in enemy countries. It was, however, small and not terribly effective. Robert Walmsley concluded: 'The atmosphere of the early days was one of bustling amateurishness and, with one exception, almost complete ineffectualness.'[77] The work of EH in 'black' propaganda did not really begin until it could absorb the expertise of Section D as part of the new SOE. Sinclair and Grand had agreed with Stuart that, on the outbreak of war, Electra House would become responsible for producing propaganda and Section D would disseminate it, if this could not otherwise be done through radio broadcasts or RAF leaflet drops. Stuart remained deeply suspicious of Section D's continued production of propaganda, and wished to take control of all propaganda operations from both Section D and the MOI.

There was, generally speaking, too much mystery about the whole affair. For instance, Colonel Grand was doing a good deal of propaganda in neutral countries. It was impossible for him [Stuart] to find out exactly what this amounted to; but if it was anti-German propaganda then he at least ought to know what was going on.[78]

Grand robustly defended himself in his evidence to the Hankey Inquiry. A consultative committee between Section D and Electra House had been established in the autumn of 1939 upon which sat the Deputy Director of Electra House, Captain R.J. Herbert Shaw, and this had jointly produced several mis-information schemes. Whilst admitting that Section D staff did still prepare propaganda material, Grand insisted that nothing was dispatched without the prior approval of Electra House. Stuart failed to appreciate that the British were not in a position to dictate content to native resistance groups and Hankey accepted the argument about the sensitivities needed to ensure that the material matched the politics and interests of the agents delivering the material. In an effort to further reduce conflict, weekly liaison meetings were now held between Section D and Electra House at the Frythe, but Stuart was reluctant to accept Hankey's view that these new liaison arrangements might have been successful.

The official response of the Ministry of Information to the Hankey Inquiry was coloured by a report that Grand had produced just ten days earlier. In this, Grand explained that Section D needed to be involved in propaganda firstly to create a favourable atmosphere in the foreign countries in which it worked, and secondly because partnership with foreign resistance groups meant that it could influence the propaganda produced by those organisations. But he bluntly concluded:

> The third reason for our doing propaganda is the fact that during the past five months the Ministry of Information has, in most cases, been completely ineffective.[79]

The first response came one week later from Jebb, who wrote to Hankey claiming that his concern was that propaganda work risked overstretching Section D and exposing its sabotage activity. Both were reasonable concerns but his complaint was also personal, believing that propaganda should be directed by 'someone other than Grand' (underlined in original).[80] Professor Carr, Head of the Foreign Publicity department of the MOI, launched a venomous defence of his organisation, claiming that Section D did not consult the MOI and had not been frank in providing information, and he concluded by essentially saying that secret propaganda was none of Section D's business and should be in the hands of an organisation that took orders from the MOI.

> The principal function of this organisation [D] is entirely unconnected with propaganda and the association of propaganda with its other work seems wholly undesirable. Moreover, the fact that this organisation is engaged on other important work of which this Ministry is quite rightly kept in

ignorance, makes it particularly easy to conceal from the Ministry things which we ought to know.[81]

But Grand was not alone in his criticism of the MOI. On the same day as Carr's submission, the Press Attaché in Belgrade, Stephen Lawford Childs, provided a glowing appreciation of Section D's work in Yugoslavia, contrasting this with the efforts of the MOI:

> As for ****** himself [Grand], I think his qualities more than outweigh his defects and that he has been over-criticised by people in secure positions. ... and as I say I know of no one who could have taken his place and done what he has done. He has broken some eggs but the omelettes were produced. ... The chief of the organisation here [Hanau] has consulted me very fully about some of his plans and particularly about those which supplement our own 'legal' action. ... As far as I know my suggestions or indications have generally been accepted. At any rate, I have no complaint to make on that score and I have always had excellent co-operation from this organisation. ... I think that the results obtained have been remarkable and I do not see how anybody else could have done better, or as well.

If this testimonial was not bad enough from the viewpoint of Section D's detractors, Childs went on to offer an unsolicited criticism of the MOI from the perspective of an end-user.

> In order that you shall get the whole picture I must confess that the tremendous difficulty of getting the MOI into efficient regional action together with a desire to keep them out of any risks has led me occasionally to try and obtain finance for certain operations from Grand's people rather than from the Ministry.[82]

Further support then came from within the MOI when Donald Hall criticised his own organisation's work in Romania.[83] Grand counter-attacked by complaining that Carr had ordered his subordinates not to cooperate with Section D and the result was a meeting between Grand, Lord Reith and Sir Kenneth Lee of the MOI. To the dismay of both Carr and Jebb, the meeting shared Grand's concerns and it was even agreed that Section D should extend its propaganda work on behalf of the MOI to produce material that appeared to be local and spontaneous in origin, rather than emanating from official channels. On the whole, the MOI was pleased with the service it received from Section D and was involved in a number of Section D schemes, not least because Grand wanted them to fund the work. In Turkey, the MOI acknowledged that they relied on the covert mechanism provided by Section D to counter the German 'whispering campaign'.[84] In Romania, Donald Hall and Grand together developed a scheme for improving propaganda that won a rare expression of enthusiasm from the Minister, Sir Reginald Hoare. In the end, the Hankey Inquiry supported the basic organisation of Section D but recommended that the Ministry should be responsible for producing the actual propaganda material, whilst Section D would be responsible for getting it into enemy countries and distributing it. This division of labour was only partly successful as Section D continued to produce propaganda in the name of foreign anti-Nazi groups. Some local Press Attachés (such as Peter Tennant in Sweden, see Chapter 9) appear to have never been aware of the full scale of propaganda work undertaken by Section D.

Early wartime British intelligence relied on an assumption that the Nazi state was fragile and could be defeated merely by interrupting its supply of war material. The veteran Italian anti-fascist Massimo Salvadori, now a Section D agent, was dismayed by this simplistic view of breaking the Nazis. Laurence Grand confidently told him that, at a given signal, thousands of rebels would rise to seize power and put an end to the Nazi dictatorship in Germany. Not surprisingly, Salvadori did not believe that Britain appreciated the hold of the fascist states over their peoples.

> They lacked experience of underground movements and comprehension of the situation in fascist countries. They had never lived under a dictatorship, and they believed that the romantic initiatives of small groups who had been able to start revolts and revolutions in the nineteenth century could be repeated in the twentieth.[85]

Even in the retreat to Dunkirk, the British and French governments were still reluctant to engage with the realities of 'total war'. Section D officers, working with French Intelligence, attempted to organise the sabotage of bridges and other installations but were blocked by the French government who had a policy to avoid damage to private property and infrastructure. It had been confidently assumed that the strength of Britain and France would overawe neutral governments, who would then 'turn a blind eye' to the sabotage of enemy targets. The fall of France changed the political landscape. Neutral governments were now wary of antagonizing Germany, while the newly occupied territories provided a buffer that made operations into Germany far more difficult. Defeatism spread within sections of the British establishment and for those looking towards a negotiated peace, the activities of Section D seemed intent on making negotiations more difficult. In June 1940 the Minister in Sweden, Victor Mallet, commented: 'You don't seem to realise, Mr Binney, that the war may be over in four or five weeks, at least that is what is being said by some of my friends at the Foreign Office.'[86] Fortunately, Churchill, as the new Prime Minister, bullied his ministers into a more aggressive war policy but elements of the Treasury and Foreign Office continued to try to discredit Section D. There were repeated delays from the Treasury and Jebb in processing payments for agreed programmes of work. On 13 June 1940 St John Bamford of the Ministry of Information wrote to the Treasury complaining that Grand had not received funding on several schemes agreed with the MOI, implying that Jebb was the source of the blockage.[87]

The Foreign Office still clung to the view that the Nazis could be defeated by economic blockade and did not want to risk any action that might strengthen the Axis by bringing neutral countries onto its side. In addition, Section D organised much of its sabotage and propaganda through funding dissident left-wing and Zionist political groups across Europe and this risked the fine balance of British diplomacy. The SOE history of Section D stressed that one of the contributions of Section D was that it firmly established the principle that sabotage and under-ground political activity were essential partners.[88] In June 1940 Grand wrote 'The Underground Counter Offensive' in which he expressed his belief that the lesson so far in the war was that

> this war is essentially a war of ideologies and that it therefore transcends national boundaries. Consequently, the opposing ideology must be sought out and defeated wherever it is found.[89]

Anyone who shared this desire to defeat the Nazi ideology was to be supported, whatever their national interest. Even within Section D such a policy could cause unease. Philby claimed that Section D officer Monty Chidson worried that the attempts to foment resistance groups in Europe would lead to anarchy.[90] The risk was that Section D was creating its own alliances to promote an anti-Nazi popular front, not necessarily equating with narrow British foreign policy. In April 1940 there was a testy exchange between Grand and Menzies on one hand and Sir Orme Sargent, deputy permanent under-secretary from the Foreign Office, on the other. Sargent believed that all sabotage schemes should be approved in advance by the local Minister.[91] Grand and Menzies retorted:

> It is obvious that no representative will think of agreeing to a policy, which, though desirable from the larger point of view, [will] embarrass his personal relations with the Government to which he is accredited.[92]

Their view was that the Foreign Office had no right to veto any sabotage scheme having Cabinet approval.[93] As a threat, they argued, disingenuously, that unless the Foreign Office withdrew its objections then Section D would be obliged to employ foreign nationals to carry out the work required by the Cabinet, falsely claiming that this was 'an extremely dangerous proceeding, and one which we have not adopted hitherto nor dare to adopt'. They believed:

> it is undesirable for His Majesty's Ministers to know anything about the activities of such persons as may be appointed for these tasks, especially if they are appointed as a result of the Cabinet overruling the Foreign Office.[94]

The Foreign Office was put in its place but dangerous enemies had been made.

Lack of resources was not seen as an obstacle to action. Grand later explained, 'if agents needed anything, you can be perfectly certain that we will do our damnedest to get it for you ... there is no activity which you are precluded from starting ... whether it is apparently within our scope or not'.[95] Nonetheless, Section D was far from the 'gung-ho' body as claimed by its enemies. Major projects went from initial discussion by the Planning Department (led by first Viscount Bearsted and then Commander Arnold-Forster), to a meeting of the SIS advisers (D/Ts), before approval by Grand, who would then seek any necessary political agreement. The project would then be handed to the head of the country section for execution.[96] Weekly reports were sent from the field and monthly progress reports then submitted to CSS.[97] In a flat structure of individual subsections, the system did, however, rely heavily on Grand's personal ability to coordinate work (Fig. 1) and there was only a rudimentary central organisation. As the organisation expanded, this became untenable. In April 1940 a more structured organisation of central services was finally introduced 'to relieve Grand of the burden of departmental detail'. There were to be four main directorates.

- Administration
- Plans
  - Potential plans
- Supplies
  - Propaganda
    - Writing propaganda material (incl. Section D/P)
    - Disseminating propaganda material abroad by clandestine means
    - Disseminating press stories through fake 'press agencies' (Section D/Q)
    - Preparing material for broadcast by foreign stations (JBC)
  - Communications
    - Travel documents and arrangements for agents
    - Liaison with SIS Section VIII
  - Personnel
    - Training (Proposed D School)
    - Cultivation of German refugee groups for use as Section D operatives
  - Technical
    - D/D research and development of devices
    - D/X laboratory section dealing with development of explosives
    - Small arms acquisition and supply
- Execution of projects

No further details have survived but in July there were further changes. George Taylor (head of the Balkans section) was brought back from Cairo to become assistant to Grand. At the same time a liaison officer was appointed from SIS to try to improve relationships.[98] He was Colonel Everard Earle Calthrop (1891–1948), formerly of the Royal Engineers but now wheelchair-bound as a result of multiple sclerosis. He was described as 'a delightful character with a tremendous sense of humour'.[99] The need for such a post was clearly indicated earlier, during the planning for the US Mail swindle (*see below*, pp. 196–9) when Section D's

Francis Ogilvy was sent to the USA but there expressed surprise to discover that there was an existing SIS organisation in the Americas.[100] On 11 August 1940, when it was still believed that Section D would continue as an independent body merely coordinated by the new SOE, plans were drawn up for a further reorganisation. Section D would now comprise five directorates, with George Taylor as 'Assistant D' (A/D) becoming the administrative head of the organisation.

1. Director of Plans: dissemination of general information to the subsections and for supplying plans and technical information on such projects as might be submitted.
2. Director of Operations: country sections and the execution of projects.
3. Director of Organisation: co-ordination of departments and for administration, etc.
4. Director of Services: co-ordinate the propaganda sub-sections, the technical sections at the Frythe and Aston House and the Balloon Warfare Station.
5. Director of Special Projects was to be responsible for those undertakings which were outside the scope of the Plans Directorate.[101]

The transfer to SOE interrupted this reorganisation but it provides an insight to the evolving sophistication of Section D. The changes were too late to save the organisation but it had come a long way from the 'shed at the bottom of a garden'.[102] The history of Section D written by SOE concluded:

D Section was not only unwelcome, but considered unnecessary by all the older established government agencies. Therefore, to prove its own worth, the Section was forced to produce results at the expense of sound organisation. It was not sufficiently firmly established to allow time to form a solid system in the field as the necessary preliminary to the achievements of result.[103]

Chapter 3

Technical Development and Training

At the beginning of 1939, little was known in this country of the principles, methods, or weapons of sabotage.

(History of the Research and Development Section of SOE)[1]

The new field of irregular warfare would rely heavily on technical innovation. Grand's first two appointments in 1938 were, therefore, highly significant: Commander John Langley was a naval explosives expert who was to command the research and supply section, while Edward 'Dead-eye Dick' Schröter was a civilian expert in telecommunications recruited from Philips. The technical innovations initiated by Section D's secret research and supply base at Aston House proved to be of enormous worth throughout the war (Figs 2, 3 and 10). A formal brief was provided by Admiral Sinclair in January 1939:

- To study how sabotage might be carried out
- To make experiments in conducting sabotage
- To produce special sabotage ammunition
- To train saboteurs
- To study methods of countering sabotage.[2]

Technical sections

John Langley, a retired naval officer and latterly a civilian employed by the Scientific Research Department of the Admiralty, was in overall charge. He first met Grand in the lobby of the St Ermin's Hotel and Langley found the proposition on offer to be 'staggering'. Nevertheless, 'I knew from the moment he shook my hand that I had met a man I would be proud to serve.'[3] His immediate task in 1938 was to study German sabotage techniques from the First World War, update them using modern technology and then devise counter-measures. Thus, early work included providing a handbook for naval boarding parties to use whilst searching merchant ships for booby traps. The analysis would then be turned into weapons of offence. As the team was expanded from late 1938, the work was organised in three sections: engineering (D/D), laboratory research (D/X), and wireless (D/E). From initial beginnings in 'a disused kitchen', by August 1939 they had set up a small experimental station and magazine at Bletchley Park

(Station X), where they had an office in the house, a workshop in the stables and a small magazine to house their stock of explosives.[4] The technical section moved to Aston House, Hertfordshire (Station XII) in November 1939 after the cryptographers complained about the disturbance caused by testing explosives. Aston House was set in a 5-acre park, with laboratories, carpentry and engineering workshops and a small explosive-filling factory. The base was known as the Inter-Service Experimental Department or the Signals Development Branch, Depot no. 4, War Office. There was no doubt considerable satisfaction when, in December 1939, MI5 could find no record of the existence of any such establishment.[5] As part of this cover, new inventions were frequently given Signals-type names. Time pencils were code-named 'Signals Relays', incendiary bombs were 'Signal Flares' and demolition charges were 'Sound Signals'. In the rarefied atmosphere at Aston House, Commander Langley recognized unease within official circles:

> None of the Defence Ministries knew of our existence; with the exception of my chief [Grand], the only high-ups in London who were aware of our activities were the Chief of the SIS and a couple of Cabinet ministers. Even so, rumours must have started to circulate. A Cabinet minister might ask himself what business the Secret Service had in running some sort of secret war. The SIS were supposed to concentrate on getting useful information, not be mixed up with a lot of piratical ruffians who might well blow up something which would sully the allied name.[6]

Dr Henry Drane, formerly of the Research Department, Woolwich Arsenal, joined Langley in late 1938 to head the D/X laboratory section, dealing with the research and development of explosives and incendiaries, together with resolving queries regarding industrial sabotage targets. In early 1939 Drane recruited his Woolwich colleague Colin Meek. Drane and Meek had both worked on the development of plastic explosives at Woolwich and the task of Section D was to develop it specifically for clandestine warfare. One of their projects was to perfect the dyeing of plastic explosive to match the colours used in German plasticine. Laboratory Assistant Arthur Christie, a former miner, was given the task of trying to bore holes in large pieces of coal in which to conceal 4oz of blackened plastic explosive. A special borer eventually had to be invented for the task.[7] Chemist Charles Bailey of University College, London, joined in February 1939, originally on a part-time/advisory basis, and invented the cigarette time delay. Bailey succeeded Drane in November 1939 and recruited Oswald Walker, another lecturer in chemistry from University College, London. Walker was a specialist on Incendiaries. Engineer John Dolphin was to characterise him as a 'typical scientist with little personality or military qualities'.[8] Douglas Barnsley, another recruit from the Woolwich Arsenal, also joined in late 1939 or early 1940. The expertise in explosives of chemist Francis Freeth dated back to the First World War. The exuberant Freeth tried to develop booby-trapped ammunition by shortening a standard no. 27 detonator with a hacksaw (!) and inserting the open end against the primer of a .303 round, then replacing the bullet. Any attempt to fire it from a rifle would cause it to blow up in the face of the user.[9] The inspiration for this somewhat dangerous experiment may have been the legend of Grand tampering with ammunition to deter theft by tribesmen.

Leslie Wood joined Section D in late 1938 to head the engineering section (D/D) and became deputy to Langley. Wood was a maverick officer who detested red tape and would not suffer fools gladly. He became CO of Aston House when Langley left rather than join SOE. The D/D and D/X sections worked closely together, with one of the results being the Tyesule paraffin incendiary (Pl. 33), as supplied to Home Defence Scheme and Auxiliary Units. These gelatine capsules filled with 2oz of petrol/paraffin mixture were invented by Freeth and Wood. At one end was a match composition which would ignite when struck – there was no time delay. They were used either on their own or were tied around magnesium incendiary devices to increase their effect. John Dolphin joined Section D in 1939 and, although an engineer, retained his original D/XE code. He was a specialist in sabotage techniques and targeting, with one of his first tasks being to provide details of possible sabotage in Germany and then providing the initial plans to sabotage the Swedish ore port of Oxelösund. In 1940 he proposed the idea of the Home Defence Scheme in Britain to Laurence Grand (*see below*, p. 179). Under SOE, he became Commanding Officer of Station IX at the Frythe, where some of his most famous inventions included the folding 'Welbike', the 'Welman' one-man submarine and the 'Welfreighter' miniature submarine. In 1950 he became chief engineer at the UK Atomic Energy Authority and continued to be a prolific inventor.

Section D did not advertise its role in the development of explosives and weaponry. Langley explained:

> And so, we did our utmost to maintain our secret cover. The people who received our weapons knew neither where they came from nor who had made them.[10]

Thus, today, the role of Section D in the development of the No. 76 Self-Igniting Phosphorus (SIP) grenade and the Northover projector that fired it has been almost completely lost. The SIP grenade was invented by Albright and Wilson Ltd of Oldbury, a chemicals company specialising in phosphorous-dreived applications, and these grenades are therefore also known as 'AW Bombs'. They consisted of a half-pint capacity glass bottle filled with a white phosphorus/benzene/water mixture and closed with a 'crown cap'. The grenade could be thrown by hand or fired from what became known as the Northover projector, after its principal inventor, Major Harry Northover, a Canadian gunsmith and inventor, then in the Home Guard. Northover's initial concept was based on his earlier design of a clay pigeon trap. He first presented the design to Churchill at Downing Street in May 1940.[11] The project was then taken over by Section D's associate, Chester Beatty (together with Charles Bailey), to the point that it was referred to during trials simply as the Chester Beatty Mortar. In mid-June, Beatty briefed Desmond Morton, Lord Swinton and Professor Lindeman on progress with the SIP grenade and Northover projector:

> Today he [Beatty] showed me [Lindemann] a projector, something like the Stokes mortar, with which beer bottles can be thrown 140 yards with reasonable accuracy. ... He thinks it should be possible to produce a thousand of these projectors a week and is anxious they should be placed in every village apt to be invaded by tanks ... He thinks in terms of tens of thousands of simple mortars to be produced in a few weeks against the War Office's hundreds.[12]

Meanwhile, staff at Aston House had taken a trial delivery of 5,000 SIP grenades from Albright and Wilson (suggesting Section D had a hand in its development) and were testing their use as smoke grenades and as incendiary grenades against tanks. They were sufficiently impressed to immediately distribute 4,000 of their stock to the Auxiliary Units.[13] This was before any demonstration to the regular forces. A demonstration of what was still termed the Chester Beatty Mortar, firing SIP grenades, was finally given in front of the Prime Minister on 28 July 1940 at Hangmoor Ranges, Pirbright, Surrey. With no thought for modern health and safety, it was tested against a moving, manned, tank:

> The first went over the tank at about 120 yards range whereas the second hit the visor of the tank and flame actually entered the tank, causing the driver to evacuate as quickly as possible.[14]

As a result of the successful trial, 2 million SIP grenades and 10,000 of what were now called Northover (Chester Beatty) Projectors were immediately ordered. Delays in production meant that the first deliveries of the Projector were not made to the Home Guard until January 1941. Approximately 6 million SIP grenades were produced by August 1941 and by 1943 around 19,000 of what were by then known simply as the Northover Projectors were in service with the Home Guard.

The establishment of the technical and research sections of Section D were amongst its most significant contributions to the war effort. The enormity of its range of inventions and production to the end of September 1940 is summarised in Figs 2, 3 and 10. By the end of 1940 almost a million each of time pencils, incendiary arrows and small incendiary bombs had been produced and supplied to European resistance groups, as well as to the British HDS, Auxiliary Units and early commandos.

The lack of official recognition of Section D provided a curious post-war postscript to the work of the scientists. In June 1939, working with Charles Bailey, Langley developed the 'Switch no. 10 Delay', more commonly known as the time pencil (Pl. 18); over 12 million were produced during the Second World War.

Figure 2. Types of materials supplied by Aston House in mid-1940. *(TNA HS 7/27)*

Time Fuses

Pencil Time Fuse — Delays of 5 mins to 5 days.

Cigarette Time Fuse — Delay fuse the size of a cigarette giving delays of a few hours, for use with chemical explosives.

Water Time Fuse — Fuse for underwater demolition giving a delay up to 48 hours. Used in limpet mines.

Clockwork Fuse — Delicate mechanism but used where precise timing was necessary.

Explosives

Plastic Explosive — High powered explosive with the appearance and consistency of putty.

Cheddite — A high explosive designed to be home-made, based on potassium chlorate and candles. Widely used by resistance forces.

Potassium chlorate/ sugar mixture — Explosive designed to be assembled from household materials.

Blasting Gelatine — Supplied by ICI to Section D, made up in continental-type cartridges.

Detonators — Commercial detonators were used, with a stock of German detonators purchased from South Africa before the outbreak of war.

Incendiary Materials

Small Incendiary Bombs — 2oz incendiary bomb for hiding amongst other inflammable materials.

Large Incendiary Bombs — 2oz bomb made from readily available materials.

Incendiary Arrows — Resembled large safety matches, c.18 inches long, with a percussion fuse at the head. Had a range of c.50 yards when fired from a longbow or catapult. Could also be dropped from aircraft.

Incendiary Liquids — Sundry incendiary liquids were supplied, the most effective being a liquid phosphorous compound, also used in Self-Igniting Phosphorus grenades.

Devices

Fog Signals — An adaption of the commercial railway fog signal, modified to fire an explosive charge that would cut a railway line. Intended for night-time use.

Pressure Switch — Designed for hiding under a railway track, so that trains could be derailed in daytime.

Limpets — Mines fitted with magnets to attach to steel or iron. Could be fitted with Water Fuse or Pencil Time Fuse.

Coal Borer — Specially designed borer for drilling a cavity in lumps of coal that could be filled with black plastic explosive and a detonator. Intended to be dropped into a railway engine tender so that it would explode and destroy the engine boiler when shovelled into the fire box.

Tree Spigot — A spigot weighing c.2lb that could be screwed into a tree trunk, pointing towards a suitable target. Used with a Time Pencil, it would fire a high explosive charge.

Secret Signalling — A celluloid filter for signalling, using polarised light, over long distances in blackout conditions.

Chemical Warfare

Abrasives — Various types of abrasives for introducing into lubrication oils, railway axle boxes and other bearings. Mainly supplied in 'toothpaste tubes'.

Noxious Liquids — Various noxious substances were produced which, when inserted into grain stores or other bulk foods, rendered them unfit for human consumption (or poisonous).

Figure 3. Explosives manufactured by Section D up to September 1940. (*TNA HS 7/5*)

254,000	Pencil time fuses.
24,974	Magnets for the application of explosives to steel surfaces.
13,656	lbs of plastic explosive.
25,290	lbs of blasting gelignite.
16,782	ft of instantaneous fuse.
62,868	ft of detonating fuse.
97,010	ft of safety fuse.
12,046	ft of match-ended lengths of safety fuse.
233,581	Fulminate of Mercury detonators.
14,705	Medium incendiary bombs.
25,474	Large incendiary bombs.
146,723	Capsules for igniting petrol bombs.
79,607	Paraffin incendiary flares.
500,000	Incendiary bombs for the destruction of crops.

Langley's inspiration was a German device of 1916 but some of his prototypes were given to the Poles and their copies then brought back by Gubbins, leading to some confusing accounts of their origin. The time pencil comprised a 5.75in-long tube made in three sections of copper, aluminium and brass, with a detonator attached over one end. A thin wire held back a spring-loaded steel striker. A glass ampoule containing an aqueous solution of copper chloride (developed by Bailey) would be broken by squeezing the copper barrel and would dissolve the wire at a set rate, determined by the concentration of the acid, and release the striker which would in turn ignite a detonator and set off the main charge. To avoid failure, the advice was to use them in pairs. In 1954 Langley made a successful claim for payment for inventing the time pencil on the basis that, as Section D did not officially exist but was instead 'an unofficial civilian technical group formed to study methods of defending Britain against attacks by sabotage and other unorthodox means', then the government had no claim on the rights to its products. He argued that at the time of the development of the time pencil 'the Claimant was not employed by a Fighting Service nor was he a Civil Servant'. As funding came from undisclosed secret service funding, Langley could even claim that 'the initial costs were not met from official funds'. Langley was awarded an *ex gratia* payment of £700.[15]

Wireless section

The use of clandestine wireless was still in its early stages in 1938 and most intelligence networks still relied on the 'grape vine telegraph' of runners and lines of communication via neutral countries, with the result that messages could take weeks to arrive at their destination. Section D was established at the same time as communications section of SIS (Section VIII) and Grand created a small wireless research section (D/E) before Brigadier Richard Gambier-Parry imposed an iron grip on all British clandestine communications. The wireless section under

Edward Schröter, with R.J. Cook, was first established at Bletchley Park before moving to Frythe (Station IX). Its main role was in research, although Schröter built at least one set for use in Norway to supplement the limited number of sets built at the time by Section VIII. The technology was crude by later war standards: some machines could only transmit and not receive, and the hand-made sets were heavy and not easy to transport. Nevertheless, the spring and summer of 1940 were crucial periods of experimentation and technological development that paved the way for the better-known wireless sets of SOE and SIS. Often overlooked, the establishment of the early SIS wireless networks on the continent, although of limited success, were vital in establishing future resistance networks. In April 1940 Guy Liddell commented on the sets sent by SIS to Norway:

> These have all been supplied by SIS, since other apparatus of the kind seems singularly out of date. The sets, I gather, are designed by [XXXXXXX] and SIS have them operating from German territory and from all over the continent.[16]

One early success of Section D as a result of wireless communications was to rescue, by fast MTB 317, three RAF pilots and a seaman after Dunkirk. They were being hidden, probably by the French 2ième or 5ième Bureau, who were in contact with Section VIII via a working two-way wireless set.[17] The records of the Section D Norwegian expedition (*see* Chapter 9) include details of the simple wireless code used before the introduction of 'one time pads'. With black humour, it used a copy of the English language *Germany: What Next?*, published by Penguin, as the code book (Pl. 29). The joke of this was probably lost on the poor wireless operator in enemy-held territory.

(a) The <u>code</u> will be <u>L.M.T.2.</u>
(b) The secret number will be 2995.
(c) The book will be "Germany, What Next?" (Penguin) as enclosed.[18]

The priority for SIS (and later SOE) was for long-range sets which, because they had to use Morse code, needed well-trained operators. As well as being able to build such sets, Schröter experimented in a different direction and, based on earlier 1930s research, invented a duplex transceiver that used voice transmission – requiring minimal training. As it operated on short wave, it was also thought that the Germans would not be searching for such frequencies. It had only a limited range and was not pursued further by SIS or SOE but it formed one inspiration for the TRD set of the Auxiliary Units.[19] Schröter also produced an advanced scrambler telephone (the 'D-Phone'), reputedly used by the 'Phantom' units in 1940. His ideas were sometimes not appreciated immediately: Schröter developed a high-powered loudspeaker to be used for the mass broadcast of propaganda. At ground level it had a range of intelligible speech of 1.5 miles and it could be deployed aerially – either automatically by drifting balloons, or by the pilot of an airplane. Such 'Psyops' were widely used after the Normandy landings but could not reach the range of Schröter's pioneering system until the very end of the war. Schröter went on to oversee the early development of clandestine wireless sets for SOE and for a period was CO of the Frythe (Station IX).[20] But he was regarded as being too focused on research rather than delivery and in late 1941 he was 'sidetracked' into the 'Schröter Section' at Imperial College where he was left to conduct pure research.[21] He then joined the Ministry of Aircraft Production to continue research on scrambler devices for the RAF.

SOE continued to rely on the skills of the Section D scientists. In June 1941 Aston House (Station XII) became the production base under Leslie Wood. The Frythe (Station IX) became a research base under Schröter (Wireless), Dolphin (Engineering) and Bailey (Explosives and Chemistry). Walker headed an Incendiaries sub-section.

Small arms section

Section D needed weapons that were not of War Office issue and could not be traced back to the British government. The small arms section was originally based at the Caxton Street HQ under Major Hugh Pollard, assisted by Mr E.J. Churchill of the London firm of gunsmiths and Armoury Sergeant Elliot. Pollard was a recognised expert on small arms and had a colourful career. An engineer by training, he had fought in the Mexican war (1910–1911) and during the First World War had served on the Western Front. In 1917 he became an intelligence officer in MI7 working on propaganda and publicity, and in 1920 he was appointed 'Press Officer' on the staff of the Police Adviser in Dublin, engaged in 'black propaganda'. This was just part of his intelligence role and in April 1921 Auto-Ordnance in the USA shipped fifteen of the new Thompson M1921 submachine guns to him for evaluation. He later confronted the inventor, John Thompson in London over the sale of their weapons to the IRA. Pollard then became Sporting Editor for *Country Life* (a post he held until 1940) and a well respected consultant on firearms but it is a moot point as to whether he was still a part of SIS. In 1936 it was Pollard (an ardent, life-long anti-communist) and another former SIS officer that flew General Franco from the Canaries to Morocco, where the latter organised the coup that began the Spanish Civil War. A continued role for Pollard within SIS is suggested by the fact that in June 1939 the MI5 Regional Officer for Kent discovered that Pollard had links to the British Union of Fascists but MI5 was ordered to 'lay off' because Pollard was working for SIS. This may relate to Grand's claim that one of his officers had compiled an exposé of Dr Buchanan's pro-Nazi 'Oxford Group'.[22] Pollard joined Section D in January 1940 and continued to have considerable dealings with Spain, using his Nationalist contacts to purchase weapons in Madrid and also leading a 'flirtation' with the idea of backing the monarchist opposition to Franco. As well as Spain, Pollard's section sourced weapons from around the world, including the USA,

Japan, Portugal and Italy, and acquired a large stock of commercial detonators of German manufacture from South Africa.[23] This work may well explain the appearance, over the summer of 1940, of adverts in US gun and hunting magazines headed 'Wanted To Buy, Arms For a Friendly Foreign Power'. A price of $40 was offered for Colt, Smith & Wesson, or similar revolvers or automatic pistols in .45 calibre, $30 for .32 and .38 automatics, $25 for smaller revolvers and .22s and .25 automatics. Similar work in 1941 is alluded to as a 'Secret Service' scheme to acquire arms from the USA.[24] The section also collected useful weapons handed in to the police. Many were second-hand and of unknown reliability, but Elliot serviced and repaired them. The work demanded care as some automatic weapons arrived with a forgotten round in the breech. Automatic pistols were particularly prized but, being unfamiliar in Britain during 1939/1940, the police tended to destroy those handed in by the public.[25] From various sources, in July 1940 alone Pollard's section acquired 30 Colt .32 automatics, 100 Luger 9mm automatics and 4 'Spanish Tommy guns'.[26] Pollard and Churchill left the section in mid-September after its transfer to SOE. Former Section D administrative officer James Tomlinson then took command and in October, having been bombed out of its existing offices, the new section moved to the Frythe and thence to Bride Hall, Hertfordshire (Station VI).

Balloons

Both the White Russian and Finnish partisans had used petrol bombs for crop-burning. Section D made a number of proposals for the large-scale burning of crops in enemy territory and by 25 August 1940 it had supplied over 103,000 incendiary bombs for aerial crop-burning to the Middle East, and over 396,000 to the RAF.[27] In addition, a section to investigate the delivery of incendiaries and propaganda via free-flying balloons was established by Walter Wren in 1938. He was unaware at the time that the RAF was also experimenting with this as a means of distributing aerial propaganda, but in October 1938 they began joint experiments.[28] In November the balloon section was taken over by Lieutenant Colonel James O'Hea, who had come out of the Army Reserve in 1938 to become CO of an RAF barrage balloon squadron. From late September 1939 O'Hea began experiments from a station established at Savehay Farm, Denham, to deploy incendiary free-flying balloons on a large scale, and was encouraged by the RAF's successful use of balloons to distribute propaganda leaflets into Germany from France. O'Hea's intention was more deadly, intended to start large-scale forest and crop fires across enemy territory. The original plan was to use hydrogen balloons but this was switched to developing hot air balloons that were built up from paper panels. In March 1940 AAF Balloon Officer and former chemist Thomas Bird joined Section D and carried out experiments using ammonia-hydrogen balloons.[29] Bird also liaised closely with experiments being conducted by the French and in April reported that in one test a 600-cubic-foot balloon carrying a 3lb load and fitted with a petrol burner had travelled 110 miles.

Experiments continued after the demise of Section D and between 1942 and 1944 Britain released 53,000 incendiary balloons to fly over Germany, each carrying a 6lb incendiary bomb. Others trailed a 270-foot-long strand of steel piano wire that was designed to catch against high voltage power lines and short-out electricity supplies.

Training

Aston House had a testing facility in an adjacent chalk quarry ('The Dell Hole') that was also used for the early, but ad hoc, training of saboteurs. In charge were Lieutenant Cecil 'Nobby' Clark, a former gamekeeper on the royal estate at Sandringham, and Lieutenant Edward Ramsay-Green, formerly of the Royal Engineers and now in charge of the design office (he also perfected the Pocket Incendiary). Ramsay-Green caused some consternation amongst trainees due to missing three fingers of one hand and with one leg amputated – the result of wounds from the First World War but disconcerting in an explosives instructor who also taught how to crimp a detonator onto a length of fuse using one's teeth![30] The training was attended by foreign agents, regional officers of the HDS and Intelligence Officers of the Auxiliary Units but the courses were short and basic.

In March 1940 Monty Chidson raised with Laurence Grand the need for a more formal training system.[31] As well as a lack of training in sabotage, the capture of Best and Stevens at Venlo had highlighted the lack of training to deal with capture and interrogation; this problem would soon be emphasised in the arrest of the Section D cell in Sweden. What was now planned was the innovative concept of a school for political warfare embracing a wide curriculum. Sabotage instructor George Hill was to later comment about Grand: 'No credit has ever been given to him for founding the first sabotage school, which was justly due to him.'[32]

Chidson, with Guy Burgess and later commander Frederick Peters and Kim Philby, formed a committee to consider a new training programme. Then on 24 June a meeting was held in Grand's St Ermin's Hotel apartment to establish cooperation between G Branch of SIS and Section D, both with interests in getting men and information in and out of enemy territory. Attending from Section D were Grand, Humphreys (France), Fraser (Scandinavia), Franck (Belgium) and Burgess (representing the putative training school), along with Commander Slocum of SIS and one other whose name has been redacted. Much of the meeting turned to discussing the need for a training school which would have a broad syllabus including espionage, counter-espionage, sabotage, propaganda, conspiracy, revolution, self-defence and communications. In his June progress report, Grand described this as the most important single item on his agenda.[33] Commander Frederick Peters RN had just joined Section D from a successful tour of duty commanding a flotilla of anti-submarine trawlers and was already earmarked to head such a school, with veteran SIS officer George Hill as the sabotage instructor.[34]

On the next day Burgess advised Valentine Vivian, deputy chief of SIS, that Section D was proposing to establish a training school for prospective foreign agents. The intention was to create 'political movements organised on a military basis', and ready to undertake sabotage when the time was ripe. Such movements were to be built 'on the highest ideals and must be imbued with a strong driving force'.[35] The influence of the highly politicised Guy Burgess is clear. Later, MI5 believed that Burgess was intending to use the school to create a para-military movement based around the European trade union organisations, an aim shared by Hugh Dalton in his early promotion of the SOE. Kim Philby joined Section D in July and gives himself credit for devising the syllabus. The motives of Soviet agents Burgess and Philby aside, the political education at the school was regarded as being of such potential value that in October (with the school now taken over by SOE) it was recommended by G Branch that other SIS trainees should attend an abbreviated course. On 9 August, before the school accepted its first students, Peters and Philby visited Guy Liddell of MI5 seeking permission to trawl for prospective trainee agents in internment camps, using the cover of visiting 'welfare officers' and for MI5 to provide a 'librarian' at the school who would keep the trainees under surveillance. The latter duty was eventually performed by Arthur Trevor-Wilson from SIS Section V (counter-espionage).[36]

The school was based at the requisitioned Brickendonbury Manor, set in 1,000 acres of parkland outside Hertford, about 25 miles north of London. Staff were appointed in July but the first course was not organised until late August.[37] Officially it was titled the 'Inter-Service Experimental Department' or Station XVII, but was usually known simply as the 'D School'. Commander Peters, the commandant, 'had faraway naval eyes and a gentle smile of great charm. ... Our trainees came to adore him.'[38] The adjutant was Major Barcroft, formerly adjutant of the Hertfordshire Regiment before retiring from the army in 1922 and becoming a property developer. George Hill was chief sabotage instructor. He also scrounged a Lewis gun to use for weapons training and for the defence of the school in case of attack. Hill had learned the techniques of espionage and railway sabotage whilst working for SIS in Russia during the First World War, had written three articles on sabotage for *The War* magazine, and published his extraordinary wartime experiences as *Go Spy the Land: being the adventures of IK8 of the British Secret Service*. Hill was recruited by Grand at a lunch at the St Ermin's Hotel, initially to develop sabotage in northern Europe, although the publication of his career as a spy limited his potential role. Before taking up his post at Brickendonbury, Hill had attended a refresher course in explosives at Aston House and then rushed over to France to supply explosives and detonators to the French and Belgian sub-sections of Section D. He escaped on the last cruiser to leave Bordeaux. Despite his well known early history as a spy in Russia, he was later sent as head of the SOE mission to the Soviets. Kim

Philby, quick-witted, perceptive and full of sound ideas (according to Hill), taught propaganda.[39] He habitually wore an old First World War tunic that had belonged to his father in an attempt to provide a more military persona.[40] Guy Burgess taught political subversion but he was ever close to a scandal, and a corporal claimed that Burgess had been 'trying to muck about with him'. In the way of the times the corporal was punished by being transferred – but no action was taken against Old Etonian Burgess.[41] Explosives expert 'Nobby' Clark transferred here from Aston House, and there was also a 'melancholy Czech printer', who had run an underground press in Prague, and an Austrian member of the SDP (Mr Werner). Teaching the skills of codes and secret inks was Professor Eric Patterson, former Principal of the Bonar Law college at Ashridge, Hertfordshire, a specialist in adult education who had somehow developed a skill in such mysteries. Graduation from the course was by written examination and practical work.[42] It is quite remarkable that two, possibly three, of the Brickendonbury staff proved to be Soviet double agents. One at least hopes that they passed on their lessons in deceit to their pupils!

In July an advance demonstration of the school syllabus was given to the Prime Minister, Professor Lindemann, Lord Beaverbrook, the assistant chief of the Imperial General Staff and other officers including Lieutenant Linge, then liaison officer between Section D and the Norwegian General Staff and later founder of the famous Norwegian Independent Company.[43] The first group of trainees did not, however, arrive until 29 August and comprised six Belgians, five Norwegians (including veterans of the Section D Norwegian expeditions), three French, and a large group of Spanish Republican refugees, totalling twenty-five in all. The Spaniards included republican *dinamiteros* from the Asturias; some had been recruited from a French Foreign Legion unit that had taken part in the Norwegian campaign and become stranded in Britain upon the fall of France.[44] Such Spanish Civil War veterans needed little training in explosives. 'All instructors are the same,' said one, 'they tell you to cut off so much fuse. We double it to be quite safe. That is why we are still alive.' Their military discipline did, however, leave much to be desired. Peter Kemp (a former Nationalist officer who joined MI(R)) later described them as a 'villainous crowd of assassins'.[45]

The training followed a six-week course including:

1. Training in Devices
The theory of sabotage and tactical training as well as practical instruction in the growing range of explosives, fuses and timer devices. There were twelve sessions of two hours each in the chalk pit at Aston, where they could study the effects of explosions from behind armoured glass.

2. Special Training
Camouflage, secrecy and security, communication lines and counter-espionage. The principal of recruiting and organisation through cut-outs, procurement and dissemination of intelligence.

3. Use of Firearms

Instruction in a wide range of small arms and grenades.

Subsequent courses were intended to include a section on wireless communications but this was not possible before the transfer of the establishment to SOE.[46] In November Colin Gubbins, formerly of MI(R), was appointed head of training in SOE. The training school at Brickendonbury was continued but, like Langley at Aston House, Commander Peters resigned rather than join SOE and rejoined the Royal Navy. He helped plan Special Operations connected with *Operation Torch* (the landings in North Africa) and later won a VC for his part in the attack on Oran harbour in 1943 but was killed just days later. Peters' place as commandant was taken by 'Nobby' Clark and the school went on to train over 1,000 agents in industrial sabotage.

Chapter 4

Western Europe: the Fascist Powers

In 1939 there was a reasonable fear that the four nations ruled by fascist dictatorship would unite as the Axis powers. Most of the efforts made against them were directed from surrounding neutral countries and are considered in other chapters. The present chapter is concerned with Section D's relationship with the native opposition groups.

Germany

In 1933 the Nazis rose to power in Germany and ruthlessly crushed all dissent. The main political opposition was fragmented between the banned Social Democrat (SDP) and Communist (KPD) Parties. Smaller, more radical, left-wing groups, notably the Socialist Workers Party (SAP), failed to convince the leaderships of SDP and KPD to join in a united anti-fascist front, but some of the younger members of SDP and those of SAP were amongst the most effective of the German opposition (the KPD being hamstrung during the period of the Hitler–Stalin Pact). Jewish youths took part in the activities of wider political groups as well as joining specific Jewish organisations. Many of those who opposed the Nazis were forced into exile across Europe but maintained secret lines of communication into Germany, making them an obvious recruitment target for Section D. A fundamental difficulty, apart from that of working within a ruthless police state, was that such opposition groups had to resolve their desire to bring down the Nazi state whilst remaining loyal Germans. The Munich Agreement had been disheartening for the German opposition and, once war was declared, many would still not work on behalf of a foreign power. Aware of the sensibilities, Laurence Grand was careful to stress that the work of Section D was directed against the Nazi state rather than against the Germans themselves, and the British origin of support to some German opposition groups was concealed. Support from German industrial workers and the trade unions was central to Grand's plans, and his wildly optimistic belief, even in June 1940, was that:

> The moment will come, possibly sooner than would seem probable at the moment, when internal disturbance in Germany on a large scale will start spreading much faster than the authorities in Germany believe.[1]

Some schemes were fantastical. Grand dreamed of RAF leaflet drops containing details of a pre-arranged signal which would advise the RAF that the target was in revolt and should not be bombed. He believed this would be practicable when 'the Army become, as become they will, disaffected, even to a comparatively small extent'.[2] He suggested dropping arms into the country from the air at random, including into concentration camps, in the knowledge that although the Gestapo would seize most of them, some would get into opposition hands. It would also tie up resources in searching for such weapons.[3] There remained limits. On 15 December 1939 Grand rejected the offer from Karl Spiecker (German Freedom Party) to organise sabotage in Nazi meeting halls in Germany. Spiecker claimed credit on behalf of his organisation for the Munich beer hall explosion carried out by George Elser on 8 November 1939 and there has remained considerable speculation as to whether Elser acted alone or as part of a wider group.

A German and Austrian section (sub-divided as D/R and D/Z) was formed under experienced SIS officer Montagu Chidson and T.S. Fairley in April 1939 and during November the two men formed a unit to liaise with émigré organisations in Britain and recruit new agents from refugee centres. The section remained small, interchangeable with Propaganda Section D/P, and mainly acting to coordinate the shipping of sabotage material and propaganda abroad by other country sections. By August 1940 Section D claimed to have established working relations with ten international political organisations having German contacts of a Labour, Catholic, Jewish or émigré nature based in Britain and over twenty others abroad. It was, however, now disheartened over the chances of any armed resistance within Germany.

Propaganda

On 4 November 1938 Grand had outlined his ideas for a propaganda organisation in Germany based on a pyramid model. One key agent in London, or in a neutral country, would pass on the mis-information to three contacts in Germany; each of these three would in turn recruit not more than three others, and so on. In this way, no agent would be able to inform on more than his recruiter and the three contacts he had made. All communications would be verbal and the British source of the black propaganda would be concealed, the material appearing to come from within the target country or from a neutral source.[4] This methodology was also used in the circulation of typed chain letters, in the hope that they would be self-generating. *Die Deutsche Kette* ('The German Chain') purported to have originated from a 'well-wisher' in the office of the personal Astrologer to Hitler and prophesied great slaughter of German troops and economic ruin if the letter was not copied and sent on to three other people.[5] Such a chain letter was found by Swedish police when they arrested Alfred Rickman in Stockholm (*see* Chapter 9).

The production section for distributing propaganda into Germany was D/P, originally under the versatile Walter Wren. The practical task of editing, printing and organising the secret distribution of German-language propaganda leaflets was in the hands of long-time SIS officer Evelyn Stamper, assisted by Clara Holmes.[6] German fonts, ink, paper, envelopes and stamps were acquired from abroad and at least 2,000 12 pfennig stamps were forged. Recipients were sourced from a large card index of addresses in Germany. A team of German refugees at the Lexham Gardens house then addressed the envelopes, using a variety of Germanic handwriting styles. Bundles of the finished product were either distributed to country sections of Section D for posting or sometimes Holmes took suitcase-loads of material to Paris, from where they were distributed in Germany via the LEX organisation of German exiles in France and Switzerland (*see below*). *Facts*, the first leaflet produced for the new German section, appeared in June 1939. Later pamphlets included *Austrian News*, *Jasomirgott Letters*, *A Magazine for German Women*, *A Magazine for Austrian Women*, *Letters to Austrian Railwaymen* and a range of subversive stickers. In all, a million leaflets were claimed to have been distributed in Germany up to 3 September 1939 by contacts of Section D. The latter also claimed credit for passive resistance, demonstrations, the chalking of anti-Nazi slogans and other disturbances, as well as strikes and other 'outrages' in Germany and occupied countries. Inevitably, German partners exaggerated any successes – particularly when paid upon results – and many claims cannot be verified. The reports did, however, fuel the optimistic vision of internal revolt within the Nazi orbit.

With the outbreak of war, Section D also became responsible for getting Electra House material into Germany. To coordinate the work, Section D/P briefly moved to Woburn House in September when Electra House was mobilised but, with only a grudging welcome from Campbell Stuart, within a few weeks it had moved to The Old Rectory in Hertingfordbury. Having lost the opportunity for direct oversight of its work, this move only added to the mystery, and Stuart complained bitterly about the fact that Section D continued to produce its own material, even though Grand maintained that all distributed material had prior approval from Electra House. The consultative committee that was established by Section D and Electra House in the autumn of 1939 jointly came up with a number of ideas for rumour-mongering that Section D agents then spread in Germany. The first, in December 1939, was to claim that one-third of U-boats were being lost at sea. Letters were circulated discrediting Professor Herlein, the head of the IG Farben chemical company and a leading expert on bacteriological warfare. Also in December, Section D/P created mischief in suggesting splits in Nazi unity by circulating photographs showing Admiral Langsdorff of the *Graf Spee* giving the military salute whilst the representatives of the German Legation in Uruguay gave the Nazi salute (Langsdorff committed suicide on 20 December 1939). It then tried to create financial instability by spreading rumours in July 1940 that the Reichbank was printing banknotes with duplicate serial numbers, in order to disguise massive economic inflation. Another rumour was that the receipt of food parcels from abroad was being taken by the Gestapo as proof that the recipients held foreign money reserves.[7]

Stuart decided to break the influence of Section D by proposing to establish his own distribution network in Germany but Lord Hankey was concerned that he displayed only a poor grasp of what was being undertaken on his behalf by Section D. Hankey tried to dissuade Stuart and warned CSS that, 'My impression is that he is not at all well informed on how much you are doing for him. ... he was certainly surprised at the scale of what you are doing for his Department.'[8] Dissatisfied with the effectiveness of the existing consultative committee, Stuart appointed a further liaison officer to Section D, Sir Hanns Vischer, a former First World War intelligence officer, recently retired from the Colonial Office. He attended weekly meetings on propaganda at the Frythe but it was clear that Stuart would never be satisfied until he had taken over the propaganda elements of Section D:

> To be quite frank he (Sir Campbell) had so little confidence in Colonel Grand's organisation that he would prefer, if it was possible, to undertake the distribution of his material himself.[9]

Whilst Stuart huffed and puffed, Stamper and Holmes got on with the job. By March 1940 Section D was claiming to deliver 70,000–80,000 pieces of propaganda per month into Germany and to be involved in three secret German printing presses. The National Archives has a collection of around fifty different propaganda leaflets produced by Section D, including posters, leaflets and stickers to deface pro-Nazi propaganda or to display elsewhere.[10] A main target was the Hitler–Stalin Pact, depicting Hitler as having betrayed German honour and sold off its assets in the east (Pl. 11). Other material encouraged friction between Germans and the Nazi party, for example by accusing the Nazis of profiting from the war while the ordinary people made the sacrifices. One cartoon showed a cold and wet German soldier in the trenches, complaining that he had received no letter from home. The answer is provided by the picture alongside which shows an SS man seducing his wife, with the caption 'NO POST ... NO WONDER ... the Home Front is in firm hands – the SS and SA are always ready for action ...' (Pl. 12). Another target was Prussia, the home of aristocratic landowners who despised Hitler and had traditionally important links to the army. There was mis-information. One official-looking leaflet, headed 'Measures against Inflation', claimed to be from the German Retailer Traders Association and urged people to follow the example of the leaders of the Nazi Party by hoarding goods before prices rose or they became in short supply (Pl. 13).[11] Other leaflets protested the anti-Christian nature of the Nazi Party. Section D also began to fund, to the extent of £150 per month, the newsletter of the German Freedom Party (DFP), *Das Wahre Deutschland* ('The True Germany'), produced from January 1938 to December 1940.[12] The DFP was a loose alliance of liberal and conservative opposition groups, founded by Karl Spiecker and Otto Klepper in Paris in early 1937. The support of Section D allowed the DFP to publish on a scale that belied the actual size of the small organisation. *Das Wahre Deutschland* (Pl. 15) was widely circulated amongst German émigrés across Europe and helped give the impression of a substantial, moderate German opposition beyond that of the revolutionary socialist SDP or SAP.

The fall of Denmark and France interrupted most propaganda channels into Germany and Austria. By the time SOE took over the German section there were still just four officers: Major R.H. Thornley (supervision of German and Austrian sub-sections, supervision of training, control of black propaganda), Major William Field-Robinson (German contacts, operations into Germany and recruiting of agents), Evelyn Stamper (handling Austrian contacts and operations into Austria) and Clara Holmes (assistant to Stamper).[13] The early optimism had dissipated and Thornley, soon to become head of SOE Section X (Germany) was, by now, pessimistic about the prospects of any organised armed resistance within Germany.[14]

International Transport Workers Federation (ITF)
During 1936 SIS established a contact in the International Transport Workers Federation (ITF), Hermann Knüfken. In an eventful life, Knüfken had deserted the German Navy in 1917 and joined the Communist Party. He hijacked a steam trawler on which he took Franz Jung and Jan Appel to the 2nd World Congress of the Comintern in the USSR, was sentenced to five years' imprisonment, and released in 1923. He then went to Leningrad but was arrested by the Soviet secret police in 1929 and returned to Germany in 1932. Forced to flee when the Nazis took power, Knüfken set up a Seamen's Action Group in Rotterdam to organise the distribution of anti-Nazi propaganda into Germany. He broke with the Communist Party in 1936 and then became an agent of SIS, informing on the activities of the ITF. As a result, in January 1939 SIS became aware of discussions within the union about interrupting the supplies of iron ore to Germany in the event of war, through Narvik, Luleå and Oxelösund. Responsibility for handling Knüfken was passed to Chidson in Section D but soon afterwards Eddo Fimmen (aged 58), the founder of the ITF and another former communist, also put out feelers to work with SIS, leading to the delicate issue of how to admit that Knüfken had been their agent for the past three years. In May Chidson contacted Fimmen in Amsterdam and it was agreed that, whilst the latter would persevere with what was likely to be slow progress towards official ITF strike action by its dockers and railwaymen, he would also support Knüfken's recruitment of individual members of the ITF to carry out sabotage. In 1948 details of work with the ITF were 'deleted on the grounds of national security' from Mackenzie's history of SOE. Some of the contacts were by then probably in East Germany, where any recognition of their role as British agents would have been dangerous.

Immediate plans by Section D to send Knüfken to Scandinavia to recruit ITF members for sabotage work in the German ports were delayed because the Gestapo had circulated his photograph to the Scandinavian governments, warning that he was 'a most dangerous and active' agent.[15] The captured Stevens later alluded to him as agent 101b from his earlier work in the Low Countries, but it was only after the war that it was realised that Guy Burgess was informing on Section D links with trade unionists to his Soviet spymasters because this posed a threat to the Hitler–Stalin Pact.[16] How much of Burgess's information was passed on to the Nazis is not known. Knüfken finally entered Sweden in October 1939 using a false Danish passport. However, Swedish police arrested him in mid-November, after he was betrayed to the police by a Swedish member of staff of the British Legation, and he was interned until 1944 (*see* Chapter 9). Johannes Jahn was one ITF member in Germany who agreed to carry out sabotage on behalf of Section D. He was recruited in January 1940 and Section D supplied him with incendiary bombs, time pencils, cigarette time delay fuses and potassium chlorate, via a contact in Antwerp. He may have had some success. In April 1940 MI5 intercepted a message from the ITF representative in Luxembourg to its HQ, now established in Kempston, Bedfordshire: 'During the past week a goods train of 120-axles [sixty wagons] was completely blown into the air between Aachen and Koln [Cologne].'[17]

LEX Organisation
LEX was an organisation of German exiles in France and Switzerland founded in 1935 by former communists Karl Otten in London and Karl Groehl in Paris, with SDP member Karl Gerold in Zurich. Foot dismissed Otten (aged 51) and Groehl (aged 44) as 'a pair of crippled German refugees' and Boyce followed this simplistic assessment in 2005 by characterising the pair as 'two eccentric old gentlemen'.[18] Although in 1940 Groehl's hearing was failing, as was Otten's sight, their appearance was deceptive and gave no hint of their history or the complexity of their relationship with British intelligence:

> GROEHL was small and deaf. His appearance was mild, a fact which worried him, since he considered that a man of his trade should be an awesome sight. Otten was professorial and became blind. He also revelled in violent activity, although possessing none of the outward characteristics generally associated with the terrorist.[19]

Karl Groehl (*aka* Stanislaw Reslaw) was a founder of the German Communist Party who fled to Russia in 1933 and thence to Switzerland (where he met journalist Karl Gerold) and to Paris, where he worked for the Comintern with Karl Otten. Groehl joined the Trotskyist *Internationalen Kommunisten Deutschlands* (IKD) in late 1933, becoming Trotsky's representative in central Europe until he apparently became a Social Democrat (although MI5 in 1938 was suspicious that he remained a Soviet agent). He was reported by MI5 in August 1938 as having a reputation for being quarrelsome and having been expelled from every left-wing group in Germany, and as 'an old-fashioned type of revolutionary who cannot be happy without a revolver in his pocket and a scheme for blowing someone up'.[20] Otten was first arrested in 1914 as an anarchist who had incited German troops to mutiny against the war. He had become a well known expressionist writer and in 1931 wrote the internationally renowned film, *Kamer-adschaft*. Forced to flee Germany in 1933, he came to Britain in 1936 and began working for the BBC. By May 1938 Groehl's LEX contacts were smuggling valuable information on German rearmament out of Germany into France, and then Groehl forwarded the information to Otten, neither realising that the 'Primrose League', as the London group of LEX was known, was under MI5 surveillance and Otten's correspondence was being intercepted as a suspected Trotskyist (the 'cut-out' between Groehl and Otten was an MI5 agent) and supplied to SIS. MI5 established that Otten was supplying the information to the Czechs at their London Legation and, although he was very hostile both to Stalin and to the Nazi regime, MI5 did not believe Otten could be trusted with confidential information, there being no guarantee that he would work exclusively for British intelligence. Nonetheless, a meeting between Grand and Otten was arranged in December 1938 to negotiate an alliance with Section D.

Otten initially claimed LEX had forty-six members within Germany and six couriers entering the country via Switzerland and the Low Countries; they were mainly professional men supposed to include one or two in the army, and, less likely, individuals in the SS. By July 1939 he was claiming that there were 200 sympathisers willing to pass on forged currency in Hamburg alone. Otten also claimed that they had previously distributed up to 25,000 leaflets per month in Germany. He admitted that the distribution of propaganda had ceased but, suspiciously, offered to restart the work if Section D would just provide £300 per month to the group. In return, LEX would give Section D full control of the material to be distributed. The relationship between Groehl and Otten was stormy. They 'lived in an atmosphere of continual mutual recriminations which generally ended in a particularly violent outburst of one against the other, after they met and all was forgiven'.[21] It became the task of Clara Holmes to act as courier and peacemaker between the two men. Holmes delivered the first batch of 2,000 leaflets produced by Section D for LEX to Groehl in Paris during early July 1939. William Berington delivered more leaflets to Brussels, which were then smuggled into Germany via seamen in the port of Antwerp. Much of the intelligence that they provided in return was of doubtful value, but included the occasional nugget of useful information. Their real value was in providing introductions to several contacts across Europe, including the publisher Bermann-Fischer, who worked on propaganda with the Scandinavian section of Section D, and, less positively, journalist Immanuel Birnbaum (later revealed as a German spy, see p. 161). They were never completely trusted and continued MI5 intercepts of their correspondence were passed to Viscount Bearsted and thence to the French section of Section D who were monitoring Groehl.

Section D encouraged LEX to progress from distributing propaganda to undertaking sabotage but was met 'with greater enthusiasm than efficiency'. Otten produced a list of likely sabotage targets and from June 1939 Section D began to supply sabotage devices to Groehl in Paris and Karl Gerold in Basle.

One of the proposed targets was an installation situated on a hill 6 kilometres north-east of Basle, the Tullinger Hugel, which Otten claimed to be the electrical and intelligence control centre for the southern end of the Siegfried Line. The targeting committee of Section D prioritised the scheme but wanted collaborating evidence. Despite his aggressive bluster, Groehl tended to shy away from specific commitments and did not wish to be seen as being directed by a foreign power, wanting his agents to be able to use their own initiative in choosing targets. Otten was persuasive and suggested a meeting at Basle between an explosives expert and the proposed saboteur, with an agreed payment of £2,000 and a USA visa for the latter. The War Office supplied aerial photography of the site and agreed with Otten's interpretation as some kind of control centre. In December the French confirmed that there was indeed some unusual activity at the site, with railway and road tunnels being bored into the hill. In the light of this accumulation of evidence, explosives were personally delivered in December 1939 to Gerold in Switzerland by Leslie Humphreys (head of the French section) and Section D then waited for the LEX agent to act.

At first there was silence and Section D suspected that it had been duped. Then reports began to circulate of a large explosion in the vicinity of the Tullinger Hugel that had taken place on 2 February. Initial delight was tempered when Groehl admitted that his agent had, in fact, taken the easier course of using the explosives to destroy a substantial munitions dump at nearby Heltingen, which was of some value but did not have the strategic importance of the designated target. Suspicion of Groehl increased as he continued to use the excuse of a lack of funds for failure to organise further action. One scheme may, however, have been more successful than was at first imagined. In March 1940 further explosives were smuggled into Switzerland for a scheme to destroy the Rheinfelden Aluminium Works. Although there was no immediate feedback to suggest sabotage at the plant, in September 1940 MI5 intercepted correspondence to Otten from Lisbon to say that the machine hall at Rheinfelden had indeed been destroyed.[22] Despite the latter, efforts to turn the LEX group into an efficient and reliable sabotage organisation had clearly failed and their claims to have distributed large quantities of propaganda in Germany might well also have been exaggeration. In March 1940 Viscount Bearsted was concerned enough about Groehl's sources to ask MI5 to increase surveillance and, if there was any doubt as to their validity, to have Otten interned. Nonetheless, their work was considered of sufficient potential for Groehl (who escaped to England following the fall of France) and Otten to continue to work with Stamper and Holmes in SOE, advising on propaganda to Germany. Doubts as to their reliability remained and MI5 maintained their surveillance, leading in early 1941 to suspicions that Groehl was passing information to a possible Soviet agent.[23] In September SOE tried to revive contacts with LEX in Switzerland, sending former Section D officer Elizabeth Hodgson to Zurich to contact journalist Karl Gerold, who was by then working for Swiss military intelligence, supplying it with reports from LEX contacts in Germany and now simultaneously passing them on to Hodgson. In return, SOE resumed smuggling propaganda and sabotage materials into Austria via LEX. Demonstrable success finally came in supplying SOE with plans of the Zeiss optical works at Jena and other factory sites in Berlin and Dresden. LEX continued to claim responsibility for sabotage attacks in Germany, but in October 1943 Gerold was betrayed to the Swiss police by his mistress and the organisation collapsed. Hodgson (now aged 58) was forced to flee into occupied France and then made her way to Spain, travelling by foot over the Pyrenees in the middle of winter. Gerold was imprisoned in a Swiss labour camp for his 'breach of neutrality' and Hodgson was sentenced, in absentia, to two years' imprisonment and banishment from Switzerland for a period of five years.[24] Meanwhile, Otten's sight deteriorated further and he became blind in 1944, marking the final end of the group.

German Social Democratic Party

The German SDP established an organisation of exiles called SOPADE (or SoPaDe). Captain Fairley made contact with them via William Gillies, secretary of the International Committee of the British Labour Party and both an inveterate opponent of the Nazis and deeply anti-communist. Gillies had long monitored Labour Party dealings with the Communist Party and it is likely that this brought him into contact with British intelligence. As with LEX, there was clearly a risk that Section D would be seen as a cash cow by SOPADE and Fairley was suspicious of its claims. In January 1940 SOPADE claimed it had an extensive organisation of about 200 reliable agents based within countries bordering Germany, and was also in contact with sympathisers still within Germany. It wanted 100,000 francs per month to increase the production of propaganda material (particularly the underground newspaper *Neuer Vorwaerts*), produce a radio programme that could be broadcast into Germany and use its contacts to monitor the effects of propaganda and economic warfare within Germany. Offers were made to produce further propaganda directed at increasing opposition to the Nazis within neutral countries and to organise counter-activities against the Ausland organisation of the Nazi party abroad. SOPADE was also looking towards a post-war settlement of Germany, offering to establish an alternative government-in-waiting and to provide for the reincorporation of Germany into the post-war world.

It was important that this was presented as a 'home-grown' German resistance and it was agreed that support should be funnelled through the Labour Party rather than admit to any funding from British intelligence. Success would be measured by how many sympathisers within Germany could be persuaded to provide active collaboration in distributing propaganda material and by those going further and conducting sabotage. Chidson negotiated the amount of subsidy down to 80,000 francs per month in March, and insisted that it be used for specific operations rather than to shore up the finances of SOPADE. The latter was, however, prepared to advise Section D on suitable propaganda material, could post bundles of letters within Germany, and would even smuggle in sabotage material for the use of Section D agents. The possibility of SOPADE mounting a sabotage campaign of its own seemed more doubtful. In one last attempt to secure a more effective partnership, in late April Fairley met in Paris with its representatives to encourage a more aggressive attitude. SOPADE still would not order its members to commit acts of sabotage to the instructions of Section D but Fairley suggested that they regard themselves as independent collaborators, rather than there be any suggestion that they were working for an organ of the British intelligence. Such progress was interrupted by the fall of France. Leading members of SOPADE managed to escape to England but the organisation was now even weaker and although communication was resumed in 1941, SOE was never able to progress Section D's initiative and focused instead on sabotaging wider German morale, infrastructure and administration. The official allied policy from 1943 of Germany's unconditional surrender naturally hampered the scope for cooperation with opposition groups and Gubbins was later to admit that SOE had achieved very little in Germany.[25]

Austria

The British government had recognized the *Anschluss* in 1938 but, based upon the opinion of long-established Austrophiles within Section D, together with pressure from Slovenian and Austrian anti-Nazi groups in the Balkans, Grand took the view that there was a large body of opinion within the country that would resist the absorption by Nazi Germany and that it should therefore be regarded as a distinct target. Austria was to be separately referenced in any radio broadcast or propaganda and 10,000 stickers and 3,000 posters were printed reading 'Neither Hitler nor Stalin – Austria for the Austrians' (Pl 16).[26] The analysis failed to appreciate both the widespread support for the Nazis within Austria and the desire for a pan-German revolution by many socialist opposition groups. The complexities of Austrian politics meant that resistance remained fragmented and divisive throughout the war. SIS officers Evelyn Stamper and Clara Holmes had served for many years in Austria and strongly believed there was the possibility of tapping into Austrian nationalism in return for an assurance that Austria would be treated differently from Germany in a post-war settlement. They also envisaged a partnership of Catholics and Social Democrats which would be able to counter any future communist ascendancy. With this special interest, all propaganda material that was sent into Austria was Section D's, rather than being produced by Electra House.[27]

The main target areas for sabotage were the Tyrol, where there were still individuals who felt bitterness towards both the Germans and the Italians, and East Austria, where there were Monarchists and Communists who, Grand believed, were prepared to work together but required arms and explosives. The first batch of 2,000 Austrian Monarchist leaflets was delivered to Groehl in Paris for distribution by LEX in July 1939. At the same time there was increasing sabotage in Austria organised from Yugoslavia and carried out by Slovenian nationalists of the TIGR (Revolutionary Organisation of the Julian March – Trieste, Istria, Gorizia and Rijeka), supported by Section D. The Slovenian nationalist movement, with members transcending the border between Italy, Austria and Yugoslavia, played a key role in the operations of Section D in the Balkans (*see* Chapter 6).

Austrian partisans continued to operate throughout the war, although most were wiped out during intensive campaigns against them in 1944. At its height, the Slovenian Liberation Front, mainly composed of local farmers in Carinthia, was organised in two battalions; at the battle of Schwarzenbach in August 1944 they managed to defeat both Wehrmacht and SS forces.

From 1940 to 1942 Holmes and Stamper unofficially edited *Free Austria*, the highest circulating newspaper for exiled Austrians, which attacked both Austrian exile groups and British politicians that held to the *Anschluss* and to a pan-German position. It was only in 1943 that the British government adopted a formal policy on Austrian independence, partly to help prevent Austria falling under the Soviet sphere of influence. It did, however, remain equivocal on the claims of the Slovenes for territorial independence. The potential for resistance, although it greatly influenced later SOE policy, never fully materialised. The resistance movement remained divided among those supported by the western powers, by the Soviets, and by the Slovenian nationalists, and for many years after the war there also remained a lingering feeling that members of the Austrian resistance had been traitors in the spirit of 'my country, right or wrong'.

Italy

Mussolini came to power in 1922 but there remained an active opposition to fascist rule. The three main opposition groups were the social democratic *Giustizia e Liberta*, the Communist Party and, in the east of Italy, the substantial Slovene minority centred on Trieste (Fig. 4), who had built up considerable resentment towards the Italians following the secession of Istria after the First World War. *Giustizia e Liberta* had been founded in 1929, had organised the Italian contingent to the International Brigades in Spain and was later to fight as partisans in Italy. The Slovenian nationalists, including TIGR and *Branizbor*, were well armed and became an extremely important reservoir of saboteurs to Section D in the Balkans, with HQs in Belgrade and Ljubljana, but in February 1940 there was concern from Lord Hankey that the Slovenes might be a potentially dangerous ally whose activities might incite Italy to enter the war.[28] Fourteen members of *Branizbor* were indeed arrested by the Yugoslavs for cross-border espionage into Italy. They had already supplied 12,000 carborundum blocks for railway sabotage to TIGR allies in Italy and some of their explosives, supplied by

Section D, were later used by the Italian resistance.[29] TIGR leader Albert Rejec recollected how he used to wait on a Belgrade street corner in the evening and meet Section D officer S.W. Bailey, who would bring a bag of explosives in his open-topped sports car. Rejec would then take the overnight train to Ljubljana, taking care to store the unwieldy bag on a luggage rack some distance from where he sat in order that he could deny ownership if necessary. TIGR would then smuggle the explosives into Italy.[30] But for the time being, the Slovenes were dissuaded from carrying out sabotage in Italy, in line with British hopes that Italy might stay out of the war.

British-born Italian Max Salvadori had opposed the Italian fascists from the outset and was first contacted by Claude Dansey of SIS in 1937, but was told at that time that the British were not prepared to promote anti-fascist propaganda. Times changed and in 1938 Salvadori worked with future Section D agent Jacob Altmaier and with Karl Spiecker in attempts to establish a 'Free German' pirate radio station, *Sender der Deutschen Freiheitspartei*, in the North Sea. The scheme collapsed in April and Salvadori went to the USA. He was urgently recalled by Dansey in August 1939 and invited to work with Section D. He was dismissive of any immediate prospect of an internal revolution as 'useless wishful thinking' and believed that a propaganda campaign was the best way forward but this was still rejected by the Foreign Office, nervous of any intervention in Italy.[31] Instead, he began to work briefly as a double agent with the Italian government, having convinced the Italian authorities that he was ready to put his country first, despite his previous opposition to the fascist regime. To this end, Section D funded a visit to Switzerland to meet an Italian emissary and he then made contact with the Italian ambassador in London. Salvadori deftly avoided any suggestion that he should inform on his friends in the Italian opposition but rather suggested that he could be a point of contact to discuss Italy's future relationship with Britain, all the while trying to gather intelligence for Section D. Nothing came of this scheme but meanwhile Section D was establishing an embryonic network in Italy itself, overseen by its French section.

Lieutenant Francis White first visited Rome in November 1939 to investigate the prospects of establishing an Italian section for the covert distribution of allied propaganda, as well as the insertion of black propaganda into Germany, aimed at disrupting good relations between the two countries. Bernard Wall was appointed as head agent in Rome, living in the Vatican City with a cover as correspondent for *The Tablet*. Wall was not optimistic of the chances of success and commented on his seven-month-long experience with Section D in Italy:

> I was to go to Rome and convert the Germans to peaceful and free ways of thinking by means of clandestine postal communications. The aim seemed desirable, though perhaps not realistic.[32]

Wall was assisted by John Verney, who worked for the British Council. Verney was, however, accused of being indiscreet and risked exposing the fact that another member of the British Council was an SIS agent. As late as mid-April 1940 the consensus of the Chiefs of Staff and Balkan ministers was that Mussolini's fascist Italy still might not enter the war on the Axis side.[33] Consequently, the Italian section worked at a minimalist level until May 1940 when it was given a short-lived permission to expand operations. Linguist Peter Hope, formerly involved in wireless broadcasting with Section VIII of SIS but transferred to the Section D propaganda section, then began to build up the Italian section while Salvadori was rushed to Paris to meet William Berington of the Paris office of Section D and make contact with exiled Italian opposition leaders. On 25 May they met leaders of *Giustizia e Liberta* to discuss their drafting and distributing of anti-German propaganda in Italy on behalf of Section D.[34] A week later *Giustizia e Liberta* was given a subsidy of £20,000 and Section D agreed to deliver 11,000 of the new leaflets to a contact in Turin. The negotiations were interrupted by the fall of Paris, but 2,000 leaflets and 35,000 stickers were sent to the Rome office. Plans were also afoot for delivering suitcases of explosives for storage in Florence. This was too little, too late. Bernard Wall reported that working in Italy was becoming increasingly difficult, it was hard to maintain communications with contacts outside Rome and virtually impossible to smuggle in propaganda from surrounding countries. As the situation rapidly deteriorated, two anxious Section D couriers found themselves stuck on a platform at Milan railway station on 30 May for a day with thirty-five cases of explosives and time fuses, waiting for a delayed train to Ljubljana in Yugoslavia.[35] Two opposition printing presses in Milan and Turin, funded by Section D, still managed to operate but the crew of the ship *Julius Caesar* were arrested for possession of leaflets 'likely to incite them to sabotage'. There was more success in the Mediterranean when Section D officer Horace Emery established a radio transmitter in Malta, which could broadcast into Italy. Ostensibly it was operated by the Free Italian movement, but it was funded by Section D, which also provided scripts. It proved so popular that a second transmitter was shipped from England.

In early June, even as Section D was making a final attempt to expand its Italian operation, the Foreign Office again banned further activity in that country for fear of providing a final excuse for a declaration of war.[36] But the speed of the German advance across the Low Countries and France convinced Mussolini to establish himself as an ally of Hitler before the war ended, allowing him to benefit from any peace settlement. Mussolini declared war on 10 June 1940. Rather naively, Grand claimed that the failure of Italian anti-aircraft (AA) guns to respond to air raids on Turin between 10 and 20 June was because the commanding officer of AA defences was a friend of one of the Section D agents.[37]

For TIGR members, the declaration of war seemed the ideal opportunity to strike and win their dreams of independence. On 20 June they approached Section D in Belgrade with an optimistic proposal for them to seize Trieste and hold it for up to five days as part of a wider allied offensive in Albania, and in return for a guarantee of Slovenian self-determination in Austria and Italy after the war. An outline of the plan was submitted to the Commander in Chief, Middle East in Cairo, but General Wavell was already greatly over-stretched and Italy would have to wait for liberation.

Spain

Spain had fought a bitter civil war from 1936 to 1939 which eventually gave victory to the rebel nationalist leader General Franco, supported by fellow fascist leaders of Germany and Italy. British intelligence played a discreet part in the outbreak of the Civil War, hoping to check the influence of anarchists and communists in the Spanish government. Franco was flown from the Canaries to Morocco by a former RAF officer, Cecil Bebb, accompanied by future Section D officer Hugh Pollard (*see* p. 47). Pollard joined Section D in January 1940 and became head of its small arms section in Caxton Street. Thanks to his contacts, Spain became an important source of unattributable weaponry for Section D. He was also involved in some of the political machinations with Spain, leading to a brief 'flirtation' in May with the idea of backing the monarchist opposition to Franco.

In February 1939 Britain and France had recognised the Franco regime in Spain and British foreign policy thereafter was a delicate balance of wooing Franco to ensure Spain's neutrality and encouraging internal opposition to hold him to that course. SIS quietly built up a substantial presence of over 150 agents across Spain. It also established secret wireless stations to monitor any movement of German troops on the French border. Initially, Section D was not expected to act beyond the covert encouragement of a united front opposition to Franco and the uncertainties of Spain's position meant that the staff of the Spanish section mainly operated at a distance from London.[38] Charles H. Phillips (aged 40) became head of Section D's Spanish section. He had been brought up in Mexico and educated in a German school, and from 1936 was managing partner of the wide-ranging merchant and insurance firm Watson Phillips & Co. Having returned to England to offer his services to the war effort, he joined Section D in July 1939 and was commissioned onto the General List in September. The sensitivity of his work may be judged by the fact that all details have been destroyed and that he was one of a small group of Section D officers recommended by Grand for a decoration at the end of the war. He was dismissed from SOE in December 1940 and it is presumed that he continued to work for SIS until June 1944, when he is recorded in the *London Gazette* as having ceased employment, granted the honorary rank of captain, and returned to Mexico.

The *Alianza Democrática Española* (ADE) was formed in December 1939 by moderate Republican exiles and was headed in London by Colonel Segismundo Casada, who had led the coup against the Negrin government in March 1939. The ADE included military officers as well as trade unionists from the UGT and

CNT but in reality, it 'was hardly anything but a cover for the activities of the British secret services'.[39] Consequently, the ADE manifesto focused on support for the Allies rather than criticism of Franco and many groups, including the nationalist Catalan and Basque organisations, refused to join. Section D was heavily involved in secretly supporting the ADE, particularly in supplying propaganda material. Grand wrote in July 1940 that 'We ... have obtained the support of many prominent Spaniards to the ADE in the belief that it is a purely Spanish movement originating in Spain.'[40] In June 1940 he ambitiously claimed that the ADE encompassed support from just right of the Communists to just left of the Monarchists.[41] In all, 350,000 copies of the ADE manifesto were smuggled into Spain by Section D from the south of France under the slogan 'Spain is for the Spaniards'.[42] The results were limited – but enough to upset the Falange. It became more difficult to distribute propaganda during the spring and in November 1940 Frank Nelson (Grand's replacement in SOE) admitted to Jebb that neither Section D nor SOE had distributed any propaganda in Spain after May.[43] This is not to say that activity had ceased. Despite the arrival of Sir Samuel Hoare as Minister in June 1940 (a person bitterly opposed to the activities of SIS and Section D in Spain), Section D began to edge towards a more forceful approach and the RAF requested Section D to organise the sabotage of German airplanes landing in Spain.[44] This plan was rejected but by the end of August 1940 Section D had shipped to Spain 219 time pencil fuses, 14 high explosive bombs (3lb), 8 magnets, 5 pressure percussion fuses, 30lb of camouflaged explosives, 150ft of safety fuse, 117 detonators, 100 cigarette-igniters, 566 medium incendiary bombs, 17 large incendiary bombs and 90 capsules for igniting petrol bombs.[45]

Contact was also made with Spanish republicans serving in the French Foreign Legion (part of a unit that had been sent by France to join the Norway campaign and had then been stranded in Britain). The aim was to train agents in the proposed school at Brickendonbury and send them to Morocco, Algiers, Tunis and unoccupied France in the hope of them being able to support a future rising in France (the Cardiff Plan). In July it was proposed to send two Spaniards to Lisbon in order to liaise with ADE in Spain. It was also decided to acquire a Spanish trawler, equip it with radio broadcasting equipment and broadcast a daily five-minute news bulletin from ADE into Spain. They were to convince Spaniards that Britain was still fighting on after the fall of France and to deter Franco from joining the Axis. It was also proposed to send an agent to South America to promote the existence of the ADE and to argue that Britain stood as the last bastion of democracy, with its survival necessary for the restoration of a democratic government in Spain. Sir Samuel Hoare eventually prevailed in his argument that British support for the ADE should be withdrawn rather than further antagonising Franco. It continued nonetheless but, after a wave of arrests across Spain, on 8 November 1941 thirty-two local organisers were tried in Valencia and ten were sentenced to death. Undeterred, their network in the

South of France became the famous 'Reseau Pat O'Leary', an escape network into Spain for many hundreds of allied soldiers and members of the Resistance through the Pyrenees. Mackenzie aptly described British policy in Spain as 'a humiliating policy, justified only by its success'.[46] In the end, recognising that Spain was exhausted by the Civil War, Franco did not follow Italy into the Axis, although fears remained that Germany might invade Spain and push through to seize Gibraltar and thereby control the Mediterranean.

Chapter 5

Western Europe: Allied and Neutral Countries

The history of secret warfare in Western Europe during the Second World War has been dominated by the story of SOE in France and the Netherlands, which has tended to focus on the heroism and tragedy of individual agents rather than strategic impact, and that narrative has found little place either for the preparatory work of Section D or for the wider intelligence operations of SIS.

France

Section D was in regular contact with French Intelligence from an early stage, but Grand believed that the French were sceptical of its work, preferring to put their faith in conventional forces. A meeting in July 1939 paved the way for a French section of Section D which was established in Paris just before the outbreak of war. It shared offices with the French equivalent, the 5ième Bureau, in its disguise as the 'Experimental Office of the Communication Staff of the Army' located in the Paris Military School. French cooperation was on the clear understanding that the British would not engage in espionage within France, only using its office as a base for operations in neighbouring countries and to liaise with the French themselves. On the day before the outbreak of war, Karl Groehl of LEX was arrested in Paris mainly, it seems, to teach the British a lesson about working with a German émigré organisation in Paris without advising the French security service. He was released at the end of the month. Section D was, therefore, unable to recruit its own French agents in anticipation of a German assault and became frustrated by the French government's unwillingness to plan in advance for a resistance. In April 1940 Grand wrote that any recruiting of agents would be 'an extremely dangerous proceeding, and one which we have not adopted hitherto nor dare adopt'.[1] The 5ième Bureau would, however, ensure that Section D agents could pass easily through France and shared knowledge on the development of sabotage devices. Foot summed up Section D's French operations in characteristically narrow terms and dismissive language:

> ineffective attempts to interfere with telephones in the Siegfried Line through a pair of crippled German refugees [Otten and Groehl], and in equally ineffective talks with Grand's opposite number, Brochu.[2]

In fact, the responsibilities of the French section extended across Europe, including insertion of propaganda and sabotage material directly into Germany and through Denmark, as well as an over-arching responsibility for Section D activities in Switzerland and Italy. In charge was the meticulous but introverted SIS officer Leslie Humphreys. On his large staff were William J.C. Berington (liaison with German and Italian anti-fascist groups in France), Frederick Elles (liaison officer to the 5ième Bureau and part-funded by them), R. Riley (Switzerland) and Francis White (Italy). In addition, George Courtauld was the French section representative at Section D HQ in London, later joined by a courier, the Honourable Anthony Samuel (son of Viscount Bearsted).[3] As early as November 1939 the Propaganda section under Douglas Saunders (D/Q) warned of the dangers of Germany trying to drive a psychological wedge between the French and British and the lack of effective British counter-measures. In January 1940 Grand and Elles (a linguist and former screenwriter), proposed to the War Office that a small dedicated Bureau was required to nullify German propaganda against the French and British and to try to subdue allied national prejudices. Nothing came of the proposal, possibly one example where a good idea suffered simply because it seemed to be part of Grand's empire-building.

It was important to ensure that the British and French sabotage plans against Germany and its interests in neutral countries did not conflict. To that end, exchange visits were organised between the senior staffs of 5ième Bureau and Section D, especially between the technical sections:

> Too much emphasis cannot be placed on the importance of the devices section in our liaison with the French. There is no doubt that the French were much impressed, both by what they saw during their visits to England and by what the devices section was able to show them during their visits to France. As a result of these visits the French tended to rely more and more on supplies from us for their own operations, while adapting our methods to their own manufacture.[4]

Section D and 5ième Bureau together acquired an armed merchantman, the *Rhin*, under the command of French intelligence but to be used jointly for sabotage in the Mediterranean. On 9 May 1940 it sabotaged the German ship *Corriente* at Las Palmas, using limpet mines supplied by Section D. After the fall of France, the *Rhin* took part in the defence of Gibraltar against Italian air attacks before sailing to Wales and being taken over by the British Admiralty as HMS *Fidelity*.

Germany invaded France on 10 May and the speed of its advance took all sides by surprise. By 25 May Section D was having to prepare for the fall of France. Grand wrote to Humphreys with suggestions for the creation of arms dumps and the organisation of stay-behind parties. He warned against the murder of German troops for fear that this would encourage undue retaliation, although he soon accepted the value of having a number of martyrs.[5] As the Dunkirk evacuation got under way, Humphreys produced a situation report: the 5ième Bureau had encountered problems in recruiting stay-behind parties and the speed of the German advance had overtaken their plans for demolition of transport links (Pl. 19).

Nonetheless, arms dumps had been established behind the current enemy lines in Belgium and in France at Chalon, Rheims, Epernay, Soissons, Compiegne, Montdidier, Beauvais, Gisors, Gournay, Rouen, Strasbourg and towards the Italian frontier. The agreed division of labour had been for the French to locate suitable sites for explosives dumps and to find and train the two 'guardians'. Section D then supplied the necessary explosives and devices and transported them to the dumps. This included 1,107lb of plastic explosives, 145lb of gelig-nite, 5,477 time pencils and 2,702 detonators.[6] Also included were translated copies of Section D's *Home Hints* and Gubbins' *Guerrilla Warfare* pamphlets. Leslie Wood was quickly sent from Aston House to work with 2ième and 5ième Bureaux in providing last-minute explosives training for saboteurs, with George Hill attempting to do the same in Belgium.[7] The saboteurs were instructed not to do anything for at least three weeks after the occupation of their village or town – a similar instruction to that given at the same time by SIS in England to the Section VII organisation and to the Home Defence Scheme (*see* Chapter 10).[8] In the final days of the battle for France, whilst simultaneously advising on the establishment of the Home Defence Scheme in Britain, George Hill was rushed to Paris and he and Humphreys proposed to 5ième Bureau that Section D should take responsibility for a sector behind Rouen, to organise the destruction of petrol dumps, bridges, etc., in the line of the enemy advance.[9] This was vetoed by the French on the grounds that it was the responsibility of the military authorities rather than either 5ième Bureau or Section D. The speed of the *blitzkrieg* negated much of the planning and the frustrated Section D office left Paris on 12 June to link up with the HQs of the 2ième and 5ième Bureaux. The Section D staff were eventually evacuated from the Gironde on 20 June. Before they left France, Humphreys and General Brochu (head of the 5ième Bureau) arranged wireless communication between SIS and elements of 5ième Bureau that would go to ground in France, which had immediate effects in the rescue of downed RAF crew who fell into 5ième Bureau hands, and Humphreys was later able to incor-porate some of the rudimentary stay-behind parties and communication lines into his successful SOE escape line.[10] The lessons of the frantic last-minute planning for French resistance were not lost on SIS planning for any invasion of Britain, and Grand mobilised the Home Defence Scheme so that a stay-behind organisation would be in place before any enemy invasion.

In July Grand submitted the 'Cardiff Plan' to SIS as a methodology to encour-age French opposition to Nazi occupation. It included the establishment on Free French territory of a 'Freedom' party of national unity which, with General de Gaulle, could establish a government not seen as acting under the influence of a foreign power. The German occupying forces were now to be provoked into undertaking retaliation in order 'to produce such German activity in occupied France as would tend to make Frenchmen realise that the enemy occupation was not as peaceful as it was made out to be', including 'the creation of a certain number of martyrs in France'. The French currency market would be manipulated to cause the depreciation of the French franc in the Vichy French empire, other than in those territories which remained on the side of the Allies. A news service would be provided for France by whatever means were possible (wireless, balloon, smuggled leaflets), including a freedom wireless station.[11] Still maintaining faith in the power of economic blockade and the fragility of the Nazi state, the ever-optimistic Grand believed that this ruthless approach would mean:

> If action on the above lines is taken it is probable that with the decrease in food stocks the French people will, by March 1941, be in a state of desperation and before that, by November/December may be prepared to receive supplies, such as explosives, rifles, etc., which will enable them to make an effective rising.[12]

The acceptance of the need for martyrs to maintain resistance was a natural development from the original Scheme D of March 1939 and was soon fulfilled.

> The first signs of sabotage were reported in the Sunday papers of 21 July, it is therefore possible that the creation of martyrs may be automatic. On the other hand it is considered that wherever possible we should stir up people, e.g. on the Breton coast, to take active measures against the Germans so that the latter will be forced to take retaliatory steps.[13]

In England, at the same time, Mike Calvert believed that the government was deliberately intending to use the Auxiliary Units to force retaliation by the Nazis.[14] It is therefore possible to see direct correlations between Section D policy in Europe and plans to meet any German invasion of Britain.

There was soon to be a return to France, albeit with tragic consequences. Major Norman Hope, head of the Belgian section, flew to France in a RAAF Walrus flying-boat to try to rescue Mme de Gaulle and her family at Carantec on 18 June 1940. Unfortunately, the plane was hit by enemy fire and crashed in a field near Ploudanie; all on board were killed. A second attempt was made the next day by fellow Section D officer Hendrik Van Riel, who sailed from Plymouth on 19 June on board MTB 29. They reached the entrance to Morlaix Bay and at dawn travelled up the channel to Carantec, where they landed at 6.00am, but Mme de Gaulle had already left and the village was occupied by the Germans. Van Riel next intended to find a French fishing boat and sail to Morlaix in the hope of finding information about the lost flying-boat, but the MTB was spotted by German aircraft and they had to return to Plymouth.[15] Despite the mission's failure, the conclusion was that the coast of France was still poorly patrolled and therefore it would be possible to land future agents.[16] Attempts were then made to re-establish communications with the French 'stay-behind' agents scattered across the country. An officer of the 2ième Bureau, Gilbert Turck, had reached England to become liaison officer between Section D and de Gaulle. He knew the location of all the Section D arms dumps in France and the whereabouts of those agents who had agreed to start operations after a few weeks of occupation, and now needed coordination. MTB 29 had been modified to better serve as a vessel to insert and recover agents and similar craft were being obtained. Fifteen French agents were recruited for Section D in the months immediately following the fall of France, although the process was complicated by the rivalries of French politics. Turck recruited several French agents from refugee camps and through the new Gaullist intelligence agency (the De Passy Bureau). In addition, Francis White made contact in London with an anti-Gaullist, Max Ridoux, who also recruited several agents. With tensions already surfacing between the exiles, an eventual distancing from the French seemed almost inevitable and 'D Section could visualise times when British military policy would be opposed to French political opinion'. The warning was repeated by the early SOE when Laurence Grand's successor, Frank Nelson, circulated a memo on 11 October 'which stated categorically that our co-operation with the French should, superficially, be complete, but that confidential matters should be kept from them in their entirety'.[17]

Efforts to re-establish operations in France (as elsewhere) were severely hampered by the lack of wireless communications. The potential was immediately evident when John Langley organised the rescue of three RAF pilots and a seaman in hiding on the Brittany coast, who had made wireless contact with Section VIII. But for the present, agents had to be landed 'blind'. Following other SIS missions to France, on 1 August came the first attempt by Section D to insert its own agents through the new Section D sea transport service under Gerard Holdsworth (which became the famous 'Helston Flotilla' of SOE). Three French agents were to be landed on the coast of Brittany near the Pointe de Primel on a three-week reconnaissance mission, but it was to prove a disappointment. The Belgian-built MTB 77 had been purchased by John Dolphin but it was to prove too slow and noisy for the work in hand. The agents V. Bernard, Marcel Clech and François Tilly were given rudimentary training at Aston House and sailed on 1 August from Penzance. Unfortunately, MTB 77 was spotted and attacked en route by a German coastal patrol, obliging it to return to Cornwall. After this failure, Marcel Clech (a former Breton taxi driver who had left his family to escape to England) made ten further attempts to land on the coast with Section D and SOE. He finally managed to land in France in April 1942 as a wireless operator but was captured in November 1943 and subsequently executed.[18] François Tilly was a merchant navy engineer who had been responsible for organising the rearguard at Le Havre, and then joined Section D. He served subsequently in the Free French Navy, the Air Force and the Marines, latterly commanding an armoured unit.

Belgium

SIS began to quietly re-establish its successful First World War intelligence networks in Belgium as soon as war was declared and they provided vital information throughout the conflict, although initially hampered by the poor early war wireless transmitters. Too late to be effective, Section D created its own Belgian sabotage section under former Shell executive Norman Hope. Explosives dumps were established at Ghent, Antwerp, Brussels and Liege, and rushed training was provided by George Hill. In May the Belgian banker Louis Franck, now a partner of the bullion trading bank of Samuel Montague and friend of fellow agent Lionel Montague, was recruited to Section D and immediately dispatched by destroyer as a special courier to the King of Belgium. He carried a special pass from the DMI to explain that Franck was travelling on behalf of the British government and should be allowed to pass freely 'without let or hindrance'.[19] On 17 May, as the Germans were entering the city, he managed to remove the remaining gold and silver reserves of the Brussel's National Bank. Having flown back to England with his cargo, he then returned to Belgium, being finally evacuated from Dunkirk on 29 May after passing through the German lines at Abbeville. He continued to work for the Belgian section until July, when he was attached to General Spears' Dakar Mission. Franck then saw distinguished service with SOE in the USA, West Africa and Italy.

Immediately following Belgium's occupation, Grand had to report that there was little information on the progress of a resistance due to the lack of an efficient wireless network.[20] Section D had at least one agent in place, Jan Bottema ('Brandy'), who operated for a period of five months from his home in Zourkamp where he was a master mariner and eel fisherman. His task was to collect shipping information but there having been no contact after the occupation, two SOE agents eventually had to be sent to re-establish contact.[21] In England Norman Hope and the newly arrived Hendrik Van Riel (formerly a Belgian army liaison officer) trawled camps of evacuated Belgian soldiers for fresh recruits to send back to Belgium, recruiting around half a dozen who continued to serve with SOE. SIS was desperate for any information on coastal defences and the conditions of German occupation. One agent was Maurice Simon (aged 37), the former sales manager for HMV gramophone records in Brussels. In August 1939 he had been recruited as an agent for Electra House; he also worked for the French 2ième Bureau, on 9 May passing them advance intelligence of the German invasion of Belgium. The information was, however, ignored. After escaping to England, he was passed on to Section D and on 16 June had the first of a series of rushed meetings with Norman Hope, Hendrik Van Riel and Louis Franck, before being sent back into Belgium at just 48 hours' notice. In a frantic time for the Belgian section, its attention was occupied by plans to rescue Mme de Gaulle and it knew that the French armistice was about to be concluded. Norman Hope was killed on 18 June during the failed rescue attempt of Mme de Gaulle, and Van Riel stayed in England just long enough to see Simon depart before he, in turn, headed for France for the second de Gaulle rescue mission. The original plans to land Simon on an isolated beach on the Biscay coast from a small boat had to be cancelled and instead he set sail on 18 June on the SS *Royal Scotsman*, heading for the Gironde to evacuate Polish troops. Carrying 40,000 Belgian francs and 5,000 French francs, his instructions were to contact Captain Marc

Fluhr of the 2ième Bureau, gather intelligence on the German occupation in Belgium and northern France and investigate the potential for an underground newspaper in Belgium. He was told 'we do not want heroes, but information'.[22] The intention was to collect him from the beach at Nieuport on the night of 17 August, or failing that on 17 September. He failed to make either rendezvous because suspicious French authorities had detained him on landing but he finally made contact with surviving agents of the 2ième Bureau. He was eventually able to establish a network in Brussels and send information into unoccupied France and thence to London. The arrival of a wireless set in Brussels in early 1941 eased the communications problem but Simon's story then becomes tangled. Following his arrest in July 1941, he was released on condition of working for the German Field Police. He became a double agent, travelling between Belgium and France, always giving those people he was ordered to arrest sufficient time to escape, and he was also involved in escape lines for allied airmen. The Germans became suspicious of his poor arrest record and Simon fled to Britain in August 1942. SIS and SOE were initially suspicious of his story, not least because of reports that his wife had become the mistress of his German controller. Eventually his remarkable story was believed, and he was recruited by the Political Warfare Executive.[23]

On 10 July an unsuccessful attempt was made to land another Belgian agent, Réné Burggraeve (aged 44), a former customs official, on the Belgian coast 5 miles north-east of Ostend. The purpose was again to gather intelligence on the coastal defences and transport restrictions, to collect samples of occupation paperwork and currency, and locate a house suitable for use as a future base of operations. As well as a signalling torch, he insisted on carrying a diminutive Belgian Bayard .25 calibre pistol with just five rounds of ammunition, although Section D would have preferred him to travel unarmed to reduce the risk of incriminating evidence. He crossed the Channel in a 70-ft MTB, accompanied by Van Riel. The motorboat anchored some 100 yards offshore and the men rowed ashore in a dinghy. They were either very unlucky or the Germans had already established regular guards along the coast, but they were immediately met with a Verey flare and returned to the motorboat. After a second flare, machine-gun fire then opened up from the dunes, followed by rounds from a light anti-tank gun. Van Riel reported that the boat was too noisy, too slow and was inadequately armed (with two AA machine guns and two Lewis guns).[24] In all, four attempts were made, unsuccessfully, to land Burggraeve along what had clearly become a heavily defended stretch of beach. It was not until July 1941 that SOE launched its first operation in Belgium, and it continued to test the coastal defences until the end of 1943 with equally little success.[25]

Holland

Little is known about Section D operations in Holland, which came, at least in part, under the orbit of Montagu Chidson's German section. Chidson had been a former SIS head of station in Holland. The kidnapping of two SIS officers

(Sigismund Best and Richard Stevens) at Venlo in November 1939, following earlier infiltration of SIS networks in Holland by German agents, had clearly placed SIS operations in the country at risk. It also caused the dismissal of the pro-allied head of Dutch military intelligence, Major General J. van Oorschot, leaving the government nervous of anything that might provoke Hitler to invade. Nonetheless, a small sub-section of Section D was established in January 1940. By March it was claiming to be smuggling, on a weekly basis, 3,000 stamped addressed letters for posting in Germany and 1,000 leaflets but only rudimentary provision had been made for a resistance organisation. It was initially agreed that Section D would organise the flooding of Schipol and Deekoy aerodromes, although this idea was subsequently dropped due to the huge number of civilian casualties that it would entail. Soon after the German occupation, Grand wrote:

> The Dutch are already, according to reports, beginning to revive and obstruction is beginning to grow. There is therefore a good possibility of creating a Freedom Party in this area. A nucleus organisation to this end was left behind together with a certain amount of material, but hitherto we have been unable to get into touch with it, a state of affairs which we hope will be corrected shortly.[26]

In August Section D agent Jan Van Driel was infiltrated by sea near Rozenburg (Zuid-Holland) to try to re-establish contact with the resistance.[27] Further details are unknown but Van Driel survived and later served with the OSS (American equivalent of SOE).

One of the most famous exploits of Section D was the rescue of industrial diamonds from Amsterdam, which earned Chidson a DSO. The official account of the mission is brief and most modern histories rely on the fictionalised version in former SIS agent David Walker's book *Adventure in Diamonds* (1955), later filmed as *Operation Amsterdam*. Chidson refused to co-operate with the book's author and it is now difficult to untangle fact from fiction. What is certain is that millions of pounds' worth of industrial diamonds were at risk of falling into enemy hands. Industrial diamonds are an essential element in precision engineering: shaping carborundum grinding wheels, making diamond wheels for grinding tungsten carbide, and in the manufacture of wire. The Germans began the invasion of Holland on 10 May and two diamond traders in England, Jan Smit and another (given the alias 'Walter Keyser' in Walker's book), offered to provide an introduction for Chidson to the diamond merchants in Amsterdam. They departed early on Sunday, 12 May in the destroyer HMS *Walpole* and steamed at full speed to Eimuiden, the nearest coastal port to Amsterdam. They landed at daybreak and made their way to Amsterdam by car. They then spent the day working with Smit's father Johan (who had refused to trade with Germany during the First World War) to convince traders to release the diamonds to Chidson when the Amsterdam Mart opened on Monday morning (the vault being protected by a time lock). Chidson spent the rest of the weekend instructing Dutch contacts in the use of explosives.[28] Supplies left for the proto-Dutch resistance included 129lb of plastic explosives, 13 magnetic mines and 145 time pencils.[29] On Monday morning they entered the vault and rescued the diamonds. The story of German paratroopers forcing their way into the building as Chidson left may be a romantic fiction and, although there was some fighting in the streets at the time, Chidson had been provided with a Dutch army escort. In 2010 journalist Paul Arnoldussen published an interview with one of the employees of J.K. Smit, which puts the episode in a more matter-of-fact context than the book or the film:

> I was picked up from my house address on that 13th of May 1940 and when I arrived at the office Mr Johan [Smit] sat behind his desk and said 'pack the diamonds'. Well, I started packing and sorting as well as listing all diamonds. But eventually that turned out too time-consuming. We then took a pillow-cover and tossed all the diamonds right in! 'Throw all diamonds in!' Mr Johan said with firm determination in his voice. Shortly after Jan, his son, came and took the whole lot with him. Outside was a Dutch soldier, with his rifle ready to shoot. And thus the largest stock of industrial diamonds on the continent was taken to London. I was there, I saw it happen.[30]

The party returned to Eimuiden, delayed by being briefly arrested as suspected fifth columnists, just in time to make the rendezvous with the destroyer. In all, up to £1,250,000 worth of industrial diamonds were rescued. It may be no coincidence that the 3 June 1940 issue of *Time* magazine contained an article reporting how Jan Smit had sent an urgent message to the J.K. Smit office in Manhattan asking how quickly they could obtain and ship 500 'diamond-cutting saws' to London. *Time* magazine assumed that this was to equip Dutch diamond-cutters who had escaped from Holland but in fact it was the diamonds themselves that had been rescued and the reference to 'diamond-cutting saws' was an element of misinformation.[31] In view of the cavalier use of *Adventure in Diamonds* as an historical source, it is worth including here the official citation for the award of Chidson's DSO, announced on 20 December 1940:

> On May 12 information reached us that an extremely important collection of industrial diamonds were located in Amsterdam. Despite the fact that this officer is on the German Black List, he insisted on going over himself. He proceeded to Amsterdam where he remained for some 24 hours, during which time there was considerable street fighting and Fifth Column activity in the town. He brought out the whole of the industrial diamonds stock and this prevented the Germans from obtaining an extremely important source of industrial activity. His action would by itself have won a recommendation to an award but considered in the light of the certainty of his fate if caught by the Gestapo, he displayed courage of a very high order.[32]

At first sight it seems reckless to send a senior Section D officer such as 47-year-old Chidson on such a mission. He had detailed knowledge of the D organisation and of its German operations, as well as having been heavily involved in the wider Jewish trade boycott campaign (*see below*). It may well have been the case that, after Venlo, there were few SIS officers left with an intimate knowledge of Holland and someone was required whom the merchants and Dutch intelligence knew personally and could trust.

Switzerland

Neutral Switzerland was bordered by Germany, Austria and Italy, and was a key centre of espionage throughout the war, with both SIS and German intelligence having a substantial presence. Switzerland's main trade partner was Germany and its large German-speaking population felt itself at serious risk. The government threatened that, if invaded, the Swiss Army would destroy the bridges and tunnels of the alpine railway system which carried materials between Germany and Italy, paralysing the connection for many years to come. As well as using Switzerland as a base from which to smuggle propaganda and explosives into Germany and Italy, Section D also focused its attention on the railways, planning to interfere with rolling stock so that it would break down within Axis territory and confuse the point of origin of the sabotage. Operations were directed by the French section but a clear sense of caution has left few details. Humphreys recruited Martin Bachtold-Acheson, a timber merchant who was at the centre of an existing anti-Nazi network in Switzerland, to build contacts for smuggling explosives into Germany for the LEX group and to develop propaganda contacts within Switzerland. The details are vague, largely because he continued to serve as an agent of SIS in Switzerland and mention of his work has been heavily redacted in the public record.

Austrian engineer and journalist Richard Strauss ('Mr Tench') was the principal Section D railway expert. He was based in Switzerland during 1939 as the foreign editor of *Modern Transport* magazine but returned to London in early 1940. His replacement was supposed to be 31-year-old Cuthbert Hamilton-Ellis, a pre-war journalist on *The Railway Gazette*, but his recruitment was plagued with problems. A railway writer and painter of Victorian and Edwardian steam engines, Hamilton-Ellis was finally recruited in March 1940, his post jointly funded by Section D and the French 5ième Bureau at a cost of £400 a year. However, the fact that he was given the code name 'Elmer T. Rudd', a play on the 1937 Warner Bros cartoon character Elmer J. Fudd, suggests that there may already have been doubts about his suitability for espionage work! When recruited, he was a private in the Royal West Kent Regiment but was on long-term sick leave. The approach was typically vague. After a 'nothing detrimental' security check by MI5 he received a short and bland letter inviting him for an interview in London from 'I.B. Wright'. The meeting was held at the offices of the Railway Research Service but he still had no idea who was recruiting him. Likewise, the members of the Medical Board who had to formally discharge him from the army were not aware of the circumstances and initially considered him to be a malingerer. After attending a short sabotage course, he was to go to Switzerland as a correspondent for *Modern Transport*. There were the inevitable delays that seemed to plague Section D, and the demobilisation process was not completed until 22 May. Then the Swiss refused a visa because they were suspicious of his new passport, which described him as a 'railway engineer' rather than a journalist. He was therefore only granted a visa for 10 days, leading Section D to warn him to be on good behaviour, to 'keep extremely clean' (i.e. not to engage in any espionage) and to try to make himself useful to the Swiss in order to be able to get a renewal. He was also to ensure that he left some unfinished business at the end of his visit, as an excuse to return.[33] He finally arrived on 8 June but could make only limited contacts within the Swiss railway industry, as befitted his journalist status. As cover, he wrote an article on 'Diesel-Electric Traction in Switzerland', published in *Motor Transport*. His instructions in case of Switzerland being invaded were to remain at his hotel until he received a message from 'Mr Longmore' but if the capital was in any danger then he was to go to the Legation or return independently to Paris.[34] However, during an invasion scare, the inexperienced Hamilton-Ellis panicked and went straight to the Military Attaché at the Legation, who, not being aware that he was anything more than a journalist, advised him to leave Switzerland as soon as possible. Lacking any contact with other elements of British intelligence in Switzerland, Hamilton-Ellis followed this advice, leaving Geneva on 17 July, and eventually arriving at Gibraltar via Marseilles. Although Richard Strauss still expressed faith in him and there was a suggestion of him being employed by the Balkans section, Hamilton-Ellis remained without a posting until September, when Humphreys, now head of SOE's French section, finally recommended his dismissal.

Jewish Boycott Committee in Europe

Writing during the 1948 Arab–Israeli war, details of Section D's work with Jewish groups was deleted from Mackenzie's account 'on grounds of national security'. Overall, he was dismissive, believing that any links had more to do with Jewish propaganda to emphasise their assistance to the British cause, and that Jewish opposition groups would have developed with or without the intervention of Section D.[35] This conclusion may have been influenced by the contemporary political situation, especially given that Section D had helped train the Haganah. Before the war Montagu Chidson had established contact with Dr Chaim Weizmann (Pl. 8), the Belarus-born, German-educated biochemist, who in the First World War had become Director of the Admiralty Laboratories and was now an adviser to the Ministry of Supply. He was also President of the World Zionist Organisation and would eventually become the first President of Israel. Weizmann had undertaken some unspecified minor missions on behalf of Section D during trips to Switzerland at the beginning of the war and then negotiated an arrangement for the joint working of the World Zionist Organisation and Jewish Agency in Palestine with Section D, opening up Jewish contacts across the USA, Europe and Palestine (*see below*, pp. 126–9).[36]

From this distinguished contact, Chidson recruited the services of Phineas Horowitz, a Russian-born but long-time British citizen, who had been one of the leaders of the original 1933–1934 anti-Nazi trade boycott designed essentially to blackmail Jewish firms into refusing to deal with Germany. In February 1940, through Frederick Matthias of the Ministry of Economic Warfare (MEW), Horowitz met Antwerp diamond trader Josef Hirschberg, who had similarly been involved in the 1933 Jewish boycott campaign, was on the Jewish Board of Deputies and also wished to work with Section D on both propaganda and sabotage. The plan was to revive the boycott under a new Central Boycott Committee to be established in London. Chidson wrote on 1 April 1940 that Horowitz was also willing to travel abroad on behalf of Section D, travelling under cover of his position as editor of *British Fur Trade*. On 11 April a planning meeting between Chidson, Matthias, Horowitz and Hirschberg agreed the division of responsibility for the boycott campaign. Chidson would get the formal agreement of the British government for the policy of distributing blacklists of firms to boycott and Section D would be responsible for the distribution of leaflets published by the Central Boycott Committee. Financial responsibility for the campaign would lie with MEW but Horowitz generously volunteered to accept responsibility for any legal damages arising from slander or libel.[37]

Horowitz believed that the Central Boycott Committee could consist simply of himself, an assistant and a secretary, run from his existing offices. The initial cost would be just £200, with a subsequent outlay of from £70 to £100 a month for the central office and £50 to £70 a month for each European country organisation. The office would undertake to prepare propaganda material suitable for each country, but Section D would then arrange its distribution. By 19 April the first draft manifesto had been produced, directed at the diamond trade in Antwerp. It named Jewish firms in Belgium which were continuing to supply industrial diamonds to Germany and called on all Jews to regard them as traitors. The intention was that this manifesto could serve as a template for other countries and other trades. On 24 April 1940 MEW agreed to supply Chidson with lists of all known Jewish firms trading with the enemy, to pass to the Central Boycott Committee for action. Grand gave his approval to the scheme on 28 April and secured the official blessing of the War Cabinet. The plan now was for Horowitz to join Hirschberg in Belgium and to visit Holland, while another agent, Blumenthal, would visit Switzerland and the Balkan countries. The initial results seemed promising and some of the results of the original manifesto were reported in the Hebrew paper *Our Community* in Brussels on 3 May 1940. Under the heading 'Diamond Merchants Beaten up', it records: 'The second days of Passover were marked by fine weather and the blows administered in numbers of Antwerp synagogues to those diamond merchants who send their stones to be cut in Germany.' The article also gave details of the lists of errant Jewish firms as supplied by the Central Boycott Committee. Chidson was pleased with this rapid reaction and from feedback received from London-based diamond merchants but the Nazi invasion of the Low Countries interrupted further plans. The Central Boycott Committee then switched its attention to the USA (*see* Chapter 10, pp. 200–1).

Chapter 6

The Balkans

[T]here is stuff in the British archives that would make your hair stand on
end ...

(Julian Amery, former Section D and SOE agent in the Balkans)[1]

British diplomatic strategy for the Balkans until the German invasion of 1941 was
to try to preserve a benevolent neutrality even though its economic or political
leverage was increasingly weak and the Balkan countries were heavily reliant
upon trade with Germany. Above all, it was fearful of any action that might
precipitate a German or Italian invasion. The focus was the River Danube, used
to transport oil from the Romanian oilfields and from Russia into Germany. The
Danube runs 2,860km (1,780 miles) from Germany to the Black Sea and passed
through what were at the time six countries, managed by the International
Danube Commission and Romania. British interest in stopping German trade on
the Danube was no secret but, characteristically, the Foreign Office could not
agree a consistent policy for Section D, 'alternatively encouraging and hindering
our efforts'.[2] Indeed, the whole British policy towards the Balkans was confused.
By contrast, Section D argued an aggressive, if simplistic, approach, to demonstrate that the Germans were vulnerable and to encourage a spirit of resistance.
Australian George Taylor, a former Shell executive, had been recruited in July
1939 to head Section D/H, covering the Balkans, Eastern Europe and the Middle
East. Sweet-Escott described him as being 'brilliant but ruthless' with a mind of
'limpid clarity' but impatient, while to Dalton he was 'belligerent, persistent and
ingenious'.[3] He played a major role in the development of Section D and later
SOE. In November 1939 Taylor concluded that the best option was to take the
offensive, believing that any German reprisals against Section D sabotage were
a way of demonstrating that neutrality was not a sustainable option.[4] It would
therefore do whatever possible to hinder the transport of supplies for the German
war effort, including blocking the Danube, destroying rail communications, oil
and grain stores, and attacking Russian shipping bringing oil into Romania and
Bulgaria. For Taylor, any delay increased the risk of local hostility and made success less likely. The British government dithered – ironically blaming Section D
in July 1940 for not acting soon enough. The later assessment by SOE of the
Foreign Office in the region was scathing:

> Fear of provoking German reactions had prevented the implementation of
> D's plans at a time when they might have been carried out, while once it was

realised that the Balkans were lost anyhow, the local position had deteriorated to such a degree that action was largely impossible.[5]

Practical results were limited but provided a test-bed for wider irregular operations in the Second World War and many officers of Section D/H later played
leading roles in SOE. The irony was that one of the most successful partisan
operations of the Second World War, under the communist Tito, played no part
in the pre-1941 operations.

Across the region, Section D created a loose alliance of disparate political
groups, intellectuals, journalists and trade unionists who criss-crossed the borders
within the Balkans into Germany, Austria and Italy. Its activities ranged from
defamation of individual Germans and organisation of anti-German demonstrations and propaganda to physical sabotage, primarily directed against industrial
targets. It forged alliances with opposition groups who did not necessarily agree
with other aspects of British foreign policy, including the Zionist Haganah, and
there was ministerial apoplexy when legation buildings were used to store explosives. Section D was, nonetheless, encouraged until the summer of 1940 by tacit
approval from some quarters within the Balkan governments and intelligence
services. To impose some sort of order in a crowded intelligence landscape,
an inter-departmental committee was established in January 1940 under Rear
Admiral Bellairs to advise on plans to disrupt the oil supplies from Romania or
Russia to the enemy, especially sabotage on the Danube. There were also high-
level diplomatic conferences to review British policy and activity in the Balkans,
to which Laurence Grand was called to explain and defend the work of Section D
to a hostile audience. The SOE history of Section D concluded:

> It was the obsession of the Foreign Office that no results could be obtained
> other than by regular and above board methods at a time when our political
> and military position was in reality so weak as to render any direct pressure
> an impossibility. When irregular action became imperative owing to the
> obviousness of British weakness, it was too late.[6]

The scale of sabotage in the Balkans and neighbouring Austria has been under-
valued as it relied on a drip feed of small-scale, undramatic operations. There was
undoubtedly a degree of exaggeration, not least because partners wished to attract
increased subsidies, and in one case a German double agent claimed entirely fictitious sabotage operations to preserve his cover. Nonetheless, in a time of general
allied failure, these were the most successful resistance operations to be undertaken in 1939–1940. They offered a small measure of encouragement to local
activists that German ascendancy was not necessarily automatic or inevitable. For
Austrian historian Peter Pirker: 'Although the D Section's development of a transnational resistance network between 1938 and 1940 was characterised by many
teething problems, this is where the foundation for future cooperation between
resistance movements, exile organisations, and allied intelligence agencies was

laid.'[7] He also acknowledged that most of the operations within the German Reich in this period were performed on the initiative of Section D.[8]

Section D/H covered Turkey, Hungary, Romania, Bulgaria, Yugoslavia, Albania, Greece and the Middle East. This was a sprawling region and difficult to manage. Until early June, Taylor controlled the region from London, assisted first by Leslie Sheridan then, from January 1940, by Arthur Goodwill. Horace Emery was supply officer but was almost exclusively concerned with operations on the Danube. Communications across this vast region depended upon couriers who travelled thousands of miles carrying diplomatic bags containing secret correspondence or explosives. Some, like Anthony Samuel, managed this with quiet discretion but the ambitions of another, Andrew Duncan, were to have dire consequences. The budget for the region's operations was equally complicated. The first suggestion for a finance officer was Leslie D'Oyly Harmar, to be based part-time in Budapest (Fig. 4) for Binder, Hamlyn & Co. as an excuse for establishing an office there, but he became entangled in the Schultz fleet scheme and his fellow chartered accountant in Belgrade, William Morgan, was recruited on a part-time basis in November 1939, originally intended to be head agent in Hungary although there was no other mention of him acting as such. He became a full-time finance officer for the Balkans in April 1940.[9] Binder, Hamlyn & Co. proved very accommodating and part-funded the salaries of Harmar and Morgan. Morgan's letter of appointment to Section D ostensibly came from the company, offering him a post in Budapest:

> For the duration of the war, you would be working only part time for Binder, Hamlyn & Co, as they have agreed to give first call on the services of their men in Belgrade and Budapest to an important Government organisation connected with the Ministry of Economic Warfare. ... The work is extremely interesting and of the greatest national importance. The connection with the M.E.W. is quite unofficial, so please do not mention it to anyone ... On the face of it, we are simply Chartered Accountants doing nothing but our professional work.[10]

In late May, in anticipation of a declaration of war by Italy, it was decided to move the Balkans section HQ to Middle East Command in Cairo (*see below*, Chapter 7). Taylor and Goodwill flew to Cairo on 29 May with most of the D/H headquarters staff, leaving Bickham Sweet-Escott and Hilton Nixon in London as liaison officer and supply officer respectively. However, in the following month Taylor had to return to London to become deputy to Grand, leaving Arthur Goodwill in overall charge (with specific responsibilities for Greece and the Middle East). Further changes came in early August when, following a wave of agent expulsions from Yugoslavia, a sub-HQ for the Balkans was established at Istanbul under S.W. 'Bill' Bailey. By now, Taylor thought future work would move away from the Balkans and be more focused on the military requirements of Middle East Command, 'in which we are simply the servants of C in C and in fact the civil half of MIR'.[11]

Figure 4. Map of the Balkans. (*Malcolm Atkin*)

In all, the Balkans section had a staff of well over sixty officers and agents. Only in Yugoslavia did Section D establish a designated head agent, the experienced SIS officer Julius Hanau. He became a high-profile target for German intelligence and there were only half-hearted attempts to create similar posts in the more hostile Romania and Hungary, where Section D relied instead on semi-independent networks which would avoid the 'domino effect' of penetration.

Yugoslavia

In 1939 the kingdom of Yugoslavia (modern-day Bosnia and Herzegovina, Croatia, Kosovo, Macedonia, Montenegro, Serbia and Slovenia) was a new country riddled by ethnic divisions and ruled by the Regent, Prince Paul, on behalf of his 16-year-old cousin Prince Peter. The government was unpopular but there was no strong pro-allied alternative and any action that destabilised the government risked precipitating a German invasion. The British Minister in Belgrade, Sir Ronald Campbell, desperate to preserve the status quo, was accused of appearing 'more interested in making sure that nothing is done to injure Yugoslav interests rather than seeing what they can do to aid British interest'.[12] For his part, Campbell regarded Section D as 'bomb-happy parvenus'.[13]

Julius Hanau ('Caesar') was born into a South African Jewish family but had converted to Christianity (Pl. 3). Now aged 54, he had been in business in Belgrade since 1920 and had lived there permanently since 1930. He was also an SIS agent with well connected friends in the Yugoslav army and government, including Major Ante Anić in the Yugoslav counter-intelligence service. Hanau had first met Grand in London during July 1938 and was formally recruited to Section D in March 1939, becoming head agent for Yugoslavia. In contrast to Sweden and Switzerland, some government officials were prepared to give tacit support to Section D's activities in Yugoslavia, which allowed a more intensive programme of operations than elsewhere. Hanau led the Yugoslav section until July 1940, by which time he was well known to the enemy and required body-guards. Until September 1939 he operated as a 'lone wolf', organising his own private war with German agents in Yugoslavia. The details have not survived but it was clearly bitter. As early as May 1939 Grand had authorised Hanau to use deadly force, 'and that for every casualty on our side, British or Serb, one Nazi should disappear. ... This put an end to violence within two months and from May 1939 to July 1940 we had no casualties in Yugoslavia.'[14]

Hanau was the most experienced and successful field agent of Section D – flamboyant, adventurous and fearless. To Alexander Glen, the joint Department of Naval Intelligence/Section D agent in Belgrade, he was 'professional, highly disciplined with no illusions'.[15] He was unable to resist any opportunity, however small, to needle the Germans, although this irritated the Foreign Office as much as the Nazis. His plans to organise a demonstration at the Germany–Yugoslav football match on 15 October 1939 in Belgrade forced a last-minute change of venue. In November he organised a demonstration outside the German Legation in support of Czech University students. In May 1940 the Berlin Philharmonic Orchestra was forced to cancel a concert in Belgrade for fear of his anti-Nazi demonstration and threatened stink-bomb attack. More significantly, in late August 1939 Hanau intercepted correspondence between the German Embassy and a German armaments firm, confirming they were about to ship a train-load of weapons across Yugoslavia to Bulgaria. The train line was sabotaged and five wagons were derailed. Once war was formally declared, he began to work in earnest with an ever-expanding team.

Hanau's headquarters were in Belgrade, covering the Danube and able to monitor Romania and Albania. To the north, semi-autonomous networks in Slovenia and Croatia, centred on Ljubljana and Zagreb, bounded Italy, Austria and Hungary (Fig. 4). A core of British officers worked with a wide range of Yugo-slav political groups, businessmen, intellectuals and journalists, together with Austrian, German, Czech and Polish refugees. Until January 1940 the priorities were propaganda and subversion. Anti-Nazi slogans were chalked on walls and 'whispering campaigns' against the Germans were encouraged. Having learned that the Germans intended to pay for a large shipment of food with a consign-ment of aspirin, Hanau flooded the Belgrade market by importing bulk aspirin from Britain. The price dropped and the Yugoslav government demanded pay-ment by other means, less convenient to the Germans. It was an irritant more than anything else but this was one inspiration for the new United Kingdom Commercial Corporation, of which Section D financier Chester Beatty became a director. In October 1939, having already been implicated in the expulsion of the Nazi propaganda chief in Yugoslavia (Dr Avender), Hanau persuaded the Yugoslav censor to ban the publication of the Nazi Party propaganda public-ation *Volkstum im Sudosten*. Hanau then discovered that Franz Neuhausen, the German Consul-General in Belgrade and chief Gestapo agent, had a criminal conviction for swindling and had served a four-year prison sentence. Hanau circulated 4,000 leaflets quoting the Bulgarian court proceedings and Neuhausen was recalled to Berlin.

Hanau built up a series of networks focused on Serbian, Slovenian and Croatian opposition groups and Czech émigrés. There was a strong nationalist movement in Slovenia which maintained cross-border links with ethnic Slovenian districts in Austria and Italy. The Revolutionary Organisation of the Julian March – Trieste, Istria, Gorizia and Rijeka (TIGR) had been formed in 1927 to achieve the annexation of Istria, the Slovenian Littoral and Rijeka to the Slovenian province in Yugoslavia. After the *Anschluss* in 1938, TIGR expanded its sabotage operations to attacks in neighbouring Nazi Germany. Despite this long heritage of subversion, Pirker has maintained that Slovenian participation in the anti-Nazi struggle in 1939–1941 can only be understood against the background of British organisation and instigation.[16] The overall contribution of TIGR to the anti-Nazi struggle was only properly acknowledged from the 1990s, having been previously suppressed by the post-war communist government.

In September 1939 Alex Lawrenson, a British Council-funded lecturer at Ljubljana University, began to build up a network of dissident groups in Slovenia and Croatia, targeting both conservative Catholics and Socialists. Not impressed by this exploitation of the British Council, the consul at Zagreb refused to pass on mail sent from Hanau to Lawrenson until ordered by the Foreign Office not to interfere. In December, having introduced Lawrenson to the leader of TIGR, Albert Rejec (a man who had taken part in the street-fighting against Mussolini's 'March on Rome' in 1922), Hanau sent Alfred Becker, a German émigré agri-cultural scientist and life-long member of the SDP, to work as Lawrenson's assis-tant and to act as a middle-man with the Slovenian groups operating in Austria and Italy and then based in Ljubljana. Becker had fled Germany in 1934, living in

Yugoslavia since 1936 as an experimental scientist with the Yugoslav Ministry of Agriculture. He became a member of Section D in the autumn of 1939, with a salary of 3,500 dinars per month plus expenses. Lawrenson's work soon became well known in Ljubljana and he became a full-time officer of Section D under the cover as vice-consul, which both provided a degree of diplomatic protection and allowed explosives to be delivered to him in diplomatic bags. His work was based around two Slovenian organisations – a Catholic grouping under Dr Julli Fellaher, which focused on intelligence-gathering, and *Branizbor* under Professor Ivan Rudolf of the Slovene Democratic Party. Rudolf became a key partner in Section D sabotage. In the 'Ostmark', TIGR also cooperated to expand Section D's range of contacts on both sides of the Yugoslavian–Italian border and into Austria.[17] As well as undertaking sabotage, TIGR provided valuable intelligence, including details of the torpedo works in Rijeka, the submarine works near Montfalcone and the Italian defences around Tobruk. They did, however, reject the propaganda leaflets produced by Section D as being too crude.[18] Lawrenson also contacted an organisation of exiled Czechs which liaised with Dr Milko Brezigar (editor of the Slovenian liberal newspaper *Jutro*). They worked closely with *Branizbor* and were equally ready to organise sabotage. The initial task of these groups was to smuggle propaganda into Austria. Apart from the value to morale of fly-posting material on walls and bridges, this was also designed to test the network before it began to undertake sabotage operations.

In Zagreb, Trevor Glanville, a chartered accountant for Price Waterhouse & Co., was also given diplomatic cover as vice-consul in early 1940 and built up a successful propaganda network with Alfred Becker and fellow SDP member Jacob Altmaier, the renowned journalist. At the time Becker and Altmaier were amongst the few German exiles of the SDP who would associate themselves with sabotage organised by Britain against their homeland. Altmaier had been an activist in the SDP since 1918 and fled Germany in 1933. He had first worked for SIS in 1938 on a German Freedom radio station in the North Sea. After moving to Yugoslavia, he established close contacts with the Serbian Peasant Party (SPP) and its leader, Milan Gavrilovitch. The SPP wanted to establish a South Slav federation of Serbs, Croats, Slovenes and Bulgarians, and opposed the Yugoslavian dependence on Germany, favouring instead an alliance with Britain and the Soviet Union. Altmaier was later described as 'unworldly' and, since he was reluctant to accept money from a foreign power, Section D had great difficulty in persuading him to accept a salary of £50 per month.[19] Becker and Altmaier would become key middlemen between Section D and the local opposition organisations. Together, they organised the publication of the Croatian nationalist anti-Nazi paper *Alarm*, which continued until May 1940. Glanville was then warned by the police that they could no longer turn a blind eye to its production. Up until this point sympathetic police officers, when ordered to confiscate copies of the newspaper, merely asked for 2,000 copies as a token gesture – and then assisted with the distribution of the rest. Becker and Altmaier also produced the nationalist Serbian *Srpski informacije* and from June 1940, to provide political balance, also produced *Novi Balkan*, a newspaper that took a pan-Yugoslavian stance. German-language Social Democratic and Catholic propaganda included the newspaper *Deutsche Mitteilungen*, which was smuggled into Austria and Germany through Slovenia and Hungary. After pressure from the local Gestapo, Becker was briefly arrested in Belgrade in January 1940 for distributing illegal propaganda but Hanau, describing him as 'indispensable', quickly secured his release.[20]

There was widespread concern that the Ministry of Information was ineffective during the first months of the war, leading the Balkan countries to doubt that the Allies could win. To improve the situation, the *Britanova* news agency, under the partnership of Section D officers S.A. Courtauld and Douglas Saunders (then head of the Section D press propaganda section, D/Q, and formerly of the J. Walter Thompson advertising agency) with Edward Hulton (owner of *Picture Post*), was registered in London as a front for distributing Section D and Electra House material. *Britanova* continued to operate worldwide until 1965. The first branch was opened in Belgrade in December 1939 under Gradimir Kozomarić, a former editor of *Vreme*; he later died in a Nazi concentration camp. Its success was immediate. Between 18 December and 15 January 295 articles were placed in local newspapers, rising to 548 over the next month, with success relying on cultivating a sympathetic journalist in every newspaper office who would push for the inclusion of *Britanova* material. Other branches were then opened across the Balkans and the Middle East. In May 1940 *Britanova* provided an interview with Arthur Greenwood on 'Britain's War Aims', which Sir Neville Henderson of the Ministry of Information declared to be the finest piece of propaganda that the Ministry had yet seen. The Ministry of Information then asked the Treasury to pay Section D £500 to translate the interview into Serbian and distribute 10,000 copies of 'Hitler Speaks'. By September *Britanova* was distributing over 68,000 words and 447 pictures per month.[21]

With propaganda work ongoing, from late 1939 the focus of operations began to switch to sabotage, assisted by the fact that, as far as possible, the Yugoslav authorities turned a blind eye at this stage. Little was ruled out in this partnership of idealistic British officers and their hard-bitten allies, although the focus was on economic targets:

> Poisoning water supplies, spreading bacteria and similar sabotage is ruled out, but introduction of foot and mouth disease, potato pests, etc., are encouraged and naturally any attacks on communications, power stations or centres of production of important manufacturers.[22]

In December five railway trucks, each carrying a Messerschmitt fighter bound for Bulgaria, went missing on the Yugoslav railway. Only one was ever found – 'lost' on an isolated railway siding. Slovenian allies also began sabotaging railway wagons heading into Germany, claiming that an average of 20–30 wagons on three trains per day were 'hot-boxed'. Section D's ally, Dr Brezigar, had devised a means of seizing wheel bearings by slipping 'carborundum blocks' (steel filings set in a small ball of pitch) into the axle boxes. Several formal protests about Hanau's activities were lodged by the German Legation to the Yugoslav government and he was publicly denounced as a British agent in the 17 December issue of *Volkische Beobachter* – but Hanau's contacts managed to get all copies confiscated in Yugoslavia. On Christmas Day Hanau wrote to Grand warning that the situation was 'a bit tricky' and the Germans were trying to have him expelled for espionage. Hanau feigned an aggrieved tone with the Yugoslav authorities, claiming that no effort was being made to restrict the activities of German intelligence.[23] To make his point, he sent copies of documents proving that the Germans had been behind recent supposedly communist agitation to the Yugoslav government. He also provided proof that a German firm had tried to bribe border guards to ease the passage of goods across the border.[24] Hanau was put under government surveillance but the Yugoslav intelligence service politely informed him of the fact and gave him advice on the best precautions to take.

To reduce tension, Hanau temporarily left the country but returned in February, relieved to find a more sympathetic attitude in the Yugoslav government to his activities, although by now it was the British minister demanding his removal. *Branizbor* agents now began working with Section D officer S.W. Bailey, a mining engineer at the Trepča mine complex in Mitrovica, Kosovo (Fig. 4), to drain ore concentrates from railway wagons leaving the mine. Bailey arranged for wagons to go for repair, during which time agents bored holes in the bottom of the wagons so that the material would slowly drain out en route to Germany. Unfortunately, the weather conditions meant that the concentrates froze in the wagons and therefore did not easily drain through the holes. Evidently the method eventually did bring some minor success as a Hamburg consignee complained to the Trepča mine of short weight on a shipment. Bailey (who to Julian Amery looked like Al Capone) served as Hanau's deputy, based part of the time in Istanbul. He too soon became a marked man with the Gestapo, eventually being obliged to sleep each night in a different hotel or apartment.[25]

The Trepča mine was a key source of iron ore concentrates and very profitable but it had become an embarrassment to American owner Chester Beatty, a major financier of Section D. The Yugoslav government had appropriated 70 per cent of the mine's output for supply to Germany in return for armaments. The rest of the production went for smelting in Europe and this too fell under increasing risk of being appropriated by the Germans. Beatty was therefore in the unenviable position of being obliged to support the German war effort or having his mine confiscated by the Yugoslav government. Beatty's response was to provide considerable private funding to Section D and to allow his organisation to be used as cover for the recruitment of its agents, including his metallurgist S.W. Bailey and engineer 'Bill' Hudson – who both oversaw the extraction of the ore and then organised its sabotage en route to Germany. Both men became a key part of later SOE operations in the Balkans. The naive Section D courier Andrew Duncan described Hudson in May 1940 as being very keen and 'already starting to make contacts'. Hudson, 'a man of serenity and strength', had evidently shared the reluctance of other agents in disclosing information to the infuriating Duncan (*see below*, p. 106) and, not appreciating his experience, Duncan suggested that Hudson be sent a copy of *Home Hints* on how to organise sabotage.[26]

This was a drip feed of minor sabotage which could at most slow down the German industrial effort but it came at a time when Britain was desperate for any disruption to the Nazi war machine. As a focus of opposition, it was something the Nazis could not ignore and in February 1940 the SS intelligence agency, the *Sicherheitsdienst* (SD), reported:

> Since the annexation of Austria to the Reich ... we have observed lively activity from the English in Yugoslavia, especially Slovenia and Croatia ... In making use of all anti-German circles, the English intelligence agency has found excellent means for facilitating its work in Yugoslavia. It avails itself of the numerous Jews, particularly in Zagreb, the Slovenian jingoists and the Czech, Polish and Russian emigres.[27]

Encouraged by the results, in late March Taylor proposed a more aggressive policy for Section D's Slovene, Czech and Austrian partners, focusing on communications, especially the proven 'hot-boxing' of railway wagons, along with attacks on Danube barges and tugs (Pl. 22), while arguments over plans for larger-scale sabotage to block the Danube continued. The Slovene organisations would work directly with Section D; the Czech groups would act independently, but supplied by Section D. In May *Branizbor* put in an optimistic request for supplies including 2,500kg of high explosives and 1,600 sub-machine guns.[28] The fact that British intelligence was building up stocks of explosives in the country was no secret. Alexander Glen, joint DNI/Section D officer at the Belgrade Legation, remembered that the early morning arrival of the diplomatic bags from London, brought by couriers Gerald Glover and Anthony Samuel, received a cheerful response from the Belgrade railway porters who were tossing them onto piles: 'Never mind the big ones,' they advised, 'it's the small ones that have the detonators, the ones you have to watch for.'[29] In February 1940 Hanau had been sent two diplomatic bags containing explosives. The courier was determined to fulfil his strict instructions to deliver the two suitcases to Hanau in person and without delay. Unfortunately Hanau happened to be in a meeting of the Franco-Serb Bank (used as a cover for administering Section D funding). The eager courier burst into the room, tripped and sent the contents of the suitcases flying across the floor. Hanau later related the incident to Glen:

> Within minutes his Serb colleagues were on the floor, opening the suitcases and examining and identifying the contents, enjoying themselves hugely as

one seized this and another that, exclaiming at the time: 'No, not that way, detonators go here,' and 'That's wrong, come on, let me do it.' Serbs love bangs![30]

By April 1940 there were explosives dumps at Marsbor, Ljubljana, Zagreb, Apatin, Novi Sad, Sombor, Sempa and Belgrade.[31]

Hanau did not only have to fight the Germans. In February 1940 the British Minister in Belgrade, having discovered that Section D was storing explosives in the cellar of the Legation, sought Hanau's removal as a destabilising influence but was overruled by the Foreign Secretary. 'Such a decision can only be regarded as a defeat for the Establishment', commented a delighted Grand.[32] The Balkan ministers maintained the pressure, however, and three months later the Foreign Office complained that the operations of Section D were confusing the policy of the official diplomatic missions and causing mischief. They again called for Hanau to be removed and for Section D operations to be suspended. The Cabinet appointed Lord Chatfield (Lord Privy Seal) and Lord Hankey (now Chancellor of the Duchy of Lancaster and Churchill's intelligence adviser) to investigate. The Foreign Office case was presented by Sir Orme Sargent and by Gladwyn Jebb (ironically, the future CEO of SOE). Sargent launched a bitter attack, demanding that the Foreign Office should have the ultimate veto over any activities of Section D. They were outflanked by Menzies and Grand, who manoeuvred Sargent into seeming to claim that the Foreign Office had the power to overrule the Cabinet in its instructions to Section D.[33] Grand provided a catalogue of the activities for which Hanau had been responsible and pointed out that 'although he could understand how embarrassing it was for the Ambassador, the very fact that the Germans were complaining only meant that the action being taken was effective'.[34] The Foreign Office was again overruled; encouraged by this, Hanau stepped up operations.

In Croatia, Trevor Glanville dropped most other Section D duties to work with the Czech émigrés, including placing incendiaries in German-bound trains, and also collaborating with staff of the Yugoslav army to prepare sabotage in the event of German invasion, as well as the denunciation of pro-German Francovci agents to the Yugoslav police.[35] In June he also organised the subsidy of the Czech newspaper *Pravica*, which the Germans made determined efforts to shut down. To compensate for the loss of Glanville for other work, in late July Lawrenson was given an assistant, G.S. Frodsham, Director of Studies from the British Council School in Zagreb. Frodsham was to become the first British Section D fatality in the Balkans.

Meanwhile, from April, the Slovenian TIGR and Austrian Social Democrat groups began an intensive railway sabotage campaign in southern Austria. The Germans suppressed any publicity about it and imposed severe penalties on any railwayman found guilty of assisting sabotage. Austrian locomotive drivers were moved to other parts of the country and were replaced by more reliable Germans, but it was still considered too risky for German locomotives to remain overnight in Yugoslav round-houses. The railway line between Vienna and Italy was a prime target, with several attacks at Judenburg. German Police records confirm attacks on goods trains on 14/15 April and, although TIGR exaggerated its successes, a report by SIS in May confirmed that the level of damaged bearings caused by 'hotboxing' on German trains meant that repairs were running at 350 per cent above normal. Further confirmation came from the German Legation, which lodged a formal protest with the Yugoslav government against the high level of 'hot-boxes' in railway wagons coming from Yugoslavia.[36] As sabotage continued, on 13/14 June the Slovenes blew up a large petrol depot on the railway line at Malburghette. There was a cost to this work. Several Slovenes had been arrested in Austria during April and May: five were later executed, including the father of one of the railway saboteurs, Alojz Knez, a deserter from the German army. Alojz escaped from Yugoslavia during the 1941 invasion and in 1943 parachuted into Slovenia on an SIS mission to the communist partisans. He was then arrested as a British spy but escaped and continued to fight with another band of partisans until the end of the war.[37] Away from the railways, 1,000 tons of hemp, purchased by Germany and worth £100 per ton, were destroyed in an arson attack on a warehouse at Sombor on 25 April. Another 2,500 tons of hemp were destroyed at Vojvina. On 17 May 500 tons of hemp were destroyed at Novi Vrbas by Dr Brezigar's Czech group.[38] A few days later they fire-bombed a German-owned textile factory at Stair Becjej. In Austria, on 26 May there was a raid on a munitions factory at Bruck an der Mur: two trucks loaded with munitions and a filling shed were blown up.

As operations developed, a triumvirate of Lawrenson, Glanville and A.H. Rogers (formerly of Shell Oil) organised work in Slovenia and Croatia as a semi-independent section, subject to Hanau only for major policy and finance. An additional agent, Stephen Clissold, another British Council-funded lecturer at Zagreb University, was appointed to develop propaganda work. He had established strong links with the student community at Zagreb and his contacts there would help distribute the new *Novi Balkan*. This all left Hanau free to focus on the Danube and broader political management. To protect the rapidly expanding work, Hanau succeeded in having Lazich, the pro-Nazi head of the Belgrade police, removed and replaced with someone more sympathetic. What was politely called a 'subsidy' of 100,000 dinars per month was paid to the new police chief for the official purpose of taking on extra police to intensify anti-Nazi activity.[39] The bribery worked. In May two Czech agents were arrested on a train near Zidanimost, Slovenia, carrying two suitcases of high explosives. They admitted that they had received these cases from Robert Head (an engineer recruited as a Section D agent in December 1939 from the Trepča mine and now Bailey's assistant). The police warned Hanau that they were about to arrest Head and he duly escaped to Romania. Soon afterwards the two Czechs were released (together with their explosives) and Head was able to return to Belgrade. Hanau triumphantly reported back to London:

> Immediately after the arrest of the two Czechs and the issue of the warrant against D/H19 [Head], I made it known to HARRY [Belgrade Police Chief] that, unless the whole affair was hushed up and the warrant against D/H19 cancelled, it would be difficult for us to go on with our work here ... I told him that the Huns were continuously doing all kinds of outrageous things, and that very rarely drastic steps were taken against them. In no measured language did I let him know that for the 100,000 Dinars a month we were paying him to support his activities, we did at least expect support by the authorities for our work, if nothing more.[40]

Robert Head was described as 'responsible for much of the less pleasant liaison work, which involved him in considerable risk'. He was finally arrested and expelled in July 1940, but continued to work for Section D as an administrative officer in Cairo and served with SOE for the rest of the war.

Yugoslavia was the base for many of Section D's plans to interrupt German trade on the River Danube. Before the declaration of war, even the nervous Minister in Belgrade, Ronald Campbell, wanted to know what arrangements were being made for blocking oil transport on the Danube.[41] This positive attitude soon dissipated. Upstream of the Iron Gates is the Kasan Pass, where the River Danube flows through a narrow gorge, one side being in Romania and the other in Yugoslavia (Pl. 21). The river narrows to 150m and reaches a depth of up to 53m. One of Section D's most daring plans, first proposed by Horace Emery in mid-July 1939, was to blow up a rock overhang on the Yugoslav side of the gorge with 120 tons of explosives, causing it to slide into the Danube and block the river to traffic. Even if the passage was not completely blocked, any rockfall was thought likely to increase the current and so make navigation difficult. Section D agent Kim Philby, for one, was not impressed by the plan. He noted: 'I had seen the Iron Gates and was duly impressed by the nerve of colleagues who spoke of "blowing them up", as if it were a question of destroying the pintle of a lockgate in the Regent's Canal.'[42] The First Lord of the Admiralty, Winston Churchill, was briefed on the plan and was typically enthusiastic, but agreed that it would be inadvisable to consult the Foreign Office at this early stage. Its reaction, in a time of peace, would be apoplectic! At the end of September Grand felt able to consult more widely. A meeting was held between the Foreign Office, including the Minister to Yugoslavia (Sir Ronald Campbell), the head of the Danube Mission (Douglas Keane), Sir Orme Sargent and Gladwyn Jebb (Foreign Office) and CSS (Admiral Sinclair). Despite the anticipated objections, Grand told the CSS that preparations should continue until the Foreign Office was ready to give final approval.[43] George Taylor urged that if the plan were to proceed, it should be done quickly – ideally in December. His prophetic concern was that the Germans would soon be placing increasing pressure on neutral governments to increase security on the Danube and any chance of sabotage on the river might then be lost.

Sinclair approved Grand's strategy and Hanau's agent, Mate Bruslja, secured a contract to mine stone from the mountain for local building work, using this as a cover to begin digging the tunnels in which to set the explosives. German agents were already looking for any sign of suspicious activity on the Danube and spotted a delivery of explosives being landed from the tug *Britannia*. The Yugoslav authorities were obliged to launch an inquiry but, in typical fashion, Hanau bribed them to conclude that the mining could not possibly be intended to sabotage the river. The frustrated Germans sent an agent from Berlin to try to murder Bruslja in a knife attack, but he successfully fought off his assailant, who was last seen being helped by two colleagues onto a train back to Berlin for hospital treatment. The SOE History wryly commented:

> Bruslja was able to disarm his opponent although in doing so he received a deep wound in the palm of his hand. However, having achieved this, he knocked the German down and trampled on him for several minutes. Bruslja weighed fifteen stone![44]

The plan was turned over to the Yugoslav General Staff, who incorporated it into their defence plans but no attempt was made to implement the scheme during the German invasion.

Upstream of the Kasan Pass at the Greben Narrows, the flow of water through a navigable channel was maintained by a retaining wall. The plan here was to blow up the wall and make deep water navigation impossible. In early November several boxes of high explosive were sunk along the wall. Although the instructions were not to detonate the charges until orders were received, later that month two Serbian assistants of Bruslja who were keeping a watch on the site panicked when they spotted a convoy of four German barges passing through the Narrows and blew a 60ft breach in the wall. Two barges were sunk and temporary inconvenience was caused to river traffic. The inevitable inquiry was in the charge of a friend of Bruslja who helpfully concluded that the breach had been an accident. Bruslja was then given the contract to repair the wall and he bricked up a new supply of explosives at its base. Unfortunately, by the time of the German invasion (fifteen months later), the long immersion had caused the firing circuit to deteriorate and the charges could not be exploded.

A second attempt to block the Danube at the Greben Narrows was based on the scuttling of the tug fleet owned by Djordje Schultz. In October 1939 Grand attempted to purchase (at a cost of £160,000) the fleet of six tugs and twenty-six barges based at Belgrade, a move which would both prevent the fleet being sold to the Germans and allow it to be later used for blocking the Danube. The deal was agreed in December 1939 and although, due to Yugoslav financial restriction, legal ownership remained an issue, the fleet was now effectively under British control and thus had some minor effect in inconveniencing German traffic. The project stalled to allow the DNI Goeland fleet scheme to proceed in Romania (*see below*, pp. 109–12). After the latter's failure, a meeting on 15 May of Cabinet members Neville Chamberlain (now Lord President of the Council) and Lord Halifax (Foreign Secretary) with Lord Hankey (Churchill's security adviser) and civil servant Sir Alexander Cadogan (Permanent Under-Secretary for Foreign Affairs) decided that 'No action must be taken which was likely to precipitate the armed occupation of the river or an early invasion of the Balkan States by Germany': action on the Danube was to be limited to impressing the need for destruction of the river passage on the Romanian and Yugoslav governments, should any German invasion occur. The barge fleet still had to be managed, with day-to-day responsibility placed in the hands of Captain Harris-Burland for the MEW and Captain Despard of DNI, with Leslie Harmar of Section D in Belgrade being responsible for the accounts. The Chiefs of Staff Committee, unimpressed by such complacency, argued that the scuttling of the fleet should be prepared immediately and in June 1940 the Cabinet finally agreed that urgent action was required. Full control of the fleet was therefore returned to Section D.

The plan was to sink twenty of the fleet's barges in the Greben Narrows as an 'accident' with the hope of blocking the channel for six to eight weeks. Grand was not optimistic and estimated the chances of success of this scheme as only 25 per cent as the barges would be empty and travelling downstream, and therefore difficult to sink with any precision.[45] With the utmost irony, on 24 July Campbell, regretting the earlier delays in carrying out the sabotage of the Danube, now demanded immediate action.[46] By then, Hanau had been finally expelled from Yugoslavia, and responsibility for carrying out the plan fell to Alexander Glen. As was typical, Campbell reversed his opinion a week later and demanded that all work on the Danube should cease. As the argument passed to and fro within the Foreign Office, on 17 August Campbell asked whether more importance should be attached to the view of the official diplomatic mission in Yugoslavia or to the work of the D organisation. Philip Broad of the Foreign Office pointed out that as the Danube scheme had been approved by the War Cabinet, 'no comments on the part of Mr Campbell could be treated as of any importance'. Late in the day, the Foreign Office recognised the desperation of the situation and on 21 August instructed Campbell that the activities of Section D (now part of SOE) would continue and that he must placate the Yugoslav government as best he could.[47]

By now it was too late. Glen had concluded that the degree of Yugoslav surveillance made the scheme impracticable, the only feasible option being to pass on the plan to Yugoslav intelligence, who agreed to scuttle the fleet if the country was invaded. The later conclusion of SOE was that the loss of Hanau was critical, 'since a man of [Hanau's] determination might have achieved in action what was impossible by negotiation'.[48] In other words, he would have taken the gamble to scuttle the fleet. The scheme was completed with limited success in 1941 by Yugoslav intelligence working with former Section D stalwart, Mate Bruslja.

A total of eight barges were successfully sunk in position with a further four destroyed by the Germans before they could reach position. The work held up German transport for six weeks.[49]

With no success in progressing major schemes to block the Danube, Section D occupied itself with minor sabotage schemes on the river. Gubbins and Emery argued over the value of such work:

> I said to Emery that there did not appear to be much point in minor sabotage on the Danube if he and the French, between them, propose to block the whole river in the near future, but he did not agree, as destruction of barges, and more particularly tugs, would always hamper the Germans in one way and another.[50]

Individual barges were successfully mined by Section D's client Czech and Slovenian groups and there was a more ambitious scheme at the end of the winter of 1939/1940 to set long-time-delay mines on tugs and barges whilst they were trapped by winter ice in one of the Danube winter harbours. Bailey and Head planned to use a Czech cell to cross the river at Belgrade to the harbour at Pancevo. The charges were planned to explode when the vessels were in Hungary, confusing the point of origin and hopefully interfering with the channel, while the use of the Czechs would provide a 'plausible deniability' for the Foreign Office. Mate Bruslja liaised with the Czech agents, providing a boat to ferry them across the river. Unfortunately, the Czechs were delayed at the rendezvous, and Bruslja panicked and left before the agents had arrived. The Czechs returned to Belgrade and before a new rendezvous could be arranged, the ice thawed and the barges were moved.

If the plans to physically block the Danube failed, more success was found in removing the human element of river traffic. The barge fleets relied on skilled pilots to guide the tugs along the difficult channels. They were employed by the International Danube Commission and could not easily be replaced. The plan to bribe the Danube pilots to refuse to work for the Germans was originally that of Lieutenant Mason of Naval Intelligence.[51] The scheme was taken forward in March by Captain Max Despard for DNI, Horace Emery and Charles Blackley for Section D, and William Harris-Burland for MEW, working with two Czech pilots, Ralph Navratil and Jaroslav Vrana. Together, they secured the agreement of fifty-four Danube pilots, whilst the French agreed to take on responsibility for a further twenty. Britain and France would double the salary of the pilots for the duration of the war on condition that they did not work for the Germans; to avoid any reprisals, their wives and families would be resettled in British Mediterranean territories.[52] Not surprisingly, news of the scheme leaked out. Some pilots were reported to have been waving bank-notes at those who still worked for a living![53] In mid-March the Treasury provided Grand with £50,000 to extend the scheme to bribe the Iron Gates pilots in Romania *en masse* 'totally to eliminate German traffic'. The scheme exceeded expectations and in April Despard wrote that matters had got somewhat out of hand, with German pilots now wishing to join.[54]

In December 1939 Hanau branched out into political subversion. The groups with which Section D worked in Yugoslavia clearly had their own political agenda but many of the British officers had been resident in Yugoslavia for several years and had personal links with local politicians and business leaders; some had Yugoslav families. The Foreign Office feared they had 'gone native' rather than being focused upon narrow British interests. The ultimate impact of this political work is difficult to judge. Many of the contact groups were small and had only limited influence. At best, their work delayed the inevitability of the German invasion but the subsequent dominance of Tito's communist partisans made much of this work ultimately irrelevant. It would, however, provide a precedent for future clandestine political operations to engineer regime change. Stephen Lawford Childs, the press attaché, had become concerned over the rising communist influence in Belgrade University. In response, Hanau organised pro-allied canvassers for the student elections, which raised alarm bells within both the Foreign Office and SIS, where Section V (counter-espionage) queried the authority of Section D to interfere in the domestic affairs of neutral countries. But Hanau became more ambitious. In the scheduled national elections, he estimated that there were 180 constituencies which were undecided between pro-allied and pro-German candidates. He thought that these seats could be bought for about £500 each, the money funnelled through sympathetic Serbian groups to conceal its British origin. Although the elections were cancelled, Grand maintained that the Foreign Office had unofficially indicated its approval, spurring Hanau onwards. In March 1940 Childs and Jacob Altmaier introduced Hanau to Milan Gavrilovitch, the leader of the opposition Serbian Peasant Party (SPP), which was already organising minor sabotage against the Nazis. The SPP was small but very active, seeking a federation of the South Slav Serbs, Croats, Slovenes and Bulgars based on peasant cooperatives. It had a seat in the Yugoslav Cabinet and Gavrilovitch was later sent as Yugoslavia's first ambassador to the Soviet Union. Section D began to provide financial assistance to its propaganda school, with the aim of encouraging a greater pro-allied content and persuading the SPP to work with Section D in expanding its sabotage operations, which included a foray into biological warfare. Together, the SPP and agricultural scientist Alfred Becker plotted to infect Yugoslav livestock bound for Germany with foot and mouth disease. Some cattle also became infected on the Yugoslav side of the border and the Yugoslav police halted the scheme. Similarly, using Section D funds, Brezigar's Czech group tried to infect cattle bound for Germany with anthrax. When he discovered this, Lawrenson was not 'at any very great pains to discourage Brezigar's activities – more especially as to do so would have certainly taken the edge off his keenness in other respects'.[55]

The links to the SPP became ever closer and its illegal printing press was shared with Section D and French intelligence. By mid-May, however, the

Foreign Office was describing the links to SPP as 'fatuous and dangerous'. On 27 May Hanau proposed a massive subsidy of £5,000 per month to the SPP, one of whose members was Minister of Agriculture and could provide high-level support and intelligence to the Allies. Grand firmly maintained that the subsidy was not to encourage an armed coup against Prince Paul but simply to support anti-Nazi operations, although suspicion remained of a wider political agenda. One officer of SIS commented that whoever was responsible 'must be quite irresponsible or have had very limited experience of Balkan political parties and affairs'. The core of Section D officers in the Balkans had lived and worked in the region for many years and it might be argued that they had a wider range of political and social contacts than the Foreign Office and the local Minister, who relied on the narrow circle of the small governing elite. More prosaically, a member of SIS Section VI (Industrial) added 'If we are considering paying £5,000 a month for buying the Peasant Party why not spend it to buy the Government instead.'[56] CSS and the Foreign Office finally approved the scheme in July, up to £3,000 per month, although Campbell continued to block the payment. Glen repeatedly had to stress that the funding was urgently needed to allow the SPP to establish a shadow organisation to Section D, in the eventuality that Germany invaded and British officers were obliged to withdraw.[57] It was not until 30 August that Campbell finally submitted and even then the first instalment was not actually paid until October, when the new SOE began supplying the SPP with weapons dumps.[58] The SPP did eventually mount a *coup d'état* against the Yugoslav government in March 1941 – a final, desperate attempt to pre-empt Yugoslavia joining the Axis powers.[59] SOE had encouraged the coup and regarded it as final vindication for the efforts of Section D, saying that the latter 'might claim to be its initiators'.[60] The coup overthrew the Regency but could not delay the German invasion. Grand drew comfort from the belief that if the Foreign Office had curtailed the activities of Section D in 1940, as it so clearly desired, then the collapse of Yugoslavia would have come much sooner.[61] By the same token, would an earlier coup to install a pro-allied government have given more time to build up allied strength in Yugoslavia?

In early June, spurred by the latest wave of attacks on railways and arson attacks on factories, SS General Reinhard Heydrich established a special commission of the Reich Main Security Office (RSHA) to investigate increasing levels of sabotage in Romania, Yugoslavia and the 'Ostmark' of Austria, and the rising anti-Nazi sentiment in Yugoslavia. It was clear that the resistance was being organised on a cross-border basis by local opposition groups allied with Section D and with the connivance of some Yugoslav officials in government and the intelligence service. The Germans had even identified the detonators supplied to Slovenian groups as being the same type as used in the Section D Norwegian expedition.[62] In April 1940 German military intelligence, the *Abwehr*, had managed to infiltrate the *Branizbor* organisation through a double agent, Alexander Herbst, in Klagenfurt. Herbst, a long-established police informer, had contacted a Yugoslav consular official who put him in contact with the Slovenian resistance and gave him the name of the president of *Branizbor*, Ivan Rudolf. Herbst was then able to falsify reports of sabotage and became the recipient of much of the demolition material destined for sabotage in the Salzburg region. Rudolf and other *Branizbor* leaders were obliged to flee from Ljubljana to Belgrade, where they lived in hiding until the German invasion.[63] It was rumoured that Heydrich then sent three Gestapo agents to Belgrade to assassinate Hanau and a bomb attempt was also made on the life of Bailey. Taylor was sufficiently worried about the security situation that he ordered Hanau and Bailey to avoid ever being in Yugoslavia at the same time (Bailey by now was regularly visiting Greece and Turkey).[64]

Hanau's role was 'blown' across the Balkans and his expulsion on 4 July was inevitable, although it was debatable whether a bullet from the Gestapo or a memo from the Foreign Office would seal his fate. Hanau himself, exhausted, acknowledged that his position had become untenable and was hampering future cooperation with the Minister, Campbell. He handed over to his assistant S.W. Bailey and then shuttled between London and Istanbul, retaining an oversight on Yugoslav affairs. Hanau continued his career with distinction in SOE until his death in Cairo in 1943. He was to perform one final service to British interests in Yugoslavia, *in absentia*. It was feared that Cvetkovik's government was about to be replaced by the Germanophile Stojadinovik but in a masterstroke Cvetkovik published a pamphlet claiming that Stojadinovik was actually an enemy of both Yugoslav and German interests, accusing him of being secretly a tool of international Jewry, Freemasonry and British intelligence. To give credence to this unlikely charge, a photograph (taken two years previously) was included of Stojadinovik with Hanau, now denounced publicly as a British spy.

The fall of France in June was a massive shock to Yugoslav confidence in the Allies; under pressure from increasing RSHA activity in the country, the government was now less prepared to turn a blind eye to British espionage. The Section D organisation began to disintegrate after the expulsion of Hanau. Bailey and Head were expelled on 8 July, and Alfred Becker was advised to leave before he could be deported to Germany. He fled to Istanbul on a false Dutch passport and continued to advise Section D on propaganda. Although still reporting to Bailey, now ensconced in Istanbul, responsibility for Section D in Belgrade was passed to the assistant naval attaché, Alexander Glen, assisted by Julian Amery (assistant press attaché) and John Bennett, a Section D officer working under cover as a consular clerk in the Legation. These all had diplomatic status and protection. Bennett, a former barrister with Yugoslav business interests, had joined Section D in January 1940 and was described as a 'loveable lumbering buccaneer' by Glen.[65] Glen officially worked for the Directorate of Naval Intelligence but in May 1940 it had been agreed that he should also act for Section D.[66] Working from Zagreb, Hudson continued to have success in organising attacks on the bauxite ships in the Adriatic, assisted by the Bishop of Jenbenik who commanded 'a good gang of toughs'.[67] As with Hanau and Bailey, Hudson was by now well known to the Nazis and pro-German Croats made an attempt to assassinate him by planting a bomb in his office.[68] German intelligence eventually found their mark on 8 September when G.S. Frodsham, Lawrenson's new assistant, was found dead in his Ljubljana flat, apparently from gas poisoning. The Germans had become aware of his work and his ground-floor flat (where he slept with open windows) proved to be an irresistible target for German assassins. Both the Section D and other SIS officers in Zagreb believed that a German agent had broken in, smothered Frodsham and then turned on the gas to make it appear to be suicide. Fortunately, the Yugoslav police did not find, or chose to overlook, the stock of 'explosive coal' that was hidden in the room.[69] The British Council, unaware of Frodsham's second profession as secret agent, sadly noted in correspondence that there was 'a tendency to believe that he worked excessively and lived none too well'.[70]

It was clearly becoming increasingly difficult for British agents to operate in Yugoslavia. On 15 August Campbell reported to the Foreign Office with some relief that Yugoslav connivance in the activities of Section D was now over.[71] Four Czech agents were arrested in Belgrade; in contrast to previous incidents, they were immediately handed over to the Germans for extradition. The atmosphere in Belgrade was likened to that of a 'bear garden', although Lawrenson, Glanville and A.H. Rogers were still managing to operate as a semi-independent triumvirate in Slovenia and Croatia. An authoritative leader was required to equal the sorely missed Hanau.[72] The first choice, Leslie D'Oyly Harmar, the chartered accountant who had worked part-time for Section D in Yugoslavia since September 1939, was rejected by the Minister. By then, the Germans were already highly suspicious of Harmar's role, although reassured of his innocence by the Yugoslav police.[73] He finally left Yugoslavia in November. As the situation worsened, Bailey established a shadow organisation of the partner Czech, Slovene and Serb groups in Yugoslavia, funded by Section D at £4,000 per month, and ready to carry on its work after the British had left.[74] Relief only came in December 1940 when T.S. Masterson was finally sent as the new SOE head agent, carrying on the work of Section D and still working under Bailey in Istanbul.

The Yugoslav army resisted the German invasion of April 1941 for just six weeks. Glen and Amery had met General Mikhailovich in August 1940 to discuss his plans for mounting guerrilla war if Yugoslavia was overrun and, with the help of Mate Bruslja, the army carried out some of the sabotage on the Danube planned by Section D.[75] Taylor, no doubt thinking back to the long history of cancelled pre-invasion sabotage plans, produced a pessimistic assessment in a debriefing following the invasion. He believed that 70 per cent of the rushed schemes for guerrilla warfare undertaken during the actual German invasion of Yugoslavia had proved ineffective due to the speed of the German advance and the inability of lightly armed guerrilla troops to counter the enemy's mechanised force.[76]

The German invasion of Russia on 22 June 1941 radically affected the pattern of the war. European communist parties felt able to enter the fray and the

Yugoslav partisans under Tito achieved dominance over Mikhailovich at the cost of a brutal civil war. The Democratic Federation of Yugoslavia was proclaimed in 1943 and much of the political manoeuvring of the early years of the war now seemed irrelevant. The crucial contribution of the Slovenian and Czech groups to mounting a resistance to the Nazis across the Balkans and into Austria, in partnership with Section D, was systematically suppressed by the post-war communist regimes in the region and was only hesitantly acknowledged in Austria, still torn by conflict over its loyalties during the war. Pirker maintains 'in as much as they are known, most activities within the German Reich were exclusively activities performed on the D Section's initiative' and were 'inspiring examples for the European countries threatened by German expansion'.[77] To men like Glen and Amery, a golden opportunity to decisively shape the direction of events had been missed in the summer of 1940 and the western Allies increasingly became bystanders in unfolding events.[78]

Romania

By 1939 Romania had become heavily dependent on trade with Germany and fears of Russian expansion appeared to make Germany the most effective protector of its independence. Britain and France remained desperate to keep the oilfields (which had strong allied commercial interests) out of German hands and in April 1939 they offered an unrealistic guarantee of Romania's freedom from German aggression. Although he had already acknowledged the inevitability of a German alliance, King Carol tried to avoid being dragged into war and in September 1939 he declared Romania's neutrality, threatening to destroy the oilfields if invaded. The Romanian government also played the role of innocent victim, using the threat of allied sabotage to deter German aggression. Precedent was on its side as British and French sabotage had put the oilfields out of action for five months during 1916. Finally joining the Axis in November 1940, the Antonescu regime went on to field the third largest Axis army and was a major supplier of its oil.

The original allied hope was a sabotage plan agreed between the Romanian General Staff and MI(R) in August 1939, in return for a bond of $60 million from the British and French governments as compensation. A team of Royal Engineers would be sent from Egypt with cover for their movement through Turkey being undertaken, in part, by Section D. They were to be supported by additional personnel infiltrated into the oilfield as 'trainees' of the Shell associate company, *Astra Romana*. The Germans learned of the plan through sympathisers in the Romanian government and used it as an excuse to interfere in Romanian security arrangements. In September 1939 Admiral Canaris, head of the *Abwehr*, met with the head of the Romanian secret service and German agents were then given free entry into Romania. In October an agreement was concluded with the Romanian secret service to protect supply routes to Germany, and in the following month the Germans provided muscle to the agreement by deploying a battalion of the

Brandenburg special forces regiment to a camp near the Iron Gates. In addition, 250 troops, thinly disguised as members of 'sports groups', were posted to the Bulgarian port of Ruse, opposite the Romanian oil terminal at Giurgiu (Fig. 4). Detachments of the Brandenburg regiment patrolled the Danube under cover as 'tourists'. They were not only to prevent allied sabotage but also to be prepared to implement their own demolition plans if the Allies landed on the Black Sea coast. A joint German–Romanian security unit was then established at Ploesti in January 1940 (Fig. 4).[79] In late June 1940 MI(R) launched a last-ditch attempt to revive its plan, this time without the knowledge of the Romanian authorities. 'Trainee oil engineers' were smuggled into the oilfields to try, with the help of sympathetic staff of the *Astra Romana* oil company, to cap the well heads with concrete and steel. The *Abwehr* easily spotted the 'oil technicians' as being army officers in plain clothes, spending extravagantly in Bucharest (Fig. 4). Romanian police raided the final planning meeting and conveniently discovered damning evidence of British explosives on the oilfield – actually hidden there by *Abwehr* agents. On 6 July 1940 the MI(R) agents were expelled from the country. The Section D organisation was left largely intact in this disaster but the *de facto* head agent W.R. Young, together with Charles Blackley, were named in documents relating to the plan (discovered by the Germans in France) – both were expelled.

Unlike MI(R), the brief of Section D was to act without reference to the Romanian authorities. Its targets were not only the transport of Romanian oil to Germany, but also Russian sea traffic carrying supplies for Germany. This meant that it worked closely with the Directorate of Naval Intelligence (DNI). Its supply lines also provided, on behalf of MI(R), a system for smuggling arms from Romania into Poland. To lessen the risks of penetration, several semi-independent networks were established, centred around the Ploesti oilfields and refinery which lay 20 miles north of Bucharest (Fig. 4 and Pl. 20). A formal head agent was not appointed until July (Gardyne de Chastelain), although there were previous half-hearted gestures towards this and W.R. Young seems to have had an informal overarching role. Oil engineer Young was recruited in September 1939. His chief collaborator was Gogu Constantinescu, an engineer at the Orion Refinery in Ploesti and friend of the politician Dr Iuliu Maniu (leader of the National Peasant Party and future leader of the Romanian resistance). Constantinescu in turn recruited several Romanian workers at the refinery. Their names were never revealed to the rest of Section D, although they might be what Section D officer Frederick Wedlake later sniffily recorded as 'crooks, down and outs, and people of doubtful character'.[80] Young also recruited Charles Blackley, a former seaman and now an engineer on the oilfields. Described as 'irrepressible' and an 'active, tough type', he carried out minor sabotage on the Danube and adjacent railways for both Section D and DNI under his cover as 'Inspector General' of the Goeland Transport Company.[81]

The initial priority was to develop anti-German propaganda. In September 1939 Leslie Humphreys of the French section and Douglas Saunders of the propaganda section discussed the possibility of using Hratchia Paniguian, a leader of the Armenian community in Romania, who was then working for the J. Walter Thompson advertising agency in Paris. Contacts within the Romanian royal family wanted him to go to Romania to produce propaganda on behalf of King Carol but Humphreys asked Paniguian in October whether he would also assist in producing anti-Nazi propaganda. Working from the Bucharest office of J. Walter Thompson, he was to use his government contacts to help get propaganda into Germany, whilst also circulating pro-Romanian propaganda amongst the German minority in Transylvania. For an initial stay of two months he would be paid a salary of £100 plus expenses. Paniguian left for Romania in November with the unimaginative code name of 'Peter Pan'. His cover was so good that Donald Hall of the MOI met Paniguian in Bucharest but did not realise that he was secretly working for Section D, and pressed for his employment by the MOI.[82] Paniguian returned to London in early February and, on the basis of his report, Grand launched a bitter attack on the efforts of the Ministry of Information in Romania to justify an expansion of Section D's role:

> ... when grave strategic necessities arise, as in the case of Rumania [*sic*], we were faced either with the certainty that nothing would be done in time or the possibility of ourselves filling the gap until such time as the Ministry of Information became effective.[83]

Section D set up a dedicated propaganda section in Romania under Gardyne de Chastelain, who had lived and worked in the oil industry in Romania since 1927 and was sales manager for the Phoenix Oil & Transport Company. Paniguian soon returned to act as his adviser, assisted by Ion Popovic ('Procopius'), who was de Chastelain's assistant in Phoenix and the Section D contact with the Polish intelligence service. They had an immediate impact and between 9 February and 9 March 1940 claimed to have increased the number of pro-allied articles and news bulletins in Romanian newspapers by 80 per cent. Grand was typically inventive, proposing the creation of a film unit and a 'showboat' travelling up and down the River Danube offering allied propaganda newsreels, although this was rejected as being too expensive.[84] From July de Chastelain, now officially head agent in Romania, worked with Maniu's National Peasant Party to secretly produce anti-German propaganda using a printing press organised by the ever-helpful J. Walter Thompson Company. The press officer at the British Legation later claimed that the Romanians never found the source of the black propaganda produced by Section D. At a less covert level, in March the newly recruited Donald Mallett was sent to Bucharest to open a branch of *Britanova* as such unofficial news agencies escaped the restrictions placed on a government press bureaux. He started his service on 23 April and in the following month the Minister in Romania, Sir Reginald Hoare, remarked that the *Britanova* propaganda was the best yet to have come from Britain to Romania. Mallett left Romania in May to help organise propaganda in Greece and Bulgaria before setting up an office in Istanbul, but the Romanian office of *Britanova* survived until September 1940, by which time it had distributed 1,571 news bulletins and 67 articles.[85]

In late March 1940 David Hacohen (leader of the Jewish Hagenah) and five of his agents went to Romania to establish a network of the 'Friends', primarily to establish escape lines for Jewish refugees but also to work more widely with Section D. He was under cover as a representative of the United Kingdom Commercial Corporation, with a letter of appointment from Chester Beatty, ostensibly to purchase timber for the allied armies in the Near East. The Minister was deeply suspicious, telling Hacohen that Legation staff had to be wary of giving recommendations 'since all sorts of people appeared from England on seemingly harmless missions, and later turned out to be intelligence agents; Romania, I should know, was maintaining a punctilious neutrality'.[86] Frederick Wedlake (aged 30) was sent to Romania in May to establish a new network based upon contacts of the 'Friends' and to liaise with the latter across the Balkans. There also appears to have been an intention to make Wedlake a formal head agent in Romania but personality clashes made this impossible. Full of criticism for the existing organisation, he proposed to leave Young and the 'old gang' to their own devices, except that he would take control of all correspondence to George Taylor and set up a new organisation based around the 'Friends' contacts.[87] Nothing came of this proposal and his work for Section D ended in mutual recriminations. In early August George Taylor reported his horror at Wedlake's poor relations with the 'Friends' and the SOE history of Section D simply says that he was 'unsatisfactory'.[88] Wedlake was in Palestine in early July when Young was expelled and it seemed unwise to continue his journey back to Romania.[89] Wedlake was recalled to Cairo and went on to join the naval planning staff of Combined Operations. Significantly, he is ignored in de Chastelain's history of Section D in Romania.[90]

The focus of Section D's sabotage efforts was on the rail traffic carrying oil to Germany. From the start of the war Young's network and a cell led by Canadian oil executive John Treacey maintained a simple but effective sabotage campaign of the oil trains by cutting brake couplings and 'hot-boxing' axle boxes by filling them with sulphuric acid or carborundum powder. They were supplied from a joint Section D/MI(R) explosives dump hidden in the British Legation, overseen by Commander R. Watson of MI(R). This was because Section D was also involved in organising shipping of explosives and other supplies into Poland via Romania on behalf of MI(R) until April 1940, when MI(R) tried to restrict shipments in order to discourage premature action.[91] The amateur saboteurs carried out operations at refineries, railway marshalling yards at Ploesti and shunting stations in Transylvania, and their success is demonstrated by the regular German complaints from November 1939 onwards regarding sabotage on trains bound for Germany. A series of explosions in the Prahova valley in early December directly led to Admiral Canaris being again sent out to Bucharest on the express orders of

Hitler to improve security. John Treacey was a 56-year-old consulting engineer and manager of an oilwell supply business in Ploesti, operating throughout the Balkans. George Taylor had recruited him in October 1939 whilst in London. His cell of enthusiastic expatriate oil workers included Cuthbert 'Jock' Anderson (oil engineer), E. Boaden (drilling superintendent of the Unira company), Charles Brasier (technical manager of the Romano Americana Refinery), and Reginald Young (chief chemist for the Romano Americana Refinery).

Treacey's saboteurs continued to operate even after King Carol abdicated and the dictatorship of Antonescu took power. In mid-September two German agents fire-bombed Treacey's house and on 25 September the Romanian Iron Guard arrested Treacey and his wife, followed by other members of the cell. In the houses of Treacey and Anderson were found incendiary capsules and bottles of sulphuric acid for making petrol bombs and cans of Vaseline mixed with emery powder and grease guns ready for 'hot-boxing'.[92] Also arrested were Charles Brasier, Reginald Young, Gogu Constantinescu and two of his men. Another Section D agent, H.C. Watts, was incriminated, as was Commander Watson, who had supplied the incendiary capsules. The men, particularly Treacey and Anderson, were badly beaten by the Iron Guard but in October a combination of diplomatic efforts by the Minister and a bribe of £5,000 organised by SOE managed to secure their release to Istanbul.[93] The fate of Gogu Constantinescu and his Romanian confederates is not known. In his history of SOE work in Romania, de Chastelain makes no mention of their arrest and believes that they simply 'laid low'.[94] Treacey's recommendation for an MBE in 1946 stated:

> His activity consisted mainly of sabotaging Axis oil transports from Romania. He recruited his own men and operated in the marshalling yards at Ploesti and at certain stations on the stretch between Ploesti and Brasov. The methods used were filling oil boxes with sulphuric acid and putting abrasives into reciprocating parts of locomotives. While it is impossible to say precisely what results were achieved, it is known that several hundred cars were operated on, producing appreciable delays in movement of trains and considerable damage to the tank cars and locomotives sabotaged.[95]

In mid-March 1940 Taylor appointed Andrew Duncan as a courier to liaise between the sprawling countries of the Balkans section, nominally on the staff of the British Legations. Young in Romania, Hanau and Bailey in Yugoslavia and Morrell in Hungary could thereby communicate with each other without having to commit messages to writing.[96] The self-important Duncan, aged 29, made the most of a vague job description and attempted to redefine his role to coordinate work across the Balkans, claiming authority direct from Taylor. Duncan built up a role collecting information on shipping movements on the Danube from the various vice-consuls, and even began recruiting his own agents. But he also saw it as his duty to provide 'constructive criticism' on the other Section D officers for Taylor, in a barrage of reports which, while useful, clearly breached the chain of command. He was fussy and tactless, described as showing 'great indiscretion in speech', and caused problems wherever he went.[97] Duncan had served as a second lieutenant in the Gordon Highlanders from 1931 to 1934, and prior to the outbreak of war was working for an advertising agency.

Duncan arrived in Romania in late April but, as elsewhere, soon discovered that agents were reluctant to take him into their confidence. He informed Taylor that he found it difficult to discover what Young was accomplishing, putting this down to his 'natural reticence'. Young did let slip to Duncan that two days previously he had put incendiary devices on an oil train heading for Germany and that these were due to explode in Hungary. There followed a schoolboyish report to Taylor: 'Am I wrong or did you say that no explosions should take place in Hungary itself?' He informed Taylor that he would go to Constanza to 'iron out' a few problems concerning Young's agents and also accused Young and Blackley of drunken indiscretions with Naval Intelligence's Minshall and Mason.[98] It was his poor opinion of the existing Section D staff in Romania that probably prompted the dispatch of Wedlake and Toyne to the country later in May, and the tensions that this then caused. Accused of being indiscreet himself, Duncan disregarded the need for a secret courier to maintain a low profile, and announced that one of his roles was to protest against anti-British propaganda.

On 1 May Duncan moved on to Yugoslavia and seemed surprised by his reception. He commented after meeting Hanau:

It may have been my imagination but he seemed resentful that I should be here at all, and rather implied that I was a case of 'fools rush in where angels fear to tread'.

A confused Hanau reported to Taylor that Duncan had claimed that his role was to 'oil the wheels of the Legations' and was 'authorised to report to you [Taylor] direct without reference to the people in charge on the spot'.[99] The easily manipulated Duncan was then drawn into a discussion with the Minister, Ronald Campbell, over the desirability of Hanau's removal.[100] Hanau was not a man to mess with and he made an immediate complaint to Taylor, demanding that Duncan be recalled. Duncan was told that he had overstepped his authority and was ordered out of Yugoslavia to Budapest, where he would receive further orders.[101] There, unfortunately, he met Blake-Tyler from MI(R) and contributed to the existing mischief in the Legation (*see* Chapter 8). Finally returning to England, he was dismissed in September 1940 as part of the SOE reorganisation.

Another unhappy decision on recruitment to the Balkans was John Toyne, who arrived in Romania in late May, just after Wedlake.[102] Toyne's later claim that he was sent to Bucharest after a personal meeting with Churchill where he was exhorted to 'win time for us' is not borne out by contemporary correspondence.[103] This former First World War intelligence agent in Russia, sometime Baptist pastor, farmer and engineer, was first interviewed for service in September 1939 by Goodwill but his recruitment was delayed whilst Toyne was nursing his sick wife Anne. After she was committed to a mental hospital in February 1940, Toyne re-established contact and was finally recruited in mid-April at a salary of £50 per month, then being sent on a naval sabotage course at Chatham.[104] For security (and possibly as a result of Duncan's damning reports), Toyne was to operate independently of the rest of Section D operations in Romania for 'special sabotage', taking instructions directly from London through Watson at the Legation. His primary mission was to hinder the sea-borne import of Russian oil into Germany but he also established weapons dumps in the Delta and in Bessarabia for supply to Hungary and Poland. Toyne's cover was as an entrepreneur seeking commercial contracts with Romania and he established a Section D-funded soap factory in the Turnu Severin district beside the Danube.[105] At first his work seemed to go well and he later received a glowing endorsement from the SIS liaison officer to Section D/SOE in London, Colonel Calthrop: 'I am informed that Toyne is the best British agent in Roumania ... CD [Nelson] has decided that he is doing such good work in the field that it is essential to back him.'[106]

Toyne's reputation had, in fact, disintegrated from late August following his marriage (arguably bigamously) to a former escort called Maria, who was suspected of having previously had relationships with German agents. His fellow agents believed he was being manipulated by her and her black market acquaintances. Toyne also became increasingly obsessed with a scheme to sell rubber to Romania, buying in return stocks of oilcake intended for Germany; that the rubber was likely to be sold to Germany was ignored. Maria was a Hungarian-born Romanian cabaret singer and Toyne was under no illusions about her previous career. He described her as a 'simple soul', claiming that he had not initially revealed that he was a British agent, declaring, with some irony given subsequent events, 'I simply don't trust woman's discretion in talking.'[107] In response to a barrage of complaints from the other Section D agents, Toyne claimed that he intended to use Maria's German contacts to obtain intelligence. To the same ends, he claimed to have also deliberately employed, as housemaid, the sister of the doorkeeper of the German Legation.

Despite Toyne's claims in his autobiography, no mention is made in his SOE file of any success in sabotaging Russian shipping. The focus of his later work was the attempt to sabotage the Yalomitsa Bridge at Ploesti but there were accusations that the planning of this was being used as a means to run a profitable black-market business selling Canadian passports and foreign currency to Jewish refugees.[108] As conditions in Romania worsened, Maria was sent to Istanbul, where she was kept under close surveillance by SIS. Having taken a luxury suite at the Park Hotel, she spent lavishly and drank heavily. Reports told of her sleeping with several men, including a member of the Turkish secret police. She made comments in bars about Toyne being head of the British secret service, and let slip the names of other British agents.[109] Maria was a security nightmare and Toyne's personnel file contains the damning conclusion that he had 'proved incompetent at his job, indiscreet and provocative in his attitude, and that there is a strong suspicion, though it is not the concern of our Organisation, that his commercial dealings were not as straight as might be desired'.[110] The final conclusion of S.W. Bailey, who was still head of the SOE Balkans section, was that 'he is either very stupid or very wicked' and should be dismissed.[111] To smooth Toyne's return to London, it was hinted that on his arrival he would be promoted and receive a decoration from the King. In fact, he was immediately dismissed and remained under surveillance by Special Branch for the rest of the war, all his attempts to secure further employment being blocked.

One of the most disastrous covert operations in the Balkans was the attempt, by Naval Intelligence, to arm the Goeland tug fleet. Section D was only involved in negotiating the original purchase of the fleet and subsequently in supplying explosives and weaponry, but it became tainted by association. The Goeland fleet of tugs and barges was owned by the Anglo-Danubian Transport Company, a subsidiary of the Anglo-Belgian company Welch, Bischoff & Finney. It comprised eight lighters, three self-propelled barges, three barges, two diesel tugs and one steam tug. In April 1939 Leslie Humphreys of Section D reported that the Germans had made an offer to buy the fleet and proposed that Section D should deny its use to the enemy by leasing the vessels through a £6,000 interest-free loan to the company, and then block the Iron Gates by sinking three of the barges, filled with stone and cement, in the narrows.[112] As the negotiations for a longer-term settlement dragged on, Bischoff was let into the secret and in July suggested that sinking three perfectly good barges was a waste and, instead, three more, cheap, barges should be purchased at a cost of £2,000, filled with stone and cement and laid up beside the Iron Gates, ready for deployment. He was also the first to suggest arming the fast tugs of the fleet to protect the operation and to resist any later German incursion along the river. In September 1939 Horace Emery was in Bucharest to buy the blocking barges. The intention was that he would become Superintendent of the fleet (to ensure it was not used by the Germans) and would take direct control of the three blocking barges as well as two tugs chartered on stand-by for the sabotage. For this, the company was to receive a retainer of £100 per week.

Grand estimated that the scheme had only a 33 per cent chance of total success – but it might block the Danube for around three months. General Gamelin (the French commander-in-chief) wanted the plan to proceed quickly but in response, Sir Alexander Cadogan of the Foreign Office told the French Ambassador that the sabotage plans could safely be postponed until the spring thaw.[113] Given such a delay, the management of a commercial fleet was now a burden to Section D and Emery agreed that the fleet should be managed through the Romanian Legation in the person of Commander Watson, the assistant naval attaché, who acted on behalf of both MI(R) and Section D. The Anglo-Danubian Company was dubious about the commercial viability of the fleet without being able to take German contracts and in December the fleet was finally purchased outright by the

Ministry of Economic Warfare. The Goeland Transport & Trading Company was created to run it as a commercial enterprise, with Captain William Harris-Burland of MEW, formerly of MI(R), as its managing director (as well as managing the Schultz fleet). Section D agent Charles Blackley became 'Inspector General' of the fleet, which was then periodically used for gun-running.[114] The French still pressed for its immediate use to block the Danube but Emery was under no illusions as to what Section D could achieve – concerns that he shared with Colin Gubbins:

> Emery tells me that he pointed out quite bluntly at the meeting [with the 5ième Bureau] that the British might be able to do something, though it would not be very much and would prejudice our position with Yugoslavia, and further, that as regards actual blocking of the Danube, the French were in a better position than the British as they owned 200 or 300 barges on the Danube in the French Company, which were at their disposal for sending whatever they liked; whereas the British had only got a hold, and that recently, on a certain number of barges, and did not actually own them.[115]

Gubbins, frustrated by his own narrow brief in MI(R), was clearly itching to get involved in a more operational way. In February 1940 he proposed allying MI(R) with a proposal by the Polish secret service for Danube sabotage, believing that 'poaching' on Section D spheres of operation could be excused if presented as a Polish scheme:

> Attached is a scheme for sabotage in Romania, handed to me by the Polish General Staff, in case it be of interest to us. It is, of course, actually a D project rather than one of mine, as it deals with Neutral Countries, but as all the action would be carried out by the Poles, and the British part would only be of materials and not even supply of money, the distinction is hardly of importance.[116]

This came amid the discussions between Lord Hankey and the DMI over the relative responsibilities of Section D and MI(R) and also cut across new plans by Naval Intelligence (DNI) to use the Goeland fleet on the Danube. It is likely that Gubbins was ordered not to complicate matters and nothing more was heard of the proposal.

The committee under Admiral Bellairs had been established to coordinate policy on the River Danube. It saw the priority for the Goeland fleet as preventing it from falling into enemy hands and to use it to counter any German naval warfare on the Danube, and therefore Bellairs decided in late January 1940 that the best use of the fleet was to follow Bischoff's earlier suggestion and arm the tugs. As a naval matter, this plan was put under the control of DNI, and Section D subsequently had only a limited role in what became a farcical venture. The scheme was planned by Captain Max Despard RN, the naval attaché for Yugoslavia and Romania. He was large and dominating, rarely revealing in public the fact that he was in constant pain from a wound received during the First World War. As was typical of intelligence agents in the region, the colourful Despard greatly alarmed the local diplomatic community. The Foreign Office assessment was that 'he is a man who is always liable to let his somewhat wild enthusiasm run away with him ... but he is unfortunately the apple of the Admiralty's eye'.[117] Despard's assistant in the scheme was Lieutenant Michael Mason, who had been sent out in January 1939 as a 'shipping adviser' to plan contingency measures in the event of war breaking out in the Balkan states. The plan had been for DNI to work with the Romanian government to ensure either the evacuation of the allied-owned barge fleets or their destruction, together with organising the disruption of German trade. As with MI(R), the presence of Naval Intelligence was, therefore, hardly a secret to the authorities.[118] Mason was joined by Merlin Minshall, under cover of being vice-consul at Galatz (Fig. 4). Minshall had been vetted for an appointment in Section D in September 1939 but instead had joined Naval Intelligence.[119]

Having claimed substantial experience of sailing on the Danube, Minshall's role in Despard's Goeland fleet scheme was to act as pilot. His actual participation differs considerably from the account in his fanciful autobiography, in which he invented a one-man espionage operation across the Balkans.[120] For Mason, Minshall was likeable but too full of bravado and confrontational, not to be trusted.[121] He had made himself a liability. On 30 March the Minister for Romania, Sir Rex Hoare, angrily reported that Minshall had threatened, with a pistol, a German medical officer in a Braila brothel.[122] The consul at Galatz, Russell Macrae, later recounted how Minshall had thrilled the 'ladies of easy virtue' with extravagant tales of British sabotage and the story became known as the 'battle of the Braila Brothels', earning Minshall the nickname 'Two Gun Minshall' and making him a well-known figure of amusement to the Germans.[123] Hoare hushed up the incident but Macrae was unsurprisingly unhappy about having Minshall imposed upon his consulate. Mason and Minshall both relished their reputations as secret agents in a quite unprofessional way:

> stories have been broadcast of wholesale British schemes of sabotage against the interests of the government with which we were on friendly terms ... The fantastic posturing of some of the young men involved gave every excuse for gossip if not for credence, particularly as some of the wildest versions can be traced to the amateur Guy Fawkes themselves.[124]

Describing them as a laughing stock, courier Duncan later claimed that Mason and Minshall had discussed the Goeland plan in great detail at 2.00am in the bar of the Athena Palace and had horrified the French 5ième Bureau who had declared 'We can't afford to have anything to do with those chattering bunglers: we will have to work alone.'[125] Ian Fleming knew both Mason and Minshall and the larger-than-life, not to say fictitious, personas that they created were likely inspirations for the James Bond character.

On 9 March 1940 Horace Emery supervised the loading of ninety-five cases of armaments onto the SS *Mardinian* in Liverpool, invoiced as spare parts to the Chrysler agent in Budapest, and sealed as 'American goods in transit to Hungary'. The shipment included 4 Vickers machine guns, 12 Lewis machine guns, 20 rifles and 50 revolvers with 25,000 rounds of ammunition.[126] There were also 600lb of explosives and 49 limpet mines. With the help of a £1,500 bribe to clear customs, the material was successfully transferred on 29 March to the lighter *Termonde* at Sulina on the mouth of the River Danube (Fig. 4) and Section D's involvement in the mission ended. On board, however, was Charles Blackley, in his role as 'Inspector General' of the Goeland Transport Company, to keep an eye on the cargo.[127]

The existing barge crews were supplemented with sixty-eight officers and men of the Royal Navy who had secretly arrived from Alexandria. The men had entered the country at Braila under the cover of being writers and artists on a sight-seeing trip but all their passports had been issued on the same day at Alexandria, and they wore identical sports jackets and grey flannel trousers. According to the horrified Consul at Galatz, the 'thinly disguised' sailors made matters worse by drawing attention to themselves and 'threatened violence in a quite unnecessary quarrel with the port authorities'. These remarkably young and fit wartime 'tourists' paraded daily to carry out naval physical training on deck.[128] The flotilla of the *Termonde* and the rest of the Goeland fleet then set off up the Danube, unsurprisingly shadowed by a steamer chartered by the *Abwehr*. The presence of Minshall as pilot, so soon after the Braila brothel incident, would alone have attracted German attention. It is hardly surprising that one of the first British tugs to arrive at Giurgiu (Fig. 4) on 3 April was searched by Romanian police at the insistence of German officers. British uniforms and a small quantity of arms were found. Although it was successfully argued that the arms were carried legitimately for personal defence, the omens were clearly not good. When the rest of the convoy reached Giurgiu the next day, the indiscretion of the British sailors in the riverside bars was enough to prompt a search of the *Termonde*. The customs seals on the crates were broken open to reveal the stock of arms and explosives. The embarrassed Romanian authorities tried to play down the affair but the vessels were ordered back to Braila, the cargo impounded and the British sailors expelled from the country. The Germans widely exploited the propaganda value of what they described as a flagrant breach of Romanian neutrality. Even *The Times* admitted that the vessels were piloted by 'an agent of the British Secret Service camouflaged as a vice-consul'.[129] This disastrous episode, loosely attributed to 'British Intelligence', was unfairly added to the MEW canon of complaints against Section D.

It had been previously agreed that Section D would do nothing that might increase surveillance on the river until Despard had completed the Goeland scheme, but the determination of the Slovene and Czech partners could not be easily contained. In early March two barges and a tug were reported by Hanau as being sunk on the Sipski Canal at the Iron Gates.[130] The seizure of the *Termonde* inevitably caused a tightening of security on the Danube and thereby hindered subsequent plans for the transport of supplies for Poland by both Section D and MI(R). Nonetheless, on 11 April Grand listed a German ship loaded with 70 tons of wheat and two barges with 1,400 tons of oil as being sunk.[131] The Romanian government was now suspicious of any British activity in the region and on 17 April the International Danube Committee banned the movement of any vessel capable of being converted into a warship and the transport of arms and explosives, also imposing control on the size and composition of crews.[132] The only armed vessels allowed were those of the riparian states. Tighter customs controls were introduced at Sulina and the Germans effectively occupied Constanza (Fig. 4). Any future attempt to block the Danube was going to be even more difficult; a further attempt to use the Goeland fleet to block the Danube was aborted (*see* p. 128), but in July there were calls for sabotage plans to be revived. Grand was worried about the practicalities of attempting this and asked Jo Holland to seek out the opinion of the General Staff.[133] An alternative plan was to destroy the towing railway beside the Sipski Canal at the Iron Gates, where barges had to be towed upstream by a locomotive pulling a rope car with a steam-driven hoist.[134] The idea was for Czech agents working with Section D to blow up at least two of the four locomotives on the railway. If successful, tugs would have to be used instead, towing smaller loads and dependent on the availability of Danube pilots. Traffic on the river was thereby anticipated to be delayed for around three weeks. The plan was still under consideration in late July but, as was typical, the Foreign Office intervened to impose fatal delays.

After the expulsion of Young in July 1940, de Chastelain became head agent in Romania and cultivated his links with Dr Maniu of the National Peasant Party. In September Grand recommended the formation of a Romanian resistance organisation under Dr Maniu, who was given a subsidy of 10 million lei for the purpose. Following the Norwegian, French and British model, the organisation would fall into two parts. The first would undertake immediate sabotage to interrupt German supplies. The second part, however, would be entirely separate; in terms reminiscent of the planning of the Home Defence Scheme in Britain (*see below*, p. 193) it would remain 'quiescent' and would only be activated following occupation by the enemy. It was firmly stressed that:

> Under no circumstances should the second organisation take any active steps at the present moment, and in territory which has been, or may be, occupied, members of the second organisation must, repeat must, remain entirely quiescent.[135]

Their role was to organise agents, hide supplies of weapons and ammunition and organise lines of communication.[136] Following Antonescu's coup, Romania officially joined the Axis on 23 November 1940 and took part in the invasion of the Soviet Union in June 1941. The new regime found Maniu too well-respected to dispose of and he maintained contact with SOE until de Chastelain parachuted back into Romania in late 1943. Antonescu was deposed in August 1944 in a coup led by King Michael, bringing Romania onto the side of the Allies and the SOE history concluded that 'Had it not been for the links established with the Opposition as long ago as 1939, it is doubtful whether the coup d'etat could have been engineered and carried through so successfully.'[137]

Albania

For most of the inter-war period, Albania was a military dictatorship under King Zog. The country was occupied by Italy in April 1939 as a 'protectorate' but no other state intervened on behalf of this remote and wild country. Until May 1940 British government policy was to do nothing that might antagonise Italy in Albania and provide an excuse to invade Greece.[138] Only when an Italian alliance with Germany seemed inevitable did the Chiefs of Staff lift the ban on planning anti-Italian subversion. Julius Hanau first asked Alexander Glen to formulate a plan for Albania but as Glen declared that he knew nothing of 'the beastly place', the task was passed on to Julian Amery (assistant press attaché).[139] Amery had been working unofficially for Section D since March and became a formal member on 6 May, although the Belgrade Legation did not officially approve the transfer until much later, which caused subsequent tensions.[140] Together with Section D officer Ralph Parker (working under cover as a *Times* correspondent), Amery made contact with Gani Beg (Gani Kryeziu), the leader of one of the opposition groups, and quickly dashed off a resumé of possibilities for working in Albania.[141] Over the rest of the month Taylor in London discussed a plan of campaign with MI(R), finally agreeing that Section D would act as a clandestine reconnaissance team that would collect intelligence and prepare supply lines ready for MI(R) to organise military guerrilla action upon a declaration of war.[142] Bailey would be in overall charge of Section D operations in Albania, with agents operating from Yugoslavia, Turkey and Greece, but dependent on the participation of disparate local opposition groups. Taylor proposed that John Bennett should provide local coordination by moving to Skopje in Macedonia (Fig. 4) but Bailey wanted Bennett to assist him in Belgrade. Consequently, it was Ralph Parker who was sent to Skopje, with Frederick Lawrence (a former Shell Oil executive who had only joined Section D in April 1940) as his assistant, under the cover of vice-consul and assistant pro-consul respectively.[143] Their main role was to assist in the smuggling of supplies to the Czech and Slovenian groups in Yugoslavia but Parker was also instructed to keep a watching brief on Albania. Meanwhile, Bailey tried to unite the various Albanian refugee groups in Yugoslavia under Jovan Djonovic, the ex-Yugoslav minister and journalist from Montenegro, focusing their activities in north-west Albania. Of the other two anti-Italian organisations already operating between Yugoslavia and Albania, that of Gani Beg was based on the north flanks of the Sar mountains. Gani Beg was a former officer

1. Laurence Grand (1898–1975). Royal Engineers major who became the charismatic head of Section D from 1938 to 1940. He managed the first offensive operations of British intelligence in the Second World War and created the basis of later SOE. Retired as a major general in 1952. (*Walter Stoneman, 1953; © National Portrait Gallery, London*)

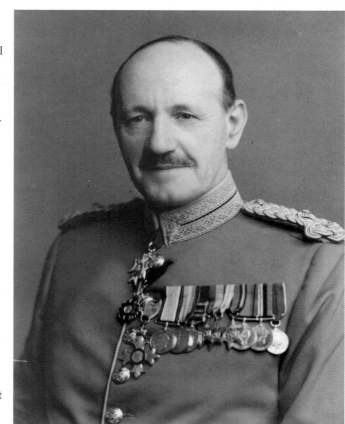

2. Neville Chamberlain (1869–1940). As Prime Minister, Chamberlain promised 'peace in our time' in October 1938, even as Section D was mobilising. In 1940, as Chief Commissioner, Chamberlain objected to the mobilisation of the Home Defence Scheme in Britain as being an illegal civilian force. In July he drafted the charter for SOE to allow it to organise similar activities on the continent. (*ACME 1940; © Getty Images*)

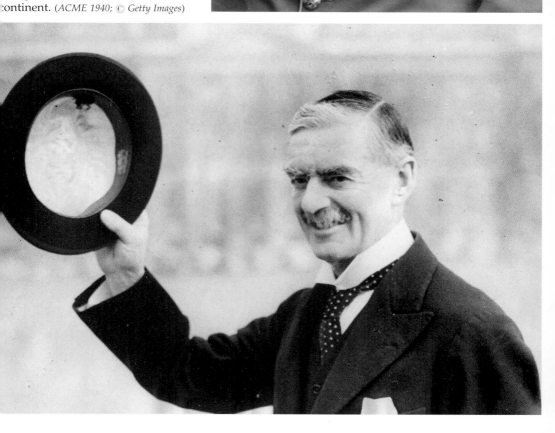

3. Julius Hanau (1885–1943). South African-born businessman and SIS agent. Became head agent for Section D in Yugoslavia and was described by Grand as 'the greatest of them all'. He became overall head of SOE's Iberian and African sectors but died of a heart attack in May 1943. Photograph from SOE file. (*Courtesy of The National Archives*)

4. Clara Holmes (1895–1992). Began working for SIS in 1917, mainly in Austria. Forced to flee the *Anschluss* in 1938, she joined Section D in May 1939, working in the German and Austrian propaganda section. She continued to work for the German section of SOE throughout the war, finally retiring in October 1945. Photograph from SOE file. (*Courtesy of The National Archives*)

5. Viscount Bearsted (1882–1948). Head of the Section D Home Defence Scheme in Britain. Later became Adviser on the Middle East to SOE. (*Walter Stoneman, 1942;* © *National Portrait Gallery*)

6. Anthony Samuel (1917–2001). Son of Viscount Bearsted. Section D courier and member of the *Operation Letter Bags* postal censorship scheme. He became a courier and administrative officer for SOE, where he wrote the official war diary of Section D. Photograph from SOE file. (*Courtesy of The National Archives*)

7. Gerard Holdsworth (1904–1985). Former director of the J. Walter Thompson Co. Advertising Agency film section. He joined Section D in early 1939 and helped organise the 'Cruising Club' to survey potential landing sites in Norway. He served as a regional officer in the Home Defence Scheme in East Anglia before creating the SOE 'Helston flotilla' to transport agents to and from France. Photograph from SOE file. (*Courtesy of The National Archives*)

8. Dr Chaim Weizmann (1874–1952) with his wife, Vera. He was Russian born, educated in Germany and became a British citizen in 1910. Weizmann was President of the World Zionist Organisation and became the first President of Israel. In 1939 he negotiated a worldwide partnership with Section D. (*ACME 1940; © Getty Images*)

9. Broadway Buildings, Westminster. HQ of SIS from 1926 and first HQ of Section D. (*Courtesy of the City of Westminster Archive Centre*)

10. St Ermin's Hotel, London (*c.*1910). SIS took over two floors of 2 Caxton Street to make it the wartime HQ of Section D, linked to a private apartment for Laurence Grand in the hotel. (*Atkin Collection*)

11. Section D propaganda leaflet distributed in November 1939 from Sweden. It appeals to German nationalism by accusing the Hitler–Stalin Pact of being a 'Sale of German Honour, Population and Property', surrendering its sphere of influence in the east. Around 6,000 were produced. *(Courtesy of Dr C.G. McKay)*

12. Section D propaganda leaflet intended to encourage division between the German army and the SS. On one side is a cold and wet German soldier in the trenches, complaining that he has received no letter from home. The reason is provided by the picture alongside, which shows an SS man seducing his wife. 'NO POST … NO WONDER … the Home Front is in firm hands – the SS and SA are always ready for action …' *(Courtesy of Lee Richards)*

13. *Schutzmaßnahmen gegen die Inflation* ('Measures against Inflation'). Section D leaflet purporting to be an official German instruction to hoard goods. (*Courtesy of Lee Richards*)

Schutzmaßnahmen
gegen die Inflation!

Der kluge Mann baut vor: In diesen schweren Zeiten der allgemeinen Unsicherheit legt der kluge Mann sein Geld in Waren von bleibendem Wert an und schützt damit nicht nur sich selbst sowie seine eigene Familie, sondern auch die Heimat gegen die zunehmende Inflationsgefahr.

Folgen Sie daher dem Beispiel der Spitzen der Partei und des Reichs.

Kaufen Sie **jetzt**, noch bevor die Preise in die Höhe gehen!

Kaufen Sie **jetzt**, solange Ihr Geld noch eine Kaufkraft besitzt

Kaufen Sie **jetzt**, solange noch Ware zu haben ist.

Kriegssparen heißt kaufen!

Aktionsausschuß der Arbeitsgemeinschaft der Industrie- und Handelskammern in der Reichswirtschaftskammer.

Alles fürs Kind

14. *Alles fürs Kind* ('Everything for the Child'). This Section D pamphlet asked German mothers to put themselves in the position of Polish mothers who had seen their children executed – 'German mothers – are you not ashamed?' – and praised the contribution of Germany to Western civilisation, now threatened by the Nazis. Five copies of this were handed in to the Munich Gestapo, who considered it too well produced for it to have been secretly printed in Germany. (*Courtesy of The National Archives*)

15. *Das Wahre Deutschland* ('The True Germany') published by Hans Alber Kluthe for the German Freedom Party from 193 to 1940 and funded by Section D. (*Atkin Collection;* © *Kate Atkin*)

16. *Weder Hitler noch Stalin! – Österreich den Östertreichern!* (Neither Hitler nor Stalin – Austria for the Austrians!) Section D propaganda sticker and poster appealing to Austrian nationalists and featuring the red/white/red Austrian flag. Approximately 10,000 stickers (8.5 × 12.5cm) and 3,000 small posters (24 × 32cm) were produced, with a similar design used in material for Bavarian nationalists. (*Courtesy of The National Archives*)

17. Skoda Works, Pilsen, Czechoslovakia, 1938. The second largest armaments factory in Europe. Laurence Grand visited here in 1938 with Czech Intelligence to discuss plans for its sabotage in case of German invasion. (*International News Photo, 1938*)

18. Top: Switch No. 10 Delay Time Pencil. Invented by Commander Langley of Section D, Aston House. The time delay was caused by acid eating through a copper wire of different thicknesses, allowing a delay of up to 20 hours. It became the standard allied time delay device of the Second World War. Bottom: Switch No. 9 L Delay which used a lead break as a time delay. Invented by Millis Jefferis of MI(R) and issued to some units of the Home Defence Scheme. (© *Kate Atkin*)

19. November 1939 press photograph showing French plans to create road-blocks by dynamiting trees across roads. The technique was simple and was taught to British saboteurs. (*ACME 1939; © Getty Images*)

20. The Romanian oilfields were a major allied target throughout the war. British attempts at major sabotage in 1939–40 were thwarted by German intelligence although Section D had some success in sabotaging rail transports from the Ploesti refineries. In desperation, the US Air Force launched major raids against the refineries in 1943. *Operation Tidal Wave* was one of the costliest US Air Force strategic operations of the war but had a minimal impact on oil production. (*Courtesy of US Army Centre of Military History, 44th Bomb Group Photograph Collection*)

1. Kasan Pass, Galati, Romania – the Iron Gates (September 1940). According to the original caption, 'It is at this point, according to German charges, that British agents had plotted to block the river by causing an avalanche with dynamite.' (*ACME 1940; © Getty Images*)

2. Barges and tugs at the port of Galatz, Romania, November 1940. The original caption states, 'There have also been reports of Danube river pilots signing two year contracts with a British company to stay off the river. Inactivity of these men would cripple anticipated transport of supplies to Germany.' (*ACME 1940; © Getty Images*)

23. Port of Narvik, Norway in October 1940. The iron-ore port was surveyed by Section D in August 1938, with a proposal to purchase a US ship, fill it with concrete and sink it to block the ore-handling quay. This was rejected and the port was the focus of a key battle during May–June 1940, during the German invasion of Norway. (*ACME 1940;* © *Getty Images*)

24. Ture Nermann, publisher of the Swedish anti-Nazi newspaper *Trots Allt*. The police surveillance of Nermann led ultimately to the discovery of the Rickman plot to sabotage the port of Oxelösund, which in turn was a major factor in the decision to close Section D and form SOE. (*Photo by K.W. Gullers, 1942*)

5. A 1930s postcard of the port of Oxelösund. This edition was used in Section D pre-planning; found in the possession of Kurtzen and in Rickman's flat by the Swedish police, it was used as evidence in court as to their plans to sabotage the port. (*Atkin Collection*)

26. Section D explosives found in the Windsor Tea Company cellar, Stockholm. (*Police photograph, 19 April 1940, Stockholm City Archives, reproduced in Björkman (2006), p. 96*)

27. The fishing boat *Wailet* being refitted as the *Lady* (V2S) for the May 1940 Norwegian expedition. (*Courtesy of The National Archives*)

28. Skipper of the V2S, Karsten Wang (left), and Section D officer James Chaworth-Musters (right) prior to the departure of the Norwegian expedition. (*Courtesy of The National Archives*)

In conjunction with arranged a transmitting station i should start functioning as fro:

We are therefore informing : lowing arrangements:-

(a) The code will be L.M.T.2.

(b) The secret number will be

(c) The book will be "Germany, (Penguin) as enclosed.

Would you kindly arrange through Head Office, all inco

Could you conveniently l mimeographed instruction shee I shall probably require thi: other agents.

Section D.
25.6.40.

9. The first Section D mission to Norway that took a wireless set used a copy of the Penguin *ermany – What Next?* as its code book. Shown here over a copy of the original signal instructions.
) *Kate Atkin*)

). Colt .32 Automatic istol. Issued to the first Iorwegian Expedition nd later described by OE as the best personal eapon for clandestine perations. Background is map of Norway, as ken on the May 1940 Iorwegian expedition.
) *Kate Atkin*)

31. Thompson M1928 sub-machine gun of the general type (with later rear sight) hidden by Section D as part of their arms dumps left by the Norwegian Expedition in June 1940 within the Voss district. (© *Kate Atkin*)

32. 'Machine-gun rattle' as issued to the HDS in the absence of Thompson sub-machine guns. (© *Kate Atkin*)

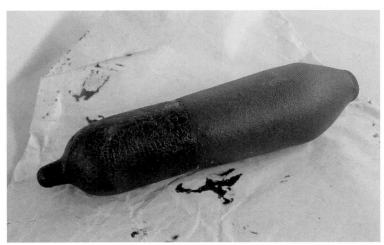

33. Tyesule paraffin incendiary, 5 inches long, as used by HDS. (*Courtesy of David Sampson*)

in the Yugoslav army who had some support from within the Yugoslav government as a possible future king of Albania. There was also the organisation of Colonel Kokosi operating on the southern flanks of the Sar. In all, a monthly subsidy of £1,500 was paid to these groups and three communication lines were established between Yugoslavia and Albania for future gun-running.

Most of the Albanian émigrés had settled in Istanbul and once the ban on activity was lifted, the retired Lieutenant Colonel Robert Cripps, 49-year-old former Inspector of the Gendarmerie School in Albania, newly arrived in Greece in early June as a cypher clerk for the MI(R) Mission, was loaned to Section D, first in Belgrade and then to establish new communication lines into Albania from Turkey. Liaison between the divided émigré communities was a thankless task which Cripps did not handle well. Over-enthusiastic, he was accused of being 'a menace to our organisation', indiscreet and guilty of entertaining 'undesirable' Albanians known to be in the pay of the Italians; he was replaced at the end of August by Lieutenant Colonel Walter Stirling.[144] Greece became an increasingly important focus of smuggling sabotage materials into Albania, but work here was especially sensitive for fears of provoking an Italian invasion. Section D agents began to build up Albanian contacts and established weapons dumps on both sides of the Greek/Albanian border, as well as smuggling propaganda from the émigré Albanian Committee in Istanbul.

Italy declared war on 10 June 1940 and began to build up strength for an invasion of Egypt against heavily outnumbered British troops. Wavell decided the risk of extending war to Greece and Albania was too great for his limited forces. On 19 June his DDMI, Brigadier Shearer, ordered a cessation of all operations in Greece directed at Albania, followed on 5 July by an order for Section D to cease all work on the Albanian borders.[145] Work only began again in earnest in October – 'a tragic loss of valuable time' according to Goodwill.[146] Undaunted, on 18 July Bailey urged the need to continue preparations for revolt, diplomatically stressing that the actual launch of the rising would be dependent on orders received from the British Middle East Command. He also proposed co-ordinating the Albanian revolt with a Slovenian rising in Istria so that the east side of the Adriatic could be properly secured.[147] Even with such a delay, the Albanians needed to be ready-armed, and Goodwill requested permission to complete a black-market deal with Yugoslav contacts for the purchase of 5,000 second-hand rifles together with 10 million rounds of ammunition and twenty-five light machine guns, all for a total price of up to £182,000.[148] The Bailey plan was dismissed by Shearer as a 'chimera' and it was not pursued. Some liaison work continued within Albania but the relationship between Section D and local ministers was already delicate and in August the inexperienced Amery was discovered inside the Tirana Legation (Fig. 4), handing over money to rebel adherents of King Zog. He was quickly removed from the country but the Yugoslav government also protested about Parker's activities in Albania, and he too had to be withdrawn. Without providing details, Alexander Glen described Parker's behaviour in Albania as 'reprehensible'. His contacts with Albanian émigrés had become well known to both the Germans and the Yugoslav authorities and he was working under considerable strain. Once in Istanbul, he wrote a letter to the Yugoslav press carelessly ('criminal' according to Glen) identifying Frederick Lawrence in Skopje as a British agent.[149] Parker's Czech mother-in-law had been arrested in Prague for allegedly passing on information to her daughter and SIS became suspicious that Parker might have been blackmailed into becoming a double agent. He was eventually cleared of suspicion but the strain of events led to family tragedy. His wife died in childbirth during the extended passage to England and the child died subsequently. Parker left what had become SOE and went to Russia as correspondent for *The Times*, becoming increasingly disillusioned with the western war effort. He eventually settled in Moscow, where he died in 1964.

The arrival in Cairo in mid-August 1940 of Walter Stirling of Section D, who was originally intended to work under Cripps in Albania, greatly improved relations with Wavell and Middle East Command. He had first been suggested for work in the Near East in May 1940 by the newly recruited Arnold Lawrence (brother of T.E. Lawrence) whilst working for the telephone censorship department. Stirling had served as Chief of Staff to T.E. Lawrence in the First World War, gaining the nickname 'Stirling the Suave', and for eight years had been an adviser to the Albanian government. Most importantly, he was a professional soldier, strict disciplinarian, and a friend of Wavell, who up until this time had regarded Section D as civilian mavericks operating beyond his strategic control. Stirling used his personal relationship to rebuild confidence in the organisation, offering Wavell something that he could not necessarily exploit using regular forces. He took evident delight in the fact that

> The D organisation ... is entirely untrammeled in its action. This organisation is an ideal tool in the hands of the C-in-C since, not being a military body, it has no scruples, few morals and is without shame. Its operations can, if necessary, be denied with an oath.[150]

Stirling clarified the division of labour between Section D and MI(R). The new SOE had not yet impinged on what were still two distinct organisations in the Middle East and Stirling proposed a new organisational chart under C-in-C Middle East and his DDMI, Brigadier Shearer. Bailey would remain in overall charge of the Balkans with Stirling taking charge of Albania. In a reversal of roles, Cripps would now be his assistant and the staff would also include another former police adviser in Albania, Dayrell Oakley-Hill. Until war was formally declared with Albania, Section D would be responsible for building links with sympathetic groups and for organising dumps of weapons. Following the outbreak of war, MI(R) would commence para-military operations using Section D's supply lines and dumps. Stirling and the D agents in Albania would officially transfer to the command of MI(R), but with Stirling still in local command and continuing to liaise with Section D in surrounding countries. The key to success would be the uniting of the Albanian groups under at least the titular leadership of King Zog. Stirling carefully concluded, 'What form of government they would eventually set up need not be discussed now.' Bailey greeted Stirling's arrival in Istanbul with a sigh of relief, believing his age and social contacts would improve relations in diplomatic circles 'where some of the younger men have already given offence'.[151] In a rare burst of optimism, Goodwill described 'a great and glorious victory out here'. He was not so sure how London would react to this division of responsibility but, 'In so far as the Middle East and Balkans are concerned, however, I cannot say how happy I feel.'[152] George Taylor was more cautious, discreetly asking Goodwill whether Shearer or MI(R) could be trusted to honour the arrangement.[153] Goodwill did not survive the new plan. His relationship with Simpson of MI(R) and Shearer had continued to deteriorate and his replacement became inevitable. George Taylor wrote an appreciative letter to Goodwill on 31 August:

> I can only say that I agree completely with everything you have done. I am extraordinarily pleased with the progress made on the two main fronts, namely 'Friends' and Albania. Nobody else has anything like your grasp of the policy, and it is a tragedy that you have to come back just when the scope of D/H Section's work is broadening so enormously, and when the need for long range policy making and organising capacity is so acute.[154]

In a last gasp of the Section D plan, on 7 April 1941 three hundred men led by Gani Beg and accompanied by Oakley-Hill (now in SOE) crossed the border into Albania from Yugoslavia. It was too late for any effective intervention and the escapade turned into more of a Yugoslav invasion than a national liberation. In the end Oakley-Hill was obliged to surrender to the Germans in Belgrade. No further SOE agents were inserted until 1943. In a final postscript, during 1949 SIS and the CIA revived the Section D plan to undermine the Hoxha regime and encourage a coup. The plan was to train Albanian exiles and then infiltrate them into the country to stir up revolt. Julian Amery and Dayrell Oakley-Hill were once more involved in what became another disaster. That other former Section D agent, Kim Philby, later admitted betraying the operation to the Soviets.

Bulgaria

Bulgaria tried to maintain its neutrality but the fear in 1939–1940 was that it might be used as the base for a German attack on the Romanian oilfields to the north or on Greece to the south. Under King Boris III, all official opposition political parties had been banned; the main opposition groups were the loosely linked left-wing Peasant Party under Georgi Dimitrov and the 'Military League' of Colonel Veltchev, together with a Communist Party which in 1940 was fiercely opposed to any dealings with the Allies. In March 1941 Bulgaria became a reluctant member of the Axis.

A series of early exploratory missions by Section D were failures. Nothing came of Jósef Radziminski's mission to Bulgaria (under cover as working for the Polish Telegraph Agency) in early October 1939. He returned to London before being sent to Hungary. Bailey from Yugoslavia and Treacey from Romania both made visits in April 1940. Treacey wanted to mount a reconnaissance of the Italian supply base at Varna (Fig. 4) but the men were unable to link up with potential contacts. Grand and Menzies put the blame for the failure to establish an organised presence in the country on the unhelpful attitude of the Minister to Bulgaria, George Rendel, although in his defence the Foreign Office brief to Rendel was clear in its support for propaganda efforts but not to allow plans for sabotage.[155] This was clearly not a view shared by some of Rendel's staff. It was decided to hand over Section D contacts in Bulgaria to French intelligence, with liaison provided by Geoffrey McDermott, third secretary in the British Legation but now 'appointed an honorary member of D organisation'.[156] In a distinguished diplomatic career, he later became Foreign Office adviser to SIS. McDermott was more accommodating than his Minister and some work continued. In May Andrew Duncan made contact with the pro-allied Veltchevist organisation which had links with the Bulgarian army. As an organisation, it refused to organise sabotage but individual members were prepared to do so through the outlawed IMRO Bulgarian/Macedonian nationalist organisation. McDermott sent them £200 as payment for an attack on the Bulgarian railway.[157] The military attaché (Alec Ross) and the assistant press attaché (Norman Davis) also continued to work on behalf of Section D. Ross worked on Section D schemes in Greece and Hungary, and in Bulgaria, at his suggestion, Grand secured approval in June for bribing several Bulgarian generals at a cost of £30,000.[158] Arms dumps were also set up along the border with Yugoslavia in anticipation of future action.[159]

The delicate work of Legation staff on behalf of Section D and against the wishes of the Minister was disturbed by Julian Amery's visit to Sofia (Fig. 4) in late August, to make another attempt to contact opposition leaders. Having already been removed from Albania because of his lack of discretion, he was now accused of undermining Ross and Davis by actively promoting the overthrow of King Boris through a coordinated coup of the Serbian and Bulgarian Peasants Parties (who wished to create a pan-Slav federation). His own version of events is that, at the instigation of the Albanian opposition leader Djonovic, all he did was pass on the views of Yugoslav and Bulgarian opposition leaders to the Foreign Office and Section D.[160] The Minister, Rendel, believed that Amery was directly involved in planning a coup behind the Foreign Office's back and Glen later explained Amery's departure as the result of 'a private and audacious plan of his own for Bulgaria that would have left Frederick Forsyth and the Jackal nowhere!'[161] Hanau and Bailey were more sanguine over the accusations and, although Amery had to be removed from the Balkans, Bailey made him his assistant in Istanbul. In the delicate period of transition from Section D to SOE, London HQ needed to minimise the risk of a further diplomatic incident and, on discovering that Amery had subsequently been sent on a mission to Bucharest, Sweet-Escott wrote to Bailey, making it clear that those concerned with establishing the resistance under Maniu should have nothing to do with him. He was recalled to Britain, where his subsequent career with SOE proved equally controversial.[162]

New Zealand-born academic Norman Davis, unemployed since the Bulgarian government withdrew support for the Institute of English Studies at Sofia University, also began working for Section D in an unofficial capacity whilst assistant press attaché in Sofia. He formally became a Section D agent in June and recruited activists from the Agrarian Union to produce propaganda, including the printer Lazar Popovski, already engaged on printing the official press bulletins of the British Legation. In August Popovski finally managed to facilitate a meeting between Bailey, Davis and Georgi Dimitrov (elusive leader of the Bulgarian Peasant Party). Suspicious of being controlled by a foreign power, the Peasant Party was initially reluctant to accept Section D funding and it was only later that they accepted SOE weapons and an explosives instructor. As the political situation deteriorated, in February 1941 Davis smuggled Dimitrov out of Bulgaria and both men were sentenced to death *in absentia*. Bulgaria joined the Axis in March 1941 and it was the communists who finally organised an effective resistance. SOE did not make effective contact again until 1944.

Chapter 7

The Aegean and Middle East

From the spring of 1940, as fears rose of Italy joining Germany in the war, British attention increasingly shifted from the Balkans to Greece and the Middle East, bringing Section D into a closer relationship with General Wavell's Middle East Command. The threat also posed practical risks for Section D in managing the already unwieldy D/H section. If the Mediterranean were closed, supply lines would have to wind around the Cape and it might become difficult to manage the region from London. Two weeks before the Italian declaration of war on 10 June, George Taylor and his deputy Arthur Goodwill moved the HQ of Section D/H from London to Cairo, relying on Bickham Sweet-Escott to maintain liaison in London. Sunderland flying boats also rushed to ship tons of explosives to a new Section D supply dump at Alexandria.[1] In Cairo, Section D worked under the alias of 'Economic Advisory Committee, Middle East', with offices adjacent to those of Middle East Command, known to the drivers of the Cairo horse-drawn taxis as 'the British Secret Office'.[2] As well as an overarching responsibility for Section D operations across the Balkans, the Cairo office had direct responsibility for activities in the Aegean and Middle East, although far less detail has survived about its operations in the latter.

Taylor returned to London in July, leaving Arthur Goodwill in charge. During his short stay in Cairo, Taylor had created a working relationship with MI(R), swapping staff between the two bodies and managing an uneasy peace with Wavell's Deputy Director of Military Intelligence (DDMI), Brigadier Shearer. The latter was formerly of the Indian army, who had served in the Intelligence Directorate in the 1920s but then became managing director of Fortnum & Masons. He likened his position with Section D as 'sitting on a volcano'.[3] Archibald Wavell, the hard-pressed head of Middle East Command, was deeply concerned that any precipitous action in the Balkans would over-stretch his resources and, in particular, would trigger an invasion of Greece. He was not opposed in principle to irregular warfare but wanted it under his control. Taylor had agreed that Section D would act as the 'civil and underground side of MIR Middle East', working under the direction of the Directorate of Military Intelligence in specific field operations where there was a clear military interest – but equally making it clear that 'he was responsible only to Grand and, through Grand, to CSS' for general instructions, and was totally in charge of Section D secret lines of communication. He particularly emphasised the civilian character of the organisation to avoid it being swallowed up by Military Intelligence.[4]

But as the work of Section D and MI(R) became more closely directed by C-in-C Middle East, this provided an attractive alternative War Office model to Hugh Dalton's dreams for an independent and civilian SOE (*see* Chapter 11).

Taylor believed that Section D would act under the DDMI in Albania and Greece (as there was the distinct possibility there of active British military involvement) but would operate elsewhere in the Balkans 'without the C-in-C having any interest in our activities'.[5] After Taylor's departure, Arthur Goodwill could not maintain the same good relations and eventually had to be replaced by his assistant, George Pollock. The combination of amateur warrior Goodwill and professional ex-Indian army Shearer was always going to be difficult. Goodwill's report on potential plans for Albania and Istria ended with the sarcastic disclaimer:

> It is desired that no statement contained in this minute shall be interpreted as an expression of opinion as to the usefulness of these proposals, of which we are not qualified to judge.[6]

A handwritten note caustically explained, 'This is for DDMI.' SOE in the Middle East was never able to shake off the departmental in-fighting that continued throughout the war.

Taylor had good reason to fear that Wavell would absorb and militarise Section D operations. In September 1939 Lieutenant Colonel I.N. Clayton had been sent by Laurence Grand to act as GSO1 (Publicity) at Middle East Command. His work was part-funded by the War Office but Section D funding was used for distributing clandestine propaganda (leaflets, gramophone records, etc.) on the Libyan border and in Transjordan and to build contacts with the tribes in Abyssinia. Clayton soon became fully absorbed within the DMI. Section D/K, under Colonel Stephen Longrigg, was formed to cover Abyssinia and wider propaganda in the Middle East; it also soon became a section of the DMI but continued to operate as a mystery in its own right. Pollock commented in May 1941: 'Longrigg kept his work very much to himself and never showed any anxiety to enlist our cooperation, as he regarded me and my section purely as experts in "thuggery".'[7] Longrigg seemed doubly ill-suited to his role, being described as both anti-semitic and anti-journalist.[8]

Greece

In April 1939, following the Italian occupation of Albania, Britain guaranteed the independence of Greece and concerns to avoid any Italian invasion of the latter coloured much of British policy in the Balkans. SIS had a substantial intelligence presence in Greece with seventy salaried agents. A small Section D presence was established immediately after the outbreak of war in September 1939 in the shape of S.R. Shotton, an employee of Ingersoll Rand Co., who worked across Yugoslavia, Turkey and Greece. He took up full-time residence in Athens in February 1940 and his limited availability was used mainly in assessing options for smuggling explosives from Greece into Yugoslavia and organising the distribution of propaganda leaflets and posters.

Section D's work in Greece did not properly get under way until May 1940 as fears of Italy joining the Axis intensified, and following a visit from Arthur Goodwill. The Ambassador, Sir Michael Palairet, would not accept the appointment of Section D officers to the Legation in Athens, fearing that it would compromise his diplomatic relations with the Greek government. Instead, Goodwill found a core of five volunteers from the large British expatriate colony, all ex-soldiers and known collectively as 'The Apostles': Meikle (Matthew), Sinclair (Mark), Saunders (Luke), Kemp (John) and Bailey (Peter). The leader was H.J. Sinclair, chief engineer of the Athens Tramway Trust and secretary of the Greek Branch of the British Legion.[9] Meikle and Kemp were directors of the Athens & Piraeus Electricity Company; Saunders was the local agent of Lloyds Insurance Company; and Bailey was head of the Lake Copais Reclamation Company. Their ambitious instructions were to:

1. establish channels of communication for smuggling material into Yugoslavia;
2. establish supply dumps in Greece;
3. identify future sabotage targets for action to follow any enemy invasion. No sabotage was to be undertaken in Greece before such an attack as it might prejudice the work of the official MI(R) Mission that was expected shortly;
4. recruit Greeks who would form a resistance after the British had been obliged to withdraw;
5. stir up revolt against the Italian rule in Albania, persuading Albanians to undertake sabotage following any Italian advance into Greece and Yugoslavia. Such work was described as 'delicate' and would only be activated following agreement with the Military Attaché;
6. establish an organisation in Corfu; and
7. organise propaganda that could not be officially supplied by the Ministry of Information 'because its character would be such as to get the British Government into trouble if it were publicly associated with it'.[10]

Sinclair was only a part-time agent but Ian Pirie arrived in Athens on 31 May as a full-time deputy. Pirie's cover was as an ARP officer in the Athens & Piraeus Electricity Company, where he could easily contact Meikle and Kemp. Pirie's previous business ventures included a pet cemetery and the manufacture of tin models of St Bernard dogs. Peter Wilkinson of MI(R) described Pirie as 'a tubby little man with a face of ageless guile'.[11] Section D officer Basil Davidson had earlier admired him for his 'charming air of boredom' whilst smuggling diplomatic bags filled with explosives into Hungary.[12] Pirie carried out his new duties with an unshakeable good humour. He once suggested improving morale after any German invasion by importing musical toilet roll holders which would play the Greek national anthem! One attempt at sabotage was to try to short circuit a secret German wireless transmitter that he had located, by causing a massive surge of electricity to the building in which it was operating. The Germans had forestalled any such problem by installing a back-up generator, but the building also contained a dentist's surgery and neither the dentist nor the patient whose tooth he was drilling were amused. One of his successes was at the expense of the War Office rather than the Germans. He managed to secretly add a quantity of 7.65mm ammunition, hand grenades and incendiary bombs to a War Office contract for ammunition from an Athens armaments factory. These were then smuggled out of the factory for the use of Section D in the Balkans. The same factory also purchased numbers of pistols and Thompson sub-machine guns on the open market on behalf of Section D.[13] Before being obliged to flee Athens when the Germans arrived, he married his girlfriend Niki Demertzi, a dancer in an Athens nightclub, to ensure her escape from the Nazis.

Pirie was assisted by a Greek, Christos Gogas (who later served in SOE as 'Chris Harris'), under cover as an agent of the Automatic Telephone & Electric Company.[14] A network of sub-agents was also established in surrounding towns. Pirie explained their function 'to lay on a Greek organisation that after evacuation would carry out widespread, continuous, small-scale sabotage'.[15] In Salonica there was the Canadian Major A.F. Menzies of the War Graves Commission, whose job took him into Yugoslavia and Bulgaria, as well as to Greece and the Aegean Islands. Pirie also recruited George Zannos, head of the Greek Red Cross and Commander Ioannis Toumbas of the Royal Greek Navy. Their task was to investigate the potential of the Free Port of Salonica for transporting material into Yugoslavia. Farrar, a keen yachtsman with a good knowledge of the Greek coastline (and a golf professional in Athens), was recruited in Patras. In the First World War he had served with T.E. Lawrence in Arabia. Wilkinson was an engineer at the reclamation works in Janina, where he recruited agents from among his employees and took charge of the main weapons dump (Fig. 4). He supplemented the stock of explosives by over-ordering supplies on his company account.[16] Another full-time officer who arrived was Reginald Barwell, who had been educated in Istanbul and had been company secretary of a pre-war shipping business there. Having returned to Britain, he had been recruited to Section D from the postal censorship department in March 1940. Barwell was sent to work in Greece under cover as an inspector for the Ministry of Wartime Transport to try to recruit English skippers and mates of ships working between Athens, Istanbul and Alexandria to carry material for Section D. He also ran the Euxinos Shipping Company as a front for Section D and bought several caiques (schooners) ready for coastal operations, focused on smuggling sabotage materials into Yugoslavia and Albania. From June onwards Barwell was based in Istanbul as shipping adviser to the British Consulate, where he managed propaganda operations in Turkey as well as acting as administrative officer for Section D in the region.

The first attempt to smuggle explosives into Albania from Greece went well. Sinclair and Wilkinson recruited a Greek doctor, Dr Karvounis, who had property in Albania and made regular border crossings. Karvounis drove into Albania during early June carrying 100kg of explosives in a suitcase, which he hid on his estate. On the second trip his car broke down and he decided to proceed by taxi. The taxi driver was curious about the unusual weight of the suitcase, looked inside and then reported the contents to the Greek border guards. Karvounis was arrested and put forward the somewhat unlikely defence that he was trying to establish a speculative trade in dynamite, taking samples to Wilkinson's reclamation works at Janina. He was banished from Greece for one year. News of the incident reached Middle East HQ in Cairo and on 19 June Shearer ordered a halt to all Albanian-related operations in Greece, for fear of providing an excuse for an Italian invasion. There was then an almost complete cessation of work, other than propaganda, within Greece. The result was a loss of morale amongst the volunteer agents, 'suffering from a lack of specific direction except of an entirely negative character'.[17] One of their propaganda triumphs was the circulation of 30,000 copies of an anti-Italian poem by Paraskos. The Italian government protested but was told that it was a Greek classic.[18] Propaganda operations were greatly strengthened by the arrival of Jacob Altmaier, newly escaped from Yugoslavia, to advise Pirie on propaganda for a month before moving on to Istanbul.[19]

Despite the ban on action from C-in-C Middle East, on 27 June Taylor reported that the C-in-C Mediterranean (Admiral Cunningham) wanted to block the Corinth Canal (Fig. 4) but was not willing to raise the matter himself 'because he thinks that it would raise a storm in the Embassy because of its political repercussions'. Section D was evidently seen as an organisation that did not care who it offended! Taylor asked Grand to seek approval from the War Cabinet but commented, 'I don't think it matters two pence if we offend the Greek Government.'[20] The intention was, with the help of the Jewish 'Friends', to sail a ship from Palestine and sink it in the canal. As ever, the scheme was dogged by extended dispute at a political level. The ISPB meeting of 5 July agreed the project but Grand put the responsibility back on the Admiralty to secure permission for the scheme, which was still under discussion when the Italians attacked Greece in October and was then dropped. A similar scheme was revived in late April 1941 when SOE sank a dinghy loaded with 2.4 tons of explosives in the canal. Unfortunately the charge failed to explode.[21]

On 15 August the Italians torpedoed the Greek cruiser *Helle* and as the diplomatic situation worsened, Pirie took over as full-time head agent. Section D began secretly supplying sabotage equipment to the Greek army but, wishing to preserve its anonymity, did so via the intermediary of the MI(R) representative, Major Barbrook. On 28 October 1940 the Italians finally launched their offensive against Greece. The network, now a part of SOE, successfully managed to carry out demolition in Salonica harbour, although work in Athens was prevented by the Greek government.

Crete

An embryonic joint Section D/MI(R) organisation was established on Crete by John Pendlebury, former curator at Knossos and now given the cover of vice-consul at Canea. George Taylor suggested that Section D should lay down dumps of demolition materials on the road from Canea to Mirabella and appoint local sabotage agents.[22] Subsequent events illustrate the confused early months of SOE. In October 1940, following the Italian invasion of Greece, Terence Bruce-Mitford and Jack Hamson also arrived on the island with supplies for an arms dump and an order to build a covert D organisation, as it was still termed. Although by now there was supposed to be a unified SOE, there was still a clear distinction between Section D and MI(R), according to GHQ Cairo. The latter decided that clandestine D activities would be restricted to the Greek mainland and Crete would be left in the more overtly military hands of MI(R), with Pendlebury operating openly in uniform. Brigadier Whiteley signalled 'D will not, repeat not, operate in Crete'. To overcome this stricture, Hamson and Bruce-Mitford installed themselves on a small island in the mouth of Suda Bay, from where they built up contacts on Crete and trained saboteurs for return to mainland Greece.[23] The British plans for clandestine operations on Crete are notable as being organised almost entirely by classical archaeologists!

Turkey

Turkey managed to remain neutral throughout the Second World War but Istanbul was a hot-bed of espionage from the warring nations. R.D. Bangay was head agent for Turkey until late June 1940, and from July it became the Section D HQ for Balkan operations under S.W. Bailey. The main effort within Turkey was to counter the efficient German propaganda effort. In April 1940 Professor Rushbrook-Williams of the Ministry of Information office in Istanbul asked Laurence Grand to provide a machinery for producing covert propaganda, believing that the MOI was too closely associated with the British Embassy to do this work.[24] In mid-June Rushbrook-Williams wanted the scheme extended to Iraq and Iran.[25] The budget for Turkey and Iran was finally agreed on 27 June and Reginald Barwell was transferred from Greece to Istanbul to manage the propaganda work as well as continuing to run his shipping operation. In August or September 1940 Denys Hamson was sent out to Istanbul to reinforce propaganda work in Turkey. He worked with the Ottoman Bank, whose management was sympathetic to the Allies, to develop a whispering campaign in Anatolia through its branches.[26] Hamson went on to work in Greece with SOE. At the same time Donald Mallett arrived to repeat his success in Romania and to set up a branch of *Britanova* as a more overt propaganda operation. A less successful Section D officer was George Lofoglu, a Greek who had worked for SIS during the period of British occupation in 1919–1923. He was sent back to Turkey in March under cover of being a special correspondent for *Reuters* and with a brief to build links with the Patriarch. Unfortunately, the real *Reuters* correspondents saw through his cover and threatened to resign. The Turks then discovered his previous history of working for the British and put him under close surveillance. He was eventually removed to Cairo in January 1941.[27] There were also attempts to link with groups in Turkey that would carry out sabotage in the Balkans on behalf of Section D. Sanction was obtained in July 1940 to work with a network of the Jewish 'Friends' in Turkey that offered to act in Bulgaria, with plans to sink four Italian tankers carrying Russian oil in Varna harbour and to blow up the railway tunnel between the ports of Varna and Ruschul. Nothing appears to have come of this plan.

Palestine

Mandatory Palestine was under British administration from 1920 to 1948. The Arab revolt of 1936–1938 had been suppressed with the aid of the paramilitary Haganah and their 'Special Night Squads' organised by Orde Wingate, but the claims of Zionists for an independent state of Israel remained politically sensitive.[28] In December 1938 Guy Burgess reported to Moscow that his first assignment for Section D was to 'work on the Jewish question and Palestine' with his friend Victor, Lord Rothschild, trying to create an alternative focus to the Zionist movement led by Dr Chaim Weizmann, President of the World Zionist Organisation and the future first President of Israel (Pl. 8).[29] It was hoped that a promotion of joint occupation by Jew and Arab would both calm Jewish–Arab tensions in the region and provide a buffer against Italian expansion into Egypt. In the end it was the Zionist groups that proved most useful to Section D, being the better organised. During the March 1939 Palestine Conference in London, Grand was instructed to meet unofficially with the leaders of the delegations. Although this attempt to bridge the Arab–Zionist gap failed, it resulted in a profitable dinner meeting between Grand, Bearsted, Lord Reading and Weizmann. Contact with Weizmann was maintained by Montagu Chidson, and Weizmann is reputed to have personally undertaken a number of minor missions on behalf of Section D at the start of the war. On 4 September Weizmann met with Foreign Minister Lord Halifax and offered assistance in the war effort in return for unhindered passage of Jewish agents between Britain, Europe and Palestine, and access to uncensored cables between London, New York and Jerusalem. With the principle accepted, on 21 September Grand met with Weizmann, David Hacohen (leader of the Haganah), David Ben-Gurion (head of the Jewish Agency) and Moshe Shertok (head of the political department of the Jewish Agency) to discuss how the Jewish Agency might cooperate with Section D in mounting underground warfare against the Nazis. Hacohen described Grand as being without prejudice in the complex problems involved in the relationship of Britain and the Zionist movement and as having great sympathy with the illegal immigration of Jews to Palestine.[30] As a result, Weizmann offered the extensive network of Zionist contacts, with Moshe Shertok as his representative in the Middle East.[31] The focus would be Palestine and the Balkans, using intelligence networks of the Haganah referred to as 'Friends'. In return, Grand agreed to significant concessions. The 'Friends' would retain their independence, giving them the right to refuse missions if they saw fit, with no interference in them assisting Jews to escape to Palestine or with the wider political ambitions of the Zionists.[32] The British authorities in Palestine were consequently assured that the frequent movements of Shertok and Hacohen in and out of Palestine were not suspicious and connected with illegal immigration, but they were, in fact, working for Section D.

A 'Friends' network was established in Romania and agents were also sent to Yugoslavia and Bulgaria to liaise with Section D in those countries. Section D officer P. Walkden in Budapest was also provided with contact details for the Zionist organisation in Hungary.[33] It was well understood that such an alliance might store up potential future political problems but for the moment all parties could agree that the priority was to defeat the Nazis. At the end of May Taylor triumphantly reported to Grand a further agreement with the Haganah on sharing intelligence with SIS:

> They have now offered in addition to place the whole of their organisation and all their influence at the disposal of the SS [Secret Service] for the collection of information in enemy or enemy-occupied territory, and in those neutral countries in Eastern Europe where there is intense enemy activity.[34]

In June the Jewish Agency's chief intelligence officer, Reuven Zaslani, became liaison officer to George Taylor while he was in Cairo, while in return the former Cambridge University archaeologist Arnold Lawrence was appointed liaison officer to Ben-Gurion and Shertok. Section D diplomatically avoided knowledge of the Haganah's wider plans but the two organisations shared ideas on possible projects against the Nazis.[35] It was agreed:

> the D/H organisation is to be regarded as an entirely separate entity from Friends (the Haganah) and while each is at liberty to make the maximum use of the corresponding organisation, they should in principle be separate, particularly in order to protect the interests of the Friends organisation.[36]

The arrangement was kept secret from the Colonial Office, Palestine authorities and Middle East Command but Section D provided an authorisation that prevented the local authorities from interfering with any of the Haganah's clandestine work on their behalf – in particular, giving the Haganah permission to stockpile weapons and conduct training. Section D supplied sabotage materials for the Haganah's secret weapons dumps, on the understanding that the dumps could be used by Section D if required. The Haganah also manufactured their own explosives and sold some to Section D through third parties to conceal their working relationship. They were also encouraged to establish contacts with Arab groups for possible future sabotage work in Iraq, Iran and Syria, which avoided Section D itself getting entwined in Arab politics. Although the practical results of the partnership with the 'Friends' during 1939–1940 were limited, Taylor was clear, in August 1940, as to the potential importance of the 'Friends' for the work of Section D in the region: 'I cannot make it too clear that I regard the maintenance of good relations with Friends as more important than any project, or anything else at all. They are our one really strong card.'[37]

Of especial sensitivity was the establishment in June of a joint sabotage training school for the 'Friends'. Section D provided a legal cover and instructors, whilst the Haganah provided the facilities. Section D officer Henry Barnes was said to be training 100 agents for distribution throughout the Middle East and the Balkans, as well as producing 'devices' through the Jewish Agency.[38] Some of the first trainees were Jewish agents sent to Romania to join the existing 'Friends' network and help organise the sabotage of the Ploesti oil wells alongside the Section D cells, as well as organising escape routes for refugees. Barnes also prepared a demolition scheme for Palestine in case of enemy occupation. He had been a film production manager who joined Section D in March 1940, aged 48, as an explosives instructor. He was regarded as a 'rough diamond' and individualistic, not to say cantankerous and quarrelsome. He returned to Britain in December 1941 and was then posted to India as an explosives instructor. There, despite his reputation as an explosives expert, he managed to first blow himself up with a Type 69 grenade and then burned his hand with a pocket time incendiary. He left SOE in July 1943.[39] No one was under any illusion that such sabotage training might later be used against the British to fight for an independent Israel. Speaking later of SOE, David Hacohen said:

> They undoubtedly knew that, in addition to operations against the enemy, we were carrying out operations and preparing plans for our own purposes, under cover of our cooperation with the British. A few of them even understood that these operations were a historic opportunity for us to advance our national needs. But care always had to be taken to avoid any clash between the two.[40]

Practical results in this period were thin and plagued with the same problems as beset most other schemes of British intelligence. Before their relationship broke down, Frederick Wedlake and David Hacohen hatched a plan to block the Danube with barges filled with 3,000 tons of scrap iron. A Greek cargo ship was chartered to sail from Haifa to Braila, where the cargo would be transferred to barges of the Goeland fleet by agents of the 'Friends', with the intention of scuttling them before they reached their destination in Budapest. In case the scuttling failed, some of the scrap iron pipes were filled with explosives. The cargo would then be sold to unsuspecting Germans in Budapest (the arrangements surreptitiously overseen by Alec Ross) so that, if the cargo ever reached Germany, it would explode in the smelting plants.[41] Loading began at Haifa on 26 June. Unfortunately, the 'Friends' over-estimated the strength of their organisation in Romania and the agents who were supposed to act as shipping agents on the

Danube panicked that the 'doctored' cargo would be discovered in heightened customs inspections. They fled, as did those who were supposed to receive the cargo in Budapest. Bad feeling resulted between Wedlake (already frustrated with the Jewish organisation in Romania) and Hacohen, which Taylor feared might sour relations overall with the 'Friends'. Wedlake described the 'Friends' as 'unreliable and muddlesome' and was removed. Hacohen then explained that several of their members, fearful of the deep-seated anti-Semitism in parts of the Balkans, were worried about working too closely with non-Jewish Balkan nationals. Reuven Zaslani said 'they would damn well have to take the risk' but, as a solution, Arnold Lawrence later suggested that all contact should be through British agents at the Consulates to insulate them from other groups.[42]

The desertion of the 'Friends' agents on the Danube meant that the ship was halted in Piraeus, Greece, until an alternative means of shipment could be found. While there, the 'Friends' agent David Hos, together with Ross from Albania, made desperate efforts to sell the cargo (via intermediaries) to representatives of German and Italian firms in Athens, but one German commented that they had secured enough scrap iron at Dunkirk to last them for two years. The situation became complicated when unsuspecting Yugoslav firms offered to buy the cargo at a higher price than that which was being offered to the Germans. The refusal to sell to neutral buyers was suspicious and in late August the scrap iron was off-loaded into a bonded warehouse at Eleusis and abandoned. It may have eventually served its purpose as the invading Italians requisitioned all scrap iron in Greece and sent it to Italy for re-smelting. It may then have exploded in some Italian smelting plant.[43] The confused organisation of the scrap iron operation was the final damning incident in Wedlake's reputation within the tension-ridden Cairo HQ of Section D and after recall to Cairo he left Section D to join the planning staff of the new Combined Operations.

Iraq

In June 1940 Professor Rushbrook-Williams of the Ministry of Information in Istanbul requested that Section D should extend its 'whispering campaign' to Iraq. The Treasury was, however, concerned that this would duplicate existing propaganda efforts. An exasperated letter followed on 1 July from St John Bamford of the MOI explaining that this issue had already been resolved and that Rushbrook-Williams 'points out that it is now two months since he began to press for "D"'s assistance'.[44] Jebb wrote to the Treasury on 16 July 1940 asking for the release of the funding but it had still not been provided to Section D, now in SOE, on 3 September.[45]

Abyssinia

Major R.C. Cliveley (Russian Section) arranged the return of Emperor Hailie Selassie to Egypt as a focus for future revolt but in June 1940 Grand concluded that although there had been some success in raising support from local chiefs, it was pointless trying to organise anything on a larger scale unless full support was given by the British government for raising a large-scale revolt against Italian occupation.[46]

*   *   *

In less than one and a half years Section D/H had created an organisation extending through a dozen countries across the Middle East, Balkans and Eastern Europe, with over sixty known staff, most of whom had little military or intelligence experience, with some shipped out immediately upon being recruited with no opportunity for training. It was forced into action without time to develop a sound organisation, system of training or a political consensus on what it was expected to achieve. Nonetheless, it created methodologies for sabotage and subversive warfare that provided the basis of such work for the rest of the Second World War, as well as making long-lasting contacts in the region. Many of the senior staff of SOE learned their trade in the section, including George Taylor. In early August 1940 he summarised the overall situation, recognising that there needed to be a brake on the earlier, frantic attempts at action in neutral countries:

> I now regard the principal function of D Section as that of preparing the way for the risings and revolts all over Europe in perhaps a year or two's time, which is in fact the only way in which we can ultimately defeat the Germans on the continent.[47]

The reversal of policy was too late. The work of Section D, however limited, had excited Churchill's imagination and led to his famous mantra to 'Set Europe Ablaze', even as such a policy was being rejected by those involved.

Chapter 8

Central and Eastern Europe

Czechoslovakia

The earliest instruction for Section D to plan specific sabotage came, according to Laurence Grand, in July 1938 when the Cabinet directed CSS, in the event of a German invasion, to 'blow up the Skoda Works at Pilsen' and Grand was ordered to explore the options.[1] He met with the Czech Intelligence Service and secretly visited the huge plant. A pyramid structure of sabotage agents was said to have been organised but there is no evidence that plans for sabotage at the Skoda Works had passed beyond a theoretical level before 17 September 1938 when large numbers of German troops moved into the Sudetenland. What Grand had promised during his visit is not clear but Peter Wilkinson later reported that the Czechs were disappointed by the level of support given by Section D at the time of the German invasion.[2] Grand again visited Czechoslovakia in October even as the Sudetenland was being surrendered to the Germans, and returned with the plans for the underground munitions factories at Zlin which were passed on to the Air Ministry and fed into the existing British plans for hidden 'shadow factories' as at Longbridge and Drakelow in the Midlands. Czech exile groups played a key role in Section D operations in the Balkans, and Sydney Morrell was appointed in Hungary specifically to liaise with the Czech resistance. By July 1940 Grand regarded the Czech resistance (along with the Slovene movement in Istria and Austria) as being the best organised in Europe. Led by General Hudecek and organised in cells of three persons, it was highly disciplined and well armed, but suspicious of making 'another gallant, but unsupported, sacrifice'.[3]

In July 1939 Colin Gubbins began to woo the exiled Czech intelligence organisation in Paris, but made it clear that the Czechs should act under MI(R) direction; in return, he promised to supply weapons and a wireless set to Czech contacts in Belgrade.[4] This was another attempt to usurp the role of SIS in operational matters and on 5 January 1940 Colonel Holland was obliged to clarify the responsibilities of MI(R) and SIS to Czech intelligence. MI(R), as a section of the General Staff, would be responsible for the coordination of Czech activities with the rest of the allied war effort, but the supply of wireless equipment and the delivery of supplies was in the hands of SIS through Section D. Gubbins was then asked to support a Czech plan to attach mines to German barges on the Danube. Gubbins wanted Peter Wilkinson to arrange for George Taylor (head of Section D/H) to supply the necessary plastic explosives and delayed action fuses but he had to admit that 'Actually all the above business is really "D"'s pigeon and not an MIR matter'.[5] It is clear that Gubbins was itching to take over the sabotage operations of Section D but there are hints that he was warned off pursuing the scheme by the Directorate of Military Intelligence, which was being asked awkward questions by the Foreign Office as to the nature of any British links to Czech intelligence. The Director of Military Intelligence, Beaumont-Nesbitt, was disingenuous to say the least in reassuring the Foreign Office of the innocence of MI(R).[6] In the end Wilkinson passed the proposal on to Julius Hanau in Belgrade, who was already working closely with Czech émigré groups. By 29 February 1940 there were more details of the Czech intelligence service scheme – which seemed to offer little in the practical sense, planning to use Yugoslav agents rather than their own men to carry out the work, with Section D providing the explosives 'and perhaps money'.[7] Discussions were still being held with Section D in April 1940 but nothing came of the plan. The main focus of official Czech intelligence was in strengthening its supply network within Czechoslovakia, but by this time Czech exile groups working with Section D were already carrying out a wide programme of sabotage across the Balkans.[8]

Hungary

Hungary (Fig. 4) was dismembered after the First World War and power fell to the right-wing Admiral Hotha, who ruled as regent. The influence of the Axis powers was strengthened by Germany and Italy restoring former territories to the country and the Hungarian police began working in ever-closer cooperation with the Gestapo. The prospects of keeping Hungary out of the war in 1939–1940 seemed slim and, as with the other Ministers in the region, Sir Owen O'Malley was criticised for his 'bitter opposition' to the work of Section D and later SOE.[9] Laurence Grand and George Taylor, whilst under no illusions over the prospect of ultimate success, took the view that Hungary was a necessary bridgehead for getting supplies into occupied Poland and that a propaganda campaign might at least delay Hungary's entry into the war.[10] In the event, in April 1941 Hotha supported the German invasion of Yugoslavia, although Britain did not formally declare war on Hungary until December 1941.

By September 1939 SIS had a network of twenty-one paid agents in Hungary. George Taylor's rambling Section D/H established its own substantial, but inexperienced, presence in the country, focused on supplying weapons and propaganda to neighbouring Poland and Czechoslovakia. As with Romania, there were only half-hearted efforts to designate a formal head agent, possibly for security reasons to avoid centralisation in a hostile environment. The first agents who arrived in October 1939, after brief training in explosives at Aston House, were the journalists Sydney Morrell (*Daily Express*) and Hubert Harrison (*News Chronicle*). In the case of Harrison, his newspaper still paid half of his existing salary. Morrell was regarded as the senior agent with a particular responsibility to liaise with the Czechs, while Harrison liaised with the Poles. They would also build up clandestine propaganda within Hungary. By the end of 1939 their propaganda, produced with the cooperation of the press attaché Frank Redward, had proved so successful that the Germans reputedly sent seventy-five agents to counter it.[11] But where the Germans failed, the British Minister succeeded; after repeated quarrels with Section D officers, he forced their operations to cease. Morrell left Hungary in April but by then virtually all of his Czech contacts in the country had been arrested. The operation to smuggle materials into Poland collapsed by the end of May after a bitter dispute with the Legation and the decision by MI(R) to slow down supplies to discourage premature action by the Polish resistance. Harrison left the next month.[12]

Basil Davidson was recruited to Section D in late 1939 and was sent to Hungary in February to further develop black propaganda within the country. Pointing out that he had never been to Hungary and did not speak the language, he was curtly told by George Taylor that there was a war on and he would do as he was told. Davidson later commented, with all the confidence of the Englishman abroad, 'but what are foreign languages, after all, except an irritation to be thrust aside?'[13] Davidson established his cover as a reporter for *Reuters* and then set up a branch of the *Britanova* news agency under the name of *Kulfuldi Hirek* ('Foreign News'). Within a month, Davidson was providing bulletins for ten Budapest daily papers, two weekly papers and five provincial papers. *Kulfuldi Hirek* survived until August 1941, although its work was closely monitored by the Hungarian government and it had to temper the pro-allied bias to the news. At the same time Davidson and his team produced and distributed an increasing amount of clandestine anti-Nazi propaganda, secretly printed at night in a government printing works:

A printer was found who was willing to do this work at night, when his plant was otherwise silent. A good Hungarian friend called George Páloczi-Horváth volunteered to write anti-Nazi leaflets, and very talented they were, while my Austro-Hungarian assistant organised a means of scattering them broadside. The idea was to suggest the existence of a large anti-Nazi organisation ... and at least we repeatedly stung the Arrow Cross newspapers to furious protest.[14]

The hope was that the false image of a substantial anti-Nazi movement might act as a brake upon the pro-Nazi sympathies of the Hotha government. The periodic tirades in the press against the 'underground trouble-makers' and the efforts made by the police to track down the source of the leaflets are a measure of their success.[15] In May 1940, with the support of the MOI, Grand secured a grant of £280 for a three-month trial period for undocumented propaganda work in Hungary but, characteristically, the Treasury delayed payment until late June.[16] Davidson was clearly also involved in political warfare and one day a parcel arrived for him via the Legation containing £500 in £5 notes. His instructions were simply that it was to be used for bribing politicians.[17] Some attempt was made to build contacts with the Hungarian Social Democratic Party and the Peasant Party but little could be achieved due to the scale of Hungarian surveillance on all opposition groups. Davidson's final success in Hungary, just as Hotha was assisting in the invasion of Yugoslavia in April 1941, was to arrange the evacuation of several of his propaganda staff, including Victor Stankovitz, the editor of *Kulfuldi Hirek*, to establish a freedom radio station broadcasting into Hungary from Haifa.

Although the official policy was not to engage in sabotage until Hungary joined the Axis, Ted Howe was appointed to prepare a sabotage network in the country, under cover as a journalist for the *London News*. His work, being especially sensitive in the post-war era, remains largely unknown, with just the briefest of mentions in official records. His assistant was a Serb, Nikola Kocijan, recruited by Hanau in Belgrade and sent by him into Hungary to build up a network of local activists using Davidson's contacts. In late April another officer, P. Walkden, was given contact details of the Zionist organisation in Hungary as a basis for possible future recruits.[18] This network did indeed mobilise after Hungary joined the German war effort but was wiped out in 1942, following an abortive attempt to sabotage the Györ armaments factory. Lajos Nadas, Davidson's former main assistant, was executed; Dezso Marton and Lásló Békeffi died in Dachau concentration camp. Other members of the network received sentences of twelve years' imprisonment. The existence of this early anti-Nazi resistance in Hungary was given little attention in the post-war communist era.

There was considerable opposition to the work of Section D and the rest of the SIS organisation from within the Legation, fuelled by MI(R). In October 1939 the military attaché, Lieutenant Colonel W.P. Barclay, wrote in almost conspiratorial tones to Gubbins about an emissary of a Polish resistance group who wished to be put in contact with SIS in Budapest. The reply included the following:

> Between you and me I mistrust PCS organisation [SIS] entirely as they always try and pinch anybody who may be of use for their undertakings without any consideration whether he might not be more useful elsewhere.[19]

The new assistant military attaché, Harry Blake-Tyler of MI(R), arrived in late April 1940 and immediately cultivated ministerial support to try to establish the supremacy of his role against Section D. His brief was to be 'chiefly concerned with the transit of stores and devices to Polish irregular organisations'.[20] Section D was the body that actually had the mechanism for transporting such materials but Harrison reported that when Blake-Tyler had first arrived in the country he had told Harrison (incorrectly) that he came with orders from Taylor to send him home. Blake-Tyler had then 'attacked him on the question of getting his supplies [redacted] saying that he should have developed safer means, and that he, that is Blake-Tyler, was busy doing so. D/H11 [Harrison] wished him luck and said he would help him in any way he could.'[21] This was Blake-Tyler telling

Harrison to go away! Worse was to come. Section D courier Andrew Duncan met with Blake-Tyler on 12 May. The latter was, at first, charming but then began a catalogue of complaints and urged Duncan to make a confidential report on the state of Section D in Hungary to the Minister, for forwarding anonymously to the Foreign Secretary. 'I began to suspect that Tyler's real aim was to get rid of the D organisation in Hungary', wrote Duncan.[22] Thwarted in this ploy, Duncan then accused Blake-Tyler of taking revenge by manipulating him into asking about potential contacts with 'Legitimists' and then making a complaint about this to the Minister. Duncan's inability to resist the temptation to tell Legation staff that he was a secret agent had already provided evidence of his indiscretion. Duncan was dragged out of bed to attend a ministerial meeting where the Minister, Owen O'Malley, exploded in typical fashion:

> The Minister then asked me what the D organisation was doing here, what value was its work anyway, and could we not operate from some other country.

O'Malley wrote to Lord Cadogan saying that he refused to have any further Section D activities in his Legation, including not only the storage of weapons and explosives awaiting shipment to Poland but also the production of subversive propaganda. Relations between MI(R)/Minister and Section D having broken down locally, Captain Douglas Dodds-Parker of MI(R) in London was left to find alternative means of supplying the Poles and sent a message to Blake-Tyler on 21 May, blaming O'Malley for the dispute:

> As existing method of delivery to Poles has broken down as result of YP's attitude now most urgent to push on with your alternative method of shipment so as be able to resume deliveries as soon as Poles can receive.[23]

Blake-Tyler's bluff had been called as he had to admit, in an irritated memo of 23 May, that he had not actually progressed any alternative ideas to those of Section D. He also realised there was a budgetary implication if he was to take over this work and he wanted to know if Section D would still pay the costs.[24] Without having time to establish the practicalities, he submitted a notional plan on the next day, involving shipping supplies disguised as crates of 'machinery parts' from Alexandria to the Free Port in Budapest, and switched on the Danube for genuine crates, with the explosives offloaded by Polish agents.[25] Peter Wilkinson commented that in late May 1940 he had to spend time dealing with 'one of those tiresome rows, typical of the intelligence community' with 'violent' telegrams being exchanged by Blake-Tyler and the established Section D representatives in Hungary.[26] Over the next week there was an evident concern to repair the damage between MI(R) and Section D at a higher level. In London, Taylor met with Jebb (Foreign Office) and Dodds-Parker of MI(R) over the matter. Taylor wanted MI(R) to call for O'Malley's request to ban Section D activities to be over-ruled 'for military reasons'. MI(R) could not support this, but it also had to acknowledge that it 'did not wish to damage relations with D/H in view of our dependence on him [Taylor] in other areas'.[27] By now, this dependence included Section D's contacts with sabotage groups, secret smuggling lines, and its supply base at Aston House. It had been intended to send out Francis Ogilvy as head agent to smooth relations with O'Malley but as the situation in France rapidly deteriorated, and an invasion of Britain became a distinct possibility, he was instead sent to organise the Home Defence Scheme in Scotland. It was agreed with Taylor that Blake-Tyler and the Minister be given a chance to try their alternative means of shipping materials into Poland, on the condition that if it did not work they would revert to the existing methods of Section D. As a measure of the agreement in London, it was Taylor who drafted the telegram for MI(R) to send to Blake-Tyler. The subsequent report by Dodds-Parker shows little sympathy for Blake-Tyler and the Minister having caused such problems: 'The Minister and B-T have their chance; it has not been necessary to coerce the Minister, though Jebb is willing. D/H is happy, having drafted the telegram.'[28]

Nothing came of the Blake-Tyler scheme and smuggling into Poland was run down by MI(R), although explosives continued to be smuggled into the Legation, to the later dismay of O'Malley. Faced with continuing opposition from the Legation, Section D agent Hubert Harrison left Hungary in June, a move which had major consequences for maintaining contact with the Polish and Czech resistance groups. Although Section D operations in Hungary were officially suspended in July, out of sight of the Minister, Ted Howe quietly continued to make plans for organising sabotage in the event of invasion. Davidson continued to produce his underground propaganda and, in concert with the SIS head of station, continued to discreetly fill the cellar of the Legation with explosives and limpet mines (brought in by Section D couriers using diplomatic bags). They were intended to be used to block shipping on the Danube following any German invasion. The military attaché discovered this in early 1941 and felt obliged to inform the Minister. Basil Davidson, now in SOE, was summoned before O'Malley, whom Davidson described as a 'gentleman of impeccable diplomacy whose views by now, well known amongst us, were that the war was probably lost and that, this being so, nothing should be done to make bad into worse, above all nothing irregular'. O'Malley was furious over this renewed exploitation of diplomatic immunity and berated the two agents:

> ... I at once ordered my military attaché to take this material and throw it into the Danube. He has done this. He has thrown it into the Danube, you understand. ... And I warn you now that if you attempt to bring in any more of such material, or in any other way act in this manner, I shall denounce you to the Hungarian police.[29]

In late August 1940 Grand argued to the new SOE that smuggling of sabotage materials and propaganda into Poland should be resumed. He also wanted to revive contacts with anti-Nazi elements in the Hungarian army which had been handed over to MI(R) but, Grand claimed, had not been pursued by Blake-Tyler. He stressed that rebuilding the organisation in Hungary could only be achieved with Foreign Office pressure on O'Malley to reverse his negative attitude towards subversive warfare.[30] Not surprisingly, there is no hint of the long-running feud between O'Malley and the intelligence services over the conduct of clandestine warfare in his autobiography, which puts his role in an altogether more positive light.[31] In the SOE history of Section D in Hungary, a special acknowledgement was made of the fact that Section D worked closely with SIS intelligence operations but otherwise the operations of Section D and MI(R) in Hungary were an organisational disaster.[32] The lack of a centralised system of networks and head agent may, as in Romania, have been thought to reduce the risk of enemy penetration but the lack of a strong leader was a severe hindrance, not least in dealing with the Legation. It is ironic that in Hungary the main threat to Section D was not the Gestapo but the British Minister and his assistant military attaché, the latter working for another branch of British intelligence.

Poland

In April 1939 Britain and France guaranteed to protect Poland's independence but the Hitler–Stalin Pact of 23 August, by giving Hitler the security of his eastern borders, precipitated the German invasion of Poland on 1 September, which in turn led to the British declaration of war against Germany on 3 September. The German invasion had been long-expected; by April 1939 both Section D and MI(R) were encouraging and supporting the development of the Polish guerrilla forces being formed by Major Charaskiewicz.[33] Small sabotage teams of three to seven men, organised in districts of seven to twenty-five patrols, would go to ground in areas of occupation following invasion, using pre-prepared arms caches, whilst larger partisan bands would raid across the front line. By July a training school had already trained 800 men. The methodology was a clear inspiration for what became Section D's standard plan for multi-layered resistance, as proposed for Norway, France, Britain and Romania during 1940, as well as for Gubbins' Auxiliary Units in Britain.[34]

Details of Section D activity in Poland is sparse, and surviving documents have been heavily redacted.[35] In July 1939 a party from the Polish General Staff, including Charaskiewicz, met in London with Section D and MI(R), prior to the re-formation of the British Mission to Poland. The Polish delegation took back with them supplies of explosives and delay devices from Section D, as well as a copy of Gubbins' *Partisan Handbook*. In the expectation of war, Section D began organising lines of supply into Poland from Scandinavia. This included Walter Wren's mission to set up direct communication lines for supplying propaganda and sabotage materials from Sweden, using Alfred Rickman's dental supply company as a cover (*see below*, p. 148).[36] Polish Intelligence remained fiercely protective of its autonomy throughout the war and was deeply suspicious (with good reason) of the motives and commitment of the allied powers. Colin Gubbins of

MI(R), head of the Polish Mission in Paris, took a similarly proprietorial attitude to the country and on 28 January 1940 he wrote to Peter Wilkinson complaining that Grand was 'playing about with our Poles'.[37] There had initially been co-operation and on 1 January 1940 Gubbins wrote to the Polish Legation in London, asking a contact to arrange an introduction for 'a friend of mine, Captain Fraser' to the Polish resistance HQ in Stockholm, as Fraser was engaged on work 'with which I am intimately concerned and of which you are aware'. Ingram Fraser was head of the Section D Scandinavian section and Gubbins asked that the Polish military attaché might be 'prepared to work in complete frankness with him immediately he arrives'.[38] The British military attaché in Stockholm, Reginald Sutton-Pratt, suggested to Fraser that he could divert some time-delay mines from a War Office contract with the Swedes, for Fraser to give to the Poles.[39] Gubbins became nervous of the burgeoning relationship of Section D and Sutton-Pratt with the Poles and on 7 April 1940 he wrote a terse complaint about Section D impinging on MI(R) interests – frustrated by the fact that he still had to rely on Section D to get material shipped into Poland via the 'wild men' of the Social Democrat and Trade Union groups who did not necessarily acknowledge allegiance either to the Polish or the British General Staff. Gubbins staked the claim of the Polish General Staff and the Polish Mission to pre-eminence:

> I have a clear-cut agreement with the Polish General Staff, in accordance with the instructions of the DMI [General Beaumont-Nesbitt], that all preparations for activities within Poland must have the agreement of the Polish General Staff and ourselves, and that all planning, demands for stores etc. should be worked out in collaboration. ... If we allow wild men to act independently they will get out of hand, and either amuse themselves with private feuds or provoke incidents before the proper time. ... I don't want to cramp your style in any way, and am very grateful for all the help you have given and are giving. But the official ruling in the W.O. [is] that as far as the Poles are concerned, we <u>control</u> and F[raser] and his master and colleagues <u>act as our agents</u>. Would you, therefore, very kindly in future send demands for materials direct to me; these I will check with the Polish G.S., and will then arrange delivery through F[raser] ... I ought to have given you a note on general policy before, but did not know that F[raser] was pushing ahead so fast; more power to him provided he doesn't exceed his charter. You had better destroy this, but it would be as well to tell Fraser that in future your demands will come direct to us, giving him the reasons.[40]

Britain's Polish Mission and the Polish General Staff had agreed that sabotage within Poland should be curtailed until circumstances favoured a general rising, with the priority being to build up supplies of weapons and explosives within the country, the main supply routes being through Romania and Hungary. It took time to properly appreciate the requirements of clandestine forces. In February

1940 Peter Wilkinson of MI(R) delivered arms to Polish contacts in Hungary on behalf of Section D, including a dozen large .45 calibre revolvers. Although concealed within bags of diplomatic mail, the box for the revolvers had been coated in creosote for water-proofing and Wilkinson commented that his sleeping car on the luxury Orient Express began to smell like a rabbit hutch.[41] When he finally reached Budapest the Polish contact complained that the revolvers were too heavy for the use of couriers and that .45 ammunition was unobtainable in Poland. To Wilkinson's chagrin, the contact therefore proposed to dump them in the Danube.[42] The Poles wanted short-barrelled .32 or .38 automatic pistols that could be unobtrusively slipped into a pocket.[43] The lesson was well learned. The iconic weapons of SOE became the .32 automatic pistol (Pl. 30) and the British Sten gun, the latter deliberately designed to break down easily into concealable parts and using continental 9mm ammunition. Up to 21 April 1940 Section D had delivered to the Poles either directly or through MI(R) the following items:[44]

4 wireless transmitters
130 revolvers
6,500 rounds .45 calibre
1,000lb high explosive (plastic or blasting gelatine)
200 pressure switches
600 delay action fuses
500 incendiary bombs

Grand, still believing that the Nazi state was fragile and liable to imminent collapse, was clearly frustrated by the official 'go slow' policy. His fear may well have been that if the Nazi occupation collapsed, and there was no active resistance, the Soviets would simply expand their area of occupation. On 20 January 1940 Peter Wilkinson wrote a hasty letter to Gubbins at the Polish Mission in Paris. At the time Wilkinson was attached to D/H under Taylor and was effectively MI(R)'s liaison officer with Section D. He warned Gubbins that the idea of the Poles spending a year in preparation before taking action,

does not suit D's book. He [Grand] sees in the Polish activities an opportunity for an immediate dividend. ... I saw an instruction from him to his agents in Budapest to say that, although the Poles had evidently received orders from their Headquarters to go slow, his agents were to do all they could to make them reconsider this decision.[45]

Grand remained determined to support the continuing resistance in Poland and to ensure that groups were adequately armed ready for any future rising. In June he called for assurance for the full support of the British Legation in Hungary to resume the smuggling of arms into Poland and requested that British long-range aircraft begin dropping supplies. He even wanted to contact the Russians to organise smuggling of arms into German-occupied Poland, using the argument that a victorious Germany would inevitably lead to the loss of Ukraine to Russia.[46] This may have been the context for Burgess's abortive mission to Moscow (*see below*, p. 145). Grand recognised that the Poles had already suffered so badly that a revolt would only take place if they were convinced that it was part of a general movement across Europe. The conundrum was that, by then, the Poles might be in such a starved condition that they would be able to do little to help.[47] In the meantime the focus shifted to sowing discord between the German and Russian occupying forces. The 5 July meeting of ISPB, attended by Grand and Holland, concluded: 'D Section was requested to investigate the possibilities of stirring up strife and murder between the Russian and German guards in Poland.'[48] This double-edged policy was in line with the intentions of the Polish 'Musketeers' resistance group and explains the interest in the links forged with it by SIS from Hungary.

Hungary was a key transit point for smuggling funds, weapons and explosives across the border into Poland and Czechoslovakia. Hubert Harrison organised the shipment of materials into Poland via couriers carrying diplomatic bags, the explosives then being smuggled across the border by the official ZWZ Polish resistance (the later Home Army). Unknown to the Minister, Owen O'Malley, the explosives were stored in the Legation; more were later stored in the flat of Section D agent Christine Granville. In early December 1939 George Taylor recruited, on a six-month trial and for a total cost of £250, the refugee Polish socialite, journalist and amateur tobacco smuggler Krystyna Gizcyka, born Krystyna Skarbek but better known by her later alias of Christine Granville. This followed an introduction from Section D propaganda officer Frederick Voigt, whom she had known for several years. She had arrived in London from South Africa with her Polish diplomat husband Jerzy Gizcyka on 6 October and had immediately sought out British intelligence. After meeting her at the Lexham Gardens safe house, the then second-in-command of the Balkans section, Leslie Sheridan, described her as 'a flaming Polish patriot ... a great adventuress ... absolutely fearless'.[49] Granville had a charisma that seemingly caused men to melt merely upon her approach, and she was evidently an accomplished actor. During an interrogation by SOE in December 1942 she left the impression of being timid and fragile, successfully acting out the role of a helpless woman who would burst into tears at the slightest criticism to excite sympathy.[50] She also admitted a fondness for telling tall stories and this has contributed to the growth of her legend as a secret agent.[51] The unreliable Kurt Singer labelled her as 'Churchill's master spy', grossly distorting the facts by claiming that she parachuted into Hungary and then served for eighteen months in Poland, organising resistance cells, sabotage groups and prison escapes.[52] On such early fiction was her legend based.

Granville already had what was described as a 'distant connection' to another Section D agent recently returned from a mission to Bulgaria, former Polish intelligence agent Jósef Radziminski. A note explained that she had worked with him previously and that he 'will do anything for her and with her'.[53] Granville offered to write a propaganda leaflet for distribution in Poland which inspired Taylor to think about expanding the existing propaganda work within Hungary to that of directly distributing propaganda in Poland. It was decided to send Radziminski and Granville to Budapest to work under Hubert Harrison and to establish new communication lines for propaganda into Poland, separate from those used for smuggling sabotage materials. Radziminski was sent out to Budapest first, on 13 December 1939, under cover as a reporter for Hulton's *Picture Post*.[54] He would be the cut-out between Harrison and Granville. She was an unknown quantity and it was stressed to Harrison that, as far as possible, she should be quarantined from other agents:

> ... she should not see you or A/H1 [Radziminski] or any other member of our organisation at all, unless there is absolute necessity for this, and that when such meetings occur, they should be arranged with every possible caution.[55]

This was a vain hope. Granville not only had affairs with three other agents in Hungary but also became a frequent visitor to the British Legation. Nonetheless, there was some success in quarantining her from the rest of Section D operations; she knew Basil Davidson as a journalist and berated him for staying in Budapest and not joining the war effort, unaware at the time that Davidson had been working for Section D in Budapest for as long as she had.[56] She also recognised one of Harrison's drinking friends as another British journalist, Ted Howe – but did she realise at this stage that he was the chief Section D sabotage agent in Hungary?

Following basic instruction in explosives at Aston House, Granville arrived in Budapest on 21 December, under cover as a French journalist, 'Madame Marchand'. A small flat, including a maid, was provided. Harrison was one of the few men whom she could not win over and probably as a consequence she dismissed him as an indiscreet alcoholic. He particularly annoyed her by using her flat as a dump for explosives in transit from London to Poland. Granville's task was to establish links with Polish resistance groups and set up communication lines for the delivery of allied propaganda and funds, in return bringing out intelligence on the state of the country. There were immediate problems with Polish Intelligence and Gubbins' Polish Mission in Paris. Polish Intelligence objected in principle to Poles being employed by a foreign intelligence service and on his visit to Budapest in February, Peter Wilkinson of MI(R)/Polish Mission tried to warn off Harrison and Goodwill from trying to send a Section D mission into Poland.[57] In order to break the deadlock, Taylor and Sheridan came to Budapest and a grudging agreement was finally reached with Polish Intelligence but Grand warned CSS that further problems might be brewing.[58] The Polish Intelligence liaison officer in Budapest refused to give Granville any contacts in Poland and warned her that 'because she was in the pay of the English' she was no longer a trustworthy Pole. With Polish Intelligence having made it difficult for her to contact the official resistance, she was also warned that 'any movement in Poland which is not our movement is an enemy one'.[59] In 1940 the Polish resistance was not united under what became the Home Army and there was considerable suspicion of the 'official' resistance supported by the Polish General Staff. Granville was still eager to go and it suited SIS to maintain alternative channels of communication with Poland. The viability of the Polish government-in-exile was still an unknown quantity, and even more important than the material Granville would take into Poland was the intelligence that she might be able to bring back. Here, the work of Section D might provide SIS with a convenient buffer against any complaints of espionage from its 'sticky' Polish allies.[60] Granville would soon find herself trapped in the mutual suspicion between the Polish and British intelligence services.

A more personal reason had arisen which made it desirable to send Granville to Poland as quickly as possible. On 11 March, the day of her departure, Grand noted 'her attractiveness appeared to be causing some difficulty in Budapest'.[61] Radziminski had become infatuated with her and when his attentions were rebuffed, he threatened to shoot himself in his genitals; he shot his foot instead. Still distraught, he threw himself into the frozen Danube, breaking his good leg.[62] Polish Intelligence now refused to work with him and Taylor decided he would have to be recalled.[63] He returned to England in late March but attempts to deploy him in other parts of Section D failed; he went to France and eventually helped organise the escape of French PoWs into Vichy France. Granville had already formed what was to be a life-long romantic affair with childhood friend Andrzej Kowerski (later known as Andrew Kennedy). He was attached to the Polish consulate, organising an escape route to Yugoslavia for Polish servicemen held in Hungarian internment camps. Whilst waiting for approval for her mission into Poland, Christine helped Kowerski break out further Polish prisoners and after Radziminski had been sent back to London, Granville recommended Kowerski as his replacement.

Granville stayed in Poland for five weeks but her report was of mixed value: mis-information and exaggeration raised questions as to her reliability and seemed to validate the concerns of Polish Intelligence. She had, for instance, claimed that 10,000 Bavarian troops had been imprisoned in railway carriages for an attempted rebellion before being taken out and shot. It was also hinted that it would be easier to organise sabotage in the Russian rather than the German occupation areas.[64] When she arrived in Poland, the official ZWZ resistance had been wary and instead she contacted a rival group. The 'Musketeers' had been founded by Stefan Witkowski in October 1939 and travelled a murky and controversial path.[65] They had a range of German contacts and had even infiltrated the *Abwehr*, which installed some of their members as agents in Soviet Russia. For SIS, this was a potentially important asset operating across Poland, Germany and Russia, but for the Polish General Staff such links were evidence of collaboration. For Witkowski, both Germany and Russia were enemies and he would play one off against the other. Granville became caught up in the intrigue and added to the complication by bringing back another lover, the ZWZ courier Vladimir Ledóchowski. Over the next few months Christine managed to balance affairs with Kowerski and Ledóchowski, while in London Section D was deflecting enquiries about Christine from her husband Jerzy.

In Budapest, Granville became a reception point for couriers of the 'Musketeers' and a contact with the Polish Socialist Party, but she was concerned that Harrison seemed offhand with her information. She was not to know that London was already worried about her reliability, whilst the value of any intelligence originating from the 'Musketeers' had been queried by the Polish General Staff, which claimed that its competitors were working for the Germans. There were suggestions of recalling her on the excuse of wishing to discuss her ideas for a Polish Freedom Radio Station. Arthur Goodwill (deputy head of D/H) admitted he was a fan of Granville but, 'If I am wrong, the sooner we part the better.'[66] Her legend could have ended there, but the instruction to return to London did not reach Granville until after Harrison returned from an extended trip to Belgrade, by which time it was impossible to obtain a travel visa.

Harrison left Budapest for good in early June, leaving Granville without a controller. She made two further attempts to enter Poland in June but both failed. Her position as a Section D agent was now ambiguous as her trial contract expired on 15 June, not least meaning she received no further payment. In late June Archie Gibson, then SIS head of station in Bucharest, recommended that Granville and Kowerski be sent back to Belgrade.[67] This did not happen and Section D finally reported losing contact with Granville and Kowerski in August. It was not until 1 December that Goodwill (now representing SOE) dispatched a telegram trying to establish Granville's whereabouts 'as she has not been referred to recently in either telegrams or dispatches'.[68] Who exactly was controlling her work in the intervening period remains unclear and confused by the fictionalisation of her activities. Kowerski claimed they blew up a barge on the Danube using limpet mines but there is no independent corroboration and such an act would be remarkable given the antagonism of their new patron in the Legation, the Minister Owen O'Malley, towards sabotage in Hungary. Their main activity appears to have been in assisting British and Polish PoWs who had escaped from Poland to reach Yugoslavia, funded by O'Malley. Wilkinson later said O'Malley 'seems to have fallen a victim to Mme's well known persuasiveness', while his daughter Kate later had a brief affair with Kowerski.[69] These relationships coloured O'Malley's praise of Granville's work in Hungary. Granville made no further attempt to enter Poland until mid-November. This was a different type of mission, attempting to rescue 18 British PoWs hiding in Warsaw (although they were found to have left before she arrived). Her unofficial contacts with Polish resistance groups, including the 'Musketeers', continued in Budapest through the autumn and winter of 1940 and it is possible that SIS quietly maintained contact with Granville, allowing its staff to continue to gather intelligence from the independent Polish resistance, against the wishes of the Polish General Staff. During October Granville passed on to Archie Gibson (now in Istanbul) details of a new Polish resistance organisation, along with its radio frequencies and communication codes, but no immediate action was taken. In view of the suspicion surrounding Granville's links, there may have been fears of exposing SIS's wireless network to a German deception scheme, but for whatever reason, de Chastelain (now in Turkey with SOE) did not request SIS to make wireless contact with this group until 10 March 1941.[70] Wilkinson later adopted a tone of righteous indignation over the matter, firmly putting the blame for the delay on Gibson. He reported on 27 April 1941 that Granville had been 'very badly let down by 15,000 [Gibson] and that her communication with Poland no longer existed'. He concluded, 'they have been treated extremely badly both by 15,000 [Gibson], by D Section and ourselves [SOE]'.[71] Granville and Kowerski were forced to flee Hungary in January 1941 and then handed to SIS in Sofia a further collection of intelligence, including microfilm that showed the build-up of German armour along the Russian border – crucial evidence of the impending German invasion.

Granville and Kowerski eventually made their way to Cairo but found an air of suspicion surrounding them in SOE, caused by a difference in opinion between those former officers of Section D and the Polish Mission over the policy to be taken towards the Polish resistance. George Taylor, now Chief of Staff in SOE, was trying to reactivate contact with the 'Musketeers' in a continuance of Section D operations, to the horror of ex-Polish Mission officers Gubbins and Wilkinson. In May 1941 a conference with General Sikorski in London finally agreed that only those Polish resistance groups owing allegiance to the government-in-exile would be supported by SOE. Consequently, Wilkinson instructed de Chastelain (now deputy head of SOE Balkans in Turkey, with responsibility for Polish liaison) to break off all contact with those independent groups with whom Section D had been in contact.[72] De Chastelain described the decision as being beyond his comprehension.[73] Having been served a catalogue of complaints by Polish Intelligence, who claimed the 'Musketeers' had been infiltrated by the Gestapo, Wilkinson recommended that Granville and Kowerski be suspended.[74] His subsequent meeting with the pair on 10 June was uncomfortable. It was not helped by the fact that Kowerski, to prove their bona fides, suddenly gave Wilkinson a 'forgotten' microfilm that Granville had been given by a Polish contact four months earlier.[75] Only later convinced of their loyalty, Wilkinson put the ultimate blame for their treatment on the Poles, concluding 'they deserved better of their fellow countrymen'.[76] Taylor was clearly upset at the treatment of his former agents, repeatedly pressing for their re-employment. In August 1942 he telegrammed, 'I would make clear we are under strongest obligation to X [Granville]. And I have personally given my word that we will not let her down again as we did in Budapest.'[77] Only slowly were they rehabilitated and it was not until July 1944 that Granville was eventually dropped into occupied France, where her exploits made her one of SOE's most famous agents. At the end of 1941 the 'Musketeers' did join the official Polish ZWZ resistance organisation (Home Army), but Witkowski refused to hand over details of his agents in Germany and Russia and was charged with treason in maintaining independent contacts in both the German and British intelligence services. He was executed by a squad of the Home Army, disguised as Germans. His killers were subsequently shot by another dissident Polish group.

Russia

The Soviet Union had long been the traditional target of British intelligence. The Hitler–Stalin Pact of August 1939 and the subsequent Soviet invasion of Poland brought fresh concern, followed by British indecision as to whether to intervene in Finland against Russia. Section D had a small Russian section (D/V) led by two veteran agents. In charge was Richard Cliveley, who had been involved in espionage against Russia from the early 1920s. He was joined by George Hill, who had spied for SIS in Russia during the First World War. In April 1940 Hill was trying to recruit agents for the Russian section from the refugee community but the section appears not to have progressed far, although it remains a possibility that records were culled during the Cold War.

One of the strangest incidents in the history of Section D was the abortive mission of Guy Burgess to Russia in July 1940, accompanied by his friend from Oxford, the Latvian-born philosopher Isaiah Berlin, who was clearly part of the cover story, later admitting not knowing the true purpose of the mission.[78] Berlin believed he was going as a press attaché to the Moscow Embassy, but the Foreign Office later denied any knowledge of such an idea and indeed said that at the time they were trying to prevent the 'intolerable' Berlin making any visit to Russia.[79] Burgess was assisted in his arrangements by Gladwyn Jebb of the Foreign Office (usually very cautious in anything connected with Section D) and Harold Nicolson of the Ministry of Information. Berlin visited Grand before departure and Stewart Menzies, the CSS, was also fully appraised of the plans.[80] Despite such high-level involvement, the Foreign Office, SIS Passport Control and SOE all later denied any knowledge of the mission.[81] Most of the records were destroyed and MI5 later concluded 'the reason or pretext for [this trip] had never been known'.[82]

At the time, Burgess was working on broadcast propaganda with the Section D front organisation, the Joint Broadcasting Committee (JBC), giving him a liaison role with Electra House and the Ministry of Information. He also cultivated close contacts with members of the Foreign Office. Consequently, Burgess managed to appear very busy without doing a great deal and offered plenty of confusion as to where he gained his authority. He was to travel to Russia under cover as a diplomatic courier but Berlin had no agreed official status. Burgess claimed that the intention was to propose that the Russians would arm non-communist resistance groups in the east and in return Britain would arm communist groups in the west.

It was an unlikely scenario but Grand was greatly concerned at this time with the problems of supplying the Polish resistance from British-controlled territory. Alternatively, Russian sources say that the idea came from Valentine Vivian of SIS to contact the Comintern and influence them against the Germans.[83] Burgess had no apparent qualifications for such high-level negotiations and there is no mention of the involvement of Cliveley's Russian section. Grand may have been carried away with Burgess's enthusiasm but the participation of CSS and Jebb remains an odd endorsement. In any event, after Burgess and Berlin had arrived in the USA, Burgess's behaviour caused such a wide range of concern that on 27 July he was recalled to London.[84] Diplomatic circles clearly felt he would be too much of a liability to the already fraught Anglo-Russian relations (not realising, of course, that Burgess was a Soviet agent). Burgess returned to Britain on 30 July and then joined George Hill in establishing the Section D Training School at Brickendonbury. Isaiah Berlin was abandoned and remained in the USA, working for the British Library of Information.

Chapter 9

Scandinavia

Scandinavia was important for its supply of iron ore and steel products such as ball-bearings, and for control of the North Sea. Nonetheless, Section D operations in the region were not extensive and the account is distorted by the failure of a single sabotage mission (*Operation Lumps* in Sweden). The latter is considered here in some detail as it had a great impact on the reputation of Section D and the surviving documentation provides a unique insight into the politics of its operations. Ingram Fraser headed the small Scandinavian section (D/G), being particularly concerned with Sweden (where Alfred Rickman was head agent), assisted by Gerard Holdsworth in Norway. Both were former advertising executives and the absence of a core of experienced intelligence officers was to prove an enormous handicap.

Sweden

Sweden had a tradition of neutrality, but it also had close economic ties to Germany and bad memories of the British economic blockade during the First World War. Whilst the British War Cabinet agonised over the issue of neutrality and the risks of precipitating Scandinavian retaliation or German invasion, Section D used Sweden as a gateway for running propaganda and sabotage materials into Poland and Germany and waited impatiently for clear direction on more direct action. There were three principal bottlenecks that might restrict the flow of iron ore to the enemy. The ore field in the far north had exits via Luleå into the Baltic and via Narvik (Norway) to the North Sea. The ore field to the south of Stockholm exited through the port of Oxelösund on the Baltic Sea. The plans for disrupting the ports of Narvik (*Operation Arctic*) and Luleå (*Operation Sub-Arctic*) never materialised but that for Oxelösund (*Operation Lumps*) was to have a far-reaching impact on the future of Section D.

Sweden had an efficient counter-espionage service and its close surveillance of any possible foreign espionage, and a lack of cooperation from the Swedish government, meant that Section D operated in a very different environment from that of the Balkans. To weaken their watchers, Section D tried the character assassination technique that had proved successful in Yugoslavia. Karl Lindquist, in the security section of the defence staff, was a known pro-German and Section D tried to frame him as being in their pay. On 16 March 1940 Ingram Fraser warned that, 'We are endeavouring to perpetrate a slight frame-up in order to compromise his position, which is very unhelpful to us.'[1] A letter of thanks to

Lindquist was posted from Germany, enclosing a sum of money but 'accidentally' addressed to Bertil Lindquist in Stockholm, who was a journalist and would hopefully pursue this invented story of police corruption.[2]

In July 1938 Alfred Rickman, aged 36 and estranged from his wife and family in Australia, was recruited to Section D. According to Cruickshank, Laurence Grand had asked Rickman's father (a barrister's clerk) if he knew of a bright young man looking for a job.[3] Rickman had no obvious qualification for intelligence work but had travelled widely in Australia and Canada, and then across Europe as business manager for the Jack Hylton Band. He became an assistant with Korda's London Film Company, from where he was recruited by Grand to gather intelligence on the Swedish iron ore industry. The fact that he knew nothing about either Sweden or the iron ore industry was not seen as an impediment. Rickman began a two-week tour of the Swedish ore fields and ports, under the cover of gathering material for a scholarly book. His work was well received within SIS, with his first report in October 1938 containing a detailed analysis of working practices at Oxelösund, Luleå and Narvik, and an analysis of future sabotage targets. *Swedish Iron Ore* was published in 1939 and established Rickman's cover and credibility as a legitimate 'expert'. In a slip of security, an entry of 21 March 1939 in the Faber & Faber ledger mistakenly identified the author as 'L.D. Grand'.[4] The Swedish press later described the book as displaying 'a profound knowledge of everything related to iron ore and further reveals an astonishing knowledge of shipping conditions in Swedish ports'.[5]

This cover had served its purpose and when Rickman took up permanent residence in Stockholm in July 1939 as head agent in Sweden it was as an entrepreneur whose businesses would allow him to travel across Scandinavia, with links into Poland, and disguise the transport of propaganda and sabotage materials. Walter 'Freckles' Wren was responsible for the initial oversight of Rickman, using his commercial background with AGA Ltd and its subsidiary, Jayandeff Ltd, as a cover, but it was Ingram Fraser, a suave Scot, who then became head of the new Scandinavian section. Fraser was a former advertising executive who went on to work with British Security Coordination in the USA. Fraser reported to Grand on 4 September that he and Rickman had discussed the range of possible sabotage targets at the ports and on the transport network, envisaging that saboteurs would be drawn from sympathetic trade unionists and organised by the German, Hermann Knüfken (*see below*).[6] The SIS head of station (John Martin) would be the main communication link, although he was working to a different agenda.[7] The military attaché, Reginald Sutton-Pratt, also worked closely with Section D; he was later denounced as having provided training in explosives and, falsely, as 'directing' its work.[8] Rickman assumed the role of managing director of A.B. Dental Material, dealing with Poland. Another trading company, Skandhamn A.B., would deal in tinned goods, acting as an agency for Wren's firm of Jayandeff. This was seen as a possible way of smuggling explosives from Britain into Norway and Sweden, hidden in sealed tins but unfortunately the experiments failed.

A subsidiary office was opened in Oslo under the Norwegian Section D agent, Helmer Bonnevie (*see below*, p. 168). As his workload for Section D increased, the need to maintain Rickman's cover meant that Section D had a new burden in having to process the legitimate shipments of goods between Sweden and Norway to reduce a stream of customer complaints for non-delivery of goods.[9]

Propaganda

In May 1939 Ernest Biggs, a British expatriate who had lived in Sweden for sixteen years, responded to an enquiry from Sutton-Pratt for anyone in the British colony who had experience in propaganda. Biggs (who had lost a leg during the First World War) was advertising manager of the PUB department store in Stockholm and had extensive contacts in the printing and publicity industry across Sweden. Sutton-Pratt forwarded Biggs's details to Rickman, who arranged a discrete introductory meeting in July whilst Walter Wren was on a brief visit to Stockholm (whom Biggs believed to be merely the financier of Rickman's business). In return, Wren invited Biggs to a supposed advertising conference in London during August, where he was recruited to Section D and returned to Stockholm as Rickman's principal assistant for propaganda, at a salary of £35 per month. Wren then passed on overall responsibility for Sweden to Ingram Fraser, who introduced Rickman to several refugees from the German Social Democrat Party who were contacts of Karl Otten's LEX group. Gottfried Bermann-Fischer, born in Silesia in 1897, had been obliged to move his influential publishing house to Sweden in 1938. Immanuel Birnbaum was a journalist, originally from Konigsberg, who worked with a Swedish producer of anti-Nazi propaganda – although well-respected, he later proved to be a German spy. In November Fraser and Rickman also met Arno Behrisch, a typesetter and trade union organiser for the International Transport Workers Federation, who agreed to cooperate in producing and distributing propaganda and later became the key sabotage agent of the network.

The first leaflets were supplied from England (Pl. 11), but the network soon began to produce its own, written as if by Swedes, highlighting the danger of the Nazis to Sweden and supporting the transit of allied troops to Finland. One had the headline 'Neutrality? Nonsense! We are doing more than any other neutral country to prolong the world war and benefit the dictator states.'[10] Rickman's network also tried to get propaganda into Germany, written in partnership with the members of the German SDP, on the proviso it was directed at the destruction of the Nazi Party rather than Germany itself. Behrisch persuaded the foreman of a printing works to allow his printing presses to be used secretly at night and other contacts would then pass the bundles of addressed envelopes containing the leaflets to couriers in Denmark. The skipper of a German ship then smuggled them into Germany where they would be posted at various locations. One was addressed to a friend of Behrisch in order to confirm that they were actually being delivered. This contact also reported that five copies of the booklet

Alles fürs kind ('Everything for the child'), an appeal to German motherhood to oppose the Nazis, were handed into the Gestapo in Munich, who concluded that they seemed too well made to have been printed clandestinely in Germany (Pl. 14).[11] Subsequent material was more crudely produced to disguise its true origin. During January 1940 alone, Rickman claimed that 43,000 leaflets had been sent to Germany. Such figures are impossible to verify, but in April 1940 the police discovered address lists for Essen, Breslau and Dresden in Rickman's flat, together with postage stamps and 3,000 addressed envelopes. There was also one of the Section D chain letters.

One of Biggs's contacts was Ture Nermann (Pl. 24), the forthright anti-Nazi publisher of the newspaper *Trots Allt* ('In Spite Of All'). From December 1939 he allowed Section D to use his printing press and to produce a small newspaper in German, but John Martin of SIS already knew that Nermann's organisation had been infiltrated by Swedish police. Kurt Singer, an Austrian Jew who was co-editor of *Trots Allt*, had been a police informant from as early as September 1938 but his controller was himself an informant for Martin. Martin's self-interested concern was to protect his source in the Swedish police and his eventual warnings to Section D were circumspect, allowing police penetration of Rickman's network to escalate. The fact that Nermann was under police surveillance was reported to Rickman in late January and he was then successfully marginalised as far as knowledge of Section D's wider work was concerned. In February Martin reported that Ingram Fraser had been observed by the Swedish police meeting Biggs and Nermann, fortunately known to them only by his alias of 'Mr Forster', but Section D still believed Martin's warning was only of a general surveillance.[12] Martin did not reveal that there was actually an informant within the organisation until 21 March, when he finally admitted that he had known Singer to be a police informant for at least eighteen months. Martin then made an extraordinary admission:

a) 36920/C [Singer] is employed by 36-land W.B. [Swedish police] and I have known this for at least 18 months

b) It is perfectly certain that everything which 36920/C has himself learnt about D.1's organisation [Rickman] is now known to 36-land W.B.[13]

In November 1939 Martin had agreed to supply Rickman with any information that seemed important to Section D operations but this clearly did not extend to his knowledge of Singer's betrayal and cooperation continued to be poor, requiring Stewart Menzies (CSS) to write unofficially to Martin in March, asking him to afford Section D full cooperation.[14] By then, the damage had been done. One redeeming feature was Section D's security practice of creating shadow networks. Another of Karl Otten's contacts, Erich Brost, a former German-Polish publisher from Gdansk but now in Stockholm, was given a fake contract from Bermann-Fischer's publishing house to write a book which provided cover for him to write propaganda leaflets; assisted by his wife Margarete, he became another centre for distribution into Germany. Brost's network did not come under suspicion until August 1940, when he fled to England and worked for the BBC.

Section D and the Ministry of Information (MOI) worked closely on propaganda in Sweden. From March 1940 Section D secretly organised the publication of the magazine *Fronten*, funded by the MOI.[15] In April the MOI agreed that Section D would produce a series of leaflets for Sweden and Norway at a rate of one a week and with a print run of 10,000. Section D would write the material but would submit inspection copies to the MOI.[16] In return, Grand provided significant funding for the official propaganda work of the press attaché, Peter Tennant. Despite denying all knowledge of Section D in his 1992 autobiography, Tennant met with Fraser and Holdsworth during April to discuss the production of propaganda by Biggs and Rickman, and urged them to increase the volume of production.[17] This included working with a pro-allied society in Sweden, the Friday Club, to revive a social democratic and pro-allied newspaper, the *Aftontidningen* ('Evening Newspaper') which would aim at a daily circulation of 75,000, in return for a start-up grant of £10,000.[18] The German invasion of Norway gave an urgency to the project and on 21 April (before he learned of Rickman's arrest, *see below*), Grand secured permission from the MOI to tell 'his people' to go ahead immediately, before any final authorisation from the Treasury.[19] Tennant later managed the scheme as an honorary, if apparently unknowing, member of Section D.[20]

Sabotage
Sweden was a hub for shipping sabotage materials into Norway, Poland and Germany, as well as for possible use in Sweden itself. It was originally intended that Hermann Knüfken (*see above*, p. 57), the exiled German ex-communist member of the International Transport Workers Federation (ITF), would organise the smuggling of sabotage materials from Sweden into Germany, linking into surviving ITF cells in Germany who would then hopefully provide a source of sabotage agents. He was, however, already well known as an agitator and as a British agent to the Gestapo, who advised Scandinavian governments to the effect that he was 'a most dangerous and active agent'.[21] He was also disliked by communist trade unionists, who were to oppose his work in Sweden. Believing him 'blown', the then CSS, Admiral Sinclair, initially vetoed his appointment but in the urgency following the outbreak of war, Knüfken was sent to Sweden on a forged Danish passport in the name of Karl Knudsen, freelance journalist, and at a salary of £40. For security, he was not to contact either the new Rickman network (at this stage envisaged as dealing mainly with propaganda) or the British Legation. But in November Knüfken contacted a German seaman, Otto Wagner, who had information on the movement of the battleships *Scharnhorst* and *Gneisenau*, as well as intelligence on hidden German aircraft factories. The information seemed sufficiently urgent for him to break procedure and to try to pass the information back

to London through the Legation. He tried to contact SIS under the pretence of applying for a British visa but one of Martin's Swedish staff in the passport control office, called Melin, recognised the Danish passport as a fake. Melin was another informant of the Swedish police and had a deep dislike of Danes. Knüfken was arrested and in his flat were found postcards of Swedish iron ore ports (Pl. 25). He was sentenced to five months' hard labour for travelling on a false passport, unlawfully collecting information and for breaches of hotel regulations.[22] It had the effect of placing more responsibility for sabotage on the Rickman network, with disastrous consequences. To their relief, Knüfken never implicated his Section D masters, thanks in some part to the fact that Chidson managed to conceal that he had been betrayed by an official at the British Legation. Knüfken remained interned until early 1944, when he was flown to England. Press Attaché Peter Tennant delivered messages to him whilst in prison but was unaware of his history with Section D, referring to him only as the 'mysterious man with the iron mask'.[23]

Martin was told about Melin's part in this affair by his police informant but again took the view that he could not act against him without exposing his source. Martin's own efforts at espionage proved no more successful. He recruited only ten agents and in January the coast-watching service he had established in October to record the tonnage and movements of German ships was discovered and five agents were arrested and imprisoned, including the head of the network, the Swede Erland Lind (British vice-consul at Ornsköldsvik), and Donald Beach, an English advertising executive in Stockholm who was revealed to be Martin's contact. They were convicted in late February of espionage and sentenced to terms of hard labour.[24] The prospects did not look good for any espionage attempts by the British.

Operation Lumps

The port of Oxelösund, 100km south of Stockholm, could handle 600,000–900,000 tons of ore per month and, although amounting to only 13 per cent of Swedish production, this was the highest grade of iron ore, making it especially valuable. In October John Dolphin (Section D targeting officer) produced the first assessment for *Operation Lumps*. He recommended that action be taken within the following six weeks whilst the port was frozen in and not fully staffed. His initial plan included the sinking of two fully laden ore ships at the wharves and the scattering of pieces of 'exploding iron ore' (ore doctored with explosives) into the rail shipments coming into the port to deter railway men from handling the cargo. The ships would be sunk with limpet mines, and incendiary bombs then used to ignite the escaping fuel oil.[25] The stakes were high, not least because of the risks of Swedish retaliation by ceasing to supply ball-bearings to Britain, and this was an operation planned at the highest levels of government. Unfortunately, the scheme was to be a catalogue of disasters from the start, and one from which no one involved emerges with any credit. Churchill, then First Lord of the Admiralty, was characteristically in favour of decisive, if illegal, action. He euphemistically wrote on 22 December that the supply of ore from Oxelösund had to be stopped by 'measures of a non-diplomatic and non-military nature'.[26] The Chiefs of Staff were also in favour, but recognised the political implications. It was then that the inability of the Cabinet to commit to a clear course of action resulted in its ultimate failure. Despite Churchill's enthusiasm, there was protracted unease within the Cabinet in acting against the neutral ports. By contrast, Churchill even saw advantage in any retaliatory invasion of Norway and Sweden by Germany, in allowing British forces to seize the northern ore fields. Stewart Menzies, the new CSS, became personally associated with the scheme, which was later to cause an embarrassment that rebounded onto the whole future of Section D.

At this time, the guard on the dock at Oxelösund was slack and all work ceased at 11.00pm, leaving cranes and loaded ships vulnerable. The sabotage was to be carried out by foreign nationals to avoid a diplomatic incident with Britain, with Rickman's role at this stage being only to store and supply the necessary explosives. On 4 November the first consignment of explosives, fire bombs and 'hot boxing' powder, hidden in a large suitcase in the back of Helmer Bonnevie's car, was delivered to Rickman by Fraser at a midnight meeting on the outskirts of Stockholm. The material comprised:

15lb plastic explosive
25 × 40-minute relays
25 × 2.5 hour relays
7 magnesium flares
100 detonators
2lb potassium chlorate
50 'cigarettes' [small time delay fuses for use with chemical explosives]
1lb fine emery powder
1lb coarse emery powder
1 (unspecified) Bickford fuse[27]

The range of material makes it clear that this was not just intended for use at Oxelösund but for a wider sabotage campaign, including ore transport by rail. The shipment was first hidden in Rickman's flat.[28] Rickman assured his girlfriend, Elsa Johansson (originally the receptionist at the hotel in which Rickman had first stayed in Stockholm, and later his private secretary), that the new plastic explosive was perfectly safe. Biggs was even more casual and asked if the explosive could be disguised as modelling plasticine, in which case he was prepared to keep a large supply in his flat, disguised as sculpture.[29] Later sabotage materials were mainly imported in diplomatic bags or in large crates marked 'Library consignment – books for the Military Attaché'. The weight of the crates was carefully adjusted, using paper-filled boxes, to match the expected weight of books. They were then transferred to the warehouse of the Windsor Tea Company, Stockholm, a firm part-owned by Ernest Biggs. Rickman hired half of the warehouse and concealed the material behind a wooden partition wall. On 6 January Sutton-Pratt reported the successful, if somewhat theatrical, transfer of one of the shipments of 'Library Books' in another midnight rendezvous outside Stockholm: 'We had great fun with the books – real Edgar Wallace stuff "in a dark dirty wood at midnight". R [Rickman] as a French chauffeur.[30]

In December a simpler, if less effective, alternative for attacking the two rail-mounted cranes and conveyor belt on the quayside was proposed. Sutton-Pratt was not convinced that it was worth the risk (preferring a scheme to entirely block access to the port).[31] The new plan received the eager approval of Churchill on 2 January 1940 but was countermanded two days later in a meeting of the Prime Minister, the Foreign Secretary, Lord Hankey and Stewart Menzies. It was agreed that further reconnaissance should be conducted on the site and a meeting on the same day was held between Fraser, an SIS officer identified as 22000 (Charles 'Dick' Ellis, head of the SIS 22000 organisation) and businessman William Stephenson (who had established a private intelligence network in Sweden).[32] The 22000 organisation was another shadowy network created by Sinclair at the time of the founding of Section D and recruited agents from business, journalism and the academic world for intelligence-gathering missions in Germany and Italy. The input of Stephenson in *Operation Lumps* was to introduce his friend, the pro-allied Swedish industrialist Axelsson Johnson. The latter owned a shipping line, was a major shareholder in Swedish iron ore mines, owner of the railway that ran from the mines to Oxelösund, and an adviser to the Swedish government. Stephenson naively over-estimated Johnson's potential involvement; although he was prepared to offer discreet advice, he would not risk his business empire to become more actively involved. Fraser and Stephenson agreed that the revised Dolphin plan was practical and a further meeting between Fraser, Ellis, Stephenson and Menzies on 8 January decided to send Fraser and Stephenson to Stockholm to reconnoitre the site and to bring back a final plan for War Cabinet approval.[33] Crucially, the meeting also agreed that, if the scheme could be carried out with minimal expense, 'it might be deemed advisable to carry out the attack without official sanction'.[34]

Menzies briefed members of the Cabinet on 17 January but misrepresented the tenor of his earlier meeting with SIS officers and Stephenson, suggesting that 'a prominent Swede' (Johnson) would organise the destruction of the gantry cranes, in which case 'the probabilities of failure were in his opinion very small'. He was hopeful that the Swede would also agree to carry out simultaneous sabotage at Luleå and Narvik. The alternative was that 'certain anti-Nazi Swedish societies' (i.e. Swedish and German Social Democrats) would carry out the sabotage, but with a substantial increase in risk. Although agreeing in principle, the Cabinet meeting asked for the sabotage to be delayed until the spring thaw, so giving less opportunity for repairs before the port would reopen.[35] But other dissenting voices were raising concern. A report of 10 January warned that the sabotage of the cranes and conveyor belt might only delay transport by two months.[36] This hardly seemed worth the political risk but a momentum, driven by Churchill and encouraged by Menzies, had been established that made it difficult to completely abandon the scheme even though Prime Minister Chamberlain wavered each time a decision was required.

On 22 January, with Knüfken now in prison, Fraser introduced Rickman and Bonnevie to *Operation Lumps*. Arno Behrisch was chosen as the chief saboteur, in return for a payment of 10,000kr (which he said would be used to support German anti-Nazi refugees in France).[37] With the harbour still frozen in, the machinery was idle and there were no guards or workmen on the quay. Fraser recommended immediate action, without waiting for agreement on plans for Narvik and Luleå, or for the end of the winter freeze. He stressed the point: 'Conditions never, repeat never, more favourable. Strongly urge your immediate authorization.' On the basis of the tacit approval given by Menzies on 8 January, Fraser ordered the sabotage to proceed, using Behrisch and two other German Social Democrats. The plan was for 15lb of explosives, hidden in canvas bicycle pannier bags (shown in Pl. 26), to be planted on each crane leg, with a time delay of 1.5 to 2 hours.[38] Behrisch, perhaps with good reason, had doubts as to whether this would bring down the cranes but was reassured by Fraser (a former advertising executive rather than an engineer or demolition expert).[39] Even while reconnaissance was in progress on 29 January, Menzies informed Fraser that a meeting with the Prime Minister and Foreign Secretary had refused to give final authorisation.[40] The postponement had a disastrous effect on Behrisch's morale and Fraser had to report to Grand, 'He no longer considers our organisation serious.'[41] With some difficulty, Rickman and Fraser managed to convince him to persevere but on 31 January Fraser, with a clear air of desperation, sent a personal telegram to Menzies pointing out that if the sabotage was not to be carried out immediately, then it would probably prove impractical.[42]

The argument continued. A Section D report, based on Stephenson's opinion, was that an attack on Oxelösund might not precipitate an invasion as feared, but that if the Allies proceeded with their plans to send troops to Finland, then the Germans would undoubtedly retaliate. The port therefore needed to be destroyed in a pre-emptive strike.[43] Seemingly convinced, formal permission to proceed was at last granted on 5 February.[44] To bolster flagging morale, Rickman decided to take part as driver. Behrisch would enter the quay with a contact identified to the British only as 'Dago', later identified by Behrisch to police as Rudolph Halbe (which may have been an assumed name). 'Dago'/Halbe was an SDP member who had fought in the Spanish Civil War and whilst there had an 'unfortunate experience' with British intelligence. Consequently, Rickman had been introduced to him as a Czech, although this fooled no one.[45] After setting the charges with a four-hour time delay, Behrisch and 'Dago' would leave a note giving directions on how to reach the target, written in Russian, at the quay in the hope that Soviet agents might then be blamed for the whole affair.[46] But the saboteurs arrived to discover that work was now in progress on a fully illuminated quay and the task was impossible. They returned to Stockholm, by which time Fraser had already left the country as part of his alibi.[47] Undeterred, they planned to return on the following weekend when it was expected that the port would be closed.[48] But the mood had already changed once again in Whitehall and whilst Grand sent his congratulations to Rickman for having made the attempt, he also ordered him not to take any further action without fresh orders.[49]

A new opportunity for success seemed to arise when the Swedes began one of their periodic round-ups of suspected communists, which would strengthen the deception that vengeful communists were responsible for any sabotage. Behrisch was briefly included in this swoop, but claimed that the Swedish police had subsequently lost interest in him. With the risk of an early spring thaw and the opportunity to blame Russia for the sabotage, Menzies again pressed the Foreign Secretary for final approval to proceed, but with no success. An exasperated Churchill summoned Grand to a meeting to explain the delays and, as a result, on 8 March Lord Hankey met with the Prime Minister and Foreign Secretary to finally agree that the scheme should proceed. With great relief, Grand sent a message to Rickman: 'Go ahead. Good hunting. Good luck.'[50]

There was, however, new frustration in Stockholm. Rickman had just discovered that the real reason for the arrest of Behrisch was that part of his payment for the Oxelösund mission had been discovered by the police. Behrisch had given it to a Swedish friend for safe-keeping but the house of the latter was raided in the search for a suspected communist. The bundle of money was discovered, left in a book borrowed from Behrisch with his name on the flyleaf. Behrisch denied all knowledge of the money, but the circumstances were clearly suspicious and the police believed the money had originated from Russia.[51] More concerned than he had earlier cared to admit to Rickman, Behrisch took advice from the committee of the German Social Democrats, admitting that he was involved in a British sabotage plan. The already disillusioned 'Dago' successfully argued that the risks of the Swedes discovering that they were working closely with the British to destroy a major Swedish asset were too great. Threatened with expulsion from the Party, Behrisch abided by this decision and the attack was cancelled. To Lord Cadogan, this was proof of the unreliability of foreigners. He minuted, 'I am afraid this is symptomatic and ominous.' Equally, Rickman admitted that the German SDP members had become nervous of 'our vacillations, incorrectness of information, and instructions to act at short notice'.[52] Undaunted, Fraser sent a message to Rickman: 'Too bad about hitch. Try again.'[53]

Despite his Party's concern, Behrisch offered to provide two other German veterans of the Spanish Civil War, not linked to the SDP, to carry out the sabotage but this was rejected.[54] Frustration reached new levels. Rickman concluded a report to Fraser on 15 March: 'For —— sake don't cancel our authority to proceed.'[55] Almost inevitably, this crossed with an instruction from Fraser: 'Prevent further attempt.'[56] Fraser's deputy, Gerard Holdsworth, arrived in Stockholm on 16 March to review the chaotic situation, with the conclusion that the only possibility of success seemed to be for Rickman, Bonnevie and himself to carry out the sabotage themselves. Menzies refused permission for British involvement, but Fraser suggested trying to recruit some willing Finns.[57] An offer from Sutton-Pratt to go to Finland to try to find volunteers was 'categorically refused' by the Minister.[58] A thoroughly disillusioned Rickman now believed that Fraser did not fully understand the problems of planning the attack or the impact of its conflicting instructions:

> We are very fully conscious of the urgency and necessity for action and the utmost is being done to hasten matters. It is possible however that the exigencies of the case as we see it may differ considerably at your end. Your advice on the subject has not since extended beyond 'do the job'. ...

Rickman wanted confirmation that the scheme really was considered urgent and important. If so, 'against my better judgement as to the chances of success in such circumstances – an attempt <u>will</u> be made.'[59] He asked whether the sabotage should be attempted 'at all costs' but the simple answer in the margin of the letter was 'No.'[60] Instead, Behrisch was asked to try to arrange sabotage by ITF union members from the port, with Rickman standing by to mount a 'sudden separate attack' in case this failed.[61]

The explosives store at the Windsor Tea Company had become an increasing risk. On 23 March Fraser advised that a new Swedish law restricting the import of tea and coffee meant that warehouses holding these goods were likely to be inspected by customs officials. Instead of ordering an immediate removal, Fraser told Rickman that new transit boxes were being made up and that a new location would be decided in the next few days.[62] In the meantime, on 30 March a new shipment of explosives was hidden in Rickman's flat – leading to future calamity.[63] Warnings of the impending German invasion of Norway brought a new tension to the situation; on 6 April Grand ordered the dispersal of the explosives to several smaller dumps scattered between Stockholm and the Norwegian border, ready for use by resistance forces in Norway or Sweden. At the same time the ice thawed at Oxelösund and ships began to leave in increasing numbers for Danzig and Stettin.[64]

On 9 April Norway and Denmark were both invaded by Germany. Fraser was captured whilst in Copenhagen and although released on the strength of his diplomatic passport, it brought added consternation. Fearing for the fate of Sweden, Rickman sought a last desperate way of undertaking the Oxelösund mission, which may have diverted him from the task of dispersing the explosives store. Ignoring previous strictures against the use of British citizens, Rickman and Biggs contacted a party of eight young English aircraft flight mechanics who were on their way back to Britain, having delivered Gloster Gladiators to the Finnish Air Force. Rickman asked for three volunteers for a 'risky job' – warning them that if caught by the police, the British Legation would not be able to help. As an incentive, the men were offered a payment of 1,000kr, and a promise of a further

£500 each when they returned to England.[65] Rickman hoped their involvement might be capable of being excused as a spontaneous operation by young hot-heads, ignoring the fact that, although travelling as civilians employed by the Gloster Aircraft Company, the men were, in reality, members of the RAF who had notionally resigned before proceeding to Finland. Rickman chose James Inward, Leslie Martin and Joseph Sayce for this last attempt on Oxelösund. It is not clear how far London was aware of this arrangement but on 11 April Rickman received a message from Grand: 'Following for D.1. from D. . . . Go right ahead. Good luck.'[66]

A final reconnaissance undertaken on the evening of Friday, 12 April was yet another disaster. The party – comprising Rickman, Johansson and the three mechanics – discovered that the gantry cranes were being operated day and night, loading ships ready for the port to fully thaw. The defences had also been strengthened. Whilst searching for a new entry into the port, their car slid into a ditch; surrounded by onlookers, it had to be pulled out by lorry. With any future alibi slipping away, their movements were then recorded at a military checkpoint. Thoroughly depressed, they returned at midnight to find yet another change in policy.

Following Fraser's arrest in Denmark, Holdsworth had been rushed from London to Stockholm to try to coordinate plans for a Norwegian resistance and to ensure that the Oxelösund sabotage would be carried out upon any invasion of Sweden. He arrived at the Legation on the morning of Saturday, 13 April to find papers already being burned in anticipation of the Germans' arrival. Sutton-Pratt and Martin both advised Holdsworth that the attack on Oxelösund was 'a lousy idea', despite Sutton-Pratt's recent offer to recruit saboteurs from Finland. Without any authorisation, Sutton-Pratt had decided to forestall the attempt by refusing to honour an earlier agreement to supply petrol for the mission.[67] This was to have unexpected consequences and once again a message from London put preparations for the Oxelösund operation on hold.[68] In the meantime Holds-worth was given a herculean task list for the small Scandinavian section, being urged to recruit 'some real toughs who don't mind taking chances', to arrange a labour strike on the docks, produce propaganda to protest the weak reaction of Sweden to the Norwegian invasion, and to create a Norwegian resistance and a mobile Free Norway wireless station.[69] Undeterred, Holdsworth asked for pistols, a wireless transmitter and incendiaries, intending to create three arms dumps 100 miles apart – one remaining in Stockholm, a stock of limpet mines on the south coast ready to attack German ships, and a third dump near the Norwegian border. The diplomatic situation was extremely tense and finally an order came from the Ministry of Economic Warfare to cease all operations in Sweden.[70] The Windsor warehouse explosives store still needed to be dispersed, but because of Sutton-Pratt's unilateral attempt to stop the previous attempt on Oxelösund, Rickman did not have enough petrol to do so immediately.

As a result of Kurt Singer's information and intercepts of German intelligence (*see below*), the Swedish police had been tapping Rickman's telephone and intercepting his post since 23 February. To Rickman's credit, this had revealed nothing of the Oxelösund plan or the store of explosives but it did place any contact with him at risk.[71] Rightly suspicious that Rickman's flat might be under surveillance, Holdsworth stayed his first night in Sweden in a hotel but, having been reassured, returned to stay the next night with Rickman, thereby linking the two men. Holdsworth had been sent in such a rush that his courier's passport was due to expire and he needed a new cover to stay in Sweden. He therefore proposed the creation of a relief fund to support Norwegian refugees, with himself as organiser. Harry Gill (an executive in the Anglo-Iranian Oil Company) was a 'cut-out' between Rickman and Sutton-Pratt, but was now instructed to break contact with the rest of the network in order to become Holdsworth's assistant in the relief fund. Holdsworth also moved out of Rickman's flat into the Grand Hotel. But before making the break complete, Gill was asked to help in finally moving the explosives dump to Ludvika, where Elsa Johansson had found a suitable cottage to rent as a hide-out.

On Wednesday, 17 April Rickman took two suitcases of explosives to Gill's flat, ready to take to the new dump by train the next day (not having enough petrol to go by car). For some reason, the move had to be postponed until Saturday, 20 April but Holdsworth now suggested that Gill should not go, afraid of compromising the cover of the relief fund. Rickman agreed to take back the explosives in Gill's flat on the evening of Friday, 19 April but he never kept the appointment. When Gill telephoned for an explanation, the cautious tone of Elsa's reply suggested that the police were present. Gill warned Holdsworth and removed all incriminating evidence from his flat, including the explosives, to the safety of the British Legation.

Gill was correct. The Swedish police began their wave of arrests of the Rickman network on the evening of Friday, 19 April. Martin's carefully protected police informant gave no warning, claiming he was engaged on German surveillance at the time.[72] The police first raided the A.B. Dental Materials office on Nächströnsgatan where they found Rickman and Johansson, together with propaganda material and four empty suitcases. Moving on to Rickman's apartment in Gärdesstaden, the visibly shocked police found gelignite, safety fuses, detonators, pistols and other sabotage material, together with a die used for forging police stamps, all being stored overnight before the intended transport to the new store at Ludvika. The police inventory of the material comprised:

6 suitcases containing 53.6kg (118lb) of gelignite
2 electrical timers
11 electric detonators
2 chisels
1 box of nails and screws

1 case containing banknotes to the value of 28,285kr (Swedish), 750kr
   (Norwegian) and 35kr (Danish)
3 pistols and ammunition
1 map of Oxelösund and three picture postcards of the port
3 Swedish passports
1 official police stamp for endorsing passports
1 manual on explosives
miscellaneous correspondence about sabotage and propaganda
   (SIS correspondence files)
1 black notebook containing notes and SIS identification codes[73]

Worse was to come. One of Rickman's employees told the police that Rickman
rented warehouse space from Biggs at the Windsor Tea Company.[74] Biggs was
arrested just before midnight; although nothing incriminating was found in his
house, this was all to change when the cellar of the Windsor Tea Company was
searched the next day. There were further arrests on the morning of Saturday,
20 April, including Holdsworth. He had presumably been seen at Rickman's flat.
He was released after less than an hour, his being the one identity which Rickman
withheld during his interrogation, and still having the protection of his temporary diplomatic passport. In the cellar of the Windsor Tea Company the police
found a further 69.4kg of gelignite, 57.3kg of plastic explosive (some disguised as
German plasticine), 8 limpet mines, 320 magnesium fire-bombs and a wide range
of other sabotage material, including Bickford fuse, potassium chlorate, carborundum tablets and powder (Pl. 26). The news of a large explosives store within
Stockholm shocked the public, who were also titillated by the news of the
personal relationship between Rickman and Johansson. What made matters
worse was that Donald Beach's court case from Martin's coast-watching spy ring
came up for appeal in the midst of the arrests, raising the profile of Britain's
unsuccessful espionage activities even further. The Minister, Victor Mallet, fearful of the Swedish reaction, was outraged at the way his Legation had been compromised and ordered the remaining sabotage materials held by Sutton-Pratt in
the Legation to be dumped in the river.[75]

Gill was not arrested until 3 May. He revealed nothing, but in the process of
interrogation it was clear he had been incriminated by Rickman and Johansson
and that the Swedish police now knew the full details of the Oxelösund affair.[76]
He was kept for two months in solitary confinement but was eventually released
with a fine of £15 for passing on messages to the espionage ring.[77] The eight air
mechanics were detained for questioning but Rickman had already given up the
names of James Inward, Leslie Martin and Joseph Sayce as being those involved
in the plot. The three were interned and the rest deported. They were only freed
after an exchange deal with German prisoners. In all, fourteen people were
arrested, although most were quickly released.[78] Bermann-Fischer was held for
five weeks and then emigrated to the USA.

The arrests increased the pressure on Holdsworth to establish the credibility of his cover story. He wrote to Grand: 'It must, Master, otherwise Humble Servant is in most peculiar position.'[79] The Lord Mayor of London eventually announced the launch of the 'King Haarkon Relief Fund' on 30 April with the Foreign Secretary, the archbishops of York and Canterbury and the Norwegian Minister in London as the principal sponsors. With wry humour, one of the first contributors listed in *The Times* on 2 May was 'Mr Graham' – *aka* Laurence Grand. Suspicions remained about the true nature of his activities and Holdsworth was clearly an embarrassment when he visited the Legation: 'If I were a charge of concentrated small-pox, I don't think they'd look much paler.'[80] The arrest of Gill on 3 May brought fresh risk and on the following day Holdsworth returned to his hotel to be warned by the receptionist that the police were waiting for him. Taking no more chances, he fled to Finland and thence back to England, where he first helped organise the Section D Home Defence Scheme in East Anglia and then established the sea transport service, before having a distinguished seaborne career with SOE (Pl. 7).

Remarkably, the long-standing surveillance of Biggs and Rickman over their propaganda operations had provided no clue about *Operation Lumps* (because all correspondence about it went via the Legation). The lead to the Windsor Tea Company explosives store only came on the night of the arrests. The sabotage scheme had therefore been viable to the end and the most damning evidence of British espionage came after the event, from Rickman's utmost carelessness in keeping the Section D correspondence files and codes in his flat, and from the fulsome confessions of the participants. Nonetheless, the arrests were indeed a triumph of Swedish counter-intelligence, with some help from the Germans. On or before 11 April, German agents had intercepted a British diplomatic bag containing material from Rickman.[81] Fraser and Rickman regularly exchanged detailed reports and if this bag had contained any such correspondence then the enemy could have passed on an alert to the Swedes. Taking no chances, the arrest, on 13 April, of Immanuel Birnbaum swiftly followed. He was not only a member of Rickman's propaganda network but also a known German spy in the SD. Birnbaum had been introduced to Biggs by Fraser in late 1939 to advise on propaganda. He was a well respected Austrian journalist of part-Jewish descent and a long-standing member of the SDP, with contacts to the LEX group. But on 8 February censors had intercepted the first of a series of letters from Birnbaum, using the signature 'Kant', to a Berlin PO Box, addressed to a 'Mr E. Kutzner'. The contents included the following passage:

> Contact with my Uncle Richard whom you have heard about, has hitherto been of little value though I feel it is promising for the future. The old chap is very suspicious and as far as he is concerned, has little to gain from his contact with me but I hope to have closer contact with his family and thus be able to win his trust as well.[82]

This was sufficiently enigmatic for the letter to be tested for invisible ink and an underlying message led straight to Rickman:

> After sustained effort, I have succeeded in determining the various members of the 'Secret Service' here. I managed to do so by getting in touch with a former acquaintance who is now in London. He divides his time between here and Norway and is in charge of an organisation for English propaganda directed against the Reich. He stamps the material here with German stamps for subsequent distribution within the Reich. ... Rickman is afraid of the Swedish authorities and camouflages everything. At present his interest is focused on Malmo. In my accounts about him I will call him Uncle Richard. Perhaps through him I shall have a chance to go to England, where I am now mobilising other acquaintances (the Press, Foreign Office).[83]

The message suggests that Birnbaum's ultimate goal was to use the Rickman contact to secure a move to Britain. At this stage he confirmed only what the Swedish police already knew regarding Rickman's propaganda work, but a letter of 8 March went further, with a warning that Rickman believed the month of May could be 'pretty turbulent' in Sweden and Norway, suggesting that Germany might not be able to obtain the same 'economic advantages' as hitherto. This hint at possible sabotage plans still did not provide enough evidence to mount an arrest. Circumstances changed following the German invasion of Norway: the Swedes could not afford further risks over Rickman's plans and it was Birnbaum's interrogation that finally prompted the arrest of Rickman and the others.

Birnbaum's explanation of his actions changed over time. First, he admitted coming to Sweden in October 1939 to collect evidence against German anti-Nazis. He then claimed to have acted under duress, persuaded in November by a German agent, Wolfgang Horst, to provide information on allied activity in Sweden so as to protect his children's future and avoid deportation.[84] Only later did Birnbaum try to maintain that his information was intended for the anti-Nazi news agency editor E. Kutzner, for whom Birnbaum had worked in Poland (and who was executed by the Nazis in 1943). At the end of the war the interrogation of Sturmbannführer Gronheim confirmed Birnbaum's identity as an agent of the Nazi security service, the *Sicherheitsdienst* (SD).[85] 'Kutzner' may have been Hans Wilkens, the Gestapo agent who from early 1939 had run a network of double agents in the Netherlands attempting to infiltrate British intelligence through émigré groups and thereby insert agents into Britain. He was now in Berlin and was known to use the alias 'Kutzner'. On 15 May 1940 Birnbaum was sentenced to eight months' hard labour for espionage on behalf of Germany. Dr McKay has concluded that this was a man whose whole career was rooted in German culture and who despised Hitler. At the same time (as certain of his former socialist friends in Stockholm believed) he was a man who, when his part-Jewish heritage deprived him of his life-style as a prominent German journalist and commentator, had succumbed to the temptation of working for German intelligence in an attempt to restore his status.[86] (Thousands of other Germans of part-Jewish descent were similarly torn as to where their loyalties or self-interest lay and around 150,000 men of part-Jewish ancestry served in Hitler's army.) At the end of his sentence the Swedes wanted to deport Birnbaum but, as a so-called 'mischling', the Nazis refused to accept him. In April 1942 he was transferred to the Smedsbo internment camp and then to a refugee centre. Eventually the deportation order was revoked and during 1945–1946 he worked for several Swedish newspapers. He eventually returned to Austria and successfully rebuilt his credentials as a progressive journalist and lecturer.

On 28 June 1940 Rickman was sentenced to eight years' hard labour but was released in 1944 on health grounds. Elsa Johansson received a sentence of three and a half years' hard labour (she served two years). They finally married in 1957. Behrisch was sentenced to three and a half years' hard labour and Biggs to five years' hard labour (reduced on appeal to 1 year). After his return to Britain in October 1941, Biggs joined the French section of SOE. Upon release, Behrisch joined the Danish resistance. The arrests revealed serious failings in SIS procedures. Rickman had (with the knowledge of the SIS Head of Station and the Military Attaché) kept the Section D correspondence files at his apartment, together with a notebook listing SIS codes and code names. The absence of any training in dealing with capture and interrogation became clear, with voluble confessions from Rickman, Biggs and Johansson. Such incompetence made Rickman a convenient scapegoat to deflect criticism from the wider failings of government and SIS. The absence of a consistent policy from the War Cabinet towards the plan is self-evident. The failure of the SIS chief in Stockholm, John Martin, to protect the operation against the police informant Singer, was extraordinary.[87] After the arrests, Martin became defensive, claiming that he had warned SIS of the risks ever since he knew Biggs was in contact with Singer.[88] Yet Martin's warning was only that Biggs was under suspicion through his connection to Nermann. Rather than lose Biggs as the lynch-pin of the propaganda operation, Rickman therefore distanced himself and Biggs from Nermann, who would only be used for 'slightly off-colour' propaganda in Sweden, working with the press attaché.[89] This meant that in February Singer was still able to report on a meeting at the Legation between Tennant, Nermann, Biggs and 'Mr Forster' (Ingram Fraser). It was not until 21 March that Martin finally advised the severing of all contact with Singer as being the source of the leaks to the Swedish police. Martin's own police informer came under suspicion once the unsuspected explosives store was discovered, for not having arrested Biggs earlier, and complained bitterly: 'previously he felt he was working with people who knew their job but now he feels large portion of 22-land [British] SIS composed of inexperienced amateurs'.[90] As Martin frantically tried to defend his actions on 26 April he falsely claimed: '36920 [police informer] ... considers it is thus through Biggs that contre-espionage department got onto tracks of rest (of) gang'.[91] He continued this defence in June:

It will be remembered that some time ago I reported 36,920 [police informer] stated unless Biggs ceased his activities he would be arrested and that 36,920 agreed to hold his hand in firm belief Biggs would be dropped by us. Since then I repeatedly urged (including verbally to D/G [Fraser] and D/1 [Rickman]) that Biggs should be dropped completely but this was not done.[92]

In fact, Martin had only warned that Biggs should no longer visit the Legation and that Rickman was to avoid being seen in public with him.[93] Biggs was warned to 'tread softly' and not to keep any incriminating material in his flat (with which he complied).[94] The court proceedings make it clear that the police had not followed a trail from Biggs to Rickman, but rather the key information had come from their interception of German intelligence through Birnbaum. The SOE history later concluded that Martin

> had never been an enthusiastic helper of the organisation, and from the telegrams he sent subsequent to the arrest of all parties, it is quite clear that he was doing his best to make a somewhat unsavoury affair appear in its worst possible light.[95]

The relationship between Section D and the British Legation in Stockholm was muddled, at times a pantomime. During March a diplomatic bag from SIS arrived at the Legation, addressed only to 36000 (Martin's internal SIS identifier). In confusion, the Minister, Victor Mallet, opened it. As the bag contained a letter for Tennant, he was next summoned and the rest of the contents of the bag were tipped out. Sutton-Pratt was summoned on the basis that this material looked 'phoney'. He arrived to find propaganda material for Rickman spread over the floor. Fortunately, 'the Boss [Mallet] did not seem to mind and has dismissed it from his mind. (We hope.)' Sutton-Pratt cheerfully passed the matter over to Martin, who was less amused and wrote to Menzies to 'get someone's knackers . . . bitten off in London'.[96] Despite the evidence being once strewn in front of him, years later Peter Tennant maintained an air of innocent bewilderment over the operations of Section D in Sweden. That Section D might have been involved in funding some of his propaganda work apparently came as a revelation.[97] For his part, Sutton-Pratt remained philosophical and wrote a cheerful letter to Fraser on 7 August 1940.

> Dear Ingram,
> I don't seem to have heard from you very recently!
> So sorry that all your hard work and plans came to nought. As it turned out, it doesn't matter, but it might and I believe would have had a big effect on the course of the war, if things had gone otherwise. . . . I remain very vexed with Freddy [Rickman] for his gross carelessness with 'documents' and feel he had no right to keep them as he did. I also feel that he spilled the beans the moment they rattled him. He even seems to have 'volunteered'

stuff. ... We often think and talk of you out here and wonder how you are and how things go and hope we may all meet again some day and laugh about it all!

Yours ever,

Reggie

Ps. I forgot to mention how near I was to expulsion from here, but that's another tale.[98]

Faced with the damning evidence of the correspondence files and the piles of explosives, Rickman, Johansson and Biggs had little option but to confirm the documentary evidence. With no training in resisting interrogation, they soon began to provide fulsome detail, including the naming of Helmer Bonnevie, now in German-occupied Norway. In August he was arrested by the Gestapo and was held until October 1940.[99] He was eventually deported to Germany in March 1942 and spent two years in a German labour camp. With some justification, Rickman blamed Fraser for pressing forward with a scheme which was not worth the risk. He accused Fraser of a lack of practical experience and declared the whole process as one of 'Order – counter-order – and disorder.'[100] This was an instance where Laurence Grand's faith in the judgement of his staff was misplaced. CSS Stewart Menzies shared Rickman's opinion and in May 1940 declared that Fraser 'has proved himself totally unfitted for controlling any agents, and his further employment is receiving my consideration'.[101] Nonetheless, he remained with the Scandinavian section of Section D over the summer and was then sent to join Stephenson at British Security Coordination in the USA. Guy Liddell of MI5 later reported that 'I cannot find anyone who has a really good word for him.'[102]

The discovery of the plot to destroy a key economic asset of a neutral country (one not prepared to brush off the incident, as in Yugoslavia) was a considerable embarrassment to the British government. Menzies, new in the post of CSS, had from the start associated himself with the planning of *Operation Lumps* and his personal embarrassment required a scapegoat. He and Grand were obliged to steadily retreat from positions of 'plausible deniability' of what were originally described as well meaning patriots with no connection to the British government. On 23 April Menzies feigned an air of puzzlement in providing an official explanation to Jebb at the Foreign Office:

As regards Mr. Biggs his knowledge of publicity, which is his profession, and his very pronounced patriotic feelings (he lost a leg in the last War), may possibly have led him to undertake privately propaganda in the Allied cause in excess of the limits imposed by the Swedish Censorship.

As regards Mr. Rickman, we are unable to account for a telegram which we have received stating that he was found in possession of 5 cwt of explosive. We do know that Mr. Rickman has always been an extremely keen supporter of the Democratic cause, and a possible hypothesis may be that he was arranging to transmit explosives to Norway. ... If the above be true then in not declaring these explosives to the Police Mr. Rickman has undoubtedly committed a minor technical offence, but in view of his extreme pro-Swedish feelings, against such an offence must be weighed the certainty that in his own mind he acted in the interests not only of Swedish neutrality, but in the interests of Sweden herself.[103]

This clumsy attempt to cover their tracks may be the origin of Jebb's accusation that Grand was 'a consistent and fluent liar'.[104] The alibi unravelled after the realisation that Section D files and SIS codes had been found in Rickman's flat. By 30 April Menzies was claiming that Biggs was a 'co-operator in work against Germany, but not ... a direct employee'.[105] Yet both Rickman and Biggs were salaried employees of Section D (Rickman at £600pa and Biggs at £420pa).[106] On 22 May Menzies wriggled again, suggesting that Rickman, although employed by Section D, had devised the scheme independently with the German Social Democrats. Menzies avoided the uncomfortable fact that the scheme had been discussed at length with the Prime Minister and the Foreign Office. Thoroughly embarrassed by having been put in such a position, Menzies wrote an angry note to Grand, blaming Fraser for allowing the SIS administrative codes to fall into Swedish hands and threatening to suspend Section D operations in the Balkans unless security was tightened.[107] Grand made a characteristically robust defence of his less-than-innocent officers, refusing to join in the condemnation of Fraser and pointing out that he had previously complained of the widespread use of SIS symbols in correspondence. Instead, Grand put the blame for the penetration of the network firmly on Martin's mishandling of his police informer.[108] But neither Martin, Fraser nor Rickman had a part in the failure of the sabotage plan itself. For this, Grand put the overall responsibility squarely on the Foreign Office in its delays in making a final decision to either proceed with or to cancel the sabotage plan.[109]

Grand was in no mood to compromise after the failure of *Operation Lumps*. He still wanted to see immediate sabotage action: 'Every endeavour must be made to block Luleå, whether by the infringement of Swedish neutrality or not.' With patience running out and his key agents imprisoned or blown, he went on: 'The effect of such an operation on Swedish opinion is not important in view of the facilities which they have given the Germans for the passage of stores up their railways and the transportation of wounded from Narvik.'[110] Less than a week after the arrests, Menzies had agreed to loan the experienced former SIS head of station in Copenhagen, Sidney Smith, to Section D to rebuild operations in Sweden. Smith's expertise was clearly welcomed by Grand, who said 'I have always wished that we could have had the benefit of your experience.'[111] Not surprisingly, this suggestion was opposed both by the Minister, Victor Mallet, and by Martin because it would cause 'confusion' (and threaten Martin's status). Instead, in July 1940 Malcolm Munthe from MI(R), who had reached Stockholm after a two-month escape from Stavanger, was ordered to establish contact with the infant Norwegian resistance and provide intelligence for SIS.[112]

The Rickman case did not have as fundamental an impact on Swedish relations as was at first feared, although it certainly led to a loss of British prestige, provided a propaganda weapon for Germany, and embarrassed Swedish intelligence enough to made it even harder for British intelligence to work in Sweden. Its real effect was on a broader scale. At the time of the arrest Rickman was supposed to have been organising supply lines into Norway and Holdsworth was planning a Norwegian resistance, but this all collapsed. The personal embarrassment felt by Menzies was a significant factor in his willingness to abandon Grand and Section D to SOE. As the SOE history acknowledges, the sabotage plan itself was sound and it may have succeeded without the vacillation of the Cabinet and the Foreign Office. Instead, it stumbled on to expose serious weaknesses in SIS procedures and became what the SOE history described as 'a study in amateur frustration'.[113]

Norway

The Norwegian ports controlled access to the North Sea, and both Britain and Germany obtained large quantities of Swedish iron ore via the port of Narvik. In August 1938, just five months after the foundation of Section D, Major H.H. Hartley sailed in his yacht to Narvik and carried out a survey of the harbour and ore-handling facilities, with a view to establishing the best way of sabotaging them in the event of war (Pl. 23). The conclusion was to sink a concrete-filled ship opposite the main ore-handling quay. It was proposed to purchase a US ship to conceal British involvement but this was dismissed as too expensive to be practical. Hartley's survey provided the inspiration for the creation of the 'Cruising Club'. The idea was to carry out a detailed coastal reconnaissance from Trondheim to Ostend, and to collect information on inland communications to establish suitable landing sites for inserting agents and sabotage materials into any future enemy-occupied territory. Under Lieutenant Frank Carr RNVR, the work would be carried out by experienced yachtsmen from the Royal Cruising Club, which had an established reputation for exploring coastal waters and would not excite any undue attention. The SOE history simply states 'There were no rules.'[114] By the time war was declared, much valuable information had been gathered for future sea-based landings. Gerard Holdsworth (who had joined Section D in February 1939 from J. Walter Thompson) and his then fiancé, Mary Thompson, had also carried out a land-based survey of possible landing places in the course of a 'walking tour' from Stavanger to Bergen.[115] Carr, with Holdsworth and August Courtauld, now switched his attention to planning how to organise the smuggling of sabotage materials from Scotland to the Norwegian coast. The Inspectors of Coastguards in northern Scotland provided isolated coastguard stations where the ships could secretly pick up their stores, and a letter from Captain Fletcher, Inspector of Coastguards in north-east Scotland, to Courtauld and Carr was headed 'Dear Pirates'. John Ratter at Cullivoe in the Shetlands, owner of Greenbank, then the most northerly licensed premises in Britain and favoured haunt of Norwegian smugglers, would be a contact with the smuggling vessels and held the key to a secret store established beside Whale Firth. Another store was established at the Torry (Aberdeen) Coastguard station.

In November 1939 Holdsworth went to Norway under cover as a sales representative of the firm Angus Watson (Skipper Sardines) to establish the landward side of the smuggling operation. Rickman would then create supply lines into Sweden. It was hoped that supplies could be smuggled into Norway in consignments of tinplate for the Norwegian canning industry and in British tinned goods where some tins had been 'doctored' to contain sabotage supplies. Neither idea was successful and most explosives were shipped in diplomatic crates, disguised as 'Library' supplies for the military attaché in Oslo. The material would then be smuggled through an office of Rickman's Skandamn company, established in Oslo under Helmer Bonnevie, a 28-year-old Norwegian and a former advertising manager for the German Telefunken company, who had a small factory printing on glass radio dials. Bonnevie had been recruited by Rickman at a salary of 500kr per month in late November. To transfer the supplies into Sweden, he purchased a 1937 Plymouth sedan modified with an additional petrol tank and a special compartment built under the front seat in which to hide explosives. James Chaworth-Musters (Pl. 28) established a separate network around Bergen in late 1939. He was a Norwegian-speaking naturalist who had the cover of vice-consul in Bergen.[116] His shadowy organisation was said to have survived after he escaped from Norway in a fishing boat on 10 May 1940 and Chaworth-Musters continued to organise Section D and then SOE operations in Norway before rejoining SIS in 1943.

Immediately after the invasion of Norway and the capture of Fraser in Denmark, Holdsworth went to Stockholm to take overall charge of Scandinavian operations. In the event, he became embroiled in the Oxelösund affair and was forced to flee but the original intention was that he would establish the basis of a Norwegian resistance with orders to contact Norwegian authorities and plan sabotage and supply dumps behind the advancing Germans, set up a new network in occupied Norway, and arrange with the local inhabitants to support a British landing at Trondheim. In the short term he was to persuade the Norwegian authorities to arrange sabotage 'as might be annoying to the Germans'. He was also to create a separate organisation that would undertake longer-term resistance following any occupation. The organisation responsible for immediate sabotage was expected to be quickly destroyed but this was not to compromise the longer-term resistance body.[117] This dual approach became the model for British resistance plans (*see* Chapter 10). Viscount Bearsted provided Holdsworth with details of pumps and petrol stations in Scandinavia both to assist British landing forces and as future sabotage targets, and instructed Shell officials to supply Holdsworth with all necessary funds.

As German forces began to occupy south and central Norway, an unnamed Section D liaison officer was sent to Norwegian HQ to continue plans to establish an organisation behind German lines. Demolition materials were to be distributed and suitable personnel recruited and trained. These may have included the young Oluf Reed Olsen and Kaare Moe, contacted by a British 'captain' said to be working for SIS in Oslo, and still in Norway in early September. Their first task was to sketch and photograph German airfields and other defensive works in the Oslo area. They were then ordered to blow up the Lysaker bridge on the western outskirts of Oslo to prevent German reinforcements reaching the area where Norwegian forces were still fighting. On the night of Saturday, 13 April Olsen, Kaare and Lief Moe laid four charges each of 16lb with a quarter of an hour delay fuse. The bridge survived but the roadway across it was sufficiently damaged to delay traffic for a few days. They were eventually captured whilst trying to steal direction-finding equipment from a crashed Heinkel 111 on Fornebu airfield. Escaping, they fled to England on 2 September in a leaking 18ft sailing boat, and after a nightmare journey of 28 days at sea they finally entered the Thames Estuary.[118]

On 3 May the Chiefs of Staff Committee asked the Inter-Services Project Board (ISPB) to consider the feasibility of raids against German-occupied Norway. Its report recommended operations to disrupt communications and force the Germans to increase coastal patrols, which might then be attacked by the Royal Navy. Clearly drafted by MI(R), operations were to be undertaken by uniformed troops landed from small motor boats released from destroyers lying offshore.[119] A gesture of resistance was urgently needed and Section D wasted no time putting its own spin on the proposal. On 11 May Fraser proposed a raid on the Voss area between the Sogne and Hardanger Fjords. The mission could also re-establish contact with Chaworth-Muster's network. CSS gave approval on 14 May and the mission was dispatched just two weeks later, after a feverish period of recruiting volunteers, acquiring and refitting a vessel and supplying it with a formidable arsenal. They set sail just as the last of the British Expeditionary Force was evacuating from Norway and, although the practical results were limited, this had great psychological value. The mission also tested the concept of what became the 'Shetland Bus', using fishing vessels to shuttle agents and supplies into occupied Norway. The plan differed significantly from the ISPB proposal. Grand advised ISPB that a 'preliminary party' would be leaving shortly to test the practicalities of small-scale landings but said that this would be a civilian 'Norwegians freeing Norway' party rather than using British troops. Grand's report was deliberately headed 'Petty sabotage . . .' as the charter of ISPB gave the freedom to conduct 'minor activities' without further reference to the Board.[120] John Dolphin's targeting section compiled a huge list of potential objectives, including underwater telephone cables, telephone lines and repeater stations, bridges and tunnels, factories and power stations. Typically over-ambitious, the party should also explore the potential for establishing a local Freedom Party and a mechanism for local printing of propaganda, together with the establishment of safe houses and weapons dumps for future operations.

For the mission, the Directorate of Naval Intelligence purchased a Danish-built fishing boat, the *Wailet* (Pl. 27), recently arrived on the Moray Firth from Norway under its captain, Mons Storemark.[121] It was a 60ft drifter, with a range of about 1,000 miles and a speed of 6–8 knots. The vessel was renamed the *Lady*, with the naval identification V.2.S. (renamed again during the expedition as the *Hospiz*). V.2.S. was taken to Aberdeen for a complete re-fitting, including the building of an extra eight bunks in the fish hold. The crew (Fig. 5), many of them whalers, were recruited by Jacob Munter from Oslo, who owned a chandler firm in London but had previously served as a major in the Norwegian army and knew the area in which the team would be operating. Unfortunately, he was out of date with the loyalty of some of his contacts in Norway. Later, agents Fjeld and Wang, just returned from Bergen, sent an urgent message back to Fraser warning him 'not to trust Mr Munte [*sic*] too far. At least one of the contacts he gave them in Bergen was now a well-known Nazi agent.'[122] Unfortunately, the Anglo-Norwegian officer who was originally due to command became unavailable and so Simon Sinclair Fjeld was put in charge. The men received only the minimum of training and it became clear that enthusiastic whalers did not necessarily make good agents. Rubin Langmoe (a 'wild' man according to his SOE personnel file) had served with the Norwegian Naval Air Service but had just one afternoon's explosives training in the Aston House chalk quarry.[123] Fortunately, the Swedish engineer Karl Kronberg had some experience of explosives and Otto Aksdal had served in the Norwegian coastal artillery. They were also sent without means of wireless communication. As was typical for the time, the volunteers were paid on a bonus system, which was later to cause great problems with SOE:

> Many Norwegians regard this work as a money-making concern: this has had to be stopped and we are now recruiting a better class of agent, and making them realise that we are merely helping them in a patriotic work; but 'as they must live' we are willing to pay them the same amount they would receive as officers in the Norwegian Army. We must not, on any account, allow ourselves to be 'blackmailed' into paying them exorbitant wages or bonuses.[124]

As a disguise, the V.2.S. carried six sets of line-fishing gear, and British, Norwegian, Danish, Swedish and German ensigns. Provisions for twelve men for fourteen days were included, along with 2,000 cigarettes, 25lb of tobacco, 1cwt of sugar, 1cwt of flour, 1cwt of coffee, and 50lb of chocolate to be used for bribes. They carried a substantial cargo of demolition materials brought from Aston House and the Aberdeen dump, which included six 'beginners' demolition packs containing explosives, fuses, incendiary bombs, detonators and delay devices, all pre-prepared by Major Hugh Pollard of the small arms section.[125] In total, the V.2.S. would carry:

730lb (331kg) plastic explosives packed in five hermetically sealed tins
130 large incendiary bombs
100 incendiary arrows
600 assorted time pencils (mainly 2 hours together with 20 mins and 20 hours)
50 pressure switches
300ft Orange Line (instantaneous fuse – 90ft per second)
300ft Grey Line (cordtex – instantaneous high explosive fuse)
1440ft Black line (Bickford safety fuse – 2ft per minute)
50ft Bickford fuse cut into 12-inch lengths
100 short lengths of match-ended Bickford fuse
15 automatic pistols with 50 rounds each (includes Colt .32 automatics)
12 'Mauser carbines' with 100 rounds each
5 sub-machine guns ('tommy guns') with 300 rounds each
2 Colt machine guns with 7,000 rounds[126]
120 Mills grenades
6 wire cutters
6 telescopes
2 pairs of binoculars
12 flashlight torches

Some of the equipment had been chosen for compactness rather than power. At least seven of the pistols were small Colt .32 automatics (Pl. 30) but the Norwegians made a last-minute request for larger-calibre Colt revolvers. Instead, seven .455 automatics were sent up to Lerwick. They also asked for two pairs of 'powerful' binoculars to supplement the existing two pairs in the inventory.[127] In the event, this extra equipment only arrived in Lerwick after the V.2.S. had sailed for Norway. Although in 1940 a reference to 'tommy guns' might refer to any sub-machine gun, a report compiled in 1941 suggests that these were from a very early issue of British Thompson sub-machine guns (Pl. 31).

It was belatedly realised that none of the crew had detailed knowledge of the target coast. Olav Leirvåg (a professional pilot) and Otto Aksdal (sailor and former Norwegian artilleryman), both recently escaped from Norway on the *Snaal*, were therefore sent down from Lerwick to join the expedition. The rest of the crew came up to Aberdeen from London under the escort of Chaworth-Musters.[128] They gathered for a final briefing by Chaworth-Musters (Pl. 28) and Fraser on the night of 24 May – the day that allied forces agreed to finally withdraw from Norway. The V.2.S. then sailed to Lerwick, where it picked up Olav Leirvåg's brother Oscar and the original skipper of V.2.S. Mons Storemark, who would serve as a second pilot. They finally left for Norway on the evening of 29 May, towing the 40ft *Snaal* and its small motor boat.

Figure 5. Section D First Norwegian Expedition Members. *(TNA HS 2/241)*

Role	Name	Weekly Salary	Notes
Original team			
Expedition Leader and First Mate	Simon Sinclair Fjeld (1910–1941)	£7 (bonus £100)	from Aal, Norway.
Skipper of V.2.S.	Karsten Wang (1905–1941)	£7	from Tonsberg, Norway.
Engineer	Karl Kronberg (1907–1940)	£7 (bonus £100)	Engineer from Malmo, Sweden.
Crew	Oscar Leirvåg	£5 (bonus £50)	from Bergen area, Norway.
	Rubin Langmoe (1920–1981)	£5 (bonus £50)	from Oslo, Norway.
	Ashjorn Kristiansen (1907–)	£5 (bonus £50)	from Tonsberg, Norway.
	Lief Olsen (1909–)	£5 (bonus £50)	from Tonsberg, Norway.
	Sigvred Pettersen (1911–)		from Tonsberg, Norway.
	Sverre Thorlup Thorsen (1915–)	£5 (bonus £50)	from Tonsberg, Norway.
	Rangvald Torgersen (1902–)	£5 (bonus £50)	from Ostjford, Norway.
	Henry Valle (1909–)	£5 (bonus £50)	from Larvik, Norway.
Added			
Pilot	Olav Martin Leirvåg (1902–1970)	£7 (bonus £100)	a pilot for 20 years in the Bergen district and the first Pastor for the Norwegian Merchant Navy.
	Otto Aksdal	£5 (bonus £50)	
	Mons Storemark (1909–1995)	£7 (bonus £50)	Skipper from Fedje, Norway.
W/T operator	Olav Wallin	£7 (bonus £100)	as agreed on return.

Their first success was during the crossing, in sinking a German mine. Olav Leirvåg and Kronberg rowed up to it and carefully hung a charge of 2lb of plastic explosive with a half hour time delay on one of the horns! On 31 May at 3.00am they landed at Stenso and hid a cache of supplies close to the shore. They also picked up six or eight refugees who had been discovered in hiding on a motor boat near Hostedal, including a Norwegian merchant seaman, Olav Wallin, who was a ship's wireless operator. A final anchorage was then made at Selvag, to the south of Sogne Fjord. The history of the mission then divides into three parties.

Party 1

The main reconnaissance party under Karl Kronberg (with Langmoe, Valle, Pettersen, Kristiansen and Olsen) was put ashore at 1.00am on 1 June. They carried a heavy load of demolition materials with a mission to survey the Voss area, hide arms caches and identify suitable sabotage targets. They first went to

Ottenstakken in two small and leaky rowing boats they had purchased for 400kr. Having passed through German lines, they rowed overnight to Gamervik but some men declared that they would rather hike over the mountains than do more rowing, and this was agreed. There were then complaints about the weight of the explosives-laden rucksacks. All but Kronberg and Langmoe reduced their load by half, leaving the rest in a cache. Complaints about the unexpected hardship continued and most of the men returned to the ship, leaving Kronberg and Langmoe to continue the mission alone. From 3 to 10 June they travelled over 200km (124 miles) in a loop to the Hardanger Fjord at Ålvik, thence to the head of Sogne Fjord and back to their boat. They travelled by foot on roads and mountain tracks, by boat and by ferry. At Torskedval an old soldier provided them with a horse and cart and seven rucksacks in which to redistribute the explosives. Two dumps, including the two heavy Colt machine guns, were left at the outskirts of Dale and, after contacting several residents and mounting a surveillance of the railway station, they went on by foot along the railway line to Horvik, where they spent the night in hiding. From here they could study the guard at the Bolstad railway station, across the water. On 5 June they moved on to Evanger, where a party of German officers in a Mercedes took their photograph as an amusing picture of Norwegian hikers – not realising that their huge rucksacks were packed with explosives (the photograph was later used as a 'Wanted' poster for the two men). At Finnteg they spent the night in the woods and hid another weapons cache. From here, they could observe the construction of an airfield at Bomoen (bombed by the RAF on the basis of their information). By now, German patrols were searching for them. On 7 June they hiked over the mountains to Ålvik, where there was a large aluminium factory served by the Bjølvefossen power station. The factory was under heavy guard but the mountainside power station appeared to be more vulnerable. They went on through increasing numbers of German troops and by 10 June they had again reached Torskedal, which they had first left on 3 June. Kronberg and Langmoe hid the remainder of their stores in Dale and then headed for their rendezvous with Fjeld. They decided that the Bjølvefossen power station would be the primary target and the three men left Grindestad on the 30km (18.5 miles) trek back to Ålvik. After going over the mountains together, Fjeld returned to the V.2.S. to make sure it would be ready for departure as soon as the two saboteurs had made their escape.

At Ålvik, Kronberg and Langmoe bought fresh clothes as a disguise and made a final reconnaissance of the area. At 1.30am on 16 June they stealthily made their way through the woods and climbed the mountainside to the power station, where they laid a series of charges that would hopefully shut down the power station and disrupt communications and power to the wider area. Some 12lb of explosives with a 20-hour time pencil were placed on each of the high-pressure water intake pipes, timed to explode at midnight on 17 June. They then moved down onto the Ålvik–Stenso road and attached a 2lb explosive charge with another time delay on to each of four telephone pylons at Trengereld. Their destruction would sever telephone links to the power station and hopefully slow down the response from the Germans. Six more charges were placed to create a landslide to block the Nyset road where it ran through a narrow cutting. Another charge would destroy a brick supporting arch for the road at Trengerweid. As a final act, they also set charges on two of the main high tension power lines running from Fröland and Ostero to Bergen. The return trip to the V.2.S. was as tortuous as the rest of the expedition. They travelled by motor boat, public bus, ferry and rowing boat to eventually reach the vessel at 9.00pm on 17 June and then made a hasty departure, narrowly evading three German patrol boats on the way and just three hours before the charges were due to explode. Despite their herculean efforts, the power station was back in action after just a few weeks and the demolition of the pylons only cut power to parts of Bergen for four days. The road was blocked for an unknown period. The action was, however, highly symbolic, coinciding with the formal surrender of Norwegian forces, and the Nazis were at first reluctant to admit the possibility of sabotage, instead blaming the damage on an air raid. Six dumps had also been left for future operations, consisting of half a ton of high explosive, 500 time pencils, 600 incendiaries, two Colt machine guns with 7,000 rounds, three 'Tommy guns', ten pistols and three carbines.

Party 2
Once the sabotage party had departed, the Leirvåg brothers and Mons Storemark attempted to return to Lerwick in the *Snaal* to report the safe arrival of the party and to request a wireless transmitter. But they got caught in a storm, the engine broke down, and they were obliged to return to the V.2.S. on 5 June.

Party 3
Early on 3 June Fjeld, Aksdal and the new recruit Wallin left the V.2.S. to make a reconnaissance in Bergen and contact survivors of Chaworth-Muster's network. Fjeld posed as a Nazi sympathiser and managed to get the V.2.S. licensed by the German authorities as the *Hospiz*, as well as making a large-scale map of the German positions in the town. His other reports, including mounting arson attacks on two factories making parachutes in Larvik (where Swedish radio did indeed report the outbreak of fires), were, however, greeted with suspicion. He told of German soldiers with bad eyesight and on drugs, poor morale, mutinies and suicides. Fjeld also reported a comprehensive plan of invasion for around 7 July, with landings along the east and south coasts of England, as well as attacks on the Shetlands and west coast of Scotland. In response to this threat, Fjeld believed he could immediately raise a partisan army of up to 600 men to raid Norwegian coastal ports, dependent on a promise of weapons and support from Britain.[129] He returned twice to Bergen on subsequent missions but feedback suggested that Fjeld had been very indiscreet, compromising his new contacts.

The three men returned to the V.2.S./*Hospiz* on 9 June. The number in the party had become unmanageable: in addition to the refugees picked up at

Hostedal, Oscar Leirvåg had gathered up four members of his family who were believed to be under threat from the Nazis. Consequently, the skipper, Karsten Wang, negotiated the use of the *Gneist*, then lying 2km away in Duusund, and had already returned in it to Lerwick, taking with him the Leirvågs, their family and six others. The progress report they delivered to Fraser included a request for a wireless transmitter for Wallin as Fjeld had already offered him a job as a wireless operator, at a salary three times that of the normal salary for Section D officers. Chaworth-Musters subsequently offered a more realistic salary of £7 per week and a bonus of £100 per trip. The confusion caused by Fjeld's extravagant offer was to cause great problems.

The *Hospiz* reached Scotland on 18 June but Fjeld and Wang returned to Bergen almost immediately for the first of two more undocumented missions. Fjeld returned to Lerwick on the night of 25 June but was soon back in Norway, returning again to Lerwick on 4 July.[130] This punishing schedule might well explain his subsequent nervous breakdown. The pressure also told on Karl Kronberg, who committed suicide in London on 25 June. Meanwhile, a further expedition to contact the Norwegian resistance was planned around Wallin, Aksdal and Langmoe. This time it would include a wireless transmitter (*see above*, p. 46 and Pl. 29). Before the invasion, some sets had been supplied to the SIS intelligence networks in Norway and it is not surprising that Section D wanted sets for its own networks. By 15 June Chaworth-Musters and Fraser had requested three transmitter-receivers for Norway. The head of SIS communications (Section VIII) said this was a 'wildly impossible demand'. They would only supply such transmitters if they received a clear operating plan, to ensure there was no conflict with their own wireless networks. Section D side-stepped the problem since Edward Schröter already had a suitable set that had been intended for the use of Clara Holmes in Paris.[131] Brigadier Gambier-Parry's other concerns over the quality of wireless operators seem vindicated by the fact that Wallin's wireless messages were never successfully received, although the set worked well for the subsequent operator, Erling Marthinson.[132]

The new expedition again used the *Hospiz*, skippered now by Mons Storemark, to cross the North Sea. They landed at Utvaer on the night of 27 June and Langmoe left on his own undisclosed mission in 'the east', returning to the Shetlands independently of the other two agents. Wallin and Aksdal headed for Fannebust, carrying the wireless set in a large suitcase. The first test transmission to England on 30 June was made after the editor of the local newspaper allowed them to rig up the transmitter in his house for a payment of 200kr. Aksdal claimed that the set worked well, ignoring the fact that they did not receive a confirmation of transmission and SIS denied ever receiving a message.[133] They then went to Tefstad, where they hired a semi-derelict house and set up the wireless, but during the next scheduled transmission on Sunday, 30 June the transmitter caught fire! They sent the *Hospiz* back to the Shetlands with all the intelligence they had gathered and a set of dates for future rendezvous, while

Aksdal went to Bergen to try to find spare parts for the wireless. A former associate of Fjeld offered to help if the set was brought to Bergen – but only in return for a substantial advance payment. Wallin and Aksdal duly brought the set to Bergen but the contact had disappeared with the money. The subsequent reports of Wallin and Aksdal are a catalogue of spiralling travelling expenses, plus the costs of trying to repair the wireless 'as you can see it is no cheap amusement being a spy'.[134] Eventually the set was repaired and Wallin set it up in a mountain farm at Setestollen, east of Bergen. There he contacted another wireless operator, Erling Marthinson, with whom he left the set and for whom it worked perfectly.[135] Meanwhile, in late June, in another undocumented mission, a wireless operator named Øverli (a trainee for the Norwegian Air Force in England) was recruited for the Trondheim area.[136]

Wallin and Aksdal organised the core of several resistance cells in the Bergen area and weapons were smuggled to them via the *Traust* and shipped into Bergen in small parcels, although the renewed claim to have 500 men ready to revolt against the Germans is typical of the optimistic claims of the early months of the occupation.[137] By now, Wallin and Aksdal had run out of money and after a month they returned to the Shetlands on the *Traust*. The mission had been fraught with difficulties but had proved the viability of the 'Shetland Bus'. Upon their return, they were sent to the new D School at Brickendonbury for further training (where Olav Leirvåg was now the Norwegian Instructor), but problems arose. Langmoe was already at Brickendonbury and the Norwegians exchanged information on their various financial arrangements. Aksdal and Wallin complained about their levels of payment, whilst the expenses they had claimed for their second expedition were greeted with suspicion. They were clearly embittered, and their knowledge of the Brickendonbury training school created an additional security risk. Despite their contribution as pioneers of agent insertion into Norway, Wallin and Aksdal were interned until February 1941, first in Brixton prison and then in the Lingfield internment camp.[138] The affair caused great damage within the new SOE over the quality and motivation of Norwegian agents, although much of the blame for the problems was put on the unstable Fjeld. Aksdal had written on 10 August from Bergen: 'Whatever happens do not let Fjeld come out again, as the Gestapo are searching for him and he has compromised our former contacts and destroyed the original foundation on which our work was based.'[139] A report of 18 September 1940 concluded:

> There is no doubt that this man, like many of his compatriots, became exceedingly swollen-headed during and after his first trip. He liked to pose as 'the big man' with any amount of money to spend and loved to throw it about lavishly. ... He also told all and sundry that he was being paid by the British Government and generally exaggerated the amount he was being paid. This exaggeration has come to the ears of the others and they complain that he was getting more than they. There is no doubt he spoilt the market.

His indiscretions were amazing and he was nothing but a very plausible rogue.[140]

The Norwegian expeditions were plagued by tragedy. Kronberg committed suicide a week after the return to England. Following their dispute at Brickendonbury, Wallin and Aksdal were interned. After his nervous breakdown, Fjeld was sent to Canada to train for the RAF but later deserted and stowed away on board a ship bound for England; it was torpedoed and he lost his life. Karsten Wang was captured on a subsequent mission for SOE and was executed in 1941. On a happier note, Langmoe joined the Kompani Linge and served for the rest of the war with SOE in Norway, while Olav Leirvåg became chaplain to the Norwegian forces in England, and appeared as a pastor in the film *The Day Will Dawn* (1942).

Many of the details of the work of Section D in Norway have been destroyed. There are, however, tantalising snippets of information to suggest at least six different missions immediately after the German invasion. Some of the intelligence gathered by the new agents was flawed and exaggerated but the first Norwegian resistance groups were indeed formed in May 1940, with a substantial organisation in Bergen. In August around a hundred suspected resistance members were arrested in the Arendal area and five were sentenced to death.[141] Grand was encouraged by the successes and a report of June 1940 considered how 'to stimulate the civilian population to undertake guerrilla warfare against the German occupying troops, and ultimately to extend guerrilla tactics to open rebellion'.[142] It looked optimistically towards a 'major effort' in the autumn, before the onset of heavy snow. The timetable was soon put back to spring 1941 at the earliest, but during August and September 1940 Fraser and Chaworth-Musters worked with the Norwegian government-in-exile in London to develop a future plan for Norwegian resistance, including provision for thirty to forty Norwegians to be recruited and trained, ready to be sent back to form resistance cells. Lieutenant Martin Linge, a former actor, was appointed as liaison officer between Section D and the exiled Norwegian army.[143] He would later command the famous Norwegian commando unit known as Kompani Linge. Frank Nelson, as Laurence Grand's replacement, tried to impose some realism into the timetable for any Norwegian rebellion and by November the schedule for rebellion had been revised back to 1942 but dependent upon the availability of resources for allied landings. Norway was not finally liberated until May 1945, when 40,000 members of the Norwegian resistance rose up to enforce the German capitulation.

Denmark

There are only the barest hints of Section D operations in Denmark. Ingram Fraser made his first visit in November 1939, later contacting Ebbe Munck of the *Berlingske Tidende* in Copenhagen who suggested a number of possible ways of smuggling propaganda into Germany but with no practical results.[144] An unnamed officer was appointed with the aim of creating communication lines into Germany, working with agents of the *Deutsche Freiheitsparte* (German Freedom Party), who arranged the posting of some of Section D's black propaganda in Germany from Denmark. The Freedom Party was a small organisation of conservative and liberal opposition to the Nazis but, eager to attract increased funding from Section D, its leader, Karl Spiecker, had laid claim to Johann Elser's November 1939 Munich Bierkellar plot. He then asked Section D in December if they would support sabotage of other Nazi meeting halls and the murder of key Nazi figures, but as the British focus was still on economic targets, this offer was rejected.[145] In April 1940 Fraser was negotiating the chartering of a ship and crew in Denmark to use as a concrete-filled block-ship at the Luleå iron ore port in Sweden but was interrupted by the German invasion on 9 April.[146] He was briefly arrested but was saved by his diplomatic passport. After the occupation, Grand was pessimistic and declared in July 1940:

> We are not hopeful of any anti-German activity in Denmark. It is, however, possible that here again a shortage of food and the destruction of their cattle and overseas markets may create some spark of resentment among the Danes.[147]

Grand believed that Section D would be able to encourage some degree of passive resistance with leaflets and radio broadcasts but the population as a whole 'were not yet fuel that would spontaneously burst into flame'.[148] This was not entirely correct but a Danish resistance was indeed slow to develop as the Germans were initially keen to showcase the country as a 'model protectorate' and conditions were more lenient than elsewhere.

Chapter 10

Britain and the USA

At our most forlorn moment when our army was pouring back from Dunkirk through gates we could never have shut against an invading enemy, Colonel Grand conceived the plan of organising throughout Great Britain a closely-coordinated sabotage and intelligence network among the civilian population who would be left behind in any territories which the German armies might temporarily be able to occupy.

(Section D Closing Report, August 1940)[1]

Britain

Despite having begun to mobilise resistance across Europe from March 1939, Section D did not turn its attentions to Britain until May 1940. Until then, the threat of invasion was not taken seriously by the government or the War Office, although in early 1940 the Secret Intelligence Service had begun to quietly create within its Section VII the cadre for a top secret nationwide resistance organisation, using trained civilian agents linked by wireless.[2] As the threat of invasion increased, using the multi-layered methodology recently developed in Norway and France, Section D constructed a second, larger organisation, the Home Defence Scheme (HDS), initially focused on short-term civilian sabotage but with an intelligence wing. With no time to train wireless operators, the latter had to rely on a 'grapevine' courier system. The War Office responded with the military Auxiliary Units, prompting an attempt to refocus the HDS into a longer-term resistance organisation that would only emerge after an enemy occupation.[3]

The British government maintained a double standard towards the concept of civilian resistance during the Second World War. It was encouraged abroad but was officially resisted in Britain as being illegal under the Hague Convention and therefore risked its citizens being executed as *francs-tireur* (literally 'free-shooters' or terrorists). It was, however, the *raison d'être* of SIS that it could engage in activities that the government could not officially support. In the face of the impending collapse of France, John Dolphin had seen an urgent need to extend the existing European 'Scheme D' into a 'Regional D Scheme' for British guerrilla warfare. The plan owed much to the Polish guerrilla organisation formed in the spring of 1939 by Major Charaskiewicz and was a natural extension of Section D's planning in Norway and France.[4] Even as Dolphin put his ideas to paper, Section D officers were hurriedly helping French Intelligence create secret arms dumps and recruit a core of future sabotage agents. Dolphin's report of 22 May

1940, entitled 'Pessimism', tried to avoid such a last-minute effort. He argued that undue optimism had led to previous disasters in the war. 'It would therefore appear wise to take the most pessimistic view about invasion of this country and prepare for successful invasion by the Germans, even though successful invasion may only be a very remote possibility.' Dolphin proposed recruiting 'everybody's reliable friends plus their friends' reliable friends, thus forming a basically sound body of men to operate particularly in the event of a successful invasion'. He called for weapons dumps to be distributed for the sabotage of enemy aircraft, bridges, communications and petrol supplies. The dumps would contain weapons suitable for use by civilians or for British troops that had been disarmed.[5] The following day MI(R) circulated a paper for the Inter-Services Project Board (ISPB) entitled 'Organisation of Civil Resistance in Belgium, France, UK and Ireland', which started from the premise that in an age of 'total war'

> the civil population of all classes should be asked to make the same sacrifices as the fighting forces. The particular kind of civil resistance which we now envisage is sabotage subsequent to occupation by the enemy.[6]

The War Office was, however, bitterly opposed to the use of civilians in combat and to any acknowledgement of possible occupation (which suggested defeatism). Dolphin and Grand first presented the Section D scheme to the ISPB meeting on 27 May and the meeting, according to Grand, declared the Home Defence Scheme (HDS) to be of 'immediate importance'. Grand needed no further urging and immediately began to mobilise the HDS prior to formal sanction.[7] Dealing with the ensuing problems of the HDS were to take up much of Grand's time over the summer.[8] The minutes of the 27 May meeting of the ISPB records:

> It was explained that it was considered desirable that arrangements should proceed immediately for irregular operations and sabotage against the Germans should they invade England. ... it was agreed that action should be taken forthwith to set up an organisation to cooperate with C-in-C Home Forces. Lieut.-Colonel Grand said he was planning to send representatives to HQ Home Forces and to Regional Commissioners to organise areas in so far as possible.[9]

HDS would organise 'technical sabotage ... requiring special equipment'. At the same time, it was hoped by MI(R) that regular defences would be supplemented with military 'guerrilla-type troops', based upon the new Independent Companies (commandos), who would allow themselves to be overrun and then attack the enemy rear and flanks. This concept devolved into the GHQ Auxiliary Units, based around the Home Guard, but it was not until July that the latter could be mobilised by the more bureaucratic War Office. In addition, Grand argued

> The whole population, whether in formed or loose formations or whether as individuals, must be instructed in the sort of contribution they can make

to assist the services, and must be encouraged to make their contribution, should the need arise, with the same ruthlessness we may expect from the enemy, whether he is provoked or not.[10]

With British troops retreating from France, the urgency might seem self-evident but there was immediate opposition to the concept of the civilian HDS. Legally, the Section D officers who would administer the organisation needed to operate as 'advisers' to the twelve regional commissioners responsible for devolved government following any invasion. Neville Chamberlain, the Chief Commissioner (ironically, who later drafted the brief for the future SOE), refused to cooperate but Grand went directly to Churchill, writing:

> The formation of an underground army was obviously important, both for the purpose of obtaining information for our own forces and later for carrying out resistance projects of all sorts. I therefore asked permission in principle and for facilities to contact the Regional Commissioners. This was refused by the Chief Commissioner on the grounds that the distribution of arms and explosives would be dangerous. The danger of invasion, however, seemed to me so great that I appealed to the P.M. (as Minister of Defence) and he gave permission to go ahead.[11]

Plans for the distribution of weapons dumps over as wide an area as possible were drawn up on 31 May. A core of guerrilla cells was then recruited, both to deliver short-term guerrilla action during the invasion campaign and, if necessary, be prepared for longer-term resistance. On 1 June Grand produced a briefing document for the thirty Section D officers who would administer the HDS. George Hill helped draw up the plan, in the midst of organising weapons dumps and training saboteurs in France and Belgium.[12] The officers included Gerard Holdsworth (just back from Sweden) in East Anglia and Francis Ogilvy in Scotland (whose orders to go as head agent to Hungary were cancelled). In charge was Viscount Bearsted, assisted by his friend and fellow banker Major the Honourable Lionel Montague and Captain W.E. Hope (Fig. 6). Bearsted had served in the First World War and had been awarded the Military Cross. He had been recruited to SIS in 1938 and co-opted to Section D in 1939 but, although he had been involved in the administration of Section D's efforts to establish intelligence networks in Scandinavia, he had no direct experience of guerrilla warfare.

Ambitiously, it was hoped to provide a wireless-equipped car for each of the twelve regional officers; the car was to include a box of cigars or cigarettes and 'plenty of chocolate' for use as bribes! The officers had to supply their own driver – who had to be 'ready for anything' – and were issued with a copy of the Section D sabotage manual *Home Hints* and a revolver. There is, however, no further mention of wireless being used by the HDS.

The instant mobilisation had by-passed formal authorisation by appealing directly to Churchill but Grand sought retroactive approval on 2 June, costing

Figure 6. Known organising officers of Home Defence Scheme.

HQ	Viscount Bearsted	
	Major the Hon. Lionel Montague	
	Captain W.E. Hope	
Regional Officers	Eric Maschwitz	East Yorkshire
	Gerard Holdsworth	East Anglia
	John Todd	Wales and South Midlands
	Francis Ogilvy	Scotland
Suspected	K.W. Johnson	
	R. Fraser	

the scheme at £3,600 for immediate expenses, with £60,000 distributed to the regional officers immediately upon notice of invasion.[13] The next day the Chief of SIS, Stewart Menzies, briefed a meeting of the intermittent Secret Service Committee 'on the part which the SIS might play in the event of an invasion of Great Britain'.[14] It is hardly surprising that on the same day the Director of Military Intelligence, Beaumont-Nesbitt, proposed that Section D should come under control of the War Office. How far Menzies had prior notice of Grand's plans is debatable. Later in the month Menzies had a meeting with the Foreign Secretary where it was noted 'D's great ideas. Doesn't seek advice before putting out schemes ... schemes not weighed sufficiently ... but C can't control him.'[15] Nonetheless, it seems unlikely that SIS would have allowed the HDS to progress further if it threatened the security of the Section VII resistance. There was, however, apoplexy in the War Office as it slowly became aware of the HDS network spreading across the country, and Peter Wilkinson (of MI(R) and the later Auxiliary Units) put his own spin on the circumstances to reinforce his hagiography of Gubbins:

> As for Section D, one of Gubbins' early tasks had been to take over Grand's civilian stay-behind organisation, hastily and unofficially set up earlier and providing a source of embarrassment to all concerned.[16]

In an effort to appease the War Office, and in line with the policy for the Balkans and the Middle East being negotiated by George Taylor in Cairo, Grand stressed that this first iteration of the civilian HDS would pass under military control when called to action.[17] He also stressed that the HDS would work in conjunction with any uniformed guerrilla activities planned by MI(R).[18] Discreetly using the term 'obstruction' to refer to sabotage, Grand's plan for the HDS was:

a) to make as many persons as possible in areas liable to invasion into conscious obstructionists, and

b) to have a nucleus of trained persons who, in the event of invasion, will remain behind and direct further obstruction under the direction of the military where such acts could aid military operations.

Under Bearsted's HQ, the HDS was organised through the twelve Section D regional officers, notionally attached to the regional civil commissioners for 'Special Duties'. They would divide the regions into sub-areas and within these, eighteen other Section D officers would recruit reliable civilians as 'Key Men'. These men would then recruit their own cell members. To maintain security, Grand suggested that cells might be self-contained units of a family or of estate workers. Grand reported:

> Recruiting went well. The qualifications were courage, intelligence, and discretion, and the bait was a certainty of execution if caught. The results were the finest body of men that have ever been collected. All classes and trades were represented, bankers and poachers, clergymen and burglars, farmers and lawyers, policemen and shopkeepers, every sort and kind of trade and interest, and the whole representing a cross section of the England that would never submit to being ruled by an invader.[19]

Volunteers were warned to avoid anything that might affect their future service in HDS, which meant that they risked being accused of not assisting the war effort. In the main, they were middle-aged saboteurs not liable to be called-up for military service, and well-established in local trades or businesses so that their movement around the countryside would hopefully not raise suspicion from occupying German forces. Both men and women were recruited, although it is likely that the women joined the intelligence network rather than as saboteurs. The regional officer for the East Riding of Yorkshire was 39-year-old Eric Maschwitz, formerly of the Section D propaganda unit. In May 1940 he was sent on a brief demolitions course at Aston House. Maschwitz had no previous military experience but in just 24 hours he found himself commissioned as a second lieutenant and expected to go to Calais with a demolition party. The operation was cancelled at the last minute and he was sent back in civilian clothes to establish a regional HQ for the HDS in Beverley. There were no written instructions and he was responsible only to the regional commissioner.

> He would recommend us to the chief constable who, without knowing exactly what we were up to, would provide us with a list of local citizens likely to prove daring and also as close as oysters. We had a secret telephone number to ring if in trouble and a garage in Yorkshire packed to the roof with various dangerous devices. For a long hot month we toured the hills and dales and seaside resorts with samples of our 'wares' (time bombs and Molotov cocktails), a couple of commercial travellers trying to 'interest' prospective customers in the prospect of death and danger.[20]

Maschwitz recruited a sizeable list of volunteers 'who had buried in their gardens, under hayricks and manure heaps, the wherewithal with which to cause the invader quite a lot of trouble'.[21] By the third week of July Grand claimed to have recruited 200 'Key Men'.[22] Some of these later became group commanders of

Figure 7. Inventory of Home Defence Scheme dumps, 31 May 1940.
('D Organisation for Home Defence', 1 June 1940, with thanks to Stephen Sutton)

Per crate	Item	Total distributed
25	Flare, Type M, fitted with 1ft of Bickford	2,000
30	match-headed Tyesules (paraffin)	24,000
1 dozen	Battery pills	800 dozen
2 dozen	Capsules	1,600 dozen
2	pint bottles of sulphuric acid	800
2	small hooded torches	1,600
4	additional batteries for torches	3,200
1	spare bulb for torch	800
6	rubber truncheons	4,800
6	sheathed knives	1,800
1	crowbar	1,000
1	each machine-gun rattles	800
1	packing case opener	1,000
6	pistols with 500 rounds	

the Auxiliary Units, although they all kept their previous work for SIS a closely-guarded secret. The 31 May inventory of the contents of the arms dumps supports the claim that 800–1,000 demolition packs were made up and distributed in the first few days. It also suggests that cells of six sabotage agents each were planned (Fig. 7). The early dumps assumed that most of the work would be incendiary in nature but Grand later appointed eighty specialist saboteurs, probably trained in explosives.

The HDS was intended to operate secretly from within the community and in his 'Preliminary Notes on Regional D Scheme' of 4 June, Grand stressed that the regional commissioners had to prevent any general evacuation from threatened areas so that the stay-behind units could hide within the general populace. If a general evacuation of the civilian population could not be avoided, the HDS would create a force of 'narks' hiding by day and operating by night, and this was the origin of the later operational bases of the Auxiliary Units. It is a characteristic that the volunteers never knew precisely for whom they were working.

'D' officers should select a suitable region-wide organisation, take the chief officers of it into their confidence, and allow them to plant the idea in the heads of their subordinates without betraying the fact that there is any official organisation behind the scheme. ... Suggest that no doubt the bloody Government, which is always years behind the times, has never thought of anything of the kind but we, the citizens of ... shire, will bloody well show them! Let each man according to his trade suggest a simple form of obstruction which he personally will do and which he recommends others to do. Take care, though, that the officials taken into confidence are reliable and are capable of 'acting up' sufficiently to plant the idea without arousing suspicion. 'D' officers in civilian clothes, if suitably introduced, might help here.[23]

No advice on specific targets was provided, but the Section D officers were to carry out an ad hoc 'policy of obstruction' towards the enemy. Grand admitted, 'So far, the scheme has been elaborated and almost initiated without anyone having been given a directive as to what to destroy', but in London John Dolphin had already carried out a survey for MI5 on likely fifth-column targets, which provided key targets for the HDS in the capital. On 6 June he produced a list of the eleven most vulnerable points for sabotage in London. Three potential sabotage targets were crossed out, as they applied only to enemy fifth column action:[24]

1. Incendiaries in the City at several points simultaneously.
2. Damage to Clapham Junction.
3. Damage to Paddington Signal Box.
4. Blowing up Maidenhead Railway Bridge.
5. Destroying pylons carrying overhead cables across the Thames near Upminster.
6. ~~Poisoning the reservoir at Staines.~~
7. ~~Spreading germs in Tubes.~~
8. ~~Firing incendiary bullets at the Balloon Barrage.~~
9. Destruction of Mount Pleasant Post Office.
10. Sabotage at the main telephone exchange in St Martins-le-Grand.
11. Main Railway Control Office.

Personal weapons were confined to pistols (each with around 130 rounds of ammunition), sheath knives and rubber truncheons. Large-scale supplies of Thompson sub-machine guns had not yet arrived from the USA and the HDS was reduced to using decoy 'machine-gun rattles' (Pl. 32). Sabotage methodology was basic, often no more than what was being proposed in the *Picture Post* by Tom Wintringham, 'e.g. putting a pick through a petrol tank, slashing tyres, piles of stone on the road, felling trees, etc.' Grand recommended that the Section D officers casually 'broach the subject of possible sabotage to men such as garage mechanics, machinists, railway men, coal miners, quarrymen etc. to establish simple and easy means of local sabotage'.[25] In March 1940 Grand had discussed tactics of irregular warfare with Finnish contacts and, in return for supplying plastic explosives, time pencils and incendiary devices, he borrowed some of their ideas about arms dumps and incendiary warfare which he now put into practice.[26] In the first weeks there was no time to train the volunteers in the use of explosives, and incendiary devices were distributed as the main sabotage weapon – easy to replenish from domestic sources and to disguise in case of enemy searches.

The inventory included pint bottles of sulphuric acid 'labelled to appear to be innocent', and a supply of chemical time-delay capsules, which Grand suggested be labelled as 'dog medicine' or similar.[27] The capsules were a gelatine capsule (later known as Capsule H) filled with potassium chlorate and sugar which acted as a crude two-hour time delay to a petrol bomb containing a small quantity of sulphuric acid. The device was hidden on the target and two of the capsules were added to the bottle to begin a chemical reaction leading to ignition. Such incendiary devices could have a more powerful impact than explosives and created effective diversions. The battery pills were a failed attempt to destroy vehicle batteries by adding tablets of platinic chloride, but issue was discontinued in July 1940. The dumps also contained Tyesules: 5-inch-long gelatine capsules filled with paraffin (Pl. 33) which could be tied around magnesium bombs to increase the impact. Some cells were more specialised: units based near airfields or flat ground potentially useful as landing sites were given special instruction and explosives with MI(R) 'L delays' – detonation devices that used a lead wire that would stretch at a known rate and break to release the striker spring – which were considered more accurate than the acid-activated time pencil (Pl. 18). The arms dumps were to be hidden in buried galvanised rubbish bins but were delivered in cardboard boxes called 'Auxiliary Units', harking back to the much-feared 'Auxiliary Division' assassination squads of British intelligence that operated in Dublin in 1920.[28] The name was inherited by the GHQ Auxiliary Units, although Colin Gubbins never publicly acknowledged its ancestry. Regional dumps were also established under military guard.[29] In the final stages there was a more general distribution of explosives as a last ditch, scatter-gun approach, in the hope of seeding additional resistance units (similar to Grand's suggestion of randomly air-dropping weapons inside Germany). Grand summarised the scale of the HDS in the closing report for Section D in August:

> Some thirty Officers of this Section went to work at high pressure and completed this organisation and distributed in several thousand secret dumps throughout the country a vast quantity of incendiary materials.[30]

Although this may be an exaggeration, the distribution was undoubtedly on a significant nationwide scale, larger than the later Auxiliary Units perhaps realised. A later US journalist reported (with a considerable degree of licence):

> I was told by a leading London gun dealer that selected personnel were called secretly to the War Office in Whitehall, given individual keys to lorries full of Bren guns, grenades and ammunition, and told to 'take the bloody stuff and bury it – we don't want records and we don't want to be able to be forced to tell where it is – and use it for resistance in the invasion'.[31]

Warwicker records in *Churchill's Underground Army* how MI5 petulantly reported that the HDS had left 'dumps of explosives all over East Anglia and the southern counties'.[32] In Hornsea, Yorkshire, a man was approached during May/June 1940 by a 'mystery man' in civilian clothing, who gave him a box of explosives and asked him to form a resistance organisation if the Germans invaded. The box was buried in the garden and was only rediscovered in 1968.[33] There is also a tale of a Lord X delivering midnight supplies to an old woman in a Scottish village, knocking so loudly on her door as to risk arousing the curiosity of the neighbours.[34] Bickham Sweet-Escott wrote how 'One of our emissaries arrived, complete with black hat and striped trousers, in a remote Scottish village, and on asking the postmaster if he would accept a parcel of stores, was promptly handed over to the police.'[35] Some of the SIS officers clearly found it difficult to shed their stockbroker image. Peter Wilkinson, first head of organisation and planning in the Auxiliary Units, reports how

> In early June 1940, army units re-forming in the south of England after their evacuation from Dunkirk reported the presence of mysterious civilians behaving suspiciously in their divisional areas. These were members of Section D who had been given the task of recruiting an underground organisation to carry out subversion and resistance behind the German lines in the event of an invasion. The appearance of these strangers in their city clothes, sinister black limousines and general air of mystery caused alarm amongst the local inhabitants and infuriated subordinate military commanders since they refused to explain their presence or discuss their business except to say that it was 'most secret'.[36]

The HDS also sought to encourage passive resistance to occupation (as was officially recommended in the Channel Islands once occupied). Officers were to encourage local communities to 'unconsciously turn their minds to the problem of dealing with the Enemy by unarmed methods'; it might include such simple tactics as non-cooperation or misdirecting enemy troops.

The intelligence wing of the HDS was 'for the purpose of obtaining information for our own forces', passing it through enemy lines to GHQ Home Forces.[37] This role was to be 'stressed equally with the "obstruction" side' and was under the direct control of Viscount Bearsted. It would later be transferred en bloc to the Auxiliary Units as the core of its 'Special Duties Branch'.[38] At a time when clandestine wireless communications were still not the norm, runners would pass on information through a 'grapevine telegraph', somehow passing through the front line. Peter Attwater, a courier for the Section VII resistance in Derbyshire, has provided an insight into how the system might have worked. Couriers would arrange rendezvous points with neighbouring cells and the beginning of a seemingly casual conversation would include a safety word to demonstrate they were not acting under duress or believed they were being followed. The message would then be passed from one cell to the next.[39] The 'grapevine telegraph' was a poor substitute for wireless communications but existing wireless sets depended on skilled operators trained in morse code and these were in short supply. Grand's early encouragement of Schröter's research into a simple duplex wireless system was intended to overcome this, by allowing untrained operators to communicate using voice transmission (*see* Chapter 3). The research would eventually contribute to the short-range TRD sets of the Auxiliary Units.

For those not yet ready to accept the collapse of traditional 'rules of war', the civilian HDS planning to fight a war from the shadows without uniform or badges of rank was both illegal and 'un-British'. It also threatened to disrupt a unified command under GHQ Home Forces if Britain were invaded. General Ironside, C-in-C Home Forces, was reported to have 'read the riot act' after learning of the distribution of the Section D arms dumps and demanded that all such activities should be under military control.[40] The CIGS and Ironside were briefed by Jo Holland of MI(R) on the origins of the HDS and won an approval in principle from Churchill and the War Cabinet on 17 June to form a military alternative, under War Office control – the GHQ Auxiliary Units.[41] They argued that the army could not fight an anti-invasion campaign on the same ground as a civilian army of *francs-tireur* acting outside its control, and made the most of the embarrassment caused by security breaches in the distribution of a small number of HDS arms dumps. But at this stage, neither the Cabinet nor the War Office had any real idea of how an alternative would operate. Two days later Colin Gubbins (who had only returned from Norway on 10 June) was in place as commanding officer of the Auxiliary Units but was wracking his brain as to how to implement his orders. The Auxiliary Units only began to properly mobilise from early July, originally only as an advisory body for the Local Defence Volunteers (renamed the Home Guard on 22 July) to create their own guerrilla units, before arriving at the system of uniformed Home Guard and army patrols operating from underground hides. Meanwhile, whatever its faults, the HDS provided the only operational guerrilla force in Britain ready to resist invasion, although there were continuing complaints over its disregard of the Hague Convention. On 21 June 1940 William Spens, the commissioner for East Anglia, harangued General Ironside over the people 'staying put' in case of an invasion. Spens was disturbed that 'we were arranging sabotage behind the lines if the Germans succeeded in landing'.[42] Gordon MacLeod, a Dorset LDV officer, who had been approached by an officer of either Section D or the new Auxiliary Units, felt so strongly that he wrote to the Prime Minister on 3 July to complain.

Sir,
Since it seems unlikely that the matter is within your knowledge, I must respectfully beg to direct your attention to the fact that LDV officers in this and presumably other areas have been approached by persons stated to represent the War Office, with a view to the organisation of a system of sabotage which could be brought into operation within the enemy lines in the event of his establishing a foothold in this country.

For the carrying out of this sabotage it is proposed that caches of explosives and the like shall be established at certain secret points, these to be utilised for *francs-tireur* operations by selected members of the LDV, who would remain behind in the occupied area for this purpose.

Quite apart from its questionable aspect under International Law, in view of the brutal retaliatory measures which action of the kind has already evoked from the enemy, in occupied territory both in this war and in that of 1914–18, and the certainty that it will similarly bring death and untold suffering to innocent non-combatant members of the community if embarked upon in this country, I cannot think that the ill-considered proposal has been made with your knowledge or approval.[43]

MacLeod's letter excited a furious denial of responsibility by the War Office for civilian sabotage operations. In discussing the letter on 30 July, General Paget, Chief of Staff to the C-in-C Home Forces, blamed Section D for the activities in Dorset and distanced the new GHQ Auxiliary Units from the concept of organising civilian sabotage in an 'occupied' area.

Mr MacLeod's misapprehension may, on the other hand, be due to the fact that there was until recently an organisation working under the SIS, of whose activities he may have heard, which was charged with the task of organising sabotage and obstruction by civilians who, in the event of invasion, would remain behind and operate locally. Special stores for this purpose were issued to selected individuals.[44]

Such comments show the gulf between what the CIGS and the Foreign Secretary had first agreed to implement in Europe in March 1939 and the more 'gentlemanly' tactics that were only acceptable to use within Britain.

It was not until 22 June that Major General Macdougall (Deputy Chief, Imperial General Staff) discovered the existence of the HDS and immediately raised concerns over its role vis-à-vis the new Auxiliary Units with Major General 'Pug' Ismay, secretary to the Chiefs of Staff Committee. Soldier Macdougall naturally assumed that the not yet activated War Office Auxiliary Units should take the lead role, without knowing any detail of the purpose of either organisation – but nonetheless suggested that SIS might fund the Auxiliary Units.

My Dear Pug,
Regarding the question of para-military activities in this country in the event of the enemy gaining a footing, the CIGS has decided that an organisation is to be set up under Brigadier Gubbins to undertake this task. The organisation will be directly under the Commander-in-Chief, Home Forces.

I now find that Lord Bearsted works under 'D' Section, and has also been charged with a similar role.

There is thus obviously great danger not only of over-lapping but more important, of considerable confusion arising as both organisations will be working in the same areas and also seeking recruits among the same personnel.

I feel that, in a matter of this nature, it is most important that there should be proper military control from the outset, as obviously these auxiliary units, whether uniformed or not, must be prepared to co-operate with and possibly even work under the local military Commander. ... That being the case, I consider that Bearsted, with whatever staff he has collected, should definitely be placed under Gubbins and work under his orders. Whatever organisation Bearsted got going could easily be absorbed if it is suitable. The only other alternative would be to close down Bearsted's show, but I think this would be a pity and there is probably no necessity for such a step. ... In view of the above, I hope you will agree that only one organisation is, not only required, but advisable and that this must be under military authority and accountable for their progress and actions to a military Commander. I would be very grateful if you could get this recognised and the necessary instructions passed to Bearsted.

A small amount of money will be required to start with, say £1,000 a month. I believe Lord Bearsted draws his funds from SIS and it would appear to be the easiest way if Gubbins could be authorised to do the same.

Yours

Ian[45]

Ismay took this up with the Director of Military Intelligence, Major General Beaumont-Nesbitt, who had almost certainly been aware of the HDS since the ISPB meeting of 27 May and was rather more relaxed about the co-existence of the two bodies as their concepts were, at this stage, very different.[46] The Chiefs of Staff Committee was another body which only belatedly became aware of the existence of the HDS and at their 8 July meeting declared that there was 'no effective control of the operations of D'. This was just the latest in a series of complaints over irregular operations being carried out without their knowledge.[47] Menzies had earlier explained to the Hankey Inquiry 'that from the earliest days S.S. [Secret Service] had, for vital reasons of secrecy, deliberately been kept aloof from regular government committees such as the Committee of Imperial Defence and the Chiefs of Staffs organisation'.[48] For his part, the CIGS had earlier approved the European-wide 'Scheme D' on the specific understanding that information was not to be shared with the Chiefs of Staff Committee. Nonetheless, as late as 5 July the Director of Combined Operations accepted Section D as being responsible for the 'Organisation of civil resistance and sabotage in the UK'.[49] Such a concept remained an anathema to many, for which the Auxiliary Units offered a legal alternative:

These men, being members of the Home Guard, will of course fight in uniform ... being a uniformed and properly organised body, its members are in no way violating 'international law' even if fighting behind the advanced elements of the invading forces, where units of regular troops will also be fighting ...[50]

The final stage of the HDS
In 1968 David Lampe rejected any idea of a significant contribution by the HDS to the Auxiliary Units:

> A few of the men who had been in Section D's resistance set-up were asked to join the Auxiliary Units organisation, but most were politely thanked for what they had been prepared to do for the nation and told simply that their organisation no longer existed.[51]

In reality, GHQ could not afford to dismiss so easily the expertise of Section D during the dangerous summer of 1940, and especially while Gubbins struggled to find a methodology for the new body he had been ordered to form. Nigel Oxenden, Intelligence Officer for Norfolk during 1940, admitted:

> most I/Os [Auxiliary Units intelligence officers] were assisted by introductions to one or two men who had already been chosen by MI5 [*sic* – Section D] ... These were generally outstanding individuals, who eventually became group commanders. Meanwhile their local knowledge made them invaluable in finding the right recruits.[52]

There was a significant overlap when Bearsted's civilian HDS continued to operate alongside, and supported, the new military Auxiliary Units. The DMI, Beaumont-Nesbitt, had been satisfied on 24 June that Gubbins and Bearsted had worked out a 'modus operandi' of working together.[53] At this time, in the spirit of MI(R), Gubbins still envisaged the Auxiliary Units intelligence officers acting mainly as advisers to local commanders of the LDV, for the latter to form small sabotage units which could also act as guides for army commandos passing through enemy lines.[54] This was a very different concept from the HDS sabotage and intelligence network which was already in place. Once his ideas crystallised, Gubbins relied heavily on Section D for supplies to his own Auxiliary Units sabotage teams, which differed from the HDS in being more focused on using professionally made explosives (there being an assumption that they would not survive long enough to need resupplying). In July 1940, in addition to distributing 300 incendiary arms dumps for the HDS, Section D supplied the Auxiliary Units with 30 demonstration demolition sets together with 400 small and 10 large explosives dumps (Fig. 8). By 25 August Aston House had supplied 7,200lb of plastic explosives, 7,470lb of gelignite, 4,000 SIP grenades, 36,020 detonators and 67,400 time pencils to the Auxiliary Units. It also supplied 200 copies of its *Brown Book* manual on the use of explosives in what became the first training manual to the Auxiliary Units.[55] Two Section D officers were loaned to the Auxiliary Units and Section D also organised some of the first training for Auxiliary Units intelligence officers at Aston House.[56] Section D's base at Aston House remained the main supply base for the Auxiliary Units for the rest of the war, continuing this role after being absorbed by SOE.[57]

Figure 8. Material supplied by Section D to Home Defence Scheme and Auxiliary Units during July 1940. (*TNA HS 8/214*)

	Home Defence Scheme	Auxiliary Units
Time fuses	4,060	46,380
Safety fuse (ft)		14,016
Safety fuse, lengths match-ended	1,810	
Detonating fuse (ft)		27,000
Instantaneous fuse		4,950
Detonators		27,020
Blasting Gelignite (lbs)		5,600
High explosive (lbs)		5,246
Medium-large incendiary bombs	450	5,270
Medium incendiary bombs	1,610	5,450
Tyesules (paraffin incendiaries)	29,479	10,124
Petrol paraffin mixture (gallons)	400	
Capsules for petrol bomb	63,540	
Acid for petrol bomb (quarts)	206	
Magnets		2,336
Fog signals		1,560
Crimping tools	42	540
Tape (15-yd reels)		1,538
Vaseline (tubes)		950
Fuzes (boxes) [Detonators]	1,540	1,571
Striker boards	1,668	
A.W. bombs		1,200
Pressure switches		50

Once the mobilisation of the Auxiliary Units finally began to get under way, Churchill was persuaded to reverse his previous agreement with Grand and formally supported the objections to civilian warfare. The Secretary of War, Anthony Eden, clarified the issue to the War Cabinet on 8 July 1940:

It is the view of the Commander-in-Chief, Home Forces, with which I am in agreement, that actual fighting should be restricted to the military and Local Defence Volunteers, and that no civilian who is not a member of these forces should be authorised to use lethal weapons. Only if this principle is accepted would it be possible to ensure control of military activities by the military authorities.[58]

At the end of July it was finally decided to absorb the HDS within the Auxiliary Units on the grounds that 'the risk of reprisals incurred by allowing civilians to engage in sabotage activities was too great'.[59] Grand recognised the fundamental change in approach:

as far as civilian obstruction was concerned, the organisation on which D officers had been forming was no longer necessary, and its place could now be taken by Auxiliary Units working openly and using as recruits uniformed LDVs.[60]

The revised methodology of the Auxiliary Units now approximated the HDS on a military basis, with sabotage teams drawn from the Home Guard, supported by army 'scout sections'. In a final attempt to preserve a rationale for the organisation, Grand proposed making the HDS less of an anti-invasion guerrilla force and more of a longer-term resistance organisation, operating only after a military surrender, when SIS would officially take on the responsibility for on-going resistance. Using the dual-level model of resistance proposed for Norway and Romania, the HDS would remain 'quiescent' during the invasion campaign and only begin to operate after the Auxiliary Units had been destroyed and the country occupied. Grand explained:

> I detailed officers to my D.M. group to work with a second organisation of special units allotted by the War Office for the same type of work. In this way we had two organisations available and one would be brought into action when, as was inevitable, the other was discovered and broken up. The D organisation was the one that was to remain quiescent at the outset.[61]

The order for the resistance organisation to initially remain 'quiescent' was also proposed in Norway, and had been given to French stay-behind parties a month earlier. It was the standing instruction for the Section VII resistance in Britain and was later recommended in Romania (*see* p. 113). Grand's proposal both suggested defeatism to the War Office and came close to duplicating the role of SIS Section VII as the main civilian resistance organisation. It was therefore quickly rejected. The Home Defence Scheme was officially disbanded, and the intelligence branch became the core of the Special Duties Branch of the Auxiliary Units. Deep in the shadows, however, the SIS Section VII resistance continued to expand and it is likely that they absorbed some of the HDS sabotage cells, surviving to 1944.[62] Some SIS officers expressed concern for the loss of the HDS. Major Maurice Petherick MP, an SIS liaison officer attached to the Paris embassy before the fall of France, wrote a blunt letter on the subject.

> Dear Grand,
> I hate to worry you but isn't it time a halt was called before the organisation which you conceived is jettisoned to national disadvantage.
>   Sincerely
>   Maurice Petherick[63]

Special Duties Branch (SDB) of the Auxiliary Units
When, in late June, Bearsted and Gubbins discussed how the HDS and new Auxiliary Units would work together, one key topic was the intelligence branch of HDS. The pressing need for GHQ in terms of intelligence-gathering in 1940 was for a ground-based early warning system that could quickly pass on information

to army commands as to the pattern of initial German landings. The main War Office solution was the deployment of the highly skilled, wireless-equipped linguists of 'Phantom' patrols of No. 1 GHQ Reconnaissance Unit, criss-crossing enemy lines. Their intelligence could be supplemented by the cruder methodology of the HDS intelligence network, although the information carried on a 'grapevine' risked being out of date before it was received and it was probably more useful in monitoring any pre-invasion 'fifth column' mutterings on behalf of MI5 and Military Intelligence.[64] Intelligence-gathering was at the heart of SIS, but its primary concern was in the expansion of its Section VII wireless network and so the rudimentary HDS intelligence branch was allowed to pass en bloc to the Auxiliary Units. Gubbins received authorisation to create an HQ 'Special Duties' on 11 July 1940, with a nominal establishment of 11 intelligence officers (not filled until 1941) but with the cryptic comment that the organisation had already commenced activities – a discreet way of referring to the HDS network.[65] None of the senior officers at Auxiliary Units HQ had experience in running agent networks and they lacked the technical expertise to provide a better communications system. In practice, the SDB continued to be managed by Bearsted and SIS over the summer of 1940, it being agreed between SIS and GHQ in July that

> While obstructive activities of the 'D' organisation are being gradually transferred to GHQ Auxiliary Units, it is considered necessary and desirable by GHQ and CSS that the Intelligence side of the activities should be maintained and developed.[66]

The SOE history of Section D concluded:

> Colonel Viscount Bearsted continued his organisation en bloc under the name of 'Auxiliary Units (Special Duties)'. It was not until the danger of invasion was relatively past that the organisation as originally planned by D section was dissolved.[67]

The paucity of references to the operation of the Auxiliary Units intelligence network during 1940 hints at the continuing influence of the ever-reticent SIS. Lampe maintained that the SDB began with 1,000 civilian agents (amounting to around one-third of the total 3,250 attained by June 1944); if this figure is correct, most of them were probably inherited from the HDS.[68] The civilian agents were something of a mystery to the military mind. One of the weekly Auxiliary Units progress meetings in July 1940 was attended by 'an equal number of strangers, officers and civilians, and even a woman'. Gubbins declared, 'You may as well get to know each other, gentlemen; you are all in the same game.'[69] These 'strangers', whilst in the same 'game', were significantly not acknowledged as being in the same organisation. The attempt to bolt together the existing HDS intelligence branch and the operational branch of the Auxiliary Units resulted in a disjointed organisation that lasted throughout the war and was a serious impediment to efficiency. Bearsted's 'Auxiliary Units (Special Duties)' survived until the autumn of 1940 when he joined SOE, and unsurprisingly it was a SIS officer, Major Petherick, who then converted the 'Special Duties' into a body that GHQ could manage directly, without jeopardising the continuing, deep-cover operations of Section VII.

Three of the four known SDB intelligence officers appointed before November 1940 show evidence of having previously served with SIS, probably in Section D. John Todd, K.W. Johnson and R. Fraser had originally been commissioned onto the General List and received their promotions to acting captain on 22 July, marking their formal transfer to the Auxiliary Units.[70] None had any known links with MI(R), the most common recruiting ground for Auxiliary Units intelligence officers but the surviving 1940 Army List entries for Todd and Johnson include the phrase characteristic of SIS officers, 'without pay and allowances' (i.e. not paid for out of War Office funds).

The Standfast Club
There was one another initiative that is worthy of mention, although it was not progressed. John Dolphin seems to have been inspired by the immediate popularity of the new Local Defence Volunteers (LDV), formed in May 1940, to suggest a body geared more to mass action in irregular warfare. He may even have had thoughts of using the LDV as the basis for his proposed 'Standfast Club' given that there was considerable uncertainty as to how the LDV should be used. As late as 22 June Churchill himself seemed unsure of the latter's purpose, writing to Eden:

> Could I have a brief statement of the LDV position, showing the progress achieved in raising and arming them, and whether they are designed for observation or for serious fighting. What is their relationship to the police, the Military command, and the Regional Commissioners? From whom do they receive their orders, and to whom do they report?[71]

On 1 July Dolphin wrote to Grand with the suggestion of a triple grade 'Standfast Club'. His idea was to encourage citizens to stay in their homes in the event of invasion. Those classed as Grade A would be given weapons and instructions on how to make defences. Grade B were people prepared to undertake sniping and minor sabotage. Grade C were those who were simply prepared to stay in their homes so as not to clog the roads with refugees and to ensure that the civilians of Grades A and B (and the HDS) would not stand out in an empty landscape. Like the LDV, the members of the 'Standfast Club' would be clearly identified with badges or armlets in compliance with the Hague Convention and Dolphin hoped that the movement would snowball into very large numbers.[72] No action was taken on this plan, as it was overtaken by the development of the Home Guard.

* * *

The British resistance was, fortunately, never called into action but the complex layering represents the most sophisticated attempt during the Second World War at creating a response to the threat of occupation, made possible by not having to be improvised in the very teeth of invasion. The methodology remained valid into the Cold War and consequently its details were subject to continued secrecy and misinformation for decades following the Second World War.

United States of America

Churchill knew that the economic support of the USA would be vital for the survival of Britain. The USA was, however, suspicious of being dragged into another European war and the allies had to tread carefully so as not to antagonise the isolationists. The Foreign Office and British Embassy were therefore initially opposed to the expansion of pro-allied propaganda in the USA for fear that it would be counter-productive. Information on the early efforts of British intelligence to both support the economic blockade against Germany and to nudge the US into the allied camp is consequently sketchy and has been overshadowed by the work of the later British Security Coordination (BSC) under William Stephenson (*see below*). But in the early summer of 1940, when the fate of Britain was in the balance and the USA was divided as to whether it was worth bolstering the British war effort, Section D broke the official agreement that British intelligence would not mount operations within the USA, and although not on an extensive scale, the British people had good reason to be grateful for its invisible presence.

The US Mail Swindle

Some of Section D's US operations were designed to cause little more than mischief and it was quickly appreciated that the potential risks to Britain's reputation were greater than the benefits of causing confusion in the Nazi state. In the summer of 1939 German Intelligence had tried to use the British postal system to distribute propaganda using addresses taken from the phone book.[73] Inspired by this, early in December 1939 the versatile Walter Wren came up with the idea that mail in transit to Germany from neutral countries via Britain could be tampered with to include propaganda that would appear to have come from the original sender. The official Postal Censorship office in Liverpool (which opened letters for examination and then clearly labelled them 'examined by censor') promised full cooperation and proved to be eager collaborators in this illegal enterprise.

> [REDACTED] of the older inhabitants of the Censors office who had done the same work in the last war greeted them with the remark 'We're glad to see you. We wondered when you were going to turn up.' [Wren] who was in charge proceeded to find as many of the last war operatives as possible (there were only two) and started to produce anew a technique that must have existed in detailed form in the last war, but of which all trace had been lost. ... Luckily, he was an officer of great ability who appreciated fully the

delicate issues involved. With first one, and later more assistants, he produced a technique which covered every aspect of secret censorship and founded what was afterwards a world-wide branch. . . .[74]

The actor and lyricist Eric Maschwitz, already working for Postal Censorship in Liverpool, was recruited to Section D and became the liaison officer to his former colleagues. An HQ for *Operation Letter Bags* was established in a suite of the Adelphi Hotel, Liverpool, with the cover that Maschwitz was developing an idea for a new theatrical revue. Adding to the deception, the team of Walter Wren, H. Montgomery Hyde, Lionel Montague, Eric Maschwitz and Anthony Samuel (son of Viscount Bearsted) threw theatrical parties and Maschwitz did indeed write the show *New Faces* in his spare time. One accidental contribution of Section D to the war effort therefore included the iconic wartime song *A Nightingale Sang in Berkeley Square*.[75]

The base of operations became the small and remote Postal Censorship office in Myrtle Street, Liverpool, which dealt with 2nd class mail that had the advantage of not being sealed, including circular material such as newspapers, samples and greetings cards. Neither the British nor the German censorship departments paid much attention to this class of mail, due to its bulk and limited security interest. Rather than tamper with the existing mail, it was decided to introduce extra mailings to Germany, supposedly coming from the USA, using envelopes of American type and bearing cancelled US postal stamps, made possible due to the US practice of allowing the purchase of 'pre-cancelled' stamps, not franked by the US Postal Service, by firms with large mailing lists. First, such stamps were roughly cut out from their original envelopes (then 'lost in the post') by three women co-opted from the Postal Censorship department – Mrs Pomeroy, Miss Ritchie and Miss Carey. An SIS laboratory in Section N (responsible for the secret opening of foreign diplomatic mail) under William Webbe (*aka* 'Steam Kettle Bill') then carefully removed the stamps and provided a gum, identical to the original, for refixing them to new envelopes.[76] Meanwhile, Viscount Bearsted had arranged the use of the Shell Addressograph facilities, which had three USA-made stencil machines, to print address labels for recipients in Germany using information from existing address lists.

The first mailing purported to be a New Year Greetings card from the fictitious 'Pan American German Friendship League' based in New York but claiming offices in Chicago, Buenos Aires and Montevideo (so allowing a spread of apparent sources for the letters). A cartoon depicted Hitler and Stalin dining off the carcasses of Finnish and Polish children, quoting from Hitler's speech that he would never be seen 'wining and dining the Bolsheviks'. Francis Ogilvy was sent to the USA in mid-January to lay a false paper trail to provide 'evidence' that the card had originated in the USA and to establish a network for further covert posting operations. The SIS station in New York was asked to cooperate but was warned that 'His contacts may possibly prove embarrassing' and therefore to avoid unnecessary contact in case the latter were engaged in other clandestine work.[77] Meanwhile, in Liverpool 2,000 envelopes containing the fake greetings cards were judiciously inserted into the US mail bags. Over two nights in the cold and draughty Myrtle Street office, the mail bags were secretly opened and the new mail inserted by the team, wearing rubber gloves so as not to leave finger-prints. Three or four appropriately addressed envelopes were carefully slipped into existing string-tied bundles of letters. No more than twenty bundles in any mail bag were so doctored. The mail bags were then resealed using forged US Mail seals. The next day the rest of the Postal Censorship staff, not aware of what had been done during the night, carried out their usual sample inspections of the US mail bags so that everything seemed normal. It took two nights with an eight-person team and, upon completion, they celebrated with a bottle of champagne.

The second mailing was intended to be of crumpled leaflets deploring the Hitler–Stalin Pact, supposedly inserted by a German worker in sample packets of coffee and cocoa sent regularly to Germany from the German-owned grocery firm of Leineweber in Brazil. At the least, this would cause some disruption as the grocery firm tried to identify the source. Unfortunately, there was a pause in the sending of suitable coffee samples and this mailing was cancelled. Instead, a third scheme was devised, purported to come from a fictitious New York literary agent, 'Oscar Finch'. 'Finch' wrote to several German doctors offering to pay them for a rebuttal of an article (actually a fake) that had supposedly been published in the *Literary Digest*, reporting on the poor state of health of the German people. The real intention was to distribute the pro-allied information contained in the fake article, sent by First Class mail (requiring a forged New York franking stamp, painstakingly stamped by hand to look as if it were machine-stamped). In the end it was only possible to complete 200 mailings of the fake article. Plans were under way for a much larger shipment of over 6,000 pieces of fake mail when, in February 1940, it was decided to abandon the operation. Francis Ogilvy had been warned by the SIS station in the USA that the paper trail he was planning to create would be too easily traced back.[78] 1940 was a presidential election year and if it were to be discovered that SIS was interfering with the US Mail, then the fact would be used by anti-war Republican candidates.

In January 1940 the secret censorship scheme was extended to Gibraltar as a joint operation with Section N of SIS. It would target mail being sent from Germany via neutral Spain and Italy to the Americas. Two officers, including H. Montgomery Hyde from *Operation Letter Bags*, were dispatched there for this purpose. Hyde travelled under cover as a Foreign Office diplomatic courier but his diplomatic bag contained not secret correspondence but instead a small kettle thoughtfully provided by 'Steam Kettle Bill' for steaming open letters.[79] Four women members of Section D were recruited for the team during May 1940. Their task was to examine transit mail seized from passing ships by the Contra-band Control section of the Royal Navy. The Section D team was based in the former porter's lodge of the Loreto convent, where it secretly opened and inspected foreign diplomatic mail as per well-established Section N routines. In addition, they identified the mailings, routed through neutral Spain and Italy, that were being used by the Germans to distribute anti-British propaganda to the USA, Central and South America. These envelopes were secretly opened and the contents replaced with pro-British propaganda before being sent on their way. Hyde commented: 'Thus, besides having an effective method of distributing our own propaganda, we had the satisfaction of knowing the Nazis were paying the postage for its delivery!'[80]

Maschwitz and Hyde were later to expand the concept of the scheme under the British Security Coordination as Station M in Canada, a more sophisticated scheme intercepting official mail to insert fake correspondence, but which was also engaged in more targeted special operations.

In 1940 thousands of tons of food parcels were being shipped to Germany across the Atlantic in US ships, frustrating British plans for a complete economic blockade of Germany. In June Grand sent Walter Hauck to the USA to insert anti-Nazi propaganda into food parcels destined for several obscure Nazi officials, identified through a 1,000-page index to Nazi party hierarchy supplied by one of the German émigré organisations.[81] An anonymous letter to the Gestapo then warned that anti-Nazi literature was being smuggled via food parcels, whereupon all shipments were held up at ports for searching – resulting in some of the food beginning to rot. It was also hoped that those officials in whose possession the parcels were found would fall under suspicion and increase the paranoia within the Nazi Party.[82] Grand also sought a more positive economic campaign. On 6 July 1940 he suggested the establishment of a fake 'Panama Corporation' to buy luxury goods from the USA for importation into the UK. He believed that this would demonstrate the economic value of an alliance with Britain, appealing to the capitalist sentiments of the US government, and simply buying-in goods would also free UK production for the war effort and provide a profit for the Treasury.

Propaganda
Based on the successful experience in the Balkans with *Britanova*, Grand proposed to establish a press bureaux in New York, the Mid-West and the Pacific coast, staffed by journalists receiving information daily from the Ministry of Information. An improvement in pro-allied reporting in the American press would also influence Latin America, and would penetrate European countries, both neutral and enemy.[83] Another avenue for improving allied influence was through the Committee to Defend America by Aiding the Allies (CDAAA), formed in May 1940 and chaired by William Allen White, newspaper editor and politician. It successfully lobbied for the provision of American material assistance for the British war effort, based on the argument that it was the best way of avoiding direct US involvement in the war. Although it was a US body, a Section D contact was inserted onto the Board of the CDAAA in London 'who could induce

the members to carry out our instructions' and ensure that the correct 'line' was carried in their newsletter, sent to the USA.[84] Although not named, this may have been Helen Parkins-Gauntlett, who was Secretary of the British 'outpost' of the CDAAA and who later worked closely with Edward Hulton in the British-based Committee for American Aid for the Defence of British Homes.

Jewish communities in America were an obvious target in pressurising the US government to take an anti-Nazi stance and to join the Allies. Despite the political risks, Section D worked most closely with the well-organised Zionist movement. Phineas Horowitz, vice-president of the British Zionist Federation, was a London fur dealer who had been one of the organisers of the 1933 anti-Nazi trade boycott and was secretary of the World Non-Sectarian Anti-Nazi League. Already working with Section D on a European trade boycott (*see* pp. 79–81), on 17 May Horowitz produced two schemes for work in the USA:

1. Re-inspire the USA anti-Nazi boycott organisation by publishing a list of Jewish firms trading with Germany and encourage moral sanctions against them in the Jewish community.
2. Mobilize American Jewish lobbying in favour of the Allied cause, which might, if thought advisable, include a campaign for direct American involvement in the war although it was important that this not be seen to be directed by allied governments.

The work would be undertaken in the USA by Horowitz, Josef Hirschberg (an Antwerp diamond merchant working with Section D in the Low Countries since February), Rabbi Perlzweig and Chaim Weizmann (President of the World Zionist Organisation and a key contact of Section D: *see* Chapter 7).

On 4 June Rabbi Perlzweig, recently returned from the USA, provided Monty Chidson with a detailed report on the US mood. He had travelled widely on behalf of the World Jewish Congress, lecturing on the Nazi threat. The British Ambassador, the Marquis of Lothian, had tried to ban overt British propaganda in the USA for fear of it being counter-productive. By contrast, German propaganda was widespread. Perlzweig wanted to harness opinion of the 5 million Jews in the United States and use this pressure to bring the USA alive to the threat posed worldwide by the Nazis. Although the Americans were still isolationists, Perlzweig believed that they were hungry for news, accepting that it was likely to be dosed with propaganda. Unsurprisingly, he also wanted the British government to display a more sympathetic consideration to the establishment of a Jewish state in Palestine. Chidson pointed out the obvious risks to Grand on 7 June that 'It was a matter of policy how far Jewish influences could be used without placing the Government under undesirable moral obligation.' Meanwhile, on 29 May 1940 Horowitz had proposed a pro-allied Jewish Fifth Column in the USA to counter the efforts of Nazi sympathisers; it was to be organised by a central committee in New York, with branches throughout the USA and in South

America. Horowitz suggested that Josef Hirschberg had the necessary contacts and personality to organise this scheme, taking direct instructions from Chidson in Section D. After providing £1,500 for set-up expenses, Horowitz believed the scheme could be run completely from voluntary donations, although the lack of a financial lever carried the risk of Section D losing control of the movement's direction. Hirschberg went on a reconnaissance to the USA in late June and established an office in New York, whilst Section D paid a four months' allowance to his wife in England at the rate of £40 a month. His first objective was to encourage the revived Anti-Nazi League under James Sheldon. Originally founded in 1933, the League had campaigned against the 1936 Olympics and the 1938 Schmeling–Louis boxing match. Hirschberg wanted to use the non-sectarian nature of the Anti-Nazi League to infiltrate and expose pro-Nazi organisations, presenting their activities as conspiratorial and anti-American – a campaign that proved most successful, providing good publicity in the US press.

It was finally decided that Perlzweig should again tour America, lecturing on the moral righteousness of the allied cause. He returned to the USA in mid-September, on the very day that Grand was sacked as head of Section D. To circumvent the ban on pro-British propaganda still imposed by the Foreign Office, Perlzweig officially went as a representative of the World Jewish Federation, although the message that he preached cut across Zionist aspirations to be firmly pro-allied. Financed initially by Section D, the mission proved to be self-financing and the later SOE considered it a great success.

Italian anti-fascists in the USA
The veteran anti-fascist Massimo 'Max' Salvadori had first worked with SIS in 1937 but in 1938 he went to the USA. On 28 August 1939 he received a telegram from 'David' (Claude Dansey) asking him to return to London, where he was recruited by Section D, first to work as a double agent with the Italian authorities and then to contact Italian anti-fascists in France (*see above*, p. 64). He found the contemporary belief in the prospects for large-scale revolt naïve and was frustrated by the Foreign Office refusal to allow Section D to build up its organisation within Italy. He returned to the USA under cover of working for Alexander Korda Films to assist the Free Italy groups that were springing up across the Americas amongst the 6 million-strong Italian community and to assist Italian exiles who were stranded in Lisbon, unoccupied France and North Africa to get to the USA. After transfer to the new SOE, he recruited exiled Italians in the USA and Mexico to return to Italy to join the resistance forces. In March 1943 he finally convinced SOE that he should be allowed to go on active service and was commissioned into the British army, becoming one of SOE's most important agents in Italy. Ironically, his father, an equally passionate anti-fascist but also a strong Italian nationalist, contemptuously described him as a 'foreign agent' when he returned home in July 1944.[85]

From Section D to British Security Coordination
In March 1940, following his failed mission to Sweden in connection with *Operation Lumps* (*see* p. 154), Menzies sent William Stephenson to the USA to establish official links with US intelligence services. He went again to the USA in June 1940 to establish the British Security Coordination organisation that brought together SIS, MI5 and SOE. Several of its early recruits, including Ingram Fraser and Walter Wren, joined later by Louis Franck as head of special operations and by Eric Maschwitz and Harford Montgomery Hyde, were former Section D officers. Of particular importance was David Ogilvy, who was working for the US Gallup Opinion Poll organisation in 1939 when recruited for Section D and could report back to Grand (and then Stephenson) on the state of US public opinion. Maschwitz further developed the concept of the secret censorship scheme in BSC's Station M in Canada, later joined by a former Section D officer from the French section, the screenwriter and photographer Frederick Elles. Other former Section D officers in BSC included Sydney Morrell from Hungary and Valentine Williams from the propaganda section. The debt of BSC to the earlier activities of Section D and the expertise of its officers was never acknowledged.

Chapter 11

Into SOE

Few in government knew of Laurence Grand's blueprint of March 1939 for encouraging a European-wide popular revolt against the Nazis using sabotage, subversion and black propaganda (*see* Chapter 2). Following the *blitzkrieg* in the Low Countries and France, Grand's ideas that had begun in a 'shed at the bottom of a garden' now emerged as a central plank of strategic planning.[1] To improve coordination, in March 1940 the joint intelligence sub-committee of the chiefs of staff had suggested the formation of the Inter-Services Project Board (ISPB) but this was only an advisory body.[2] On 25 May, with the fall of France imminent, the chiefs of staff concluded that popular revolts in occupied countries now needed high-level direction and a new system was needed to achieve this:

> we regard this form of activity as of the very highest importance. A special organisation will be required and plans to put these operations into effect should be prepared, and all the necessary preparations and training should be proceeded with as a matter of urgency.[3]

Out of military weakness, bombing and economic blockade, coupled now with subversive warfare, were still optimistically seen as obviating the need for a large-scale military intervention. Even as the Dunkirk evacuation was under way, Gladwyn Jebb of the Foreign Office collated a report which predicted the collapse of the German home front within weeks.[4] Hugh Dalton, the new Minister for Economic Warfare, similarly predicted that within six months Europe would be faced with 'Famine, starvation and revolt, most of all in the slave lands which Germany had overrun.' On 14 June he declared that the Nazi pall would soon dissipate 'like the snow in spring'.[5] Here was the context for Churchill's enthusiasm in expanding the concept of Section D to create a more powerful Special Operations Executive (SOE) to 'Set Europe Ablaze' and encourage immediate large-scale popular revolt. By July Section D comprised up to 300 officers and agents, operating across Scandinavia, Western Europe, the Balkans and within Britain. It is not surprising that critics viewed it as a private army beyond military or ministerial control – ripe for the picking. But in carving out a role for the revolutionary Section D, the innovative Grand had made too many dangerous enemies across the government, SIS and the War Office for him to have a place in this new era. The success of Section D in organising propaganda irritated the Ministry of Information and Electra House. In June 1940 Grand stepped on the toes of GHQ Home Forces by suggesting a reorganisation of UK defence into small 'All-Arms Brigade Group' areas. At the same time he proposed a new 'Ministry of Progress' to improve efficiency of the implementation of government decisions.[6] There were few sections of government that he had not antagonised! As Grand's reputation was being systematically destroyed, his revolutionary concepts and even his language were appropriated by Hugh Dalton, newly responsible for the Ministry of Economic Warfare.

The War Office was the first department to set its sights on Section D. On 3 March 1940 the new Director of Military Intelligence, Major General Beaumont-Nesbitt, wrote to Major General Ismay, Secretary to the Chiefs of Staff Committee, complaining that the small MI(R) still remained an organisation largely dealing only with the theory of irregular warfare but

> It has been left to SIS to put any projects into force. In many cases, too, such projects have been put forward and developed by SIS with little or no reference to Service Departments. To my mind this is fundamentally wrong and is not the way to secure maximum results.[7]

Beaumont-Nesbitt's predecessor, Henry Pownall, had suggested the division of labour between Section D and MI(R) but the rapid collapse of army operations in Europe had prevented MI(R) from developing its remit of organising military guerrilla warfare. In June Beaumont-Nesbitt proposed bringing all irregular operations under the control of a new directorate of the War Office, responsible to the Chiefs of Staff Committee (hitherto excluded from a role in secret warfare).[8] Ismay agreed, having confidently asserted in early May, 'As I see it, the War Office would normally be the predominant partner in any sabotage business or other form of irregular warfare.'[9]

At around the same time, at the Foreign Office Lord Cadogan (Permanent Under-Secretary) suggested to his Private Secretary, Gladwyn Jebb – the official who had the difficult job of being the buffer between Section D and the Foreign Office/Treasury – that Jebb should become Controller of all D schemes, putting Grand under direct Foreign Office supervision. Sir Campbell Stuart of Electra House supported the proposal, reassuring Jebb by saying that such an appointment was merely a stepping stone to getting rid of Grand completely and then he would be in full charge.[10] Jebb rejected the idea, ironically, in view of his future position as CEO of SOE, admitting he did not have the temperament or training for such a post. He believed that sabotage should be under the control of a 'tough and intelligent soldier' and also feared that Grand would simply avoid telling him what was going on.[11] In late June Stewart Menzies, chief of SIS, met with the Foreign Secretary and discussed the future of Section D. The embarrassment over *Operation Lumps* in Sweden and current complaints over the Home Defence Scheme would have been fresh in the mind. The objectives of Section D were so at odds with the primarily intelligence-gathering role of SIS that it risked exposing, or at least unbalancing, the organisation. Unlike his predecessor, Admiral Sinclair, who had worked closely with Grand as mentor and ally, Menzies (renowned as a weak manager) could not control his dynamic subordinate and was floundering. Although Menzies received monthly written reports from Grand during 1940 and was directly involved in the organisation of some projects (including the disastrous *Operation Lumps* in Sweden), a pencilled note of the meeting explains:

> C says responsibility too much for him. 'D' represents his own views as 'C'. D's great ideas. Doesn't seek advice before putting out schemes ... Schemes not weighed sufficiently ... but C can't control him.[12]

Hugh Dalton, the new Minister for Economic Warfare, eager to restore the flagging reputation of his Ministry, also sought to take a ministerial coordinating role over the existing work of Section D, MI(R) and Electra House. The Ministry of Economic Warfare (MEW) in the early months of the war had been characterised by feverish administrative activity that 'gave a fallacious sense of achievement'.[13] By March 1940 it was criticised in both the press and Parliament, described as the 'Ministry of Wishful Thinking'.[14] Section D was already, in practice, the secret executive arm of the MEW, commissioned to undertake projects that supported the economic blockade. Grand's report of 10 June 1940, 'The Underground Counter Offensive', must have whetted Dalton's appetite. Grand admitted that efforts to date were 'grossly inadequate' and needed the additional authority that being under direct ministerial control would provide:

> They have had to be achieved by means of isolated sanctions, each little item being judged by whatever Department, whose co-operation was essential, on its merits, but not being judged in relation to a wide conception which would draw in the complete machinery of government to the assistance of a field of battle ... these activities will require the full attention of a Minister of the Crown in order that the requirements may be represented to the War Cabinet and the general line of policy approved in each case and the necessary directions given to Government Departments for the provision of such co-operation as may be required. ... The general line of policy must of course derive from the Committee of the Privy Council, but after that the Minister responsible will be more in a position of a commander-in-chief than the political head of a Department.[15]

Grand's proposed 'Fourth Arm' would require £250,000 per month, provided on the Secret Service budget to avoid parliamentary audit. The task of underground propaganda and radio broadcasts into Germany would be taken over from the Ministry of Information and the Minister would be represented on the Joint Planning Committee to ensure adequate liaison with the other fighting services.[16]

The machiavellian Hugh Dalton used his party political relationship with Clement Attlee to persuade Churchill that he was the man to lead any new organisation. In a period of popular dislike for the Conservative 'Guilty Men' who were held responsible for the outbreak and early conduct of the war, it was an obvious tactic for Attlee to request that the new intelligence post should be in the hands of a Labour minister such as Dalton. Putting an explicitly socialist spin on Grand's long-standing analysis, Dalton argued that as the proposed work would include the encouragement of strikes and subversion, boycotts and riots, the main allies were likely to be among the European Left and a Labour minister was the obvious choice to lead such a movement.[17] General Dallas Brooks blamed Harold Laski, the chairman of the Labour Party, 'clever but a liar', for first pushing the case for Dalton.[18] Dalton was neither well-liked nor well-regarded, not least by Churchill. Gladwyn Jebb described him as 'the reverse of easy', not a good organiser, energetic but regarded by many as heavy-handed and a bore.[19] For Robert Bruce Lockhart he was 'vain and patronising'.[20] The complaint of the joint director of MEW, Professor Sir Noel Hall, was that Dalton was 'no good, never gets beyond generalities'.[21]

To counter the claims of the War Office, Dalton's diary for 1 June announced that a plan to reorganise Section D was being 'concocted' and Campbell Stuart of Electra House was said to be 'very agreeable'.[22] Section D had been a successful rival to Stuart's Electra House, itself now facing criticism. The Political Intelligence Department of the Foreign Office described the German propaganda produced by Electra House as 'extremely crude' and the Italian propaganda as 'fatuous'.[23] On 9 June Dalton tried to recruit Jebb as his informer with 'an instruction to investigate everything and question everyone on this field, and to report. This should pave the way for his taking charge under whatever political direction shall be decided upon.'[24] In turn, Jebb raised the removal of Grand with Cadogan, on 13 June writing 'Frankly what is wanted at the moment is the removal of D', but warning that Grand had the backing of Lord Hankey and Desmond Morton.[25] Success seemed to be in the offing, for on 21 June Dalton records that Jebb and Cadogan were considering a scheme whereby he and Eden would share responsibility for a new organisation.[26] Dalton may have pressed his case too hard for on 28 June Cadogan wrote: 'Dalton ringing up hourly to try to get a large finger in the sabotage pie', and he now counter-proposed that this should come under Beaumont-Nesbitt's Directorate of Military Intelligence. Worried that the tide was turning against him again, Dalton wrote in his diary, 'I concert counter-measures and invoke the aid of Attlee'.[27]

On 1 July (the day that the German army occupied the Channel Islands) there was a large meeting with Lord Halifax (Foreign Secretary) in the Chair. It was attended by Lord Lloyd (Secretary of State for the Colonies), Lord Hankey (Minister without Portfolio), Hugh Dalton (Minister for Economic Warfare), Sir Alexander Cadogan (Permanent Under-Secretary at the Foreign Office), Major General Beaumont-Nesbitt (DMI), Stewart Menzies (CSS), Desmond Morton (representing the Prime Minister) and Gladwyn Jebb (Cadogan's Private Secretary). There was considerable support for Cadogan's proposal to put Section D under the control of the DMI. This may have been spurred by the agreement of 3 June by which Section D in the Balkans and Middle East now partly acted under the instruction of the Director of Military Intelligence, Middle East Command, with Section D and MI(R) forming 'virtually two halves of the same body'.[28] Dalton opposed such military control, saying that he wanted an organisation to promote 'chaos and revolution – no more suitable for soldiers than fouling in football or throwing when bowling at cricket', holding that 'there was a clear distinction between "war from without" and "war from within" and that the latter was more likely to be better conducted by civilians than by soldiers'.[29]

This conclusion was dismissed by MI(R) as being 'amateurish' and proved not to be sustainable.[30] Hankey saw no problem in principle with the existing shared responsibilities and blamed any failure of Section D's schemes on 'the reluctance of the Foreign Office to authorise them, or at any rate to authorise them until too late'.[31] Lord Lloyd agreed, telling Halifax 'You should never be consulted because you would never consent to anything; you will never make a gangster.'[32] Morton was a long-time supporter of Grand but was not impartial: he was living in an apartment paid for by Section D. The meeting could only reach a vague agreement that a coordinator of existing departmental activity was required at a ministerial level.[33] But Dalton saw potential for his future ambition in the decision that,

> Whether any reform of the existing machinery was required could safely be left to him [the ministerial coordinator] to decide, after he had some experience of its working. He should in any case devote his whole time to the work.[34]

This was the licence that later allowed Dalton to go beyond the agreement to appoint a coordinator of existing services and create SOE as an independent body. He wasted no time and on 3 July suggested himself to Attlee and Halifax as the coordinating minister.[35] Meanwhile, attacks on Section D continued at the Chiefs of Staff Committee meeting, complaining that there was 'no effective control of the operations of "D" which needed to be brought under the control of the joint intelligence sub-committee'.[36] The War Office repeated the proposal that Section D and Electra House should come under the DMI, leading Dalton to believe that he might still be outflanked; he therefore stepped up the pressure by urging members of the Cabinet to support his bid to take over 'ungentlemanly warfare'.[37] The War Office could not compete with this political manoeuvring but in his diary for 10 July Dalton recorded: 'There has been a great to-do today. Beaumont-Nesbitt has been pulling every string. Chiefs of Staff Committee – always apt to be girlish – and Ismay threatening to resign.'[38]

In fact, on 7 July Halifax had met Churchill and, despite the latter's reservations, they had agreed that Dalton be given ministerial control over Section D and MI(R). On 19 July Neville Chamberlain's draft Charter for the Special Operations Executive (SOE) was circulated to the War Cabinet and on 22 July it was approved.[39] Dalton was to chair an organisation 'to co-ordinate all action by way of subversion and sabotage, against the enemy overseas'. The decision was not envisaged as affecting the structure of Section D, MI(R) or Electra House which 'will, for the time being, continue to be administered by the Ministers at present responsible for them'.[40] But Dalton wanted more than a coordinating role and Holland, forever the champion of uniformed irregular warfare, commented in the MI(R) War Diary for 22 July: 'It looks a little as though the Army has missed the bus, so to speak, and has allowed para-military activities to be carried on outside its jurisdiction.'[41] Dalton had earlier exploited Campbell Stuart's opposition to Grand but now wanted rid of a potential rival within the existing organisations.

> I have become convinced that he [Stuart] is so widely disliked, both in the Service Departments and in some political circles, that his continued presence here as head of Electra House would be a constant source of friction and disharmony. This I am most anxious to avoid at the outset of my new coordinating work.[42]

He made his attack whilst Stuart was absent in Canada (negotiating the site of a new BBC radio transmitter). Dalton repeated to Churchill a second-hand story accusing Stuart of having gone to Canada to make preparations for evacuation. On 25 July Churchill agreed to Dalton's suggestion that Stuart be sent a telegram saying that in his absence a decision had been made to reorganise propaganda services and that his post had been suppressed.

George Taylor (now the effective administrative head of Section D under Laurence Grand) wrote to Arthur Goodwill in Cairo on 2 August, informing him of the new regime. The constitution was vague, there was no organisational chart and 'It has not got a name yet or rather it has had several which have been discarded', but he sounded cheerful about the prospects under a Minister reporting directly to the War Cabinet.[43] It was not until 16 August that Dalton and Halifax agreed that SOE should take over direct responsibility for Section D.[44] Even then, there was no simple transfer of power and as a measure of the confusion, on 4 September Menzies wrote to Jebb that he had only that day become aware of the transfer of control.[45] In an effort to clarify the relationship of SOE to SIS, Jebb and Menzies met on 15 September. Jebb explained, 'it became obvious that the spheres of "C" and "D" must be defined on paper and I therefore drafted, and got the CSS to agree to, a document'.[46] It began:

> C and D have agreed as follows:
>
> D is a separate, secret organisation, forming part of a larger organisation [SOE] under the control of Mr Dalton. The function of this organisation is the promotion of subversion. For general purposes of administration and discipline, therefore, the D organisation comes under Mr Dalton and not under the Foreign Secretary.[47]

Although it was drafted by Jebb, he was seriously outmanoeuvred by Menzies in an agreement which was to cause problems for the rest of the war. It established the pre-eminence of SIS intelligence gathering over the work of SOE, and the appointment of agents required the approval of SIS. Any intelligence gathered by SOE was to be passed to SIS before being circulated any further and all secret communications would remain under the control of SIS. The agreement between Jebb and Menzies confirmed the continuing distinct nature of Section D which had continued with little alteration up to 18 September, when Grand was unceremoniously sacked. In the Middle East the C-in-C seemed oblivious to the changes and the old distinctions and rivalries between Section D and MI(R) continued for the rest of the year. It was not until 23 October 1940 that a new name was decided, with George Courtauld, formerly of Section D and now chief administrative officer of SOE, announcing to staff that the new designation within SOE for the D organisation was SO2 (although it was later simply known as SOE).[48] Some officers were recorded as remaining with Section D until January 1941; the SOE file of Chidson recorded the abolition of the 'Statistical Research Centre' on 31 December 1940.[49]

Similarly, on 19 August Dalton asked that the subversive functions of MI(R) be transferred to SOE.[50] MI(R) had been unhappy from the start. Taylor reported that 'MIR is furious at the new arrangement and are fighting it in every possible way.'[51] The absorption was not finally agreed by the War Office until 3 October – by which time as many as possible of the fourteen officers had been transferred to other branches of the Directorate of Military Intelligence, including Millis Jefferis and the small MI(R) technical section. Jo Holland was transferred back to the Royal Engineers and SOE therefore absorbed only the rump of MI(R), thus making it almost entirely dependent on the former Section D, including its technical sections. Few MI(R) officers had senior positions within the new SOE, the main exceptions being Gubbins and Wilkinson, who only joined in November 1940 from the Auxiliary Units.

Despite Dalton's frustrations, the long shadow of Laurence Grand and Section D continued to fall over the new SOE. The story of a purge of Section D staff became part of the myth of SOE, necessary for its invented narrative of having started its campaign of irregular warfare virtually from nothing. Undoubtedly aware of the true facts, Wilkinson initially maintained: 'Soon after taking over as CD, Frank Nelson had dismissed most of the former staff of Section D and MI(R).'[52] Kim Philby also claimed there was a general purge of Section D staff by Nelson, 'gleefully' assisted by Claude Dansey and David Boyle in SIS.[53] In July 1940 Section D had around 300 officers but only 25 are listed as being dismissed by 1 October, as more of a token gesture to satisfy Dalton. One list has survived:

Just to keep you au fait with how we are proceeding in our cleaning up process the following were given their conge [dismissal] yesterday –
George Butler
Mr G. Glover
Major Douglas Saunders

Mr H.S. Knowles
Major R. Cliveley
Mr F. Ogilvy
Mr J.W. Hackett
Captain Duncan
Lieutenant F.L. White

There will be others to come – probably 2 or 3 more, including one Burgess, who is now employed in the School.[54]

A number of the officers on this list came from the propaganda section: John Hackett's SOE file revealed how he was irritated by being dragged out of civilian life and given an emergency commission, but then being dismissed soon after, following Nelson's incorrect explanation that the new SOE was no longer engaged in propaganda – an indication of early confusion within SOE between SO1 (propaganda) and SO2 (sabotage).[55] Hackett was reinstated at the insistence of Philby and later commanded the joint SOE/PWE propaganda school. George Butler was also from the propaganda section and first transferred to SO1, then joined PWE. Gerald Glover went on to be chief regional officer for MI5. Saunders had been head of the D/Q press propaganda section and was a founder of *Britanova*. He went on to serve in the public relations department of the War Office. Cliveley became head of the Russian section of MEW. Francis Ogilvy, regional officer for the HDS in Scotland, reappeared in SIS under cover as a senior RAF intelligence officer in the Cabinet War Rooms, with the rank of wing commander. He also became one of Churchill's speech writers. Guy Burgess was dismissed for 'irreverence' and re-joined the BBC. Some senior officers refused to work under Dalton and withdrew to SIS, including Commander Langley at Aston House and Commander Frederick Peters at Brickendonbury. Hugh Arnold-Forster, head of the technical planning department of Section D, became Head of SIS Section III (Naval Intelligence). Such exceptions apart, the new SOE continued to rely heavily on former Section D officers in its senior management for much of the war (Fig. 9).

Grand remained in operational charge until 28 August, with Taylor still as his deputy, when Sir Frank Nelson (formerly of SIS) took up overall command of the sabotage section of SOE and Grand became his deputy.[56] A memo of 8 August from Jebb to Grand showed the early necessity for SOE to appease Grand:

My dear Grand,
With reference to our talk over the telephone, I write to say that there was, of course, never any intention of excluding you from the reformed Projects Board. On the contrary, the whole point was that the whole-time officers suggested should assist you personally, and appear on the Board with you.
    Yours ever,
    Gladwyn Jebb[57]

Figure 9. Section D Officers who became senior managers of SOE.

Name	Section D role	SOE Post
S.W. 'Bill' Bailey	Head of Balkans section	Head of Balkans section
Viscount Bearsted	Head of HDS Intelligence wing	Special adviser to Middle East
John Bennett	Yugoslav section	Head of Yugoslav section
Gardyne de Chastelain	Head of Romanian section	Head of Romanian section
George Courtauld	French section liaison	Chief Administrative Officer
John Dolphin	Tasking officer	CO of Station IX (The Frythe) and Head of Engineering
Julius Hanau	Head agent in Yugoslavia	Head of Central and West Africa section
Robert Head	Yugoslav section	Head of Iberian section
Elizabeth Hodgson	Austrian section	Head of SOE in Zurich
Gerard Holdsworth	Home Defence Scheme, East Anglia	Head of 'Helston Flotilla'; Head of SOE Italy
D.T. 'Bill' Hudson	Yugoslav section	SOE Mission to Mihailovic
Leslie Humphreys	Head of French section	Head of French section; Head of SOE escape section
Ian Pirie	Head of Greek section	Head of Greek section
Edward Schröter	Head of wireless research	Head of wireless research to 1941
Leslie Sheridan	Head of propaganda section	Head of propaganda section
Bickham Sweet-Escott	Liaison officer, Balkans section	PA to Taylor; regional director for Balkans and Middle East; Chief of Staff, Force 136, SEAC 1945
George Taylor	Head of Balkans section; Assistant D	Chief of Staff to Nelson; first Director of Operations; Head of SOE Far East
R.H. Thornley	Head of German section	Head of German section
John Todd	HDS regional officer	Head of SOE East Africa Mission
James Tomlinson	Head of small arms section	Head of small arms section and Station VI (to 1941)
Leslie Wood	Head of D/D section	CO of Station XII (Aston House)

Even after becoming Nelson's deputy, Grand retained the code name D and still, it seems, maintained direct control of the 'D Section'.[58] Philby described Nelson as 'a humourless businessman' and 'austere and magisterial'.[59] Nelson's views on the exuberant Grand were mixed. He was impressed with Grand, but complained that existing projects were not near completion and the organisation was uneconomic, needing a 'radical overhaul'. He therefore recommended that Grand be placed 'outside the organisation'.[60] This was something of a foregone conclusion as it was unrealistic to have expected Grand, never shy of expressing his opinions, to take a subordinate position in the organisation that he had effectively created. Moreover, Dalton barely concealed his dislike for the man he called 'King Bomba' and was looking for any excuse to be rid of him.[61] On a personal level, Grand had angered Dalton by refusing to mount a mission to extract the socialist politician Leon Blum out of France. Grand said he would only risk his men's lives in doing so if Dalton obtained approval from the War Cabinet, which Dalton would not do.[62] By mid-September Dalton had finally lost patience and on 18 September he brusquely dismissed Grand. The final excuse was an accusation of disloyalty to Nelson on the evidence of two unnamed army officers who were unwilling to put anything in writing, suspiciously like the vague accusations used earlier to remove Campbell Stuart:[63]

> I have given further thought to the arrangements concerning the D organisa-
> tion and have reached the conclusion, with regret, that, under the reorgani-
> sation on which I have now decided, there will be no further opportunity for
> the use of your services. I must, therefore, ask you to take such leave as is due
> to you as from September 20th, and to consider yourself, as from that date,
> no longer a member of the D organisation.[64]

More sympathetically, a note was appended to the letter of dismissal by a civil servant in the Ministry of Economic Warfare to say 'a word of thanks would not have come amiss'.[65] Jebb justified the change because of Section D's unpopularity in Whitehall, claiming it 'spent much of its time conducting subversive opera-tions less against the enemy than against a rather similar outfit operating under the War Office known as MI(R)'. This is a distorted view of the undoubted rivalries, as previous chapters have demonstrated. Jebb did, however, acknowl-edge that Grand was 'an able man who inspired loyalty'.[66] In his autobiography Jebb admits that 'Unfortunately the Doctor [Dalton], though immensely active, did not himself have any great sense of organisation.'[67] In other words, the same charge that was levelled against Grand. Dalton wanted Grand sent as far away as possible and he was posted to the north-west frontier of India, leaving in November 1940.[68] For his part, Grand was to say in 1973 that 'I was damned glad to return to ordinary soldiering.'[69] His career did not suffer from what was only a brief sojourn in the murky world of intelligence during a long army career. He was promoted to major general in 1949 and retired as Director of Fortifications and Works in 1952. The dismissal of Grand was symbolic but there were to be no swift changes in direction. Grand was immediately succeeded as deputy to Nelson by George Taylor, providing essential continuity as the officer in charge of operations. Taylor's importance both in Section D and in establishing the early SOE is often overlooked. He became responsible for SOE country sections, propaganda, plans and the training centre, served as chief of staff to three suc-cessive heads of SOE and ended the war as Director of SOE in the Far East.[70]

Churchill's simplistic exhortation to 'Set Europe Ablaze' caused a confusion of unrealistic expectations in the new organisation, although Bickham Sweet-Escott (now Taylor's personal assistant) maintained that few within the organisation were told of the slogan at the time.[71] In practice, to the frustration of Churchill, the priority for SOE was to contain expectations until allied strategy required large-scale rebellion to support an invasion. SOE retained the SIS atmosphere of an 'old boys' club' until September 1943 when it moved away from the dream of

Grand and Dalton as a 'fourth arm' and under its new head, Colin Gubbins, became a military organisation.

The dismissal of Grand certainly did not end the internecine warfare over control of subversive warfare, nor did it lead to the dramatic changes that seem to have been expected. In August 1941 the propaganda wing of SOE (SO1) was hived off to become the Political Warfare Executive (PWE) and the idea of a unified organisation to control all aspects of subversive warfare disintegrated. Robert Bruce Lockhart, head of the new PWE, continued the old accusations, writing to the Foreign Secretary Anthony Eden: 'most of the energy which should have been directed against the enemy has been dissipated in inter-departmental strife and jealousies'. Cadogan was also disappointed by the limited impact of the changes that he had helped introduce, writing in January that Special Operations 'don't seem to me much good. They can produce nothing but the old schemes.'[72] Dubious of Dalton's claims of successes, Cadogan commented on an early report 'I have a salt cellar by me when I read it'.[73] Churchill lost interest in the new SOE once it was clear that it could not immediately deliver the successes that Dalton had promised and SOE gets barely a mention in his classic *History of the Second World War*. Thus, SOE found itself facing the same criticisms as the old Section D, with far more tragic consequences due to its operations within occupied countries. A Dutch parliamentary commission concluded its report on SOE's failure in Holland in familiar terms: 'a catastrophe ... caused by lack of experience, utter inefficiency and the disregard of elementary security rules'.[74]

Conclusions

> The impression left by a study of D Section's operations is one of great energy and ingenuity spread thinly over an immense field ... There were therefore many people who were anxious to make a case against D Section, for not achieving what no one could have achieved in the conditions of the time ... on the whole there are few departments which did much better in 1939–40.
>
> (William Mackenzie)[1]

Mackenzie's conclusion, written in 1948 as part of the official history of SOE (but not published until 2000), still holds true. Between March 1939 and September 1940 Section D operated across more than twenty countries and many operations remain shrouded in mystery, some still considered matters of 'national security'. There were determined efforts to destroy the reputation of Section D, through fear of this new 'ungentlemanly' arm of warfare and jealousy from rival agencies. Section D paid the price for what seemed, at times, to be a rushed and chaotic series of operations, particularly *Operation Lumps* and the Home Defence Scheme, but its work must be considered in the context of the fraught conditions of the time. By the time Section D formed the core of the new SOE in 1940, Laurence Grand had established the potential of clandestine warfare that others could develop with better resources. Arguably, civilian-based sabotage was the least strategically significant element of this legacy, although attracting the most attention in the false romance surrounding the SOE. This was an era of British intelligence dominated by amateur, untrained, agents from 'good' schools and families and there was a steep learning curve in the need for rigorous training. In the arena of political warfare and subversion, however, Section D employed some of the finest experts from the worlds of advertising, journalism and commerce to find innovative ways of shaping ideas and opinions.

Much of the criticism was directed at the dynamic personality of Section D's head, Laurence Grand. The organisation was undoubtedly coloured by his eternal optimism and sense of purpose. During his period of attachment to SIS he antagonised colleagues in the War Office and Foreign Office not by lack of ability but simply by the nature of his task. But in his enthusiasm and drive, Grand was not afraid to go beyond his brief and offer inventive, if sometimes tactless, suggestions as to how other departments could improve their performance. Former Section D officer and future Foreign Secretary Julian Amery wrote 'Grand's disregard of Whitehall conventions, his love of the Nelson touch, and his ruthless ways of cutting through red tape had made him a thorn in the side of the Government machine', but 'a large part of the credit for Britain's acknowledged pre-eminence in the waging of Resistance and subversive warfare belongs to Grand'.[2] In the face of almost insurmountable odds, the ability of Section D to force an acceptance of this new form of warfare, which had been decried as terrorism when used against the British army, was a triumph. Grand felt the pressure: 'Examining such an enormous task one felt as if one had been told to move the pyramids.'[3]

Grand was a professional army officer who had spent four years in the War Office dealing with the administrative detail of procurement; an engineer used to precision, whose citation for a CBE in 1943 praised him for his organisational abilities, and who ended his career as a major general and the British army's Director of Fortifications and Works. He was not the chaotic figure implied by his enemies and in later histories. Unfortunately, the necessarily rapid expansion of Section D led to a multiplicity of sub-sections whose demarcation was not always clear and which overwhelmed the original organisational structure. Grand was left trying to shoulder too much of the responsibility for coordination whilst at the same time fighting political battles in Whitehall and at the War Office. It was necessary to delegate responsibility, with checks being provided by a structured system of reports and project authorisation (including consultation with the wider SIS and political approval) but Grand's renowned loyalty to his staff could sometimes blind him to their limitations. It was only from April 1940 that a more sophisticated administrative structure began to be implemented, relying heavily on George Taylor. Taylor came from industry with no intelligence or military experience but was a huge influence on the direction and management of Section D. He went on to be the lynchpin of SOE as chief of staff until 1943 (when he went to head SOE's Far East operations). It is notable that the decision to send him to Cairo to directly manage Section D/H in the field was rescinded after only a month so that he could return in July to assist Grand. By then it was, however, too late to save the organisation.

Given the lack of a modern selection procedure it is not surprising that, in the mushroom growth of staff, some did not live up to Grand's expectation. As with the rest of SIS, there was a preponderance of advertising executives or journalists – enthusiastic but not necessarily natural spies or saboteurs. A few were incompetent or egotistical rogues, two were Soviet spies, but others were highly experienced intelligence officers. For Basil Davidson, the amateurishness of Section D was an advantage:

> Such was more or less how we began, a handful of us scattered around distant countries; and it remains a fact of some interest, at least archivally, that this hopeful amateurism brought results in the early years of the war ... One reason for this relative success, I believe, was precisely the ingredient of

amateurism, if only because the enemy would never have thought it worth-while to attend to us.[4]

However romantic a notion, the amateur nature of British intelligence could not compete with the professionalism of the German or Swedish counter-intelligence services. The problems were certainly not confined to Section D (as the Venlo incident and the Goeland fleet disaster showed) but the breaches in security surrounding the Oxelösund debacle brought the issue into sharp focus. Most of the successful sabotage was undertaken by contracted Czech or Slovenian agents whose skill was borne out of experience fighting the fascists in an underground war for, in some cases, up to eighteen years. One of the most significant legacies of Section D was a realisation of the need for more careful selection and training of British intelligence officers and agents. The pioneering training school at Brickendonbury laid the foundation for the intensive training programmes of SOE and SIS. Similarly, the technological advances made by Aston House laid the basis of sabotage techniques and supply for the rest of the war.

British Intelligence remained disjointed throughout the war, bedevilled by inter-departmental rivalry. With the death of Admiral Sinclair, Grand lost a shrewd guiding hand in the development of Section D and it was a pity that the partnership of Grand and Jo Holland (MI(R)) did not survive the outbreak of war and the organisational divide between SIS and the War Office. In 1940 Section D was accused of spending more time on battling MI(R) than the Germans but the guilt was at least equally shared (as clearly demonstrated in Hungary) and the problems owed much to the ambition of Colin Gubbins, who resented having to rely on Section D. In June 1939 Grand had first presented the vision of an integrated department of clandestine warfare, but it proved to be an elusive dream and although the principle was later seized on eagerly by the War Office and Hugh Dalton, the concept did not survive Section D for more than a few months.

Section D worked as part of the contemporary government and intelligence assessment that the Nazi state would swiftly implode under internal social and economic pressure coupled with risings by peoples in occupied territories. As late as 4 April 1940 Neville Chamberlain could confidently maintain his view that Hitler had 'missed the bus'.[5] The task of Section D was to prepare for that

Figure 10. Extract of Supplies to 25 August 1940. (*TNA HS 7/5*)

	Time Pencils	Plastic Explosives (lb)	Camouflaged Explosives (lb)	Gelignite (lb)	Detonators
Balkans and Poland	65,492	1,573	55	4,410	6,365
France	5,477	1,107	247	145	2,702
Scandinavia	2,327	1,273	126	1,180	3,520
Auxiliary Units, Britain	67,400	7,200		7,470	36,020

immediate but illusory collapse by building supply lines capable of delivering arms to the home resistance groups and latterly to the occupied territories. Its role as the facilitator and organiser of the supply chain of sabotage materials and propaganda should not be under-estimated (Fig. 10). By the summer of 1940 it was becoming clear that such an optimistic vision was a false hope. The speed of the German advance through Europe, the recognition that Germany was more united and more resilient under Hitler than had been hoped, and the scale of collaboration in the occupied countries were huge blows, placing great pressures on the need for Section D to develop and meet the rapidly-changing nature of the threat. S.W. 'Bill' Bailey believed Section D 'was expected to run not merely before it could walk but before it was out of the cradle'.[6]

Britain did not stand as defiantly united in 1939–1940 as the popular myth suggests. There was widespread political division and complacency until the fall of the Low Countries and France. The vision of Admiral Sinclair and Laurence Grand to prepare, in 1938, for total, uncompromising and 'un-British' warfare did not fit easily within this environment. Even in 1940 there was a gulf between what the government was prepared to accept in foreign countries and the unwelcome possibility that Section D could unleash a guerrilla warfare that might, to paraphrase Churchill's famous dictum, 'Set Britain Ablaze'! Throughout late 1939 and 1940 Section D had been encouraging and instigating civilian resistance across Europe. Although SIS had already secretly begun developing the core of a deep-cover civilian resistance in Britain, Section D began to expand this concept in May 1940 to form a new guerrilla organisation (Home Defence Scheme). It drew upon the pre-war plans for Poland and Czechoslovakia and its own rushed attempts to create a resistance in advance of occupation in Norway, the Low Countries and France. The result was a multi-layered system, based upon civilian resistance, that fortunately never had to be deployed. As on the continent, the deepest levels of secrecy comprised the intelligence networks of SIS, linked by wireless and to be protected at all costs, offering as they did the potential of communication to a government-in-exile. Above this was the shorter-term sabotage and more crude intelligence network to be organised by Section D. The civilian volunteers were warned to remain 'quiescent' during the actual invasion – waiting until the organised military campaign was over and Britain apparently defeated. At the uppermost level, around the coast there were the uniformed guerrilla units of the Auxiliary Units, designed only to support the military during the actual invasion campaign but potentially able to mislead the Gestapo (and indeed modern historians) into believing that this was the British 'resistance', so diverting enemy attention from the more deeply hidden SIS organisation.

Churchill's exhortation for SOE to 'Set Europe Ablaze' was the last gasp of the optimistic policy of European revolt that had seen the foundation of Section D. It became a curse for future operations. Although such a notion appealed to Churchill, Grand and Hugh Dalton, the strategic need by autumn 1940 was to restrain European resistance groups until the time was ripe for large-scale military intervention – now recognised to be years away. MI(R), under the more calculating Jo Holland, and latterly even Section D issued warnings to European allies now under enemy occupation not to act prematurely but to protect their resources for when they were needed at a strategic level. This viewpoint was summarised by George Taylor following the German invasion of Yugoslavia, when he offered a warning of the difficulties of resisting invastion by guerrilla warfare in Europe and stressed the need to focus on unobtrusive political warfare and propaganda, whilst preparing for a more strategic sabotage campaign:

> The events in the Balkans have proved that in Europe, guerrilla activities are of little use in modern warfare. The enemy moves too fast and is too well-armed for light irregular forces to be able to stand against him. . . . Mr Taylor does not believe that any effective form of guerrilla warfare could be carried on in Europe as was done in Abyssinia. . . . S.O. [Special Operations] activities in the political and 'propaganda' field are however likely to be very useful, and preparations for long term sabotage and subversive action should be carefully made.[7]

Section D operated primarily within neutral countries and success was dependent on the attitude of those governments. There was at least a degree of support from Balkan governments and their intelligence services that was notably absent in Switzerland and Sweden. The creation of a swathe of occupied territories by the autumn of 1940 created a new landscape of war in which SOE faced problems operating in territory where any action resulted in large-scale reprisals. Despite its own misgivings, in pandering to Churchill's love of the dramatic gesture, and in trying to maintain the morale of the resistance activists, SOE contributed to the deaths of many hundreds of innocent hostages across Europe, murdered in reprisal for ad hoc sabotage that, with rare exceptions, had little impact on the course of the war. The resentment towards the resistance felt by large sections of the native population in France and elsewhere is an uncomfortable fact that veterans have naturally had difficulty in accepting, and does not fit the post-war narratives of national unity. When the time came to prove their strategic worth, many of the resistance networks had been fatally compromised. In a vindication of Jo Holland's original thesis of guerrilla warfare being organised on a military basis, irregular operations to support the D-Day landings were based around the new insertion of the Sussex and Jedburgh teams, and the 2,000-strong SAS brigade. The concept of mass revolt as envisaged by Grand and Dalton had little success. Section D had been most successful in organising sabotage in the Balkans and resistance there did develop into mass partisan warfare. It is, however, ironic that this occurred without input or direction from Section D or SOE. It was led by the communists who had played little part in opposing the Nazis in 1940 and even there it was the decisive intervention of the Red Army rather than partisan warfare that finally triggered the German collapse.

During the war SOE acknowledged the debt that it owed to Section D and the continuing influence of the latter's staff, not least because the internal history was written by a former Section D officer, Anthony Samuel. The legend of Section D incompetence owes much to the post-war sanctification of Gubbins and SOE by its historians, with the opinion of M.R.D. Foot casting a long shadow. To make SOE seem more impressive, they accused Section D of being ineffective. They seized on Jebb's picturesque tirade against Section D in June 1940, describing it as 'a laughing stock', claiming 'to pit such a man [Grand] against the German General Staff and the German Military Intelligence Service is like arranging an attack on a Panzer division by an actor mounted on a donkey'.[8] Once given un-critical credence in the literature, such opinions are difficult to shift. Yet German intelligence was obliged to deploy a special unit in the Balkans against the un-remitting effect of the sabotage campaign on the railways and the Danube. For all its weaknesses, there was no alternative body to carry out this new form of warfare and, in a time of desperation during 1939–1940, too much hope was placed on it as a central plank of strategy. The sabotage was small-scale and undramatic, a drip-feed aimed at industrial targets to support the economic blockade, but at the time it was at least a symbol of continuing resistance to what seemed an un-stoppable war machine and a test-bed for future techniques. The pioneering attack on the Norwegian power station at Bjølvefossen established the principle of infiltration of sabotage agents and tested the methodology of the 'Shetland Bus'. Likewise, the early attempts to land agents in France led to the formation of SOE's 'Helston Flotilla' under Section D's Gerard Holdsworth. It was also Section D's Leslie Humphreys who created the highly successful escape lines of SOE's Section D/F, based upon the communication lines established in the closing weeks of the campaign in France. Section D worked primarily through the agency of established native opposition groups, where British involvement was not always apparent, and in the Balkans the value of those groups was syste-matically suppressed by post-war communist regimes who wished to promote the work of the later communist partisans or were redacted by the British govern-ment concerned to protect the safety of their former agents. Popular historians have been less interested in the undramatic work of such groups than in the individual heroism of British SOE agents who suffered torture and death – but who did not necessarily achieve significant results.

Jebb's opinion after the war, freed from political machinations, became more charitable, saying simply that 'the great criticism of the old D Organisation had been that nobody knew what it was up to and that none of those departments which should have been consulted was consulted'.[9] Even this is not borne out by the documentary evidence, which reveals that some schemes were discussed almost *ad infinitum* with the Foreign Office, with the issue being not a failure to consult, but the inability of the Foreign Office to reach a decision – or even to hinder projects. The Ministry of Information also acted in concert with Section D to a much greater degree than its detractors, envious of its comparative success, were willing to admit. Following the death of Admiral Sinclair in November 1939, the new CSS, Stewart Menzies, did not have the same interest and was prepared neither to fight the case of Section D nor to exercise clear management control over his energetic subordinate. Indeed, the reputation of Grand as a maverick may well have been welcome to Menzies as a means of covering his own failings in overseeing Section D, particularly in his role in the *Operation Lumps* debacle in Sweden.

The sabotage might have been little more than an irritant to the Germans in the broad strategic sense, but for the Foreign Office it risked the delicate diplomatic balance with neutral countries. A gulf developed with local British ministers who at times appeared to oppose Section D more fiercely than the Nazis. Some agents were threatened with being turned over to local police and sabotage materials were thrown into rivers. The problems had their origin in the Foreign Secretary having agreed the D Scheme in March 1939 but making it clear that he wanted to protect plausible deniability by not wishing to hear further details. Grand took this as a licence to pursue a single-minded crusade against the Nazis wherever he could attack their influence but it caused problems when the Foreign Office was obliged to confront this policy head-on. The traditionally minded Foreign Office seemed increasingly out of step with the wishes of the Cabinet and War Office to pursue an aggressive war policy that cast aside diplomatic convention, and the problems continued into the era of SOE.

As important as its pioneering of state-supported sabotage was Section D's development of 'black' propaganda, starting operations before the Ministry of Information and Electra House came into being (much to their irritation). Huge resources were devoted to propaganda during the Second World War but its impact is difficult to quantify. For the Nazis, it was a central tool for shaping the beliefs and loyalties of its population, whipping up anti-Semitism and fear of an international communist conspiracy to provide a common enemy. Britain and the USA used propaganda to reinforce national identity and to provide key messages on industrial production and security. After 1940 it was also used to bolster the morale of those in occupied countries and to counter the German propaganda that Britain had abandoned them. Less successful was propaganda designed to alter the beliefs of the enemy, and in the main overt propaganda by a foreign power was viewed with cynical suspicion. Instead, Section D tried to insert 'black' propaganda into Germany and Austria under the pretence of it being produced by native anti-Nazis and to incite divisions and disruption, particularly surrounding the Hitler–Stalin Pact and creating discord between the German army and ordinary people against the SS and the Nazi party (Pls 11–16). It also funded the publications of existing continental anti-Nazi groups (Pl. 15). Its various attempts to interfere with the passage of mail between the USA and Germany were designed to unsettle confidence in the regime but, whilst inventive, were on too small a scale to have a serious effect. The effect within Germany was probably minimal, mainly reinforcing the morale of the activists – there was no mass

German revolt against the Nazis. 'Black' propaganda was most useful in the neutral countries, focused on challenging pro-German sentiment, and the need to either maintain neutrality or foster pro-allied beliefs.[10] It was especially important in 1940 when Germany looked set to win the war. Section D's work in pioneering propaganda through the distribution of leaflets and radio broadcasts is frequently overlooked but a clear indicator of its sensitivity is the continued redaction of many documents in The National Archives related to its propaganda work, including the work of the clandestine radio stations and the long-lived news agency *Britanova*.

The most controversial role of Section D was in political warfare where, by supporting opposition groups in the Balkans and the Haganah in Palestine, it seemed to be formulating its own foreign policy at odds with that of the British government. From the outset, this was an integral part of its work, arguably more far-reaching than its efforts in sabotage, and the belief of members of Section D that they could override the view of the Foreign Office was an attitude that continued into SOE. Laurence Grand saw his work as an explicit crusade against the Nazis but not against the German people, and he established widespread links with dissident German individuals and groups, albeit with limited results. The control of the Nazi state over its people was greatly under-estimated and the dissidents tended to over-exaggerate their influence and potential in their desperation for any support from the allies. There was always the risk of enemy infiltration; work could be overshadowed by distrust and complicated relationships, as the LEX group demonstrated. This effort was all but abandoned by SOE and the work was made more difficult as the war progressed, culminating with Roosevelt's demands for a policy of unconditional surrender in 1943.

The anti-Nazi forces across Europe were far from united, which assisted the dictatorial Nazi state. Nowhere was this worse than in Poland, where resistance forces were deeply suspicious not only of their foreign allies but also of rival groups. Dalton wanted to develop Grand's ideas into an explicitly socialist civilian movement but this concept did not outlive 1940 and the original ideal of a cohesive department of irregular warfare, as sought by all parties to the formation of SOE in the summer of 1940, was dashed first by the original subdivision of SOE into SO1 (Propaganda) and SO2 (Special Operations) and then by the creation of the Political Warfare Executive in August 1941. The Yugoslav coup in March 1941 was seized upon as a rare early triumph of SOE in shaping political events, based upon the early work of Section D – although any benefit was quickly overtaken by the German invasion and occupation. Everywhere, nationalism drove the struggle. Few saw it as a war to protect the Jews, the gypsies or the other minorities persecuted by the Nazis. In 1940 Section D found itself trying to recruit from three separate French groups and the lack of unity of the French resistance continued throughout the war and beyond. The Foreign Office was driven by the need to pursue British interests and was fearful of the risks of trying to influence the course of national politics in 1939–1940, retreating to a policy of vacillation, trying to maintain the status quo in neutral countries even when those governments were likely to fall into the Axis camp. For Grand, this lack of commitment to total war against the Nazis was intensely frustrating, and he declared that no department of war had ever been 'more domestically cramped by the domestic timidity with which we entered upon this Herculean struggle than this Section, if only because its activities by any standards other than those of total and lightning warfare are peculiarly disreputable'.[11] Undeterred, Section D bribed officials and politicians, and it supplied arms and training to opposition groups whatever their political complexion, sometimes realising (as in the case of the Haganah) that this might later be used against Britain.

The political work of Section D was on a limited and disjointed scale but set an important precedent. As the war progressed the allies came to believe that they could use their support (or otherwise) of resistance organisations to help shape the direction of post-war national politics. Indeed, Gubbins came to see political warfare as the main vehicle with which to try to ensure SOE's survival after the war, but it was not a policy that could be easily admitted.[12] In September 1944 a meeting between the Foreign Office and SOE acknowledged that there was a 'tendency for officials, and even Ministers, to say that Britain has never interfered in the internal affairs of other countries, and never will do so'.[13] The long-standing reluctance to engage with the topic, dating back to the original presentation of Scheme D in March 1939, meant that any objective analysis of the methodology had progressed little since the early discussions of Laurence Grand and Jo Holland. In the twenty-first century the arguments continue about the morality of trying to externally engineer regime change.

The overall impact of irregular warfare in the Second World War is mired in myth and romance. In particular, an admiration of the bravery of individual SOE agents has distorted an objective assessment of what they achieved. Keegan, Hastings and Williams, amongst others, have questioned if the sacrifice was worthwhile.[14] Against this view, those involved at the time would argue that the moral importance of maintaining defiance was as important as any practical effect. Section D did not invent the concept of *francs-tireur* or resistance fighters but it did legitimise their use by the British government. Recognising the implications of 'total war', Laurence Grand and Admiral Sinclair introduced the use of civilian saboteurs as part of official military strategy, accompanied by political warfare to remodel opinions and to encourage regime change. The 1939 Scheme D explicitly accepted that it would use the methods of the IRA, including show executions – and the government agreed to look the other way. Later, in planning the outline of a French resistance, Grand coldly considered the need to create martyrs – a disturbing feature of clandestine warfare that SOE discovered to its cost.[15] The main targets in 1939–1940 were economic rather than human, although the suggestion of using biological warfare was a warning for the future. This strategy for clandestine warfare was conceived out of military weakness but it had dangerous implications. Nigel West concluded in his 1992 account of SOE that the work of Section D 'was transformed into a global organisation that actively assisted despotic tyrannies to seize power in so much of Eastern Europe'.[16] Max Hastings later concluded:

> The most baleful consequence of Resistance was that it represented the legitimisation of violent civilian activity in opposition to local regimes, of a kind which has remained a focus of controversy throughout the world ever since.[17]

The nervousness of the British government in 1940 to avoid the charge of sponsoring civilian *francs-tireur* in Britain (though the status of resistance fighters abroad was treated more casually) now seems to be the last gasp of a concern to cling to a 'gentlemanly' conduct of warfare. From 1938 to 1940 Laurence Grand, with the men and women of Section D, brushed aside such academic, legalistic or even moral arguments. Their vision was simple. Created at a time when the dominant government view was one of appeasement, they saw themselves as part of an international crusade to eradicate Nazism by whatever means were necessary, supporting any group that shared that basic aim on the simplistic principle of 'the enemy of my enemy is my friend'. In effect, the conservative Grand had reinvented the concept of the Popular Front abandoned by the Communist Party during the Spanish Civil War. Their work was unpopular to many in the British establishment but they deserve recognition as idealistic pioneers of a new form of warfare, whose consequences, for good or ill, remain with us to this day.

Notes

Preface

1. 'Laurence' and 'Lawrence' are used interchangeably in the literature but I have used the preferred family spelling throughout.
2. Seaman (2006), pp. 18–19; Dalton to Grand, 18 September 1940 (Dalton papers LSE/DALTON/7/3, quoted in Bennett (2009), p. 262).

Introduction

1. D Section Early History to September 1940: TNA HS 7/3.
2. Duncan Stuart, 'Of historic interest only: the origins and vicissitudes of the SOE archive', in Seaman (2006).
3. D Section Early History to September 1940: TNA HS 7/3 and HS 7/4; memo of 4 December 1943 to D/CR in Samuel SOE file: TNA HS 9/1306/1.
4. Walker (1957), p. 9.
5. Quoted in Helm (2005), p. 353.
6. Hill (2014), p. 3.
7. Sweet-Escott (1965), ch. 1; Foot (1984), pp. 15, 17, 23.
8. Cruickshank (1977), p. 5.
9. Lett (2016), p. 140.
10. Lindeman (2016), p. 50; Foot (2004), p. 6.
11. Davies (2004), p. 119.
12. Seaman (2006), p. 19.

Chapter 1.   Creating the 'Fourth Arm' – 1938

1. Notes and Lessons by Laurence Grand, 1946: TNA HS 7/5.
2. Analysis of the Defence Requirements Committee, 1933, reported in Collier (1957), pp. 25–6.
3. Seaman (2006), p. 8.
4. Seaman (2006), p. 8.
5. Sweet-Escott (1965), p. 24.
6. Hankey report on Section D, 11 March 1940: TNA CAB 63/192.
7. Notes and Lessons by Laurence Grand, 1946: TNA HS 7/5.
8. Notes and Lessons by Laurence Grand, 1946: TNA HS 7/5.
9. Information from Lady Bessborough, with thanks.
10. Philby (1968), p. 4.
11. Jeffery (2010), p. 352.
12. Astley (2007), pp. 20 and 37.
13. Maschwitz (1957), p. 131.
14. Sweet-Escott (1965), p. 20.
15. Astley (2007), p. 21.
16. Wilkinson & Astley (1993), p. 35.
17. Mss note, Jebb, 13 June 1940: TNA FO 1093/193.
18. Gladwyn (1972), p. 101.
19. TNA WO 373/79.

20. Notes and Lessons by Laurence Grand, 1946: TNA HS 7/5.
21. Gladwyn (1972), p. 103.
22. Notes and Lessons by Laurence Grand, 1946: TNA HS 7/5.
23. Great Britain's Only Successful Experiment In Total Warfare, by Laurence Grand, August 1940: TNA HS 8/214.
24. Recommendations with regard to the control of extra-departmental and para-military activities, 5 June 1939: TNA HS 8/305.
25. D Section Early History to September 1940: TNA HS 7/3.
26. Notes and Lessons by Laurence Grand, 1946: TNA HS 7/5.
27. D Section Early History to September 1940: TNA HS 7/3.
28. SOE War Diary, quoted in Mackenzie (2000), p. 5.
29. Ryan to Tallents, 30 September 1938: TNA FO 898/1.
30. The MOI was not actually created until 4 September 1939. Likewise, Electra House, although commissioned on 3 April 1939, was not mobilised until 1 September 1939.
31. Ryan to Tallents, 30 September 1938: TNA FO 898/1.
32. Ryan to Tallents, 30 September 1938: TNA FO 898/1.
33. Ryan to Tallents, 5 October 1938: TNA FO 898/1.
34. Henniker-Heaton to Tallents, 17 October 1940: TNA FO 898/1.
35. TNA FO 898/2; Howe (1982), p. 38.
36. Memo from an officer of SIS, 11 May 1942: TNA FO 1093/155.
37. Notes and Lessons by Laurence Grand, 1946: TNA HS 7/5.
38. Great Britain's Only Successful Experiment In Total Warfare, by Laurence Grand, August 1940: TNA HS 8/214.
39. He only formally transferred from the MOI to 'War Office ("D")' in June 1940: minute of Leigh Ashton, 16 June 1940: TNA INF 1/27.
40. TNA FO 395/646.
41. W.J. West (1987), p. 114.
42. D Section Early History to September 1940: TNA HS 7/3.
43. W.J. West (1987), p. 118.
44. Note of 1 May 1939: TNA HS 8/305.
45. Notes and Lessons by Laurence Grand, 1946: TNA HS 7/5; Hyde (1982), p. 18.
46. Sweet-Escott (1965), p. 21.
47. Amery (1973), p. 159.
48. D Section Early History to September 1940: TNA HS 7/3.
49. *News of the World*, 2 October 1938.
50. D Section Early History to September 1940: TNA HS 7/3.
51. Notes and Lessons by Laurence Grand, 1946: TNA HS 7/5.
52. Great Britain's Only Successful Experiment In Total Warfare, by Laurence Grand, August 1940: TNA HS 8/214; interview with Grand in 1973 quoted in Howe (1982), p. 33.
53. 'Comre-rendu de Mission à Londres, 30 January–1 February 1939', quoted in Jeffrey (2010), p. 322.
54. TNA HS 7/3; Gladwyn (1972), p. 103.
55. Great Britain's Only Successful Experiment In Total Warfare, by Laurence Grand, August 1940: TNA HS 8/214.
56. D Section Early History to September 1940: TNA HS 7/3.
57. Boyd Tollinton of the British Council was instrumental in recommending lecturer Arnold Lawrence to Section D.
58. Turner (2011), p. 16.
59. Bailey to Goodwill, 28 January 1941: TNA HS 3/244.
60. TNA HS 1/145; see Atkin (2017b).
61. Turner (2011), p. 14.

62. Howe (1982), p. 33.
63. TNA HS 9/642/4.
64. Philby (1968), p. 2.
65. Berington SOE file: TNA HS 9/1182/7.
66. G.H.N. Seton-Watson, 'Afterword: Thirty Years After', in Auty & Clogg (1975), p. 284.
67. Liddell Diary for 19 April 1940 in West (2009), p. 77.
68. *Nottingham Evening Post*, 10 September 1940.
69. Hyde (1982), p. 22.
70. Mackenzie (2000), p. 13.
71. Interview with Grand in 1973, quoted in Howe (1982), p. 34; Atkin (2017b).
72. Sweet-Escott (1965), p. 21.

Chapter 2.   Section D goes to War

1. Sweet-Escott (1965), p. 17.
2. Atkin (2017a); D Scheme: TNA HS 8/256.
3. Minutes of meeting, 19 October 1940: TNA HS 8/268.
4. D Scheme: TNA HS 8/256; Atkin (2017a).
5. Foot (1984), p. 12.
6. Notes and Lessons by Laurence Grand, 1946: TNA HS 7/5.
7. D Scheme: TNA HS 8/256.
8. Recommendations with regard to the control of extra-departmental and para-military activities, 5 June 1939: TNA HS 8/305.
9. Wilkinson (2002), p. 87.
10. Wilkinson to PCO, 4 February 1940: TNA HS 4/31.
11. Astley (2007), p. 21; information from Lady Bessborough, with thanks.
12. Astley (2007), p. 19.
13. D Scheme: TNA HS 8/256.
14. Notes and Lessons by Laurence Grand, 1946: TNA HS 7/5.
15. Special Operations 1938–1945, July 1946: TNA HS 7/1.
16. Astley (2007), p. 20.
17. Holland and Grand were promoted major on 18 January 1933 and 28 September 1937 respectively. Holland was then promoted to brevet lieutenant colonel on 1 January 1938 whilst Grand was only appointed an acting lieutenant colonel on 3 September 1939.
18. Wilkinson & Astley (1993), p. 34.
19. Gubbins Papers 3/2/57: Imperial War Museum (quoted in Lindeman (2016), p. 46).
20. Astley (2007), p. 41.
21. Atkin (2017a).
22. Mackenzie (2000), p. 9.
23. Scheme D, 20 March 1939: TNA HS 8/256.
24. War Diary of MIR, Appendix A/9, Romania: TNA HS 8/263; Notes on MIR history: TNA HS 8/263.
25. Notes and Lessons by Laurence Grand, 1946: TNA HS 7/5.
26. Astley (2007), pp. 20–1.
27. D Scheme: TNA HS 8/256 and Appendix 2.
28. D Scheme: TNA HS 8/256 and Appendix 2.
29. Sweet-Escott (1965), p. 24.
30. Notes and Lessons by Laurence Grand, 1946: TNA HS 7/5.
31. Notes and Lessons by Laurence Grand, 1946: TNA HS 7/5.
32. Notes and Lessons by Laurence Grand, 1946: TNA HS 7/5.
33. Report for July 1940: TNA 8/214.
34. Memo from an officer of SIS, 11 May 1942: TNA FO 1093/155.

35. Read & Fisher (1984), p. 12.
36. Recommendations with regard to the control of extra-departmental and para-military activities, Grand, 5 June 1939: TNA HS 8/305.
37. Wilkinson (2002), p. 63.
38. Astley (2007), p. 27. A D/M section remained within Section D as a liaison unit.
39. Quoted in Seaman (2006), p. 13.
40. TNA CAB 127/376; West & Tsarev (2009), p. 201.
41. Young (1980), p. 100.
42. Young (1980), p. 259.
43. MI(R) War Diary for 20 September 1939: TNA HS 8/263.
44. MI(R) War Establishment: TNA HS 8/257. These figures did not include staff transferred to the Polish Mission or Auxiliary Units.
45. Lownie (2015), pp. 112–13.
46. Costello & Tsarev (1993), pp. 241 and 243.
47. Liddell Diary, 4 December 1944: TNA KV 4/195, f. 307.
48. Hyde (1982), p. 19.
49. Cadogan to Sir John Dill, 23 July 1940: TNA FO 1093/135.
50. West (1983), MI6, p. 251.
51. D Section Early History to September 1940: TNA HS 7/3.
52. Howe (1982), p. 34.
53. Atkin (2017b).
54. Notes and Lessons by Laurence Grand, 1946: TNA HS 7/5.
55. Interview with Grand in 1973 quoted in Howe (1982), p. 34; Atkin (2017b).
56. TNA HS 8/214.
57. Grand to Jebb, 8 August 1940: TNA HS 8/334.
58. D Section Early History to September 1940: TNA HS 7/3.
59. TNA FO 898/2.
60. TNA HS 9/1145/4.
61. Langley to Grand, 2 April 1940: TNA HS 4/31. By April 1940 SIS had established a system of numerical codes for their training and experimental bases, continued by SOE.
62. Sweet-Escott (1965), p. 19.
63. Bennett (2009), p. 263.
64. Unpublished entry in Dalton Diary for 16 December 1940, quoted in Bennett (2009), p. 264.
65. Grand to Jebb, 5 August 1940: TNA HS 8/334.
66. Great Britain's Only Successful Experiment In Total Warfare, by Laurence Grand, August 1940: TNA HS 8/214.
67. D Section Early History to September 1940: TNA HS 7/3.
68. History of SOE, 1946: TNA HS 7/1.
69. Mackenzie (2000), p. 14.
70. TNA CAB 63/192, p. 71; evidence of Morton to Hankey, 17 January 1940: TNA FO 1093/193.
71. Evidence of Beaumont-Nesbitt to Hankey, 8 January 1940: TNA FO 1093/193.
72. Hankey Report, TNA CAB 63/192, f. 66.
73. Hankey report, 11 March 1940: TNA CAB 63/192.
74. Minutes of ISPB Meeting, 14 May 1940: TNA HS 8/193.
75. Hankey Report, 11 March 1940: TNA CAB 63/192.
76. Hankey to Jebb, 7 February 1940: TNA FO 1093/193.
77. Robert Walmsley quoted in Howe (1982), p. 44.
78. Evidence of Campbell Stuart to Hankey, 2 February 1940: TNA FO 1093/193.
79. 'Propaganda' by Laurence Grand, 5 February 1940: TNA HS 8/305.
80. Jebb to Hankey, 14 February 1940: TNA CAB 63/192.
81. Carr to Lee, 15 February 1940: TNA CAB 63/192.

82. Childs to Jebb, 15 February 1940: TNA CAB 63/192.
83. Report on visit to Romania. Part 2, Propaganda, February 1940 by David Hall: TNA FO 371/24988.
84. TNA FO 1093/137.
85. Salvadori (1958), p. 133.
86. Tennant (1992), p. 206.
87. St John Bamford to Brittain, 13 June 1940: TNA FO 1093.137.
88. D Section Early History to September 1940: TNA HS 7/3.
89. The Underground Counter Offensive, 10 June 1940: TNA HS 8/255.
90. Philby (1968), p. 7.
91. Memorandum on the issue of Sabotage Schemes in Neutral Countries by Sir Orme Sargent, 11 April 1940: TNA FO 1093/138.
92. Menzies and Grand, undated, April 1940: TNA FO 1093/138.
93. Sargent, 18 April 1940: TNA FO 1093/138.
94. Menzies and Grand, April 1940: TNA FO 1093/138.
95. Draft letter Grand to Smith, 25 April 1940: TNA HS 2/264.
96. Note of 26 October 1939: TNA HS 2/263.
97. Report VIII, July 1940: TNA HS 8/214.
98. D Section Early History to September 1940: TNA HS 7/3.
99. Johns (1979), p. 16.
100. D Section Early History to September 1940: TNA HS 7/3.
101. D Section Early History to September 1940: TNA HS 7/3.
102. Great Britain's Only Successful Experiment In Total Warfare, by Laurence Grand, August 1940: TNA HS 8/214.
103. D Section Early History to September 1940: TNA HS 7/3.

Chapter 3. Technical Development and Training

1. History of the Research and Development Section of SOE: TNA HS 7/27.
2. History of the Research and Development Section of SOE: TNA HS 7/27.
3. Quoted in Turner (2011), p. 14.
4. TNA HS 8/214.
5. Edward Schröter SOE file: TNA HS 9/1329/1.
6. Turner (2011), p. 33. When SOE took over Aston House, Langley transferred to SIS Section XIII at Whaddon.
7. Turner (2011), p. 154.
8. TNA HS 9/1551/5.
9. Turner (2011), p. 153.
10. Turner (2011), p. 33.
11. Northover to Churchill, 27 March 1942: TNA PREM 3/428/10.
12. Prof. Lindemann to Churchill, 3 July 1940: TNA PREM 3/428/10.
13. Report VIII, July 1940: TNA HS 8/214.
14. Report of demonstration of anti-tank devices, 28 July 1940: TNA PREM 3/428/10.
15. TNA T 166/119/17.
16. Liddell Diary for 24 April 1940 in West (2009), p. 78.
17. Turner (2011), pp. 26–8.
18. Memo from Section D to G.C. & C.S., 25 June 1940: TNA 2/241.
19. Schröter confidential report for 1941: TNA HS 9/1329/1; Atkin (2015), pp. 113–17.
20. D Section Early History to September 1940: TNA HS 7/3.
21. CD to CEO, 28 April 1941: TNA HS 8/334.
22. — to Valentine Vivian, 23 June 1940: TNA HS 9/1200/5; Notes and Lessons by Laurence Grand, 1946: TNA HS 7/5.

23. Great Britain's Only Successful Experiment In Total Warfare, by Laurence Grand, August 1940: TNA HS 8/214; History of the Research and Development Section of SOE: TNA HS 7/27.
24. Edwards, William, 'Guns in our "Bundles for Britain"', *Gun*, December 1959, p. 33; TNA WO 199/3049.
25. Station VI history: TNA HS 7/27.
26. Report VIII, July 1940: TNA HS 8/214.
27. Great Britain's Only Successful Experiment In Total Warfare, by Laurence Grand, August 1940: TNA HS 8/214.
28. Ryan to Tallents, 5 October 1938: TNA FO 898/1.
29. D Section Early History to September 1940: TNA HS 7/3.
30. Maschwitz (1957), p. 136.
31. Minute of 15 March 1940 (destroyed), quoted in Mackenzie (2000), p. 14.
32. George Hill, Reminiscences of Four Years with the NKVD, Hoover Institution Archives (1968), p. 13: unpublished MSS quoted in O'Connor (2014), p. 11.
33. The Underground Counter Offensive, 10 June 1940: TNA HS 8/255.
34. MI5 report on Burgess, 13 November 1953: TNA KV 2/4110.
35. MI5 report on Burgess, 13 November 1953: TNA KV 2/4110.
36. Philby (1968), p. 7; MI5 report on Burgess, 13 November 1953: TNA KV 2/4110; Milne (2014), p. 102.
37. Notes and Lessons by Laurence Grand, 1946: TNA HS 7/5.
38. Philby (1968), p. 8.
39. O'Connor (2014), p. 1.
40. Muggeridge (1973), p. 125.
41. Quoted in Lownie (2015), p. 112.
42. Report VIII, July 1940, TNA HS 8/214.
43. Report VII, July 1940, TNA HS 8/214.
44. Notes and Lessons by Laurence Grand, 1946: TNA HS 7/5; They were Republicans who had originally been interned in France after escaping at the end of the Spanish Civil War. They were given the choice of either serving in the Foreign Legion or being deported to Spain. They would later form the basis of the SOE 'Sconce' units.
45. Philby (1968), p. 9; Kemp (1958), p. 50. Kemp had fought for the Nationalist side in the Spanish Civil War and was implicated in the execution of International Brigade prisoners. He later joined MI(R) and then SOE.
46. D Section Early History to September 1940: TNA HS 7/3.

Chapter 4.   Western Europe: the Fascist Powers

1. The Underground Counter Offensive, 10 June 1940: TNA HS 8/255.
2. The Underground Counter Offensive, 10 June 1940: TNA HS 8/255. Disaffected German soldiers did indeed work with the Channel Islands resistance.
3. Note, Appendix B: TNA HS 8/214.
4. Great Britain's Only Successful Experiment In Total Warfare, by Laurence Grand, August 1940: TNA HS 8/214.
5. Leaflet P54: TNA FO 898/486.
6. TNA HS 1/145.
7. Letter to RAD Brooks from Valentine Williams, 7 July 1940: TNA FO 898/70, quoted in Richards (2012), p. 11.
8. Hankey to Menzies, 6 February 1940: TNA 63/192.
9. Sir Campbell Stuart evidence to Hankey Enquiry, 2 February 1940: TNA CAB 63/192.
10. Hankey Inquiry on SIS, March 1940: TNA CAB 127/376; see Richards (2010a), Appendix III for catalogue of Section D propaganda taken from TNA FO 898/486.

11. Leaflet P50: TNA FO 898/486.
12. Memo to Leeper, 18 September 1940: TNA HS 8/305.
13. TNA HS 7/145.
14. TNA HS 7/145.
15. D Section Early History to September 1940: TNA HS 7/3.
16. N. West (1983), p. 250.
17. TNA HS 6/642.
18. Foot (1984), p. 16; Boyce (2005), p. 108.
19. D Section Early History to September 1940: TNA HS 7/3.
20. Groehl MI5 file: TNA KV 2/2171/2.
21. D Section Early History to September 1940: TNA HS 7/3.
22. Otten MI5 file: TNA KV 2/1123/2.
23. Groehl MI5 file: TNA KV 2/2171/1.
24. TNA FO 371/60516.
25. Gubbins (1970), pp. 105–6.
26. Catalogue of subversive leaflets produced by D Section, P1a: TNA FO 898/486.
27. Outline of recent propaganda activity by Section D, Grand to Leeper, 18 September 1940: TNA HS 8/305.
28. Hankey Report: TNA CAB 63/192.
29. D Section Early History to September 1940: TNA HS 7/4.
30. Earle (2005), pp. 23–4. Albert Rejec (1899–1976) studied law at Padua and Rome Universities and took part in the street fighting against Mussolini's march on Rome. He was one of the founders of TIGR in 1927. Forced to flee Italy in 1929, he settled in Ljubljana and continued his work for TIGR. He led the joint working with Section D in 1940 and in 1944 joined Tito's partisans – but was arrested because of his earlier links to British intelligence. From November 1945 to July 1948 he was translator at the press office of the President of the Slovenian government, then until 1959 researcher at the Institute for Ethnic Studies in Ljubljana.
31. Bailey (2014), p. 25.
32. Wall (1969), p. 106.
33. Memorandum by Chiefs of Staff Committee, 26 March 1940 and 'Aide Memoire', 6 April 1940: TNA FO 371/24888.
34. Despite pleading with Dansey to secure a British army commission, Salvadori then returned to the USA and worked with British Security Coordination before joining SOE.
35. Sweet-Escott (1965), p. 31.
36. The Underground Counter Offensive, 10 June 1940: TNA HS 8/255.
37. Report VIII, July 1940: TNA HS 8/214.
38. Report VII, July 1940: TNA HS 8/214.
39. Heine (1983), pp. 35–6.
40. Report VIII, July 1940: TNA HS 8/214.
41. The Underground Counter Offensive, 10 June 1940: TNA HS 8/255.
42. Minutes of ISPB Meeting, 10 June 1940: TNA HS 8/193.
43. Nelson to Jebb, 22 November 1940: TNA H S8/305.
44. Minutes of ISPB Meeting, 10 June 1940: TNA HS 8/193.
45. Great Britain's Only Successful Experiment In Total Warfare, by Laurence Grand, August 1940: TNA HS 8/214.
46. Mackenzie (2000), p. 33.

Chapter 5.   Western Europe: Allied and Neutral Countries

1. Laurence Grand, 14 April 1940, quoted in Foot (2004), p. 52.
2. Foot (1984), p. 16.
3. D Section Early History to September 1940: TNA HS 7/3.

4. D Section Early History to September 1940: TNA HS 7/3.
5. Report VIII, July 1940: TNA HS 8/214.
6. Great Britain's Only Successful Experiment In Total Warfare, by Laurence Grand, August 1940: TNA HS 8/214.
7. Turner (2011), p. 60.
8. Atkin (2015), p. 140.
9. Report of 29 May 1940 quoted in Mackenzie (2000), p. 224; D Section Early History to September 1940: TNA HS 7/3.
10. D Section Early History to September 1940: TNA HS 7/3; Foot (2004), pp. 7–8.
11. Report VIII, July 1940, and Note, Appendix to Report VII: TNA HS 8/214.
12. Note, Appendix to Report VII: TNA HS 8/214.
13. Report VIII, July 1940: TNA HS 8/214.
14. Mike Calvert (XII Corps Observation Unit) believed that part of the government anti-invasion strategy was to accept widespread reprisals against the civilian population in order to harden British resolve and convince the Americans of the justice of joining the Allies. Quoted in Warwicker (2008), p. 68.
15. D Section Early History to September 1940: TNA HS 7/3.
16. TNA HS 9/1509/4.
17. D Section Early History to September 1940: TNA HS 7/3.
18. Information from Paul McCue, from his Valençay 104 project, with thanks.
19. TNA HS 9/538/2.
20. The Underground Counter Offensive, 10 June 1940: TNA HS 8/255; Report VIII, July 1940: TNA HS 8/214.
21. Foot (2001), p. 195.
22. Mission statement, 5 November 1940: TNA HS 9/1362/6.
23. TNA HS 9/1362/6.
24. TNA HS 9/1509/4.
25. Foot (2001), p. 243.
26. Report VIII, July 1940: TNA HS 8/214.
27. TNA HS 9/1504/1.
28. Notes and Lessons by Laurence Grand, 1946: TNA HS 7/5.
29. Great Britain's Only Successful Experiment In Total Warfare, by Laurence Grand, August 1940: TNA HS 8/214.
30. Paul Arnoldussen, *Het Parool* (2010).
31. *Time* magazine, no. 23, 3 June 1940, p. 68; discussion with Michael Van Moppes in 2016 suggests that the use of 'diamond-cutting saw' was a mistake.
32. TNA WO 373/16/272.
33. Memo of 3 June 1940, D/FX to Humphreys: TNA HS 9/477/7.
34. SOE file of C. Hamilton-Ellis: TNA HS 9/477/7.
35. Mackenzie (2000), p. 32.
36. D Section Early History to September 1940: TNA HS 7/3.
37. Frederick Matthias, born 1891 in Australia, had a long history in the diamond industry and in 1940 proposed to establish a diamond-processing centre in Palestine to avoid the risk of the industry falling into German hands following any invasion of the Low Countries.

Chapter 6.   The Balkans

1. Quoted in Onslow (2005), p. 17.
2. D Section Early History to September 1940: TNA HS 7/3.
3. Sweet-Escott (1965), p. 21.
4. Taylor to Grand, 1 November 1939, quoted in SOE History: TNA HS 7/3.
5. D Section Early History to September 1940: TNA HS 7/3.

6. D Section Early History to September 1940: TNA HS 7/3.
7. Pirker (2012), p. 778.
8. Pirker (2012), p. 777.
9. SOE personnel file: TNA HS 9/1060/8; letter of 29 November 1939: TNA HS 9/1060/8; SOE personnel file: TNA HS 9/1060/8.
10. Letter of 29 November 1939: TNA HS 9/1060/8.
11. Taylor to Goodwill, 2 August 1940: TNA HS 5/497.
12. Hanau SOE file: TNA HS 9/653/2.
13. Campbell to London, 30 July 1940: quoted in Onslow (2005), p. 34.
14. Notes and Lessons by Laurence Grand, 1946: TNA HS 7/5.
15. Glen with Bowen (2002), p. 36.
16. Pirker (2012), p. 768.
17. Pirker (2012), p. 773.
18. Earle (2005), pp. 27–8.
19. Bailey to Sweet-Escott, 19 September 1940: TNA HS 3/244.
20. Hanau to Taylor, 1 February 1940: TNA HS 9/112/4.
21. D Section Early History to September 1940: TNA HS 7/3.
22. Clissold Papers, MS Eng C2683, A. Lawrenson report, 12 June 1945, quoted in Onslow (2005), p. 20.
23. Hanau SOE file: TNA HS 9/653/2.
24. D Section Early History to September 1940: TNA HS 7/4.
25. Amery (1973), p. 167.
26. Davidson (1987), p. 78; Report on 35-Land, Duncan to Taylor, 1 May 1940: TNA HS 9/458/2.
27. Quoted in Pirker (2012), p. 769.
28. Notes and Lessons by Laurence Grand, 1946: TNA HS 7/5.
29. Glen with Bowen (2002), p. 37.
30. Glen with Bowen (2002), p. 37.
31. D Section Early History to September 1940: TNA HS 7/4.
32. Notes and Lessons by Laurence Grand 194: TNA HS 7/5.
33. Menzies and Grand, undated April 1940: TNA FO 1093/138.
34. Notes and Lessons by Laurence Grand, 1946: TNA HS 7/5.
35. Report on 35-Land, Duncan to Taylor, 1 May 1940: TNA HS 9/458/2.
36. D Section Early History to September 1940: TNA HS 7/4.
37. Earle (2005), pp. 102–15.
38. D Section History: TNA HS 7/5.
39. D Section Early History to September 1940: TNA HS 7/4.
40. Hanau to Taylor, 22 May 1940: TNA HS 9/684/4.
41. D Section Early History to September 1940: TNA HS 7/3.
42. Philby (1968), p. 4.
43. Draft Notes by Grand: TNA HS 7/5.
44. D Section Early History to September 1940: TNA HS 7/3.
45. The Underground Counter Offensive, 10 June 1940: TNA HS 8/255.
46. D Section Early History to September 1940: TNA HS 7/3.
47. D Section Early History to September 1940: TNA HS 7/4.
48. D Section Early History to September 1940: TNA HS 7/3.
49. Activities of SOE in the Balkans: minutes of meeting of 25 June 1941: THA HS 8/957; MX to M, 13 June 1941: TNA HS 4/198.
50. Gubbins to Holland, 3 February 1940: TNA HS 4/193.
51. Draft Notes by Grand, TNA HS 7/5; in his not entirely reliable autobiography *Guilt-Edged*, Merlin Minshall of Naval Intelligence claimed the idea as his own.
52. TNA FO 1093/137.

53. D Section Early History to September 1940: TNA HS 7/3.

54. D Section Early History to September 1940: TNA HS 7/3; TNA FO 1093/137.

55. Clissold Papers, MS Eng C2683, A. Lawrenson report, 12 June 1945 quoted in Onslow (2005), p. 19.

56. SIS internal correspondence of June 1940 quoted in TNA HS 7/4.

57. Glen to Sweet-Escott, 31 July 1940: TNA HS 5/872; Glen to Sweet-Escott, 19 August 1940: TNA HS 5/872.

58. Campbell to Hopkinson, 30 August 1940: TNA HS 5/872; Brittain to Broad, 26 October 1940: TNA HS 5/872.

59. Taylor to SO2, 23 March 1941: TNA HS 5/938.

60. D Section Early History to September 1940: TNA HS 7/4.

61. Draft Notes and Lessons by Grand, 1946: TNA HS 7/5.

62. German sources quoted in Pirker (2012), p. 768.

63. Rudolf then escaped to the Middle East on a false British passport. There, he helped recruit and train Slovenian parachutists for the SIS. After the war he became a teacher in Trieste.

64. Taylor to Hanau, 18 June 1940: TNA HS 5/497.

65. Glen with Bowen (2002), p. 40.

66. Glen to Bailey, 30 September 1940: TNA HS 5/965.

67. D Section Early History to September 1940: TNA HS 7/4.

68. Obituary by M.R.D. Foot in *The Independent*, 14 November 1995.

69. Report by Glen of 16 September 1940: TNA HS 5/965.

70. David Shillan to British Council, 17 September 1940: TNA HS 4/31.

71. D Section Early History to September 1940: TNA HS 7/4.

72. Bailey to Sweet-Escott, 19 September 1940: TNA HS 3/244.

73. Glen to Bailey, 30 September 1940: TNA HS 5/965.

74. Sweet-Escott to Glen, 23 July 1940: TNA HS 5/872; Brittain to Broad, 26 October 1940: TNA HS 5/872.

75. Amery (1973), p. 179.

76. Activities of SOE in the Balkans, June 1941: TNA HS 8/957.

77. Pirker (2012), p. 777.

78. Amery (1973), p. 183.

79. Deletant (2016), pp. 70–1.

80. Wedlake SOE personnel file: TNA HS 5/498.

81. TNA HS 9/160/6.

82. Report on visit to Romania, 8 March 1940, Part 2, Propaganda by Donald Hall: TNA FO 371/24988.

83. Propaganda by Laurence Grand, 5 February 1940: TNA HS 8/305.

84. Propaganda in Romania, Laurence Grand, 4 March 1940: TNA FO 371/24988.

85. Bailey to Sweet-Escott, 19 September 1940: TNA HS 3/244.

86. Redacted letter, 21 March 1940: TNA HS 3/201; Hacohen (1985), p. 100.

87. Wedlake SOE Personnel File: TNA HS 5/498.

88. Taylor to Goodwill, 2 August 1940: TNA HS 5/497; D Section Early History to September 1940: TNA HS 7/3.

89. Reports of Wedlake: TNA HS 5/498.

90. De Chastelain history of SOE in Romania: TNA HS 7/186.

91. Report on activities between British and Polish institutions in Romania, MI(R), 7 April 1940: TNA HS 4/193.

92. Treacey statement: TNA HS 9/1481/6.

93. De Chastelain history of SOE in Romania: TNA HS 7/186; letter of P. Broad to Brittain, 26 November 1940: TNA HS 5/830.

94. De Chastelain history of SOE in Romania: TNA HS 7/186.

95. Treacey SOE file: TNA HS 9/1481/6.
96. Goodwill to Young, 11 April 1940: TNA HS 9/458/2.
97. D Section Early History to September 1940: TNA HS 7/4.
98. Duncan to Taylor, 16 April 1940: TNA HS 9/458/2.
99. Hanau to Taylor, 1 May 1940: TNA HS 9/458/2.
100. Report on 35-Land, Duncan to Taylor, 1 May 1940: TNA HS 9/458/2.
101. Taylor to Hanau, 6 May 1940 and Taylor to Duncan, 6 May 1940: TNA HS 9/4582.
102. History of SOE in Romania: TNA HS 7/186.
103. Toyne (1962), p. 3; TNA HS 9/1480/1.
104. Toyne to Holmes, 7 February 1940: TNA HS 9/1480/1.
105. Memo of Watson to Goodwill, 22 October 1940: TNA HS 5/824.
106. Memo of D/T, 7 September 1940: TNA HS 9/1480/1.
107. Toyne to Sweet-Escott, 11 September 1940: TNA HS 5/824.
108. Memo by Bailey, 3 January 1941: TNA HS 5/824; SOE Report of 10 October 1941: TNA HS 9/1480/1.
109. TNA HS 5/824.
110. Report of 15 April 1941: TNA HS 9/1480/1.
111. Letter of Bailey, 23 January 1941: TNA HS 9/1480/1.
112. D Section Early History to September 1940: TNA HS 7/3.
113. Zundel to Humphreys, 5 October 1939; TNA HS 5/199; D Section Early History to September 1940: TNA HS 7/3.
114. TNA HS 9/160/6; Watson to Gubbins, undated but January 1940: TNA HS 4/193.
115. Gubbins to Holland, 3 February 1940: TNA HS 4/193.
116. Gubbins to Holland, 3 February 1940: TNA HS 4/193.
117. Barker (1976), p. 37.
118. TNA FO 371/23752.
119. TNA HS 9/1039.
120. Minshall (1975).
121. Glen with Bowen (2002), p. 50.
122. Letter of Reginald Hoare to Nicholls, Foreign Office, 30 March 1940: TNA FO 371/24988.
123. Events in Romania as seen from Galatz, R. Macrae, November 1940: TNA FO 371/29990.
124. Events in Romania as seen from Galatz, R. Macrae, November 1940: TNA FO 371/29990.
125. Report on 14-Land, Duncan to Taylor, 21 April 1940: TNA HS 9/458/2.
126. D Section Early History to September 1940: TNA HS 7/3.
127. TNA HS 9/160/6.
128. Quoted in Barker (1976), p. 38.
129. *The Times*, 9 April 1940.
130. D Section Early History to September 1940: TNA HS 7/4.
131. Notes and Lessons by Laurence Grand, 1946: TNA HS 7/5.
132. Gorove (1964), p. 34.
133. Grand (presumed) to Holland, 22 July 1940: TNA HS 5/199.
134. In 1967 a dam was constructed making the towing railway obsolete and a huge lake now covers the course of the railway.
135. Grand to Nelson, 7 September 1940: TNA HS 3/147.
136. Grand to D/O and Nelson, 7 September 1940: TNA HS 3/147.
137. History of SOE in Romania, 1945: TNA HS 7/186.
138. Chiefs of Staff Meeting, 4 December 1939: TNA CAB 79/1.
139. Amery (1948), p. 24.
140. SOE personnel file: TNA HS 9/28/7.
141. D Section Early History to September 1940: TNA HS 7/4.
142. Memo to Section D staff, 29 April 1940: TNA HS 5/60.

143. D Section Early History to September 1940: TNA HS 7/4.

144. Minute, Glen to Bailey, 15 July 1950: TNA HS 5/60; Minute of 22 July 1940 from 797 to D/H, H/H2 and D/HR: TNA HS 5/60.

145. Pirie, History of SOE in Greece, ch. 1, p. 16: TNA HS 7/150; History Albanian Activities, 25 August 1940: TNA HS 5/60.

146. Annotation by Goodwill to Potential rising in Albania and Istria, 19 July 1940: TNA HS 5/60.

147. Some notes on subversive activities in Albania, Istria and Austria by D/H2, 18 July 1940: TNA HS 5/60.

148. Potential rising in Albania and Istria, 19 July 1940: TNA HS 5/60.

149. Glen to Bailey, 30 September 1940: TNA HS 5/965.

150. Stirling to Goodwill, 19 August 1940: TNA HS 5/60.

151. Bailey to Stirling, 19 September 1940: TNA HS 3/244.

152. Report of August 1940: TNA HS 5/60.

153. Taylor to Goodwill, 31 August 1940: TNA HS 9/600/3.

154. Taylor to Goodwill, 31 August 1940: TNA HS 9/600/3.

155. Menzies and Grand, undated April 1940: TNA FO 1093/138.

156. D Section Early History to September 1940: TNA HS 7/4.

157. Report on 11 Land (Bulgaria), 4 May 1940: TNA HS 9/458/2.

158. Report VII, June 1940: TNA HS 8/214.

159. Report VIII, July 1940: TNA HS 8/214.

160. Amery (1973), pp. 174–85.

161. Glen with Bowen (2002), p. 40.

162. Sweet-Escott to Bailey, 8 September 1940: Amery SOE personnel file: TNA HS 9/28/7.

Chapter 7.   The Aegean and Middle East

1. D Section Early History to September 1940: TNA HS 7/4.

2. Amery (1973), p. 204.

3. Shearer to Beaumont-Nesbitt, 1 September 1940: TNA HS 9/896/4.

4. Taylor to Grand, 5 June 1940: TNA HS 5/497; Minute on D activities in the Middle East, 7 August 1940: TNA HS 5/60, and HS 3/147.

5. Taylor to Grand, 5 June 1940: TNA HS 5/497.

6. Potential rising in Albania and Istria, 19 July 1940: TNA HS 5/60.

7. Pollock to Nelson, 19 May 1940: TNA HS 5/60.

8. TNA HS 9/938/5.

9. Report of August 1940: TNA HS 5/60.

10. Pirie, History of SOE in Greece, p. 16: TNA HS 7/150.

11. Wilkinson (2002), p. 117.

12. Davidson (1987), p. 54.

13. Pirie, History of SOE in Greece, p. 23: TNA HS 7/150.

14. Gogas personnel file: TNA HS 9/595/4.

15. Pirie, History of SOE in Greece, p. 34: TNA HS 7/150.

16. Pirie, History of SOE in Greece, p. 4: TNA HS 7/150.

17. Potential rising in Albania and Istria, 19 July 1940: TNA HS 5/60.

18. Pirie, History of SOE in Greece, p. 27: TNA HS 7/150.

19. Taylor to Grand, 27 June 1940: TNA HS 5/497; Bailey to Sweet-Escott, 19 September 1940: TNA HS 3/244.

20. Pirie, History of SOE in Greece, p. 35: TNA HS 7/150.

21. Minutes of ISPB Meeting, 5 July 1940: TNA HS 8/193; Pirie, History of SOE in Greece, pp. 35, 106–8: TNA HS 7/150.

22. Taylor to Shearer, 26 June 1940: TNA HS 5/497.

23. Pirie, History of SOE in Greece, p. 38: TNA HS 7/150.

24. Rushbrook-Williams to Jebb, 5 April 1940: TNA FO 1093/137.
25. Propaganda in Turkey, Iraq and Iran, note of a meeting of 12/13 June: TNA FO 1093/137.
26. Bailey to Sweet-Escott, 19 September 1940: TNA HS 3/244.
27. Bailey to Goodwill, 28 January 1941: TNA HS 3/244.
28. Wingate was a visiting lecturer at the Osterley Home Guard Training School and future leader of the Chindits in Burma.
29. Costello & Tsarev (1993), p. 239; Purvis & Hulbert (2016), p. 108.
30. Hacohen (1985), p. 105.
31. Redacted letter, 21 March 1940: TNA HS 3/201; Hacohen (1985), p. 104; Harouvi (1999), p. 35.
32. Hacohen (1985), pp. 97–9; draft letter from D/L to D/H, 21 March 1940: TNA HS3/201.
33. Taylor to Walkden, 30 April 1940: TNA HS 3/201.
34. Taylor to Grand, 29 May 1940: TNA HS 3/201.
35. Stoil (2013), p. 157.
36. Memo of meeting, Haifa, 13 July 1940, quoted in Stoil (2013), p. 157.
37. Taylor to Goodwill, 2 August 1940: TNA HS 5/497.
38. D Section Early History to September 1940: TNA HS 7/4.
39. Personnel file: TNA HS 9/91/8.
40. Hacohen (1985), p. 127.
41. Taylor to Grand, 27 June 1940: TNS HS 5/497; Hacohen (1985), p. 101.
42. Arnold Lawrence to D/H1, 13 August 1940: TNA HS 9/896/4.
43. Pirie, History of SOE in Greece, p. 19: TNA HS 7/150; TNA HS 5/498.
44. Bamford to Brittain, 1 July 1940: TNA FO 1093/137.
45. Baggallay to Hopkinson, 3 September 1940: TNA FO 1093/137.
46. The Underground Counter Offensive, 10 June 1940: TNA HS 8/255.
47. Taylor to Goodwill, 2 August 1940: TNA HS 5/497.

Chapter 8.   Central and Eastern Europe

1. Notes and Lessons by Laurence Grand, 1946: TNA HS 7/5.
2. Wilkinson to Holland, 7 January 1940: TNA HS 4/31.
3. Report VIII, July 1940: TNA HS 8/214.
4. TNA HS 4/31.
5. Gubbins to Wilkinson, 2 February 1940: TNA HS 4/31.
6. Beaumont-Nesbitt to W. Strang, 1 February 1940: TNA HS 4/31.
7. Wilkinson to Hanau, 29 February 1940: TNA HS 4/31.
8. Record of meeting of Holland, Gubbins, Wilkinson, Fisers and Moravec on 5 January 1940, made on 22 January 1940: TNA HS 4/43; Langley to Wilkinson, 2 April 1940: TNA HS 4/31.
9. Draft SOE Hungarian Section History: TNA HS 7/162.
10. SOE History, Hungary: TNA HS 7/162.
11. Redward had served in the Danube flotilla during the First World War and had been a press officer at the Legation since 1920. He served temporarily with SOE and returned to Hungary in 1945.
12. Report on 15-Land, Duncan to Taylor, 26 April 1940: TNA HS 9/458/2; D Section projects in Hungary, 22 August 1940: TNA HS 4/93.
13. Davidson (1996), p. 19.
14. Davidson (1987), p. 56.
15. Draft SOE Hungarian Section History: TNA HS 7/162.
16. E. St John Bamford to Brittain, 13 June 1940: TNA FO 1093/137.
17. Davidson (1987), p. 55.
18. Taylor to Walkden, 30 April 1940: TNA HS 3/201.
19. Gubbins to Barclay, 5 October 1939: TNA HS 4/193.
20. MIR War Diary, 22 April 1940: TNA HS 8/263.

21. Duncan to Taylor, 16 May 1940: TNA HS 9/458/2.
22. Duncan to Taylor, 16 May 1940: TNA HS 9/458/2.
23. MIR to M.A. Budapest, 21 May 1940: TNA HS 4/193.
24. M.A. Budapest to DMI, 23 May 1940: TNA HS 4/193.
25. M.A. Budapest to DMI, 24 May 1940: TNA HS 4/193.
26. Wilkinson (2002), p. 92; Blake-Tyler was commissioned into the Royal Berkshire Regiment as a second lieutenant in April 1939. By May 1940 he was a major. He was promoted lieutenant colonel on 20 January 1941. By 1943 he was First Secretary at the British Embassy in Washington DC, USA.
27. Memo re Blake-Tyler and D, by Dodds-Parker, 25 May 1940: TNA HS 4/193.
28. Memo re Blake-Tyler and D, by Dodds-Parker, 25 May 1940: TNA HS 4/193.
29. Davidson (1987), pp. 78–9.
30. D Section operation in Hungary, 22 August 1940: TNA HS4/93.
31. O'Malley (1954).
32. Draft SOE Hungarian Section History: TNA HS 7/162.
33. MI(R) report, 20 April 1939: TNA HS 4/193.
34. Minutes of a meeting with Major Charaskiewicz, July 1939: TNA HS 4/193.
35. TNA HS 4/168 is completely redacted.
36. Police file available at http://www.stockholmskallan.se/PostFiles/SSA/Arkiv/SE_SSA_0140/SE_SSA_0140_06_03_Protokoll_1940_2_Rickman_2.pdf.
37. Gubbins to Wilkinson, 28 January 1940: TNA HS 4/43.
38. Gubbins to Kwiecinski, 1 January 1940: TNA HS 4/193.
39. Sutton-Pratt to Fraser, 6 January 1940: TNA 2/261.
40. Gubbins to Sutton-Pratt, 7 April 1940: TNA HS 4/193.
41. Wilkinson (2002), p. 88.
42. Wilkinson (2002), p. 89.
43. TNA HS 4/193.
44. TNA HS 4/193.
45. Wilkinson to Gubbins, 29 January 1940: TNA HS 4/193.
46. The Underground Counter Offensive, 10 June 1940: TNA HS 8/255.
47. Report VIII, July 1940: TNA HS 8/214.
48. Report VIII, July 1940: TNA HS 8/214; Minutes of ISPB Meeting, 5 July 1940: TNA HS 8/193.
49. 'Fryday' (Sheridan) to Taylor, 7 December 1939: TNA HS 9/612.
50. Report of Trusykowski, 16 December 1942: TNA HS 9/612.
51. Mulley (2012), pp. 305–6.
52. Singer (1953), pp. 210–13.
53. 'Fryday' (Sheridan) to Taylor, 7 December 1939: TNA HS 9/612; D/H (Taylor) to D/H11 (Harrison), 20 December 1939: TNA HS 9/612.
54. Goodwill to Taylor, 8 December 1940: TNA HS 9/1224/6.
55. Taylor to Harrison, 20 December 1940: TNA HS 9/612.
56. IWM Sound archive 8682, quoted in Mulley (2012), p. 75.
57. Goodwill to Harrison, 17 February 1940: TNA HS 9/612.
58. Grand to CSS, 11 March 1940: TNA HS 9/619.
59. Harrison to Goodwill and Wilkinson, 11 March 1940: TNA HS 9/612.
60. Report by Grand, 11 March 1940: TNA HS 9/612.
61. Granville personnel file: TNA HS 9/612; Grand to CSS, 11 March 1940: TNA HS 9/619.
62. Wilkinson (2002), p. 90.
63. Taylor to Harrison, 27 March 1940: TNA HS 9/1224/6.
64. Report of Harrison, 14 April 1940: TNA HS 9/612.
65. Witkowski had commanded an anti-tank unit armed with long anti-tank rifles nicknamed 'muskets'.

66. Goodwill to Taylor, 22 April 1940: TNA HS 9/612.
67. Memo, 30 June 1940: TNA HS 9/668/8.
68. Goodwill to Hawkins, 7 December 1940: TNA HS 9/588/2.
69. Wilkinson to Gubbins, 10 June 1940: TNA HS 4/198.
70. Memo of de Chastelain, 10 March 1941: TNA HS 9/588/2.
71. Note on XYZ Group, Wilkinson to Gubbins, 27 April 1941: TNA HS 9/588/2.
72. Wilkinson to de Chastelain, 7 May 1941: TNA HS 9/588/2.
73. De Chastelain to Norton [Jerzy], 12 August 1941: TNA HS 9/588/2.
74. Wilkinson to de Chastelain, 28 May 1941: TNA HS 4/198.
75. Masson (1975), pp. 112, 125.
76. Wilkinson (2002), p. 122.
77. Telegram, Taylor to Tamplin, 3 August 1942: TNA HS 4/612.
78. Draft letter 21 June 1940 to Lord Halifax; letter to Lionel Curtis, 9 July 1940: Hardy (2004), pp. 302–3, 312.
79. Marquis of Lothian (Washington Embassy) to Foreign Office, 1 August 1940: TNA FO 371/24847 and TNA KV 2/4105.
80. Hardy (2004), p. 335, fn. 2; Burgess MI5 file: TNA KV 2/4105.
81. Memo of 8 January 1941: TNA FO 371/24847 and TNA KV 2/4105.
82. TNA KV2/4117.
83. Lownie (2015), p. 108.
84. Telegram, Foreign Office to Washington Embassy, 27 July 1940: TNA FO 371/24847 and TNA KV 2/4105.

Chapter 9.   Scandinavia

1. Fraser to Rickman, 16 March 1940: TNA HS 2/264.
2. Grand to Fraser, 7 March 1940: TNA HS 2/261.
3. Cruickshank (1986), p. 28.
4. McKay (1986), p. 975.
5. CXG 277, 11 May 1940: TNA HS 2/264.
6. Fraser to Grand, 4 September 1939: TNA HS 2/261.
7. Martin to Fraser, 31 October 1939: TNA HS 2/261.
8. CXG 648, 20 June 1940: TNA HS 2/264.
9. Rickman to Fraser, 1 March 1940: TNA HS 2/264.
10. Cruickshank (1986), p. 49.
11. Leaflet P41 in TNA FO 898/486.
12. CXG 846, Martin to Grand, 16 February 1940: TNA HS 2/261.
13. Martin to Rickman, 21 March 1940: TNA HS 2/261; Singer, an Austrian Jew, was born in 1911. In 1933 he started an anti-Nazi newspaper in Berlin and was eventually forced to flee to Sweden. His anti-Nazi credentials were, therefore, impeccable. After the war, he rewrote his personal history several times, whilst becoming a successful writer on intelligence.
14. Fraser to Grand, 10 November 1939: TNA HS 2/261; Rickman to Fraser, 20 March 1940; Fraser to Rickman, 30 March 1940: TNA HS 2/264.
15. Randall to Jebb, 8 March 1940: TNA FO 1097/137.
16. Jebb to Brittain, 8 April 1940: TNA FO 1093/137.
17. CXG 825, Fraser to Rickman, 4 April 1940: TNA HS 2/263; Report of Holdsworth, 20 April 1940: TNA HS 2/264; Cruickshank (1986), p. 48.
18. Fraser to Holdsworth, 26 April 1940: TNA HS 2/264.
19. Lord Hood to Kirkpatrick, 22 April 1940: TNA FO 1093/137.
20. Cruickshank (1986), p. 60.
21. Referred to as Agent 101B in the German intelligence summary of early 1940, see N. West (1983), p. 250; Early History, TNA HS 7/3.

22. McKay (1993), p. 120.
23. Tennant (1992), p. 89. In 2016 file TNA FO 371/24865/6379 on Knüfken remained closed on national security grounds.
24. Fraser to Grand, 10 November 1939: TNA HS 2/261; Section D Minute of 4 February 1940: TNA HS 2/261.
25. Dolphin to D/T, 23 October 1939: TNA HS 2/263; Dolphin to Fraser, 26 October 1939: TNA HS 2/263.
26. Note by Churchill, 22 December 1939: TNA CAB 301/34.
27. Report of Fraser, 12 November 1939: TNA HS 2/261.
28. www.stockholmskallan.stockholm.se/PostFiles/SSA/Arkiv/SE_SSA_0140/SE_SSA_0140_06_03_Protokoll_1940_2_Rickman_1.pdf.
29. Notes of meeting between Rickman and Fraser, 12 November 1939: TNA HS 2/261.
30. Sutton-Pratt to Fraser, 6 January 1940: TNA HS 2/261.
31. Memo, 'Horace' (Sutton-Pratt), 22 December 1939: TNA HS 2/263.
32. Referenced in report of 18 March 1940: TNA HS 2/263.
33. Report of Fraser, 4 January 1940: TNA HS 2/263; Stephenson was recalled from Sweden on 30 January after his failed mission to recruit Johnson (CSS to Stephenson, 30 January 1940: TNA HS 2/263). He went to the USA in March and played no further part in the Oxelösund scheme. An exaggerated account of Stephenson's role in the *Operation Lumps* plan was first contained within his biography, *The Quiet Canadian*, by H. Montgomery Hyde (1962), p. 21. Tennant also emphasises Stephenson's part in the affair in his autobiography *Touchlines of War*, but being unable to consult official documents, he wrote his account on the basis of Stephenson's fiction.
34. Report of meeting by Fraser, 8 January 1940: TNA HS 2/263.
35. Note of a meeting at 10 Downing Street, 17 January 1940: TNA FO 1093/208 and CAB 301/34.
36. Answers to Questionnaire on Oxelösund, 10 January 1940: TNA HS 2/263.
37. Stockholm police files, available at www.stockholmskallan.se/PostFiles/SSA/Arkiv/SE_SSA_0140/SE_SSA_0140_06_03_Protokoll_1940_2_Rickman_1.pdf.
38. Fraser to Grand, 29 January 1940: TNA HS 2/263.
39. After the war the Swedish army was called upon to demolish the cranes but, with far greater resources, failed at the first attempt: information from C.G. McKay, with thanks.
40. CXG 694, CSS to Fraser, 30 January 1940: TNA HS 2/263.
41. CXG 803, Fraser to Grand, 31 January 1940: TNA HS 2/263.
42. Rickman to Holdsworth, 2 February 1940: TNA HS 2/263; CXG 802, Fraser to CSS, 31 January 1940: TNS HS 2/263.
43. Report of ?Grand, 3 February 1940: TNA HS 2/263.
44. Fraser to Grand, 5 February 1940: TNA HS 2/263.
45. Rickman to Fraser, 1 March 1940: TNA HS 2/264.
46. CXG 801, D/G to D/G1, 30 January 1940: TNA HS 2/263.
47. CXG 835 and 35, Fraser to Grand, 7 and 9 February 1940: TNA HS 2/263.
48. CXG 830, Rickman to Fraser, 9 February 1940: TNA HS 2/263.
49. CXG 711, Grand to Rickman, 9 February 1940. This message was reiterated in Grand to Rickman, 16 February 1940: TNA HS 2/263.
50. CXG 762, Grand to Rickman, 8 March 1940; Hankey to Jebb, 9 March 1940 and Jebb to Hankey, 15 March 1940: TNA FO 1093/232.
51. Rickman to Fraser, 7 March 1940: TNA HS 2/263.
52. Jebb to Cadogan with marginal note by Cadogan, 18 March 1940: TNA FO 1093/232; Rickman to Fraser, 15 March 1940: TNA HS 2/264.
53. CXG 768, Fraser to Rickman, 12 March 1940: TNA HS 2/263.
54. Rickman to Grand, 10 March 1940 (received 16 March): TNA HS 2/263.
55. Rickman to Fraser, 15 March 1940: TNA HS 2/264.

56. CXG 943, 16 March 1940: TNA HS 2/263.
57. CXG 786, Fraser to Rickman, 18 March 1940; CXG 407, Fraser to Bonnevie, 21 March 1940: TNA HS 2/263.
58. CXG 979 Holdsworth to Fraser, 3 April 1940, and CXG 991, Martin to Fraser, 8 April 1940: TNA HS 2/263.
59. Report by Rickman to Fraser, 23 March 1940: TNS HS 2/263.
60. Report by Holdsworth, 26 March 1940: TNA HS 2/263.
61. Fraser to Rickman, 26 March 1940: TNA HS 2/263.
62. Rickman to Fraser, 20 March 1940: TNA HS 2/264; Fraser to Rickman, 23 March 1940: TNA HS 2/264.
63. Fraser to Rickman, 30 March 1940: TNA HS 2/264.
64. CXG 657 93500 to London, 8 April 1940: TNA HS 2/263.
65. www.stockholmskallan.stockholm.se/post/18931.
66. McKay (1993), p. 57.
67. Report of Holdsworth, 20 April 1940: TNA HS 2/264; Stockholm police files available at www.stockholmskallan.se/PostFiles/SSA/Arkiv/SE_SSA_0140/SE_SSA_0140_06_03_Protokoll_1940_2_Rickman_1.pdf.
68. CXG 873, Grand to Holdsworth, 14 April 1940: TNA HS 2/263.
69. CXG 886, Grand to Holdsworth, 16 April 1940: TNA HS 2/263.
70. D/XE1 to Fraser, 16 April 1940: TNA HS 2/263.
71. McKay (1993), p. 61.
72. CXG 161, Martin, 26 April 1940: TNA HS 2/264.
73. McKay (1993), p. 58.
74. Björkman (2006), p. 95.
75. CXG 637, 19 June 1940: TNA HS 2/264.
76. Holdsworth report, 20 May 1940: TNA HS 2/264.
77. TNA FO 1093/291.
78. CXG 129, 23 April 1940: TNA HS 2/264.
79. Section D Early History to September 1940: TNA HS 7/4.
80. Holdsworth to Fraser, 26 April 1940: TNA HS 2/264.
81. CXG 858, Holdsworth to Rickman, 11 April 1940: TNA HS 2/261.
82. Cruickshank (1986), p. 42 mistakenly conflates these events to 13 April. *See* McKay (1993), p. 59.
83. McKay (1993), p. 60.
84. Björkman (2006), pp. 94, 170–1.
85. McKay (1993), note 25, p. 265.
86. Discussed under his code name 'Kant' in McKay (1993), pp. 58–61. I am grateful to Dr McKay for his comments (2016) on Birnbaum's role in the Rickman affair.
87. Message of Martin to SIS, 27 December 1940: TNA HS 2/263.
88. CXG 135, Martin, 23 April 1940: TNA HS 2/264.
89. Fraser to Rickman, 30 March 1940: TNA HS 2/264.
90. CXG 290, Martin to CSS, 12 May 1940: TNA HS 2/264.
91. CXG 161, Martin, 26 April 1940: TNA HS 2/264.
92. CXG 514, 7 June 1940, from Martin: TNA HS 2/264.
93. Fraser to Rickman, 28 and 29 March 1940: TNA HS 2/264.
94. Fraser to Rickman, 30 March 1940: TNA HS 2/264.
95. D Section Early History to September 1940: TNA HS/4.
96. Sutton-Pratt to Fraser, undated: TNA HS 2/264.
97. Tennant (1992), p. 129.
98. Sutton-Pratt to Fraser, 7 August 1940 from: TNA HS2/264.
99. CXG 277, 19 September 1940: TNA HS 2/261.

100. A concise report on operations in Sweden 1938–1940 and certain deductions there by A.F. Rickman, 11 July 1944: TNA HS 7/4.
101. Memo CSS to Grand, 12 May 1940: TNA HS 2/264.
102. *Liddell Diary*, 1939–1942, for 6 June 1942: West (2009), p. 264.
103. Menzies to Jebb, 23 April 1940: TNA FO 1093/231.
104. Quoted in Jeffrey (2010), p. 352.
105. Menzies to Sir Godfrey Thomas, 30 April 1940: TNA FO 1093/231.
106. Holdsworth to Taylor, 13 September 1940: TNA HS 9/1257.
107. CSS to Grand, 12 May 1940: TNA HS 2/264.
108. Grand to CSS, 13 May 1940: TNA HS 2/264.
109. Notes and Lessons by Laurence Grand, 1946: TNA HS 7/5.
110. The Underground Counter Offensive, 10 June 1940: TNA HS 8/255.
111. Fraser to Holdsworth, 24 April 1940; Grand to Smith, 25 April 1940: TNA HS 2/264.
112. Cruickshank (1986), p. 60.
113. D Section Early History to September 1940: TNA HS/4.
114. TNS HS 7/4.
115. Cruickshank (1986), p. 46.
116. Notes and Lessons by Grand, 1946: TNA HS 7/5. This contradicts the start date in Chaworth-Musters' SOE file: TNA HS 9/1080/7.
117. TNA HS 7/4; Gerard Holdsworth later ran the 'Helston Flotilla' for SOE, running agents in and out of Brittany, and had a distinguished career with them.
118. After serving as a pilot on convoy escort duty out of Iceland, Reed Olsen retrained as an agent for SIS and was parachuted into Norway in April 1943. His wireless station was one of those providing vital intelligence on the movements of the *Tirpitz* and its defences. He was eventually forced to flee to England but returned in May 1944.
119. Irregular Activities in Norway, report of ISPB to COS Committee, 8 May 1940: TNA CAB 80/10.
120. Petty sabotage in Denmark, Norway, Holland and Belgium, Laurence Grand, 19 May 1940: TNA HS 8/193.
121. TNA HS 2/241.
122. Inglis to Fraser, 28 June 1940: TNA HS 2/241.
123. Rubin Langmoe personnel file: TNA HS 9/886/2.
124. The Norwegian Project, 3 November 1940: TNA HS 2/128.
125. TNA HS 2/241.
126. Five small crates of Russian ammunition were included in the stores, suggesting that the Colt M1895 machine guns may originally have been part of a batch, built by Marlin, as part of a Russian contract in the USA that was cancelled by the Russian Revolution.
127. Signal of 27 May 1940 from Naval Officer IC Lerwick to SIS: TNA HS 2/241.
128. TNA HS 2/241.
129. TNA HS2/242.
130. TNA HS 2/242; MacEwen to Fraser, 27 June 1940: TNA HS 2/241; TNA HS 7 /174.
131. Hankey Report, 11 March 1940: TNA 63/192; Liddell Diary for 24 April 1940 in N. West (2009), p. 78; D/G Sec to D, 16 June 1940: TNA HS 2/241.
132. Marthinson was eventually captured by the Nazis and executed in October 1943.
133. TNA HS 2 /242.
134. TNA HS 9/17/1.
135. Report by Major Maltby, Section VIII, SIS: TNA HS 9/17/1.
136. Fraser to Grand, 28 June 1940: TNA HS 2/241.
137. TNA HS 9/17/1.
138. Report by Wallin: TNA HS 9/1553/6.
139. TNA HS 2/242.

140. TNA HS 9/17/1.
141. Gjelsvik (1979), pp. 10–11.
142. Cruickshank (1986), p. 55.
143. Chaworth-Musters to Taylor, 17 August 1940: TNA HS 2/240.
144. Cruickshank (1986), p. 49.
145. D Section Early History to September 1940: TNA HS 7/3.
146. Minute by Jebb, 11 May 1940: TNA FO 371/24832.
147. Report VIII, July 1940: TNA HS 8/214.
148. Cruickshank (1986), p. 57.

Chapter 10. Britain and the USA

1. Great Britain's Only Successful Experiment In Total Warfare, by Laurence Grand, August 1940: TNA HS 8/214.
2. This had no known name but was organised within Section VII. Its existence was first revealed in Jeffery (2010), pp. 361–2 and is discussed in Atkin (2015), ch. 11.
3. The first detailed history of the Home Defence Scheme was published in Atkin (2015), ch. 4.
4. Minutes of a meeting with Major Charaskiewicz, July 1939: TNA HS 4/193.
5. Pessimism by John Dolphin, 22 May 1940: Document provided by FCO SOE Adviser 1997, with thanks to Stephen Sutton for making it available to this author.
6. Organisation of Civil Resistance in Belgium, France, UK, and Ireland, by MIR, 23 May 1940: TNA HS 8/193.
7. Minutes of ISPB Meeting, 27 May 1940: TNA HS 8/193.
8. Sweet-Escott (1965), p. 38.
9. Minutes of ISPB Meeting, 27 May 1940: TNA HS 8/193.
10. Minutes of ISPB Meeting, 27 May 1940: TNA HS 8/193.
11. Report of meeting of 14 May 1940 in Draft Notes, Section 19 by Grand: TNA HS 7/5.
12. D Organisation for Home Defence, 1 June 1940. Document provided by FCO SOE Adviser 1997, with thanks to Stephen Sutton for making it available to this author.
13. Notes on Regional D Scheme, 2 June 1940 and *Preliminary Notes on the Regional D Scheme*, 4 June 1940: TNA HS 8/255.
14. Note on First Meeting of the Secret Service Committee, 3 June 1940: TNA FO 1093/193.
15. Jeffery (2010), pp. 352–3.
16. Wilkinson & Astley (1993), p. 72.
17. D Section, Early History to September 1940, p. 14: TNA HS 7/3.
18. Regional D Scheme Briefing, 2 June 1940: TNA HS 8/255.
19. Notes and Lessons by Laurence Grand, 1946: TNA HS 7/5.
20. Maschwitz (1957), p. 136.
21. Maschwitz (1957), p. 136.
22. TNA HS 8/214.
23. Preliminary Notes on Regional D Scheme, 4 June 1940: TNA HS 8/255.
24. Preliminary Notes on Regional D Scheme, 4 June 1940: TNA HS 8/255; Targets in London by John Dolphin, 6 June 1940: TNA HS 8/255.
25. Preliminary Notes on Regional D Scheme, 4 June 1940: TNA HS 8/255.
26. TNA CAB 63/89, f.43.
27. Preliminary Notes on Regional D Scheme, 4 June 1940: TNA HS 8/255.
28. D Organisation for Home Defence, 1 June 1940. Document provided by FCO SOE Adviser 1997, with thanks to Stephen Sutton for making it available to this author.
29. TNA HS 8/255.
30. Great Britain's Only Successful Experiment In Total Warfare, by Laurence Grand, August 1940: TNA HS 8/214.
31. Edwards, William, 'Guns in our "Bundles for Britain"', *Gun*, December 1959, p. 33.

32. Warwicker (2008), p. 178.
33. Williamson (2004), p. 13.
34. Lampe (1968), p. 105.
35. Sweet-Escott (1965), p. 38.
36. Wilkinson (2002), p. 100.
37. Notes and Lessons by Laurence Grand, 1946: TNA HS 7/5.
38. Preliminary Notes on the Regional D Scheme, 4 June 1940: TNA HS 8/255; D Section, Early History to September 1940: TNA HS 7/3.
39. Atkin (2015), p. 148.
40. Interview with Peter Wilkinson by Mark Seaman, 1993: IWM Audio Interview, Cat. No. 13289 reel 5.
41. Minutes of War Cabinet, 17 June 1940: TNA CAB 65/7/65.
42. Macleod & Kelly (1962), p. 368.
43. Letter of A. Gordon MacLeod to the Prime Minister, 3 July 1940: TNA CAB 120/241.
44. Letter of General Paget to Captain Sandys, 30 July 1940: TNA CAB 120/241.
45. Major General Ian Macdougall to Major General 'Pug' Ismay, 22 June 1940: TNA CAB 21/1473.
46. Beaumont-Nesbitt to Ismay, 24 June 1940: TNA CAB 21/1473; Gubbins, circular letter to LDV commanders, 5 July 1940: TNA CAB 21/120; Atkin (2015), p. 69.
47. TNA HS 8/258.
48. TNA CAB 63/192, f. 108.
49. Offensive and Irregular Operations, Appendix I (paper to COS Committee): TNA HS 8/258.
50. General Paget to Captain Sandys, 30 July 1940: TNA CAB 120/241.
51. Lampe (1968), p. 68.
52. Oxenden (2012) (typescript 1944), p. 2.
53. Beaumont-Nesbitt to Ismay, 24 June 1940: TNA CAB 21/1473.
54. TNA CAB 120/241; Atkin (2015), pp. 69–71.
55. Great Britain's Only Successful Experiment In Total Warfare, by Laurence Grand, August 1940: TNA HS 8/214.
56. Report VIII, July 1940, p. 23: TNA HS 8/214; Turner (2011), p. 96.
57. Turner (2011), pp. 22–3.
58. TNA CAB 67/7/27.
59. D Section Early History to September 1940, pp. 17–18: TNA HS 7/3.
60. Report VIII, July 1940: TNA HS 8/214.
61. Notes and Lessons by Laurence Grand, 1946: TNA HS 7/5.
62. In 1943 a team, under cover of being part of the local Home Guard, hid a cache of weapons including a Thompson M1A1 sub-machine gun in a well in Mellor, Cheshire. Another arms cache was hidden in Birmingham during 1944. For further details *see* www.mwatkin.com.
63. Major Petherick to Laurence Grand, 15 July 1940, quoted in Warwicker (2008), p. 190.
64. Atkin (2015), pp. 111–13.
65. TNA WO 260/9.
66. Report VIII, July 1940, p. 4: TNA HS 8/214.
67. Section D: Early History to September 1940, pp. 17–18: TNA HS 7/3.
68. Lampe (1968), p. 127.
69. Oxenden (2012) (typescript 1944), p. 2.
70. TNA WO 260/9; thanks to Will Ward for information on the early IOs.
71. Churchill to Eden, 22 June 1940: quoted in Churchill (1953), p. 147.
72. TNA HS 8/255.
73. Propaganda by Laurence Grand, 2 June 1939: TNA HS 8/305.
74. Notes and Lessons by Laurence Grand, 1946: TNA HS 7/5.
75. Maschwitz (1957), pp. 129–30.

76. The secret censorship department, known as 'Room 99', also dealt with the opening of diplomatic mail for Section N of SIS.
77. Memo to SIS Station New York, 1 January 1940: TNA HS 9/1117/3.
78. D Section Early History to September 1940: TNA HS 7/3.
79. Hyde (1982), p. 28.
80. Hyde (1982), p. 35.
81. Great Britain's Only Successful Experiment In Total Warfare, by Laurence Grand, August 1940: TNA HS 8/214.
82. Notes and Lessons by Laurence Grand, 1946: TNA HS 7/5.
83. D Section Early History to September 1940: TNA HS 7/3.
84. Report VII, July 1940: TNA HS 8/214.
85. Salvadori (1958), p. 190.

Chapter 11.   Into SOE

1. Great Britain's Only Successful Experiment In Total Warfare, by Laurence Grand, August 1940: TNA HS 8/214.
2. COS (40) 271, 21 March 1940: TNA CAB 80/9.
3. British strategy in a certain eventuality, 25 May 1940 (Report by chiefs of staff), circulated to the War Cabinet as WP (40) 168: TNA CAB 66/7.
4. Summary of Secret Reports regarding internal conditions in Germany, Gladwyn Jebb, 30 May 1940: TNA PREM 3/193/6A.
5. Dalton Diary, 3 and 14 June 1940.
6. TNA HS 8/255.
7. Beaumont-Nesbitt to Ismay, 3 March 1940: TNA CAB 21/1425.
8. The coordination of all irregular operations …, 6 June 1940: TNA HS 8/256.
9. Ismay to Beaumont-Nesbitt, 5 May 1940: TNA CAB 21/1435.
10. Jebb to Cadogan, 13 June 1940: TNA FO 1093/193.
11. Jebb to Cadogan, 13 June 1940: TNA FO 1093/193.
12. Report VIII on the activities of D Section during July 1940: TNA HS 8/214; quoted in Jeffrey (2010), p. 352.
13. Medicott (1952), p. 44.
14. Medicott (1952), p. 46.
15. The Underground Counter Offensive, 10 June 1940: TNA HS 8/255.
16. The Underground Counter Offensive, 10 June 1940: TNA HS 8/255.
17. Dalton (1957), p. 368.
18. Young (1980), p. 79.
19. Gladwyn (1972), p. 104.
20. Young (1980), p. 71.
21. Young (1980), p. 84.
22. Pimlott (1986), p. 33.
23. Memo D/F1 to D/F, 30 August 1940: TNA HS 8/305.
24. Pimlott (1986), p. 37.
25. Mss memo of 13 June 1940, Jebb to Cadogan: TNA FO 1093/193.
26. Pimlott (1986), p. 45.
27. Dilks (1971), p. 308; Pimlott (1986), pp. 50–1.
28. Minute on D activities in the Middle East, 7 August 1940: TNA HS 5/60, HS 3/147 and HS 3/154.
29. Minutes of meeting of 1 July 1940: TNA FO 1093/193; Garnett (2002), p. 30.
30. Meeting of 1 July 1940 to discuss the direction of sabotage: TNA FO 1093/193; MI(R), *An aide-memoire on the co-ordination of subversive activities in the conquered territories*, 6 July 1940: TNA HS 8/259.

31. Minutes of meeting of 1 July 1940: TNA FO 1093/193.
32. Pimlott (1986), p. 52.
33. Minutes of meeting of 1 July 1940: TNA FO 1093/193.
34. Minutes of meeting of 1 July 1940: TNA FO 1093/193.
35. Mackenzie (2000), p. 68.
36. TNA HS 8/258; MI(R), *An aide-memoire on the co-ordination of subversive activities in the conquered territories*, 6 July 1940: TNA HS 8/259.
37. Pimlott (1986), p. 57.
38. Pimlott (1986), p. 57.
39. Memorandum by the Lord President of the Council, 19 July 1940: TNA CAB 66/10.
40. Churchill to Dalton, 16 July 1940 quoted in Mackenzie (2000), p. 69.
41. MI(R) War Diary for 22 July 1940: TNA HS 8/263.
42. Dalton to Churchill, 24 July 1940: TNA PREM 3/365/6.
43. Taylor to Goodwill, 2 August 1940: TNA HS 5/497.
44. Gladwyn Jebb, Minute, 27 March 1942: TNA FO 1993/155.
45. Menzies to Jebb, 4 September 1940: Mackenzie (2000), p. 70.
46. Memo of H.M. Gladwyn Jebb (CEO of SOE), 28 March 1942: TNA FO 1093/155.
47. 'Subversion, Annex II', copy of minutes of a meeting between Menzies and Jebb, 15 September 1940, Gladwyn Jebb, 5 October 1940: TNA HS 8/334; TNA FO 1093/155.
48. Courtauld to all Section D staff, 21 October 1940: TNA HS 8/334. SO1 became the designation for the propaganda wing.
49. Chidson SOE file: TNA HS 9/306/7.
50. Para 3, Annex I (dated 19 August 1940) to paper on Subversion, October 1940: TNA HS 8/334, quoted in Mackenzie (2000), p. 70.
51. Taylor to Goodwill, 2 August 1940: TNA HS 5/497.
52. Wilkinson & Astley (1993), p. 77.
53. Philby (1968), p. 12.
54. Nelson to Jebb, undated: TNA HS 8/334.
55. Correspondence of 6 December 1940, 11 April 1940, 31 May 1941 and 1 June 1941: TNA HS 9/642/4.
56. D Section Early History to September 1940: TNA HS 7/3.
57. Jebb to Grand, 8 August 1940: TNA HS 8/334.
58. Nelson to Broad, 6 September 1940: TNA HS 8/305.
59. Philby (1968), p. 11.
60. Seaman (2006), p. 17.
61. Pimlott (1986), p. 85.
62. Howe (1982), p. 34.
63. Pimlott (1986), p. 83.
64. Dalton to Grand, 18 September 1940: quoted in Seaman (2006), p. 19.
65. Seaman (2006), pp. 18–19; Dalton to Grand, 18 September 1940 (Dalton papers LSE/DALTON/7/3, quoted in Bennett (2009), p. 262).
66. Gladwyn (1972), p. 101.
67. Gladwyn (1972), p. 101.
68. Pimlott (1986), p. 85.
69. Howe (1982), p. 34.
70. Nelson to all staff, 23 September 1940: TNA HS 8/334.
71. Bickham Sweet-Escott, 'SOE in the Balkans', in Auty & Clogg (1975), p. 6.
72. Dilks (1971), p. 349.
73. Cruickshank (1986), p. 61.
74. Quoted in Deacon (1969), p. 301.

Conclusion

1. Mackenzie (2000), pp. 36–7.
2. Amery (1973), p. 222.
3. Notes and Lessons by Laurence Grand, 1946: TNA HS 7/5.
4. Davidson (1996), pp. 19–26.
5. Speech to Conservative Party, Central Hall, Westminster, 4 April 1940.
6. S.W. Bailey in Auty & Clogg (1975), p. 279.
7. 'Activities of SOE in the Balkans', June 1941: TNA HS 8/957.
8. Mss note, Jebb, 13 June 1940: TNA FO 1093/193.
9. Gladwyn (1972), p. 103.
10. I am grateful to Lee Richards at www.psywar.org for discussion of wartime propaganda throughout the course of researching this book.
11. Great Britain's Only Successful Experiment In Total Warfare, by Laurence Grand, August 1940: TNA HS 8/214.
12. Tasks for SOE in Peace and War, by Colin Gubbins, 22 September 1945: TNA HS8/202.
13. Minutes of SOE–Foreign Office meeting, 13 September 1944: TNA HS 8/281.
14. Keegan (1989), p. 484; Williams (2013), p. 243.
15. General Paget to Captain Sandys, 30 July 1940: TNA CAB 120/241; Report VIII of July 1940: TNA HS 8/214.
16. N. West (1992), p. 6.
17. Hastings (2009), p. 474.

Bibliography

Amery, Julian (1948), *Sons of the Eagle* (Macmillan, London).

Amery, Julian (1973), *Approach March* (Hutchinson, London).

Astley, Joan Bright (2007), *The Inner Circle: A View of War at the Top* (The Memoir Club, Stanhope (first publ. 1971)).

Atkin, Malcolm (2015), *Fighting Nazi Occupation: British Resistance 1939–1945* (Pen & Sword, Barnsley).

Atkin, Malcolm (2016), *Myth and Reality: The Second World War Auxiliary Units* (online at https://independent.academia.edu/MalcolmAtkin).

Atkin, Malcolm (2017a), *The D Scheme, March 1939* (online at https://independent.academia.edu/MalcolmAtkin).

Atkin, Malcolm (2017b), *Officers and Agents of Section D, SIS, 1938–1940* (online article at https://independent.academia.edu/MalcolmAtkin).

Auty, Phyllis and Richard Clogg (eds) (1975), *British Policy towards Wartime Resistance in Yugoslavia and Greece* (Macmillan Press, London).

Bailey, Roderick (2014), *Target Italy* (Faber & Faber, London).

Barker, Elizabeth (1976), *British Policy in South-East Europe in the Second World War* (Macmillan Press, London).

Bennett, Gill (2009), *Churchill's Man of Mystery: Desmond Morton and the World of Intelligence* (Routledge).

Björkman, Leif (2006), *Säkerhetstjänstens egen berättelse om spionjakten krigsåren 1939–1942* (Hjalmarston & Högberg, Stockholm).

Bond, Brian (ed.) (1974), *Chief of Staff: The Diaries of Lieutenant-General Sir Henry Pownall, Vol. 2* (Leo Cooper, London).

Boyce, Frederic (2005), *SOE's Ultimate Deception: Operation Periwig* (Sutton Publishing, Stroud).

Boyce, Frederic and Douglas Everett (2003), *SOE: The Scientific Secrets* (Sutton Publishing, Stroud).

Brown, Anthony Cave (1988), *The Secret Servant: The Life of Sir Stewart Menzies, Churchill's Spymaster* (Michael Joseph, London).

Churchill, Winston (1953), *The Second World War: Triumph and Tragedy* (Cassell, London).

Collier, Basil (1957), *The Defence of the United Kingdom* (HMSO, London).

Costello, John and Oleg Tsarev (1993), *Deadly Illusions* (Century, London).

Cruickshank, Charles (1977), *The Fourth Arm* (Davis-Poynter, London).

Cruickshank, Charles (1986), *SOE in Scandinavia* (Oxford University Press).

Cunningham, Cyril (1998), *Beaulieu: the Finishing School for Secret Agents* (Leo Cooper, London).

Dalton, Hugh (1957), *The Fateful Years: Memoirs 1931–1945* (Frederick Muller Ltd, London).

Davidson, Basil (1987), *Special Operations Europe: Scenes from the Anti-Nazi War* (Grafton Books, London).

Davidson, Basil (1996), 'Goodbye to Some of That', *London Review of Books*, Vol. 18, No. 6, 19–26).

Davies, Philip H.J. (2004), *MI6 and the Machinery of Spying* (Cass, Abingdon).

Deacon, Richard (1969), *A History of the British Secret Service* (Frederick Muller Ltd, London).

Deletant, David (2016), *British Clandestine Activities in Romania during the Second World War* (Palgrave Macmillan, Basingstoke).

Dilks, David (1971), *The Diaries of Sir Alexander Cadogan, OM, 1938–45* (Cassell, London).

Earle, John (2005), *The Price of Patriotism* (The Book Guild, Sussex).

Foot, M.R.D. (1984), *SOE: An Outline History of the Special Operations Executive 1940–46* (BBC Books, London).

Foot, M.R.D. (2001), *SOE in the Low Countries* (St Ermin's Press, London).

Foot, M.R.D. (2004), *SOE in France* (Cass, Abingdon (revised edn; first publ. 1966)).

Garnett, David (2002), *The Secret History of PWE* (St Ermin's Press, London).

Gjelsvik, Tore (1979), *Norwegian Resistance 1940–1945* (C. Hurst & Co., London).

Gladwyn, Baron (1972), *The Memoirs of Lord Gladwyn* (Weidenfeld & Nicolson, London).

Glen, Alexander with Leighton Bowen (2002), *Target Danube: A River Not Quite Too Far* (The Book Guild, Sussex).

Gorove, Stephen (1964), *Law and Politics of the Danube* (The Hague).

Gubbins, Colin (1970), 'SOE and Regular and Irregular War', in Michael Elliot-Bateman (ed.), *The Fourth Dimension of Warfare, Vol. 1* (Manchester University Press).

Hacohen, David (1985), *Time to Tell: Israeli Life, 1898–1984* (Cornwall Books, USA).

Hamilton-Hill, Donald (1975), *SOE Assignment* (New English Library, London (first publ. 1973)).

Hardy, Henry (2004), *Isaiah Berlin: Letters 1928–1946* (Cambridge University Press).

Harouvi, Eldad (1999), 'Reuven Zaslany (Shiloah) and the covert cooperation with British intelligence during the Second World War', in Hesi Carmel (ed.), *Intelligence for Peace* (Frank Cass, London).

Hastings, Max (2009), *Finest Years: Churchill as Warlord 1940–45* (Harper Press, London).

Heine, Hartmut (1983), *La oposición política al franquismo. De 1939 a 1952* (Barcelona).

Helm, Sarah (2005), *A Life in Secrets: Vera Atkins and the lost agents of SOE* (Little, Brown, London).

Hill, George (2014), *Go Spy the Land: Being the Adventures of I.K.8 of the British Secret Service* (Cassell, London (first publ. 1932)).

Hinsley, F.H. and C.A.G. Simkins (1990), *British Intelligence in the Second World War, Vol. 4* (HMSO, London).

Hinsley, F.H. *et al.* (1979), *British Intelligence in the Second World War, Vol. 1* (HMSO, London).

Howarth, Patrick (2000), *Undercover: The Men and Women of the SOE* (Phoenix Press, London (first publ. 1980)).

Howe, Ellic (1982), *The Black Game: British Subversive Operations Against the Germans during the Second World War* (Michael Joseph, London).

Hyde, H. Montgomery (1982), *Secret Intelligence Agent* (Constable, London).

Ismay, Lord (1960), *The Memoirs of General The Lord Ismay* (Heinemann, London).

Jeffery, Keith (2010), *MI6: The History of the Secret Intelligence Service 1909–1949* (Bloomsbury, London).

Johns, Philip (1979), *Within Two Cloaks: Missions with SIS and SOE* (William Kimber, London).

Keegan, John (1989), *The Second World War* (Hutchinson, London).

Kemp, Peter (1958), *No Colours or Crest* (Cassell, London).

Lampe, David (1968), *The Last Ditch* (Cassell, London).

Lett, Brian (2016), *SOE's Mastermind: an Authorized Biography of Sir Colin Gubbins* (Pen & Sword, Barnsley).

Lindeman, A.R.B. (2016), *Rediscovering Irregular Warfare: Colin Gubbins and the Origins of Britain's Special Operations Executive* (University of Oklahoma Press).

Lownie, Andrew (2015), *Stalin's Englishman: The Lives of Guy Burgess* (Hodder, London).

McKay, C.G. (1986), 'Iron Ore and Section D: The Oxelösund Operation' (*Historical Journal*, Vol. 29, Issue 4, 975–8).

McKay, C.G. (1993), *From Information to Intrigue: Studies in Secret Service based on the Swedish Experience 1939–1945* (Frank Cass, London).

Mackenzie, William (2000), *The Secret History of SOE* (St Ermin's Press, London).

Macleod, Roderick and Denis Kelly (eds) (1962), *The Ironside Diaries 1937–40* (Constable, London).

Maschwitz, Eric (1957), *No Chip On My Shoulder* (H. Jenkins, London).

Masson, Madeleine (1975), *Christine: a search for Christine Granville* (Hamish Hamilton, London).

Medicott, W.N. (1952), *The Economic Blockade, Vol. 1* (HMSO, London).

Milne, Tim (2014), *Kim Philby* (Biteback Publishing, London).

Minshall, Merlin (1975), *Guilt-Edged* (Bachman & Turner, London).

Muggeridge, Malcolm (ed.) (1947), *Ciano's Diary 1939–1943* (Heinemann, London).

Muggeridge, Malcolm (1973), *Chronicles of Wasted Time: The Infernal Grove* (Collins, London).

Mulley, Clare (2012), *The Spy Who Loved: The Secrets and Lives of Christine Granville* (Macmillan, London).

O'Connor, Bernard (2014), *Sabotage in Holland* (Lulu).

O'Malley, Owen (1954), *The Phantom Caravan* (Murray, London).

Onslow, Sue (2005), 'Britain and the Belgrade coup of 27 March 1941 Revisited' (*Electronic Journal of International History*, 1–57).

Oxenden, Nigel (2012 reprint), *Auxiliary Units: History and Achievement 1940–1944* (BRO Museum, Parham (typescript 1944; first publ. 1998).

Paucker, Arnold (2015), *German Jews in the Resistance 1933–1945: The Facts and the Problems* (German Resistance Memorial Centre, Berlin).

Philby, Kim (1968), *My Silent War* (Macgibbon & Gee, London).

Pidgeon, Geoffrey (2003), *Secret Wireless War* (UPSO, East Sussex).

Pimlott, Ben (ed.) (1986), *The Second World War Diary of Hugh Dalton 1940–45* (Jonathan Cape, London).

Pirker, Peter (2012), 'Transnational resistance in the Alps-Adriatic Area in 1939–40 . . .' (*Acta Histriae*, Vol. 20, 765–88).

Purvis, Stewart and Jeff Hulbert (2016), *The Spy Who Knew Everyone* (Biteback, London).

Read, Anthony and David Fisher (1984), *Colonel Z: The Life and Times of a Master of Spies* (Hodder & Stoughton, London).

Richards, Brook (2012), *Secret Flotillas, Vol. 1* (Pen & Sword, Barnsley).

Richards, Lee (2010a), *The Black Art* (www.psywar.org).

Richards, Lee (2010b), *Whispers of War* (www.psywar.org).

Salvadori, Max (1958), *The Labour and the Wounds* (Pall Mall, London).

Schellenberg, Walter (2001), *Invasion 1940: The Nazi Invasion Plan for Britain* (St Ermin's Press, in association with Little, Brown & Company (first publ. 2000)).

Seaman, Mark (ed.) (2006), *Special Operations Executive: A New Instrument of War* (Routledge, London).

Singer, Kurt (1953), *Spies and Traitors: A Short History of Espionage* (W.H. Allen, London).

Stafford, David (1975), 'Britain looks at Europe, 1940: some Origins of SOE' (*Canadian Journal of History*, No. 2, August, 231–48).

Stafford, David (1980), *Britain and European Resistance 1940–1945* (Macmillan, London).

Stafford, David (2010), 'Secret Operations versus Secret Intelligence in World War', in T. Travers and C. Archer (eds), *Men at War: Politics, Technology and Innovation in the Twentieth Century* (reprint; first publ. 1982, pp. 119–36).

Stoil, Jacob (2013), 'Structures of Cooperation & Conflict: Local Forces in Mandatory Palestine during the Second World War' (*Ex Historia*, Vol. 5).

Soulier, Dominique (2013), *The Sussex Plan: Secret War in Occupied France* (Histoire & Collections, France).

Sweet-Escott, Bickham (1965), *Baker Street Irregular* (Methuen, London).

Tennant, Peter (1992), *Touchlines of War* (Hull University Press).

Tittenhofer, Mark A. (1969), 'The Rote Drei: Getting Behind the "Lucy" Myth' (*Studies in Intelligence*, Vol. 13, Issue 3, 51–90).

Toyne, John (1962), *Win Time for Us* (Longmans, Toronto).

Turner, Des (2011), *SOE's Secret Weapons Centre: Station 12* (The History Press, Stroud (first publ. 2006)).

Van der Bijl, Nick (2013), *Sharing the Secret: A History of the Intelligence Corps 1940–2010* (Pen & Sword Military, Barnsley).

Wake-Walker, Edward (2011), *A House for Spies: SIS Operations into Occupied France from a Sussex Farmhouse* (Robert Hale, London).

Walker, David E. (1955), *Adventure in Diamonds* (Evans Brothers, London).

Walker, David E. (1957), *Lunch with a Stranger* (Allan Wingate, London).

Wall, Bernard (1969), *Headlong into Change* (Harvill, London).

Warwicker, John (2008), *Churchill's Underground Army: A History of the Auxiliary Units in World War II* (Frontline Books, London).

West, Nigel (1983), *MI6: British Secret Intelligence Service Operations 1909–45* (Weidenfeld & Nicolson, London).

West, Nigel (1992), *Secret War: The Story of SOE, Britain's Wartime Sabotage Organisation* (Hodder & Stoughton, London).

West, Nigel (ed.) (2009), *The Guy Liddell Diaries, Vol. I: 1939–1942* (Routledge (first publ. 2005)).

West, Nigel and Oleg Tsarev (eds) (2009), *Triplex: Secrets from the Cambridge Spies* (Yale University Press).

West, W.J. (1987), *Truth Betrayed* (Duckworth, London).

Wilkinson, Peter (2002), *Foreign Fields* (I.B. Tauris Publishers, London (first publ. 1997)).

Wilkinson, Peter and Joan Bright Astley (1993), *Gubbins and SOE* (Pen & Sword, London).

Williams, Heather (2013), *Parachutes, Patriots and Partisans: The Special Operations Executive and Yugoslavia, 1941–1945* (Hurst & Co., London).

Williamson, Alan (2004), *East Ridings Secret Resistance 1940–44* (Middleton Press, Sussex).

Wylie, Neville (2005), 'Ungentlemanly Warriors or Unreliable Diplomats? Special Operations Executive and "Irregular Political Activities" in Europe' (*Intelligence and National Security*, Vol. 20, No. 1, 98–120).

Young, Kenneth (1980), *The Diaries of Sir Robert Bruce Lockhart, Vol. 2, 1939–45* (Macmillan, London).

Index